Profiles In Sanctification

Maturing In One's Personal Relationship With Christ

Profiles In Sanctification

Maturing In One's Personal Relationship With Christ

Chris S. Sherrerd

Portions of this book may not be copied or reprinted for commercial gain or profit without written permission. However, except for direct quotations from other authors, the use of short quotations or occasional page copying for personal or group study is permitted and encouraged. Permission will be granted upon request.

Unless otherwise identified, Scripture quotations are from the New American Standard Bible, © 1960, 1962, 1963, 1968, 1971, 1972, 1973, 1975 and 1977 by The Lockman Foundation. Used by permission.

Take note that the name satan and related names are not capitalized. We choose not to acknowledge him, even to the point of violating grammatical rules.

ISBN 0-9714361-2-6
Copyright © 1979, 1983, 2000 and 2003, All Rights Reserved
by Shulemite Christian Crusade, SAN 254-3931
Web Page: http://www.chrissherrerd.com
Published by Destiny Image Publishers
167 Walnut Bottom Road, PO Box 310
Shippensburg, PA 17257-0310

SHULEMITE CHRISTIAN CRUSADE

Sharing
The Sure Word Of Prophecy
... 2 Peter 1:19-21

1420 Armstrong Valley Road, Halifax, PA 17032
717-896-8386   Fax 717-896-8676
email: sherrerd@epix.net

Many writers change the exact transliterations of Hebrew words into more pronounceable forms. But nobody knows how ancient Hebrew was pronounced, since it ceased twice in history to be a spoken language. A precise way to transliterate Hebrew is to use capital letters to represent actual Hebrew letters, with lowercase letters added in certain cases. Following that practice, we have used throughout this book the following the Hebrew transliterations:

Hebrew Letter	English Trans.	Hebrew Letter	English Trans.
א	Ah	ל	L
ב	B	מ (ם)	M
ג	G	נ (ן)	N
ד	D	ס	S
ה	H	ע	I
ו	W	פ (ף)	Ph
ז	Z	צ (ץ)	Ts
ח	Ch	ק	Q
ט	T	ר	R
י	Y	ש	Sh
כ (ך)	K	ת	Th

Cover

The cover gives for illustration four samples of believer's profiles in their maturing in intimacy with Christ Jesus. The vertical scale suggests a measure of intimacy, with zero before the cross, to some maximum "measure" attainable in this life. The horizontal scale is relative time, from the moment one accepts what Christ has done for him/her on the Cross, until he/she physically dies and goes home to be with Him.

Each profile shows some of the inevitable but temporary ups and downs that result from forces which briefly get our eyes off of Christ. Believer (1) is the weakest most of his/her life until late when he/she receives the Baptism into the Holy Spirit and enters into a very significant level of intimacy with Christ as a result. Believer (2) starts out a bit stronger, and ever seeks to grow close to Christ, soon receiving the Baptism into the Holy Spirit and continuing to grow thereafter. Believer (3) starts out yet a bit stronger, but does not seek to grow further in intimacy with Christ, and hence remains stagnant throughout his/her live. Believer (4) parallels believer (2), starts out the strongest, but at first does not seek to grow closer to Christ. However he/she finally seeks to and hence receives the Baptism into the Holy Spirit, and ends up the most intimate with Christ in this life.

"... the exhortation which speaks to you as sons: 'My son, do not despise the chastening of the Lord, nor be discouraged when you are rebuked by Him; for whom the Lord loves He chastens, And scourges every son whom He receives.' If you endure chastening, God deals with you as with sons; for what son is there whom a father does not chasten? But if you are without chastening, of which all have become partakers, then you are illegitimate and not sons. Furthermore, we have had human fathers who corrected us, and we paid them respect. Shall we not much more readily be in subjection to the Father of spirits and live? For they indeed for a few days chastened us as seemed best to them, but He for our profit, that we may be partakers of His holiness. Now no chastening seems to be joyful for the present, but painful; nevertheless, afterward it yields the *peaceful fruit of righteousness* to those who have been trained by it. Therefore, strengthen the hands which hang down, and the feeble knees, and make straight paths for your feet, so that what is lame may not be dislocated, but rather be healed. Pursue *peace* with all people, and ***holiness, without which no one will see the Lord.***" [Hebrews 12:5-14]

"I am the true vine, and My Father is the vinedresser. Every branch in Me that does not bear fruit He takes away; and every branch that bears fruit He prunes, that it may bear *more* fruit. You are already clean because of the word which I have spoken to you. Abide in Me, and I in you. As the branch cannot bear fruit of itself, unless it abides in the vine, neither can you, unless you abide in Me. I am the vine, you are the branches; he who abides in Me, and I in him, bears much fruit; for without Me you can do nothing. If anyone does not abide in Me, he is cast out as a branch and is withered; and they gather them and throw them into the fire, and they are burned. If you abide in Me, and My words abide in you, you will ask what you desire, and it shall be done for you. By this My Father is glorified, that you bear much fruit; so you will be My disciples." [John 15:1-8]

Dedication

This volume, and the other six volumes of the series *Where Do You Fit In? Practical Commitments in the Body of Christ*, is dedicated to the local leaders of the new wave of God that is beginning to move throughout the Body of Christ. Throughout the Body, there is a general awareness that our Lord Christ Jesus is now about to do something drastically new among us. Many are desperately seeking to become more *intimate* in their personal relationship with Christ Jesus. In fact, that is or Lord's very *purpose* in His dealings with us.

This volume addresses those very dealings. It is dedicated to the local leaders of the Body of Christ. It is they who must (a) personally live this message first; (b) teach it to others so they may properly respond to the Lord in the days ahead; (c) discern the spiritual needs of fellow Christians and help them discover how they can benefit by this message; and (d) help others walk in this message as they respond to God's voice themselves.

Acknowledgements

Original text references were: for the Old Testament Hebrew, *Biblia Hebraica*, edited by Rud. Kittell, published by Wurttembergische Bibelanstalt, Stuttgart, Germany; and for the New Testament Greek, *Interlinear Greek-English New Testament* (which uses the *Received Text)*, by Jay P. Green, published by MacDonald Pub. Company, MacDill AFB, FL.

For original text concordances: I primarily used *The Exhaustive Concordance of the Bible ... with ... Dictionaries of the Hebrew and Greek Words* by James Strong, STD, LLD, published by Abingdon Press, Nashville, Tennessee; I also made extensive use of the *Analytical Concordance to the Bible* by Robert Young LLD. published by Wm. B. Eerdmans Publishing Company, Grand Rapids, Michigan. For Hebrew lexicons: I primarily used *The Analytical Hebrew and Chaldee Lexicon* by Benjamin Davidson, published by Samuel Bagster & Sons Ltd., London, England; I also used *A Hebrew and English Lexicon of the Old Testament* by William Gesenius, translated (into English) by Edward Robinson, published by Oxford University Press, London, England. For Greek lexicons: I primarily used *Greek-English Lexicon of the New Testament*, translated and revised and enlarged by Joseph Henry Thayer DD, published by Zondervan Publishing House, Grand Rapids, Michigan; plus also *The Analytical Greek Lexicon*, compiled by the publisher, Zondervan Publishing House, Grand Rapids, Michigan. I also made limited use of *An Expository Dictionary of New Testament Words* by W. E. Vine, MA, published by Fleming H. Revell Company, Old Tappan, New Jersey.

Contents

Preface..xix

Part I: Do You Care?......................................1

Chapter One   What *Is* Sanctification?...............3
1. Relationship, Not Religion!.........................5
2. The Human Spirit, Soul And "Flesh"..............8
3. Human Triparte Nature As Created................12
4. Sanctification of The Human Triparte Nature....18
5. Sanctification By Emptying Trials................23

Chapter Two   What Does Christ's Crucifixion Mean To Us?..................................27
1. By Grace We Are Saved Through Faith..............28
2. Salvation: Personal Relationship With God In Christ Jesus.....................................29
3. Eternal Life - What Is It?.......................32
4. Grace - The Causative Agent: Having Christ, Crucified, In Us.................................37
5. Faith: Total Abandonment.........................39
6. Passover & Lord's Supper: His Crucifixion Into Us..45
7. The Shed Blood of Christ Jesus...................47
8. This Cup Is My Covenant..........................49
9. Crucifixion Stages Of The Salvation Process.....52
10. How: The Effectual Power Of The Cross..........56

Chapter Three   Our Qualifying Paradigm: That We Intensely Desire Him!.......................61
1. Qualifications For Grace.........................62
2. Qualifications For Ministry.....................63

3. His Vested Interest In Us..67
  4. The Impact Of Our Thoughts And Motives...............70
  5. The Necessary Vision And Perspective
       For Motivation..74
  6. Christ Must Be Central To Our Thinking..................75

Chapter Four   God's Ultimate Intention....................85
  1. Our Oneness With God's Overall Plan......................86
  2. Were We Created To Be Redeemed?.......................90
  3. Historical Unfolding Of God's Ultimate Intention......99
  4. Constraints Under The Adamic Curse 104
  5. The *Work* Of The Cross..109
  6. The *Way* Of The Cross..111
  7. Kids, Grow Up!..118
  8. Maturing In Our Personal Relationship With Christ.119
  9. Chastened As Sons...121
  10. Purification Of Our Faith Through Fire...............123
  11. Meekness, Honesty And Love...............................131
  12. Pleading The Shed Blood Of Christ Jesus............136

Part II   The Holy Spirit Our Sanctifier.............143

**Chapter Five   Roles of the Holy Spirit
                    In Believers....................................145**
  1. Specific Workings Of The Holy Spirit....................146
  2. A Word On The Word's Word "Word"....................151
  3. Charismatic Cybernetics: Me *vs* Christ In Me.........154
  4. Cleanses Our Kidneys As Well As Our Hearts........158
  5. Holy Spirit Empowerment Of Healing Repentance..161
  6. Is It Actually Possible?...163

Chapter Six Receive Ye The Holy Spirit
 In His Fullness...169
  1. Baptism Into The Holy Spirit?.............................170
  2. Old *vs* New Covenant Baptisms..........................174
  3. Baptism Unto The Presence-Glory of God............175
  4. Regeneration *vs* Baptism Into The Holy Spirit.........176
  5. Mount Sinai A Type...178
  6. That The Body Of Christ Be Matured....................180
  7. The Charisma Of Our Callings.............................181
  8. Heart Circumcision And Soul Release...................182
  9. Cutting Asunder The Soul-Spirit Barrier................184
  10. Unto The Kingdom Of God.................................187
  11. Forgiveness Unto Regeneration *vs* Purity By Fire.....188

Chapter Seven   The Experience Of The Baptism Into
 The Holy Spirit............................193
  1. First We Must Be Born Again..............................193
  2. Experience Of The Baptism Into The Holy Spirit....194
  3. A Person, *Not* An "Experience"............................197
  4. That We *Know* Him..199
  5. Some External Evidence 201
  6. What Does It Mean To Be "Filled" With
   The Holy Spirit?..202
  7. "Peace Offering": QRBN of ShLM........................204
  8. Necessity & Commitment, *Not* Option/Luxury........205
  9. Point Of No Return..206
  10. Not Instant Maturity..208
  11. Have We Two Natures Or One?...........................214
  12. The Biblical *Fulness* Of The
   Baptism Into The Holy Spirit...............................215
  13. What About Speaking In Tongues?......................218
  14. Our Present Condition: Saved But Immature......225

Part III   Profiles In Sanctification....................229

Chapter Eight   Experiencing Sanctification..............231
  1. The Sanctification Process Takes Time...................232
  2. Sanctification Ladders?..234
  3. Shifts In Influences During Sanctification..............237
  4. The *Process* Of Sanctification................................246
  5. Reconciliation *vs* Consecration *vs* Sanctification......253
  6. Take Up Your Cross...258
  7. Follow Him..262

Chapter Nine   Maturing Through Soul Affliction...265
  1. "Torrents", "Classes", "Planes" & "Degrees"...........267
  2. The Repeated Cycle...272
  3. Purging Of Self..276
  4. Outward Prayers *vs* Inner Poise Of The Soul.........282
  5. Other Basic Lessons, Again & Again.....................286
  6. Balance Between Two Conflicting Truths..............289
  7. How Many, How Long?... 289
  8. The First Stage: Law And Labor............................291
  9. The Second Stage: Holy Spirit Empowerment.......295
  10. Unto Spiritual Reality..297
  11. Initial Filling And Spirit Release...........................299
  12. Unto Mount Moriah..301
  13. Inner Heart Healing..302
  14. Personal Characteristics Of Second Stage.............305
  15. The Third Stage: Emptying & Outpouring...........308
  16. Emptying Of Our Self-Nature: Our
       Atonement Offerings...309
  17. Baptism With Fire..312
  18. Complete Emptying Of Self.................................316
  19. Standing In The Divine Presence..........................317

Chapter Ten   Divine "Three" 323
  1. In Love With Jesus 325
  2. Our Unfolding Love Relationship With
          Christ Jesus 326
  3. Spices, Fragrances And Fruit of Love 333
  4. Visibility Of Our Message Of Christ 335
  5. Growing In Christ-Likeness 336
  6. Growing In Communication With Him 338
  7. New Testament Believers Are To Offer Offerings ...339
  8. The Primary Essence Of Offerings 342
  9. Levels Of Offerings 344
  10. This Cup Is My Covenant 352
  11. Kings And Priests - A Holy People 357
  12. Anointings 367
  13. Overcoming Temptations 369
  14. Pilgrim's Progress 372
  15. Mary, Mary, Mary! 378
  16. Some Other Authors' "Divine Threes" 380

**Part IV   Typological Perspectives And Personal
            Examples** 397

Chapter Eleven   Divine Perspectives 399
  1. The Tabernacle: Holiness In Perspective 400
  2. Esther Story: Psychological Perspective 415
  3. Psalms Of Degrees Of Ascent:
          Our Walk In This World 419
  4. Several Types Of The Sanctification Process
          Time Sequence 425
  5. Israel's Holy Convocations: Our Separation
          From The World 425
  6. Remembrance Aspect In The Exodus-Joshua
          Story: Theological Perspective 430

   7. Personal Aspects: Our Progress In
                     Spiritual Maturing..............................431
   8. Prophetic Aspects: God's Patience As
                     Reflected In Dispensations.................433

Chapter Twelve   Our Cloud Of Witnesses.................439
   1. Meanings Of Old Testament Names.....................441
   2. Abraham: Unto Faith...445
   3. Jacob: Unto Righteousness...................................455
   4. Joseph: Unto Forgiveness.....................................463
   5. Moses: Unto Overcoming People's
                Ungodly Demands............................468
   6. Wandering Israelites: Singleness Of Purpose..........474
   7. David: Unto Victory...483
   8. Elijah: Prophet's Testings.......................................494
   9. New Testament And Other Examples.....................500
   10. Those Who Saw Not The Vision Fulfilled.............502

Epilogue..507

Appendix One   The Human "Heart".......................511
   1. Body, Soul And Spirit...511
   2. The Human Spirit In The Bible.................................513
   3. The Human Soul In The Bible..................................515
   4. The Human "Heart" In The Bible..............................516
   5. The Human "Flesh" In The Bible..............................519
   6. But What Are They, Really?.....................................522

Tables, Figures And Charts

Table One:	Fruit And Spices Of The Holy Spirit In Our Hearts	72
Figure One:	God's Ultimate Intention	100
Figure Two:	Influences On Our Hearts	239
Sanctification Stages Chart One		249
Sanctification Stages Chart Two		254
Sanctification Stages Chart Three		260
Table Two:	Maturing Through Soul Affliction	271
Sanctification Stages Chart Four		324
Sanctification Stages Chart Five		340
Sanctification Stages Chart Six		360
Table Three:	Our Three Great Temptations	371
Sanctification Stages Chart Seven		381
Sanctification Stages Chart Eight		386
Sanctification Stages Chart Nine		389
Sanctification Stages Chart Ten		402
Figure Three:	Tabernacle General Layout	403
Sanctification Stages Chart Eleven		420
Table Four:	Christian Maturing Concepts In The Ascent Psalms	421
Figure Four:	Types Of The Sanctification Process Time Sequence	426
Table Five:	Israel's Holy Convocations And Their Typological Aspects	427
Sanctification Stages Chart Twelve		440

Preface

This book belongs to the Lord Jesus Christ. It is His. I of course am responsible for the no-doubt many ways in which true inspirations from His indwelling Holy Spirit have been degraded by mixture with elements of my yet-far-from-perfected self. But the book itself is His doing.

The basic theme of the book is that the spiritual growth of Christian believers is a multi-stage process with common elements but also as varied in detail as there are believers.

The Biblical concept of the Body of Christ is that of a deep personal intimate relationship with God the Father and Christ the Son. In John 17:3, Jesus defined "eternal life" as **knowing** Him - **gnosko** or intrinsic, inner, intimate, even mystical knowledge of Him. But in most Christian contexts, intimate relationship with Him has long been replaced by doctrinal knowledge **about** him, together with religious structures according to the traditions of men.

This first occurred to me in January of 1968, some four months before I received the Baptism in the Holy Spirit. During the previous year I had been led by the Lord across denominational barriers and through accompanying doctrinal confusions; and I began to see that no single denomination emphasizes all Biblical aspects of spiritual growth through to maturity. I also recognized that the spiritual growth of each individual believer is strongly influenced by the particular Biblical teachings to which he is exposed.

By early Summer 1968 I envisioned that each individual Christian believer has a unique profile to his sanctification, and that at any one point in time he has spiritually grown along his profile only up to a particular and unique point. Yet I was curious as to what *common* aspects of the profiles of all believers are taught in the Bible, and to what degrees do various believers' profiles actually vary one from another.

By early Autumn of 1968, as I was meditating upon my own spiritual growth up to that point, I became cognizant of a certain phenomenon that actually had repeated itself several times in my life. At each step of my searchings for maturity in my walk with the Lord Christ Jesus, I would be able to assimilate only those teachings and experiences commensurate with my particular level of growth at that time. I had to be fed milk when a babe and bread when a toddler; I needed to grow a bit before I was ready for meat. So, the Lord would place me at the feet of some leader who had been called by Him to the level of ministry of Christian counseling and Bible teaching that I needed at that time. After a while I would have assimilated all that I could from that leader's ministry. I would seek out (and the Lord would lead me to) another leader's ministry at the next level of spiritual growth appropriate for me at the time. Invariably this meant leaving one particular Christian fellowship or set of doctrines, even in some cases crossing denominational barriers. As I did so, the leader under whose ministry I had grown thus far and to whom I was deeply grateful, would invariably oppose (usually with sharp hostility) my seeking to grow further beyond *his* ministry.

Preface

It was not until two years later that I began to understand *why* this phenomenon was a necessary part of the ***Lord's*** ways. But it taught me how ***provincial*** are the ministries of a single person or a single denomination, no matter how mature and anointed be its emphases, and also how each ministry or denomination ***hinders*** spiritual growth by individual believers ***beyond*** its own particular level. Individual ministries, fellowships, churches and denominations vary tremendously in the upper bounds of the particular levels of spiritual growth they practice and foster within their flocks.

I here state *Sherrerd's Law Of Christian Dignity*: **A Christian's soul is far too precious to our Lord Christ Jesus to be forever restricted to a single person's or denomination's ministry!**

In December 1969, the Lord specifically burdened me with a then-quite-future writing/teaching ministry and indicated to me several specific subject areas that that would entail. ***Profiles In Sanctification*** was one of those specific subject areas, with those exact words. But I had not yet grown significantly in my understandings of spiritual growth. It was not until during early 1971, when I read some books by Jessie Penn-Lewis, Watchman Nee, A. W. Tozer and DeVern Fromke, that I ***began*** to research out and grow in understandings of the Bible teachings of this subject.

The winters of 1970-71 and 1971-72 saw the "First-Fruits" of my teaching ministry as the Lord led and anointed. It was during the Winter 1971-72 sessions that the Lord guided and anointed me in developing and teaching the basic material of much of Parts III and IV of this Volume. But still some vital details eluded me, and because of my misguided efforts to *force* the basic sanctification pattern into the doctrinal positions of much of evangelical Christianity, some serious distortions were embedded in my teaching notes of that time.

The subject laid dormant in my heart for the following year. In late June 1973, during a conversation of sharing with a fellow believer who had been heavily dealt with by the Lord, I fully realized in my heart the vital missing point: the end goal of our spiritual growth from the Lord's point-of-view is our utter, total dependence *upon* Him *experientially*, and *not* upon our understandings *about* Him *intellectually!* "Eternal life" is *life*, and *life* is far more than intellectual understanding. It is *knowing Him*, not just knowing *about* Him. It is a *flowing* of His light, life and love, first *into* us, and then *through* us unto others!

In August 1973, the Lord instructed me to proceed forthwith in the actual writing on this (and other) subjects. He anointed me to develop a full overview, abstract, and table of contents by mid-September 1973.

But I yet had far to go. The Lord's emphasis on my life again shifted. In October 1974 He gave me the full insights of another book, "From Sheepfold To Bride: Christ Maturing His Church" (now Volume III of this series). I prepared and taught extensively on that subject in 1975 through 1976.

On top of that, He gave me the insights of still another book, "Unto The Mountain Pass". The subsequent years until mid-1981 were devoted to actually producing it. That original manuscript has now been incorporated into this ***Where Do You Fit In?*** series, the prophetic portions constituting

Volume VI, and the underlying spiritual and social issues scattered through Volumes IV and V.

Profiles In Sanctification remained dormant from late 1973, until late August 1981 when He again quickened His anointing for it. Late 1981 through 1982 saw the completion of six chapters plus five appendices, with the extensive Biblical exegetical research that entailed.

I do not write upon my own initiative, but rather strictly respond to what I believe are the leadings of our Lord Christ Jesus. His anointing is a very *specific* life-flow. It is not a general state of my personal being or activity *per se*, but rather He flowing in a *specific* activity or ministry *through* me. I seek that it be not I, but Christ living in me (Galatians 2:20), Who both wills and effects His Perfect will through me (Philippians 2:13). So, if He waits many years before again pouring out His anointing for a given task, then I also wait those many years.

So once again the manuscript was set aside unfinished. A further 9 years was to pass before this work was to resume, and then as part of this ***Where Do You Fit In?*** series. When during 1990 and 1991 this entire series unfolded and the first four volumes were completed, the proper context of ***Profiles In Sanctification*** became settled as very early in the series. Volumes IV, V and VI of ***Where Do You Fit In?*** address general issues in the Body of Christ that apply to both individual believers and to local groups: IV - spiritual realities that we must ***dramatically embrace*** if we are to be part of that "new work"; V - ***social implications*** thereof; and VI - the ***clarion call*** that our Lord Christ Jesus is now beginning to do a "new work" in our midst. But first, in "Profiles In Sanctification" we address some of those powerful Biblical truths discussed in Volumes IV and V, specifically as they are worked out in the lives of *individual believers*.

The story still doesn't end there. During the winter of 1990-91, through researching the writings of Dr. Larry J. Crabb and others, I at long last apprehended another vital missing link in my Biblical understandings and teachings. Although the Lord had blessed me with to-me-remarkable understandings of His ways and will, I simply did not know *how* to apply those Biblical principles - particularly those related to *repentance* - to my own personal needs and to the needs of other Christians. Just *how* can we *actually* live the Christian life?

Now at last I learned specifically how the natural human heart, so utterly self-deceiving in its self-seeking and self-protecting, works in the very opposite direction from repentance unto servanthood. The original sin runs so deep in all of us, that even after years of "walking in the Spirit" as Christians we are still largely self-seekers rather than Christ-bearers. Even though the Tree (source) of Life (Christ Himself) is available to us (actually lives within us), we still partake of the Tree (source) of Knowledge so that we can serve ourselves by self-seeking. We don't *really* believe or take seriously the fact that Christ Himself actually lives in us, or if we do believe that fact, we slap Him in the face by thinking that His Presence is not enough for us! That is the depth at which we must repent! Our obtaining ultimate victory from our inner hurts and "hangups" and "secret sins", etc., all boils down to this: truly repenting from self-seeking and from receiving our "empowerment" from the "Tree of Knowledge"; and truly walking in faith, which is total dependence upon and obedience to Christ Indwelling our Tree of Life. We must trust in Him meeting our own needs, and not seek to have our needs met *by our own efforts!*

But true repentance at that depth is so difficult a step for us to make, that most of us don't even try; just to consider it, only increases our inner sense of guilt. It's extremely difficult because, first of all, we don't know *how*, and second, when we find out how, it's excruciatingly painful. So we just continue to hide our inner hurts by various ways of covering up, pretending to be holy Christians by our actions, and coping with inner hurts by various "defense mechanism" maintained to distance ourselves from others who we sense might otherwise further hurt us. We remain oblivious to the fact that the inner pain itself was created in us by God for the very purpose of driving us to total dependence upon and obedience to Christ indwelling.

Further research along this theme gave me vital insights on how, *via* the inner workings of the indwelling Holy Spirit of Christ Jesus, the inner healing process is actually possible. Even then, however, I still had a ways to go: I myself had to actually walk through that painful process personally . And my discoveries by that walk were utterly amazing to me. Six full chapters on this deep surrender repentance unto inner heart healing, two on its exegetical foundations and four on its experiential aspects, appear now as Chapters 5 through 10 of Volume I of this series: *The Christian Marriage - A Sixfold Covenant Of Love-Motivated Servanthood.*

As I then proceeded to delineate the three-stage model of the sanctification process that we present in Chapters Eight through Twelve herein, I realized I had had a basic misunderstanding between the "second" and "third" general stages. The "first" general stage indeed begins upon regeneration, and the "second" general stage indeed begins upon our receiving the Baptism into the Holy Spirit by our Lord Christ Jesus. However, in the model I have finally settled upon herein, I somewhat arbitrarily define precisely where the second ("natural" or "soulical") stage ends and the third ("spiritual") stage begins. This is because both the latter part of the second stage and the early part of the third stage involve one or more cycles of vision-loss-struggle-surrender-revisitation-consummation, which we delineate later in Chapter Nine. (I had originally included all such emptying cycles in the "second" general stage.) For illustrative purposes, we herein define the second stage to "end" when the vision first experienced upon Baptism into the Holy Spirit reaches some form of "consummation". This is a slight modification of the Guyon-Penn-Lewis concepts referenced in Chapter Nine. Using this concept, the second stage includes at least one, and usually two, of these cycles, and likewise the third stage begins with at least one, if not more, such cycles.

We need to emphasize that our purpose for delineating such a three-stage general model of sanctification, is **not** to give the reader a program for him/her to follow. This volume was not written to provide the reader with a "three or twelve step self-help program" by which one can achieve spiritual maturity. (Indeed, none of us would knowingly *seek* the emptying cycles of the second and third stages.) Rather it has been written to provide the reader with understandings of the dealings of the indwelling Holy Spirit of Christ Jesus in our lives, so that he/she may more freely be able to cooperate therewith, and be encouraged to endure the emptying cycles of those dealings.

Remember: the *purpose* for our seeking inner heart healing, and for our enduring all of the other loss-striving-surrendering-revisitation-consummation cycles of the sanctification process to which he chooses to subject us, is not *our being blessed;* rather it is that we become pure vessels/channels for He to pour Himself through unto others. Any other motives we might have than that, are motives that yet need those very cycles in order to remove from us! Jesus Christ is Lord! He, alone, is worthy of our entire commitment. His Will for us is the *only* issue of importance to us. To Him, alone, is the Glory!

So, this book is the second of the series of seven volumes under the title, *Where Do You Fit In? Practical Commitments In The Body Of Christ.* That series as now configured is as follows (not in order of publication):

Volume I addresses our marriage relationships, the most *crucial* area for the purging work of the Holy Spirit within the Body of Christ today. This volume II delineates several dozen biblical portraits of three general levels of the maturing process in our *individual* relationships with Christ. Volume III delineates 12 parallel stages of the *corporate* maturation of the Body of Christ (right now, we are functioning at "stage four" at best). In Volumes IV and V we study many foundational aspects of our relationship to Him *as a spiritual reality*, and with one another in *local social contexts*. Volume VI examines our eschatological vision for the current purging moves of the Holy Spirit and God's *purposes* behind them. Volume VII exposes the many current forms of *deception* common within the Body of Christ today.

Part I

Do You Care?

"Sanctification" - what *really* is it? Is it a "crisis event" or a "growth process"? Is it a "Work of Grace" or something *we* must strive and work for? What is meant by "spiritual growth" anyhow? Are we merely to "wait for the rapture", witnessing of the Gospel of Jesus Christ to others as best we can in the meantime? Or are we to seek a "deeper life" of "spiritual power" while still in this life? What does God really want of us, here and now, once we are "saved"?

To address these concerns, we need to first study several foundational Biblical concepts. Being a Christian is having a personal relationship with Christ Jesus, in the *spirit*. We each have a human spirit, distinct from our soul and flesh, that makes that possible. And sanctification is our increasing in that spiritual relationship with Christ Jesus while decreasing in physical relationship with self and the world. That is the full meaning of our being crucified *with* Christ. But none of this will take place unless we *care*, and care very deeply, to grow in that relationship with Him. Our growth in our spiritual relationship with Him is the essence of God's ultimate intention behind creation in the first place. Yes, we are strongly admonished to grow up in Him!

Chapter One

What *Is* Sanctification?

The Body of Christ is divided along doctrinal issues related to several questions pertaining to sanctification. One great barrier to fellowship of believers is doctrinal controversy. So often we refuse to welcome into our own circle of Christian fellowship others who have a vibrant testimony of Jesus Christ but who interpret the Scriptures differently than we do *re* our favorite doctrines. Rather than "unity in the Spirit", we foster doctrinal parochialism, which in turn strongly hinders our own spiritual growth.

As an example, we often distort the word "holiness" to mean xenophobic isolation from the world into our particular Church denomination - all others being of the "world" and hence, *ipso facto*, "unbelievers". For, after all, does not the Bible admonish us to "stand firm in the doctrines of the Gospel" (John 7:16-17; I Timothy 4:6, 13 & 16; Titus 2:1-10)? Are we not to be on guard against "ravenous and savage wolves" (Matthew 7:15-16 & 24:24; Acts 20:28-30)? Are we not duty bound to defend God's Word against the encroachments of scientific atheism, humanism and pagan philosophies? And is not our own particular doctrinal position solidly founded upon the Written Word of God?

In I Corinthians 1:10-25 and 3:3-9 and 11:18-29, Paul talks *against* this very thing. The word "heresy" in the Greek (actually the Greek word itself) does *not* mean a "wrong doctrine"; rather, it means a *division* due to a legalistic, doctrinal *dispute:* i.e., a *"litigation"*.

Yet even if we recognize this, we still tend to think that since our own doctrinal position, founded in the Scriptures, is "right", other denominations are *doubly* wrong: (a) by disagreeing with us, hence in error exegetically; and (b) by causing divisions in the Body of Christ as a result. After all, since our doctrines are *Biblical*, we can't be in the wrong! Or can we?

In the decades of the 1950's through 1970's, the Lord Jesus Christ did a work in His Body to destroy this parochalism. In many places, the so-called "Charismatic Movement" arose spontaneously and increased in momentum, with its most significant characteristic being unity of believers of all denominational backgrounds in Spirit-led worship and Christ-oriented fellowships. Yes, the *Lord* was tearing down our doctrinal (as well as cultural) barriers!

Did this mean that our doctrinal steadfastness was *not* of the Lord, that it *conflicted* with the Lord's Will for us? Yes, partly! Our trouble is that we fail to realize God's balancing of *truth vs personal experience* in our spiritual growth, both in timing and priority.

Four vital principles in particular we tend to lose sight of are:

(1) No one believer, group nor denomination ever possesses *all* revealed truth. To acquire a fullness and proper

balance of all revealed *Biblical* understandings, one must assimilate much of the doctrinal emphases of many Christian denominations and movements.

(2) According to such vibrant Scriptures as John Chapter 3, the essence of being a Christian is having received *eternal life*. "Eternal life" is *life!* It is not intellectual understanding and acceptance of correct *doctrine*. Nor is it personal *emotional* experience. Nor is it denominational *institutional* structure. It is *life*. It is a dynamic two-way interaction, *via* Christ Jesus, with the domain or realm of spiritual reality within which everything we know and are is intrinsically embedded.

(3) True spiritual growth of every Christian believer *requires* that unity in *Spirit*, both with Christ Jesus as Lord and with fellow believers, *precede* unity in *truth*. The *humble* walk in the Spirit of God must be experienced *first*. For when truth precedes the Spiritual walk, spiritual *pride* axiomatically results.

(4) The Biblical essence of being a Christian in the first place is not being a member of some *religion*, albeit based on *truth;* but rather is having a *personal relationship* with God through the Holy Spirit of our Lord Christ Jesus indwelling, and manifested in *love-motivated and Spirit-empowered servanthood!*

1. Relationship, Not Religion!

In Christ there is virtually no limit to the promised blessings that we believers can theoretically apprehend in this life. But we attain to *only* those promises that we actively seek; and at any moment we have fulfillment only to the extent of our *actual* pursuits. He wants us to seek Him, to seek Him above all other interests, to seek Him intensely enough to be willing to put aside all other conflicting desires of the flesh and self, and to yield to Him in total dependence and obedience.

The deepest longing in each of our hearts is the true inner peace and joy of knowing with certainty that all is "right". Now, it *is* possible to approach full satisfaction of that longing in this life. It is possible though Christ Jesus. But it requires more than merely being a regenerated Christian: it requires a full personal companionship *knowing* Him in intimacy and *yielding* to Him indwelling us, so that He actually lives His Life and effects His Will *through* us (Philippians 2:13).

Christianity is *relationship*, not religion! Our walk in Christ has never been intended by Him to be a walk in religion, i.e., in a social organization structured to meet human (albeit "spiritual") needs. Rather, our walk in Christ is a matter of being in personal relationship with God through Christ Jesus. And Christian maturing is a constant growing and deepening and expanding in/of our personal relationship with Him.

To recognize Christ as one's personal saviour, but to not yet know Him in depth and to yield to Him, commits a Christian to a way of life that is *impossible!* That way of life *also* requires the *power* of the Indwelling Holy Spirit of Christ (which flows only as we respond by *yielding* to Him). It is not enough, though necessary and important as it is, to just know *via* the Scriptures that a Christian must repent, accept, yield, and grow. We must still actually *do* the repenting, accepting, yielding, and growing.

Now it usually isn't too difficult to repent of our *sins*: it should be quite obvious that by ourselves we humans are in a wretched mess. To *receive* and *accept* Jesus as our personal saviour is a little harder: that involves blind faith in the very things - supernatural realities - that our intellect wants to deny. But to *yield* to Him is *extremely* difficult: to want *only* and *entirely* to do His will requires a total and agonizing denial of our self, including all of our personal idols and dreams and psychological crutches. Yet, we grow in Christ only to the extent we indeed love Him, seek Him, and regard Him as **Lord**.

Hence the regenerated but yet immature Christian can easily become caught up in a frustrating cycle. We need *three* things in order to overcome the conflicting desires of flesh/self *vs* spirit and to flow in oneness with Him: (1) the *indwelling* Holy Spirit of Christ Jesus (Who comes upon our regeneration); (2) a conscious *awareness* of that indwelling (that should come upon a "Baptism Into The Holy Spirit"[1]); and (3) a *determined* dependence upon Him and obedience to Him. Until we actually flow in that dependence upon the Holy Spirit of Christ indwelling, it is very difficult for us to overcome the worldly diversions and temptations enough to seek Him with sufficient determination.

Although these aspects of grace are free gifts that we cannot earn nor merit, nevertheless they come to us only to the extent we really *seek* them in Him. So, He must deal with our *motives*. He must bestow His peace upon us, and at the same time *discipline* us, iteratively, step-by-step. That is a life-long *process*, a process called "sanctification", that involves both "crisis experiences" and periods of growth under His hand of loving chastisement (Hebrews 12:5-11).

Once we turn to Christ Jesus and yield to His Saving Grace, from that point on in our lives He deals with us, in many diverse and baffling ways, toward one objective: to bring us into utter and total *intimacy* with Him. That ever requires our *dependence upon and obedience to Him*.

The root meaning of the New Testament Greek word translated "faith" is an "empowering dependence". The word is used to depict our utterly depending upon Christ Jesus as Lord in "real time" (i.e., when and as we need), whereupon we receive the abilities and power to do and be whatever He Wills for us at that particular moment.

However, because of the particular nature of human psychology as God Created us, one of our greatest hindrances to this empowering dependence *upon* Him is our mental understandings *about* Him. We tend to trust only that which we understand and to avoid that which we do not understand - the very reversal of true "faith".

2. The Human Spirit, Soul And "Flesh"

Of all of the Biblical teachings that are *basic* to the Christian walk, I know of none so essential to our understanding of God's dealing in our lives, than the *triparte* nature of the human psychological makeup.

We have been created in the image of God. The "image" of God is the Holy Trinity. So is our "image" a triparte one. And God's disciplinings and chastenings of us can be explained only in the context of three major and distinct aspects of our salvation that correspond to the three aspects of our triparte psychological nature.

This emphasis on each of us having been created with a human *spirit* as well as soul, so thoroughly scriptural, is totally denied in almost all Christian doctrine and thinking today, and has been for over 1700 years. Edwards[2] gives an excellent brief summary of why this is so:

> "Why have we heard so little on this central issue of man's being *spirit*, as well as soul and body? Why is man seen almost universally as (only) body and soul? Why an almost total void of any reference to man as partly spirit? Why so little known about the human spirit? Why, for most of the last 1,700 years, have scholarly Christians been teaching that we are body and soul, when we actually are spirit, soul and body?
>
> "Well, the problem all started in *places* you probably never heard of. ... All those men ... were of Greek origin, and they were all heathen. They are the grandfathers of a (pagan) school of Western thought called the *Pythagorean school of philosophy.* ... concluded that man was body and soul. And so it stuck. And *every* philosopher since has accepted that view and speculated on what "soul" meant. ...
>
> "... Their profound ideas certainly should never have come over into the Christian faith! But they did! And there is an excellent chance the Christian faith at large will never recover from this sad event. ...
>
> "... Man has a body, and it interfaces with man's soul; man is a soul, but the soul interfaces with man's spirit. Soul and spirit so interlock that *only* an indwelling Lord can distinguish soul from spirit.

"Man's humanity rests in his soul. The Lord Jesus' main place of residence in the believer is in his spirit.

"Heathen philosophers had absolutely no idea of such a view. They could not have comprehended such a thing had they heard it. ... the heathen philosophers of the second and third centuries who became believers perpetrated this view on fellow Christians. One of these diametrically opposed views had to go. Unfortunately the idea of man as 'body and soul' won out over 'spirit, soul, and body.'

"... It happened on this wise: Around the middle of the second century (c. A.D.150), a few philosophers, all of them 'sons' of Plato and Aristotle, began to convert to Christianity. They came into the Christian faith bringing their philosophical and pagan mind-set with them. ...

"... these philosophers-turned-Christian began applying the dialectics and logic of Aristotle to the analysis of the Christian faith. In so doing, they offhandedly declared man to be soul and body. ... The Christian faith might have been untouched by this corruption except for ... (certain) men. These men were all stepped in Greco-heathen philosophy *and* at the same time they claimed to be Christian (and probably were). ...

"Among other things, the concept of man as *body and soul* reigns unquestioned in theological circles to this very day."

Edwards[3] lists several such men: Origen, Tertullian, Augustine, Pseudo-Dionysius, Thomas Aquinas, Martin

Luther, John Calvin, and the author/editor of *The Baptist Commentary*. (Yes, Protestant leaders also.) Edwards then summarizes some of the sad results of this[4]:

> "Virtually every Christian commentary ever written takes up the theme that man is body and soul, and is flavored with the view of the soul as seen by Thomas Aquinas. ...
>
> "But the saddest part is not only the loss of the spirit, but the fact that the intellect of man is that which is seen as his most spiritual part. No wonder we have no idea of what 'the spirituals' means. An indwelling Lord simply has no place anywhere in all these writings. ... An understanding of the human spirit's being one with God's Spirit exists almost wholly in 1 Corinthians and never in theology. ...
>
> "Moreover, when psychiatry and psychology entered into Christian theology (by way of something dubiously called 'Christian counseling'), it also carried with it the pagan/heathen humanistic concept of man as body and soul. ...
>
> "Christian counseling, self-centric by its very nature, has left us trying to solve soul problems with the soul! ... but most of our problems of the soul will be solved only within our spiritual faculties. ...
>
> "The ***proper abode*** for the believer is a difficult matter for man to lay hold of. 'To walk in your spirit' and to 'live in your spirit' began way back two thousand years ago as terms that came out of experience that was real!

"It was not until the twentieth century that ... (certain mature Christian teachers) pointed out that we are spirit, soul, and body. Until then, almost no one had noticed the cavernous disparity. Even then men looked, thought, and soberly declared, 'Perhaps there is a difference in soul and spirit, but whatever the difference, it is of no great significance.

"Not significant? Only the difference between Jesus' life and our life. The difference between this realm and the realm of the spiritual. Only the difference in our Adamic inheritance and our divine inheritance."

Our starting point, then, in understanding just how sanctification works out in practice is studying the Biblical depiction of the human "heart" including the human spirit: the totality of the "psychological" or non-physiological portion of man.

3. Human Triparte Nature As Created

The Biblical triparte portrait of the human "heart" is spirit plus soul plus flesh. Spirit, soul, flesh: *human* spirit, human soul, human flesh. Throughout the Old Testament, three distinct Hebrew words are used for these: RWCh for "spirit", NPhSh for "soul", and BShR for "flesh". The corresponding New Testament Greek words are Pneuma for "spirit", Psuche for "soul", and Soma for "body". Paul also often uses the Greek word Sarx for "flesh" to refer to the psychological power of the appetites of the physical body.

However, this distinction of the three separate aspects of the human psychological nature was not clear to Old Testament writers; only occasional such understanding appears prior to the time of Paul. Indeed it is to the Holy Spirit through Paul that we primarily owe this understanding.

The Old and New Testaments also use the words LB and Cardia respectively (translated "heart") to refer to the human soul, not spirit[5]. It does not of course refer to the physical organ that pumps our blood, but to the "innermost" or central "core" of our consciousness or psychological nature. It refers to the seat of all emotional, intellectual, volitional and moral functions. Our heart determines our personality. It is not only where God dwells, but also where satan directs his fiercest attacks.

BShR in the Hebrew basically means "flesh" in the physiological sense, i.e., muscle, bone, "meat", etc. In the Greek, Soma means the body in an overall sense: our entire being; but Sarx specifically refers to our **carnality**, that is, the **appetites** of our physical body and how they influence our feelings, thoughts and decisions.

In Appendix One we go into the use of these Hebrew and Greek words in some detail.

Our Human Spirit

Let's look at these three parts in further detail. First, our human spirit. Our human spirit is our seat of *God*-consciousness. It is that which God has created into us (uniquely among the entire "animal kingdom") in order to enable us to be in two-way communication with Him.

The functions of the human spirit include: ***intuition*** - an ability to know things of God, spiritual truths and other facts in a way other than by what we have learned in our mind; ***conscience*** - an ability to know moral truths and to know God's will for us in specific situations; ***guilt*** - God's way of warning us of our violations of His laws; ***grieving*** - deep discomfort that causes us to seek God more earnestly; ***love***, both Agape (self-sacrificing) and Eros (passion); ***yearnings*** - subtle motivation to abandon ourselves unto Him; ***praise*** - the drive to thank God for what He has done for/unto us; and ***worship*** - actual Spiritual union with God.

Since all of these functions are empowered and amplified by the Holy Spirit of Christ Jesus ***dwelling*** in our human spirits, the phrase "house of the Lord" means our human spirit. The full meaning of ***grace*** is the dwelling of Him therein.

The human spirit links man with the higher intelligences of the spiritual domain, with both evil spirits and the Godhead. It is the highest part of man, and it is the seat of reception of, or "quickening by", the Holy Spirit of Christ Jesus (1 Corinthians 15:47, etc.). But the soul and the flesh are normally much ***stronger*** forces in the human experience, and are in conflict with the Holy Spirit's workings through the believer's spirit.

In the unregenerated man, the human spirit is so suppressed by the soul-flesh combination, that it often loses its distinction in manifestations from the soul. Nevertheless, the human spirit ***still exists*** as part of his nature. Intuition and conscience still operate, and a "religious" force or yearning for a "god" is a powerful drive in the non-christian.

Our Soul, Self And Sin

Our soul is the seat of our *self*-consciousness: that which appears to us to be our "self". Although the true and full "me" consists of my human spirit *plus* my soul, the totality of my direct *awareness* of my self is my soul alone. All functioning of my spirit cause me to be aware of God, not of my self.

The functioning of our soul include: our *mind* - our ability to consciously and rationally think, reason, plan and calculate; our *emotions* - our ability to *feel* and emote; and our *will* or *volition* - our ability to deliberately determine and choose to act or not act.

Allender[6] gives what I regard to be an excellent experiential understanding of the human soul:

> "The concept of the self is an intuitive rather than scientific notion. What is the self? How do we define the word *soul* or *self* or, for that matter, the idea of life? There is something inside us that provides continuity and cohesion to the divergent experiences of life. ...
>
> "But what is me? I have no idea. All I know is that I am connected to that boy (who I remember was me twenty-five years ago), and he is connected to a man I can see twenty-five years from now ... the slow, overweight, balding man I will (probably) become as the years transpire. I am not my body, but my body is as much me as I know anything else to be. I am so much more than my body; nevertheless, I am at least the totality of all that I have experienced in my body. Confused? Maybe that is partly God's intention. My

being can never be defined outside relationship with God. I am an orphaned child of Adam and an adopted child of the King (Christ). My identity and being find their beginning and end in something outside myself, but if I am numb to my hunger and thirst, I will never look outside of myself for meaning or life.

The soul and the flesh are distinct. The soul, with its will function, actually controls all that we think and do.. When the soul yields to the power of sin in the flesh, the results are the manifestations of the flesh. To be delivered from the power of sin means the soul has to reckon the flesh to be dead, i.e., having no influence over the soul. The self-life of the soul has to be dealt with by the cross apart from basic regeneration.

As long as we are in this body, it is possible for the soul to yield to the power of sin through the flesh. We never in this life reach the state where it is *impossible* for us to sin. We *cannot* cleanse the flesh. Subduing the flesh through asceticism is not God's way either. Until the redemption of our bodies (Romans 8:23 and Philippians 3:21), we must trust in faith that Christ *via* His Holy Spirit in us is continually giving us the power to reckon the flesh of no account (Romans 6:6 and 1 Corinthians 10:13).

In our "natural" state, i.e. before complete sanctification by the Holy Spirit of Christ Jesus, our soul is the power of self that is in *actual* control of all we think and do. *Self* is the real king enthroned in our "hearts". Satan through sin-power, working through our flesh, is vying for control against the Holy Spirit in our spirits. Christ, through His Holy Spirit in our human spirits, is also vying for control against him. Thus the warfare Paul so aptly describes in Romans Chapter 7.

Paul also uses such phrases as "old man", "old nature", "old creature", etc., to refer to sin-power working through our flesh to dominate our soul; it means a soul yielding to the power of sin. (Note for example Romans 6:6, 1 Corinthians 5:7-8, Ephesians 4:22 and Colossians 3:9. Note also 2 Peter 1:9.)

In contrast, we find in the Bible such phrases as "new man", "new nature", "new heart", "new creation", etc., to refer to the Holy Spirit ruling us through our human spirit, to which our soul is yielding. (See for example 2 Corinthians 5:17, Galatians 6:15, Ephesians 4:22-24 and Colossians 3:9-10.)

We also find the expression "inward man" referring to the human spirit (Romans 7:22, 2 Corinthians 4:16 and 7:15, and Ephesians 3:16) and the expression "outward man" referring to the soul and body of flesh (Matthew 23:28, Romans 2:28, 2 Corinthians 4:16 and 1 Peter 3:3).

"Flesh"

Lastly, our flesh is the seat of our *world*-consciousness: all of our abilities to know the physical context of our lives. It includes more than simply our nervous system and the five physical senses. It is of course closely linked with our nervous system and our glands. But it also includes the *influences* of those physical senses on our soul functioning.

Our "flesh" or carnality is a real and distinct part of us, distinct from both our corporeal body and our soul, but nevertheless closely linked to both. That is why the Bible uses a distinct Greek word (Sarx) for it, in addition to the word (Soma) for "body. In practical experience, our carnality is the realm of our bodily *feelings*. i.e., the feelings of consciousness of the physical body.

4. Sanctification Of The Human Triparte Nature

Each of these three aspects of our psychological nature has a power of its own, apart from God if not in Him. The flesh has the power of *sin* in a direct sense; it is the area of our lives most directly under satan's control, except to the extent we reckon it crucified with Christ. The soul has a tremendous power in its own right, far more so than we realize. And our spirit is the power to directly communicate with the "spirit world", with satanic spirits if not with God.

Each must be dealt with separately and in totally *different* ways. There is a time-sequence of our sanctification given in 1 Thessalonians 5:23: our human spirit *first;* our human soul *second;* and our flesh *last.* We delineate this sequence briefly here, and study it in depth in Chapters 8 through 13, below. The reader is also referred to Ebaugh[7] for an easy-to-read parallel discussion.

Salvation Of Our Human Spirit

Briefly, our human spirit is sanctified upon *regeneration*, when the Holy Spirit of Christ Jesus comes, *in His entirety*, to dwell in our human spirit, placing us in two-way communication with God and hence enabling us to "know" Him and possess "eternal life". This is a single or "crisis" event in our lives, although not necessarily one we are *consciously* aware of at the time[8].

What Is Sanctification?

Our soul is *sanctified* by the *process* of our increasingly yielding our soul-functions of mind and emotions and will to that Holy Spirit Who already indwells our human spirit. *Baptism* into the Holy Spirit means that our *soul* is initially *immersed* into that Holy Spirit. Our soul is the totality of our consciousness; hence this is the first time when we become *experientially aware* of He Who is already dwelling in us.

Our bodies are sanctified upon final redemption in conjunction with Christ's Parousia return when we become established fully in Him (Philippians 3:21).

Our carnality (Sarx) can *never* be sanctified; it must be *reckoned as crucified;* it must die! Romans Chapter 6 addresses this issue in conjunction with water baptism. In fact, it is only to the *extent* that we indeed reckon our Sarx dead that we progress in our soul-sanctification.

Hence the first to be "quickened" is our human spirit. That is the issue upon regeneration: receiving "eternal life". Eternal life is the Holy Spirit of Christ Jesus dwelling in our human spirit and enabling us to communicate with God Himself. That communication is two-way - both to and from Him - and is *via* intuition, conscience, guilt, grieving, love, yearning, praise and worship and joy.

Eternal life is imparted unto us by our Lord. The expression used in the Bible for that impartation is "breathe into". Adam and Eve had that Spiritual knowledge of, and direct communication with, God immediately upon God breathing it into them in Genesis 2:7. Christ Jesus breathed it into the disciples in John 20:22. He readily imparts it to us, in response as we repent and seek Him.

The key to becoming born-again is *belief* upon Christ Jesus as the resurrected Son of God (John 1:12, 3:15-18). But "belief" or "faith" (Greek: Pistis) means not just mental acknowledgement of the truth of certain Biblical statements or promises, but rather *trust* in, *dependence* upon, and *obedience* to, the Person of Christ Jesus. If we trust in Christ, then these passages give us the certainty (since they are from God's Word) that somewhere along the line we did become born-again. John 3:3-8 is not given as a practical guide for *how* to become born-again, but rather is a statement of theological understanding of what happens *when* we do.

Since rebirth involves our human spirit, and initially not our soul, it is not something *by itself* of which we are necessarily consciously aware. Since "eternal life" involves the Holy Spirit of Christ Jesus coming to indwell our human *spirit*, He does not necessarily immediately dominate our self-consciousness.

But our human wills must operate in repentance and seeking of Him in order for Him to impart regeneration unto us. Though we can never earn nor deserve so great a salvation, we nevertheless must qualify for it, and that qualification is repentance. Hence, what we call a *born-again experience* is better called a *repentance experience*, since that involves certain soul-functions of which we *are* vividly aware: conviction of our sinfulness and its consequences; desperate begging of Jesus for forgiveness; and release of our burden of guilt.

If a believer is brought to Christ in this way, then he will know that he is born-again. But many genuine believers exist in non-evangelical environments who have never been *taught*

What Is Sanctification?

John 3:3-8 and the words "born-again".

How About Sanctification Of Our Soul And Self?

He purposes that we allow His Holy Spirit to completely control our entire beings - that He live His life in and through us as He wills, unhindered by our self-interests and desires. But our soul functions of mind and emotions and will can (and usually do at first) remain independent of that now-indwelling Holy Spirit in our spirit. He does not override our wills. So, our soul functions must determinedly *yield* to that indwelling Holy Spirit. Subsequently to our receiving this new quality of life, He is ever dealing in our lives and hearts to entice us to increasingly choose to yield to His will. It is those subsequent dealings by Him in our lives, that the Bible refers to as ***sanctification***.

The human soul must be ***denied*** (Matthew 10:38-39 & 16:24-26; Luke 17:32-33; Mark 8:34-36; John 12:25), ***cleansed*** by that denial and by renewal (Romans 12:2), ***purified*** by obedience to truth and through prayer (1 Peter 1:22) and ***hated*** or ***mistrusted*** (Matthew 10:37 and Luke 14:26).

Specifically what must be denied, cleansed, purified, hated, distrusted, etc.? The three most powerful and deep-seated motivational forces of our soul/self are drives to seek, or protect ourselves from failure to obtain a sense of personal identity, purpose and acceptance, and to seek that by any other route than our personal relationship with Christ Jesus. We need an "inner heart healing" for full sanctification of our soul/self. That inner heart healing is discussed in great detail in Volume 1 of this series[9].

As we yield our wills and minds and emotions to Him, the result is that He increasingly saturates our self-consciousness (soul) with a sense of His indwelling *presence.* This is the root meaning in the Greek of the phrase "be *filled* with the Holy Spirit". Luke 1:15 and Acts 2:4, 4:8, 4:31, 9:17 & 13:9 use the Greek word Pletho that has the fuller meaning of "to satiate", "to take possession of", or "to fulfill". Ephesians 5:8 uses the Greek word Pleroo that means "to cause to abound" or "to furnish liberally". These words do not refer to an initial receiving or being filled with the Holy Spirit, but rather to a subsequent being *saturated* with Him Who is already in us.

It is our *soul* that needs to be thus "filled" with the Holy Spirit in these passages. Our human *spirit* already became filled with Him upon regeneration. But now our mind, our emotions, and most particularly our will, need to be saturated with Him, that He exercise complete control over our behavior and mind. "Be (continuously being) filled with the Holy Spirit" in Ephesians 5:18 refers to an on-going continuous *process* wherein we ever allow the Holy Spirit of Christ Jesus, Who indwells our human spirits since regeneration, to satiate our soul functions - mind, emotions and will - so that Christ Jesus can live His life in and through us as He wills.

Dealing With Our "Flesh"

Finally, how about the "flesh"? Eventually we will receive immortal bodies like His (Philippians 3:21). But "flesh" (Gr. Sarx) as used by Paul means our physical carnal desires and drives. As such, our flesh now is so corrupt that it can in *no* way be purified unto Christ or given eternal life. No, our physical drives must be rendered of no effect, reckoned as dead through crucifixion (Romans 6:1-21, Galatians 5:24,

Philippians 3:3-4 and 1 Peter 3:21) so that we no longer yield to carnality but only to Christ indwelling.

5. Sanctification By Emptying Trials

The most difficult of these three components to be brought to full yielding to the Lord Jesus Christ is the human *soul*. It is the seat of the self, the "I", the Adamic Nature. No matter how strongly we desire (and pray for) being yielded to the Lord, the soul will continue to dominate our behavior and to suppress the human spirit (until, that is, the soul determines to yield). The human mind demands understandings; the human will demands that understanding *precede* commitment; and our emotions confuse and deceive us. Furthermore, the Lord has chosen to never *force* us into anything against our will; so He *draws* us unto entire soul sanctification through a combination of: (1) enticing us by His *love* (to soften our emotions); (2) physical *miracles* (that our mind can *not* understand) such as speaking in tongues, healings and victories over our passions (to weaken our *mind's* dominance); and (3) trials and tribulations in the circumstances of our daily lives (to redirect our *will*).

Trials and tribulations? In I Peter 1:6-7 they are compared to a refiner's fire, wherein our "faith" is "tested" to be found precious as gold. This "testing" of our "faith" in essence means *"tempering"* (purifying and strengthening) our "direct and obedient dependence upon our Lord Jesus Christ in His *Spiritual* reality. The dross being removed from us in this purifying process refers to our natural tendencies to depend upon ourselves, our own abilities, our mental understandings, our cultural or traditional conditioning, the social contexts of our ministries, etc. We never *really* depend upon Christ Jesus beyond that with which we are familiar and which we understand, until the circumstances of our lives and ministries leave us with no other alternatives. Only then can our soul fully *yield* to Him. Then can we begin to really grow in *spiritual* understanding!

But even such testings would not accomplish this purification - indeed in many cases would lead only to a more hardened and embittered heart - unless the Lord effects two things in us at the same time: both things that *we* must consciously and willfully *seek* (but that He does the doing in response to our seeking):

(1) A saturation of our consciousness (soul) with the Holy Spirit, so that we have the power and abilities to endure the trials and grow by them; and

(2) A praise relationship with the Person of Christ Jesus, so that we are vividly conscious both of His Personal Presence in and undergirding of our lives and of His total Love for us.

The first step in our spiritual relationship with Christ (i.e., basic regeneration) is "easy" - wide is the way and easy the path. But Truth - and *He* is The Truth - is expensive: it costs us our *everything*. Narrow and steep is the way to *discipleship* and to *submitting* to the Kingship of Christ Jesus.

* * * * * * * *

This book is dedicated to a study of the pattern of general spiritual growth. The human condition and God's dealings with it are first studied in depth exegetically. Then Biblical typologies and examples are used to demonstrate that pattern from many different viewpoints.

Each individual believer is dealt with by the Lord in unique ways and in unique timings, although with a basic common pattern. Each of us has a distinct

Profile In Sanctification.

"Commit thy way unto the Lord; trust also in Him, and He shall bring it to pass" ... (Psalm 37:5).

End Notes: Chapter One

[1] We are *not* referring here to "speaking in tongues". We study the "Baptism Into The Holy Spirit" and "speaking in tongues" in Chapter 7 later in this Volume II.

[2] Edwards, Gene, *The Highest Life* (Wheaton, Illinois: Tyndale House Publishers, Inc), pp. 168-174. Copyright © by Gene Edwards.

[3] *Ibid.* pp. 171-178.

[4] *Ibid.* pp. 179-181.

[5] Most Bible scholars have long regarded "heart" to refer to the entire human psychological makeup, including human

spirit, soul and carnality (See Appendix 1 later in this volume.) However, the 779 Old Testament uses of LB and 157 New Testament uses of Cardia refer to functions which parallel the functions which the scriptures associate with the human *soul,* and do *not* parallel the functions which the scriptures associate with neither the human spirit nor carnality *per se.* The scriptural word used for the entire psychological make-up is the New Testament Greek word Nuos (or Noos), which literally means "our innermost sanctuary".

6. Allender, Dan B. *The Wounded Heart - Hope For Adult Victims Of Childhood Sexual Abuse,* (Colorado Springs, Co.: Navpress, 1990), pp. 105-106. Copyright © 1990 by Dan B. Allender. Used by permission of NavPress. All rights reserved. For copies, call 1-800-366-7788.

7. Ebaugh, David P., *The Third Salvation,* (Harrisburg, PA: David Ebaugh Bible School, 102 Park Terrace, Harrisburg, PA 17111).

8. As was the personal experience of this author: it was not until over six years later that I became literate of what had actually happened.

9. Sherrerd, Chris S., *The Christian Marriage - A Six-Fold Covenant Of Love-Motivated Servanthood,* Volume I of the series "Where Do You Fit In? Practical Commitments In The Body Of Christ" (Shippensburg, PA: Treasure House, Destiny Image Publishing Group, 1994). Copyright © 1994 by Shulemite Christian Crusade.

Chapter Two

What Does Christ's Crucifixion Mean To Us?

The apostle Paul, in writing to the believers in Corinth, regarded the crucifixion of Christ as a most important aspect of the gospel message: "... but we preach Christ *crucified*, to Jews a stumbling block, and to Gentiles foolishness" (1 Corinthians 1:23). "For I determined to know nothing among you except Jesus Christ, and Him *crucified*" (1 Corinthians 2:1).

Christ's crucifixion is certainly the most crucial and absolutely necessary *foundation* for salvation. The Adamic curse of death (Genesis 2:17, 3:3 and 3:19) had to be fulfilled before man could again have fellowship with God. "... without shedding of blood there is no forgiveness (remission) of sins" (Hebrews 9:22). Before we come to Christ, we are hopelessly cut off from God (Ephesians 2:1-3 and 12); but by shedding His blood on Calvary, Christ Jesus has now brought us near to God (Ephesians 2:5-8 and 13). Such is our *only* possible route to salvation; there is no other way (Acts 4:12)!

But are not the resurrection (He lives!) and ascension (Ephesians 1:2-23) of even greater ultimate significance? That *we* are now (positionally) seated in Heavenly places with Him (Ephesians 2:6)? That He, now, is our High Priest, interceding on our behalf with God the Father (Hebrews 4:14 and 7:25)? Yes!

Why, then, is the *crucifixion* of Jesus Christ at Calvary regarded by Paul to be of higher importance than our position and abiding in the *Living and Indwelling* Christ? Or does he?

To understand the proper context and significance of crucifixion in a Christian's life, we must first examine what is really meant by "salvation", "grace", "receiving eternal life" and "faith". These most basic of Christian concepts are much under-understood in most Christian circles today.

1. By Grace We Are Saved Through Faith

One of the most succinct statements of fact in the Scriptures regarding the basic aspects of our personal relationship with God is Ephesians 2:8-10. In eight brief words, Paul states: "For by grace, we are saved, through faith." He then follows that fact with two parenthetical concepts: (1) that it is done in such a way that we have no basis whatsoever for taking any of the credit; and (2) God's purpose for it all is that we walk and function in *righteousness*.

Note the sequence here. Grace (whatever that is) is a causative agent; being saved (whatever that is) is the end result; and faith (whatever that is) is a necessary intermediate factor. Grace, saved, faith - what do they mean? Also, just what is "eternal life" and how does it fit in? Putting aside the usual religious jargon and cliches that we are so quick to speak, what is *really* meant by these and related words?

2. Salvation: Personal Relationship With God In Christ Jesus

We are being called by our Lord Christ Jesus to be brought into a personal companionship relationship of oneness with Him, and to fully understand in our hearts the ***full basis*** for that relationship. To be a Christian is not to be religious, but to be in personal relationship with God through and in Christ Jesus.

Exactly how and why are we ever brought to oneness, in any sense, with the Very God? We assert that that full-basis relationship is what "salvation" is really all about!

"Salvation" in both the Old Testament Hebrew (YShWIH and ThShWIH) and the New Testament Greek (Soteria) means to "preserve life from perishing". It implies that without it our "life will perish". Romans 6:23 does specify "death" as a consequence of sin. And John 3:16-18 links "receiving life unto not perishing" to "believing or trusting in Christ", on one hand; and "being judged unto perishing" to "not believing or trusting in Christ", on the other hand.

But perish how, and from what? What kind of death does this mean? Certainly not physical death, for we observe that truly born-again Christians, who indeed have Biblical "salvation", still experience natural death.

"Life" in Genesis 2:7 is in the plural in the Hebrew. That implies that originally God implanted at least two kinds of life to

Adam, physical life obviously being one of them. We often call the other form "spiritual life", and we glibly say that "perish" here means loss of that "spiritual life". But that's not quite accurate. The phrases "spiritual life" and "spiritual death" are *not* Biblical! The Biblical phrase is "*eternal* life", and it means far more than just "spiritual existence" or "living forever in time" (although those are properties of it). "Eternal life" also involves having direct *communication* with and experiential *knowledge* of God the Father and Christ Jesus the Son!

Still, "perishing" has strong implications beyond just "not knowing God", and we need more than mere word definitions in order to understand it. What is it we perish *unto*, and what is the factual basis for that perishing?

It is the *Adamic Curse*! (Genesis 2:17 and 3:4, 17, 19, 22, & 24).

Exactly what is the essence of that curse? Loss of direct communication with and knowledge of God? Yes, certainly loss of a face-to-face walk with God. But in Genesis 6:3, which pertains to a time about 1400 years after the Fall of Adam and Eve, we see strong implications that God's Spirit still abode in and dealt with men, implying that man still had the capacity to know God and to communicate with Him for some years under the Adamic curse.

"In the day ye partake thereof, death becomes a certainty to you." Did Adam and Eve actually physically die "in the day they partook thereof"? Both lived for many hundred years after that moment. We could argue that "1000 years is like a day unto the Lord" (2 Peter 3:8), and say, "Yes, they did." But

What Does Christ's Crucifixion Mean To Us?

what would have been the significance of a curse that said "You will die sometime in the next 1000 years"? Something even more was involved in the Adamic curse, that is lost to us unless we become "saved" through Christ Jesus. What?

Physical immortality was one of the properties that mankind lost in the Fall. Genesis 3:22 says "... lest ... and they live forever." And it is physical immortality that we, who abide in Christ Jesus, will finally regain (1 Corinthians 15:51-56 and Philippians 3:21). Being "Saved" in John 3:16-18 and Ephesians 2:8 therefore includes regaining physical immortality through knowing and trusting God through Christ Jesus.

Salvation is a *process* whereby the Adamic curse we are under is nullified and we are restored to the full personal relationship with God that Adam had in the Garden before the Fall.

Salvation involves many stages: first being brought into a child-of-God relationship (through becoming "born again"); then maturing in the righteousness of Christ; and finally, upon physical redemption, being fully established ("adopted" - Romans 8:11) as God's sons and joint heirs with Christ (Romans 8:23 and Ephesians 1:5).

The essence of "salvation" is not "getting to heaven after we die", but rather becoming "complete in Christ" and ruling and reigning with Him throughout eternity (Ephesians 1:18-23). The Kingdom of God is not merely heaven after death, but Christ being King and Lord in our lives, here as well as there, now as well as then. The requirement is faith in Christ (Luke 23:42-43), inner honesty with God (Luke 16:20-25), and righteousness in interpersonal relationships based on love (Hebrews 11:31 and 12:1).

3. Eternal Life - What Is It?

"Unless a man be born again, he cannot see the Kingdom of God." "... God gave His only begotten Son that whosoever believes in Him shall not perish but have eternal life." (John 3:3 & 16).

"Born again...." "Eternal life...." Common expressions on the lips of many Christians; indeed most of us testify to a personal *experience* of these concepts. But what do they really mean? As we briefly mentioned in the opening section of Chapter 1 above, "eternal life" is *life!* But what actually *is* "eternal life", what is its significance, and how do we acquire it?

We say, "eternal life is living forever with God." Well and good: that indeed is a characteristic or property of it; and in the context of evangelistic outreach to non-Christians, that is an appropriate concept or aspect of eternal life to emphasize. But eternal life means far more than that.

We can see that eternal life means more than "forever in time" by three elementary arguments. First, do not the damned souls life forever (in hell)? Yet they do not have "eternal life".

The Greek word used for "eternal", Aionion, does not mean "forever in time", but rather means "related or pertaining to the (present) eon or age". So, "eternal life" is literally "that life that pertains to (God's purposes) in the (current) eon." What are those current purposes of God? Ephesians 1:10 gives us a clue: "to sum up *all* things in Christ". Although the full meaning of that phrase is far from clear and obvious, we can argue that "eternal life" is that quality of life that pertains to God currently bringing us into unity with Christ Jesus.

A third argument is Jesus' definition of eternal life. In John 17:3 He defines it as "knowing God the Father and Christ the Son". This is not just *mental knowledge about* God and Christ, but is *intrinsic, intuitive, inner experiential* knowledge of Him as a *Person*. In what sense do we know Christ experientially? As Christ indwelling, living in us (Galatians 2:20)!

So, eternal life is not simply a *quantity* of life (i.e., going on forever in time), but a *quality* of life: a dynamic *relationship* (of a specific type) with God the Father and Christ Jesus the Son, here and now as well as in Heaven bye and bye. It is *not* intellectual understanding and acceptance of correct *doctrine*. It is *not* personal *emotional* experience. It is *not* denominational *institutional* structure. It is *life*. It is a dynamic two-way interaction, *via* Christ Jesus, with the domain or realm of spiritual reality, within which everything we know and are is intrinsically embedded.

The key essence of eternal life, then, is a dynamic *relationship* with Christ-indwelling! More specifically, eternal life is the Holy Spirit of Christ Jesus dwelling in our human spirits. And He enables us to communicate with God Himself. The Holy Spirit's main function here and now is to reveal God the Father and Christ Jesus the Son to "all whosoever ...". That communication is two-way - both to and from Him - and is *via* the functions of intuition, conscience and worship of our human spirits. We enter into that communication through study and meditation of His Written Word, prayer, praise and worship.

As a result, we learn to know Him and His ways. Hallelujah, what a privilege!

When did the Biblical personages receive eternal life? Adam and Eve had that experiential knowledge of and direct communication with God immediately upon God breathing it into them (Genesis 2:7). Christ Jesus knew God before the foundations of the world were laid (John 1:1). His mission today is to impart that dynamic quality of knowing Him, to "all whosoever...". He imparted it to the disciples in John 20:22 (an event that occurred before His ascension, and hence at least ten days prior to Acts Chapter 2). And He readily imparts it to us, in response to repentance and seeking of Him on our part.

The expressions "being born again" and "receiving eternal life" do not appear in the Bible until the *fourth* Gospel, i.e., in John Chapter 3. In the first three Gospels, the emphasis is on what *we* must do - repent, change our thought patterns, and seek Him. It is not until we come to the Gospel of John that we find the emphasis on Jesus' divine mission of imparting eternal life to us. The mention of "eternal life" in John Chapter 3 is a theological explanation to Nicodemus as to what actually happens in us, i.e., what Jesus actually effects in us, when we obey His command to repent. That is indeed a conscious experience, both in our realization of our need for Christ as our Saviour and in our sensing His forgiveness of our sins!

However, since "being born again" primarily involves our human spirit rather than our human soul, the *full effect* is one of which we are ***not necessarily cognitively aware of.*** As in the physical realm, the immediate result of birth is an immature (but very much alive) baby, and at the moment of regeneration we are but mere babies in our relationship with Christ (1 Corinthians 3:1, Hebrews 5:13, 1 Peter 2:2 and 1 John 2:1 & 12-13). We are very definitely members of the "Household" or "Family" of God, and totally objects of His love, protection and provision; and we should never lose sight of that, even though we seldom "feel" it. The Biblical concept of Christ the Great Shepherd and we the sheep of His flock also emphasizes His total love, protection and provision toward us.

But He also wants us to grow up in Him. It is one thing to be a baby at the age of one day, and it is another thing to still be a baby in thoughts and actions at the age of 21 years! So we are in His sanctifying process of *maturing*, wherein He, Christ Jesus, day by day and minute by minute, works in us to deepen our apprehension of Him and our dynamic personal relationship with Him.

Christ purposes that we allow His Holy Spirit to completely control our entire beings - that He live His life in and though us as He wills, unhindered by our self-interests and desires. But He does not dominate our self-consciousness (i.e., the mind, emotions and will functions of our human *soul*). Our human will must operate in repentance and seeking of Him in order for Him to impart it unto us. Our soul functions must determinedly *yield* to that indwelling Holy Spirit. Otherwise our soul functions can and alas usually do remain independent.

He does not override our wills. But, subsequently to our receiving this new quality of life, He is ever dealing in our lives and hearts to *entice* us to increasingly choose to *yield* to His will. It is those subsequent dealings by Him in our lives that the Bible refers to as "sanctification".

Underlying this is the fact that God, on His initiative, has chosen to work out His purposes through imperfect men. He doesn't have to do it that way - He could clobber us all, as we indeed deserve, and bring forth a new creation of His choice. But He has chosen to work through *us*.

As we indeed *yield* our wills and minds and emotions to Him, *then* He increasingly saturates our self-consciousness (soul). This is the root meaning in the Greek of the phrase "be *filled* with the Holy Spirit". Luke 1:15 and Acts 2:4, 4:8, 4:31, 9:17 & 13:9 use the Greek word Pletho that has the fuller meaning of "to satiate", "to take possession of", or "to fulfill". Ephesians 5:8 uses the Greek word Pleroo that means "to cause to abound" or "to furnish liberally". "Be (continuously being) filled with the Holy Spirit" in Ephesians 5:8 therefore means "ever allow the Holy Spirit of Christ Jesus, Who indwells our human spirits since regeneration, to satiate our soul functions - mind, emotions and will - so that Christ Jesus can live His life in and though us as He wills". It is our *soul* that is being filled with the Holy Spirit in these passages; our human *spirit* became filled with Him upon regeneration, but He has no control over us except and until our souls yield.

Along these same lines, the meaning of Hebrews 4:12 is that the **Word** of God (Rhema or dynamic dealings of God in our lives) is constantly striving to break the dominance that our self-consciousness (soul) has over the seat of His indwelling (i.e., our human spirit), so that He through our spirits becomes dominant in our lives as He wills.

Other phrases used in the Bible to denote our souls yielding to Him indwelling, are "heart circumcision" and "crucifixion of self". Also the Baptism into the Holy Spirit, the main emphasis of which being that we yield our human wills to the indwelling Holy Spirit of Christ Jesus. In fact, if we are truly yielding our wills and lives to Him indwelling, since His main characteristic is Agape love, it is that *love* that will be the *main* manifestation in our lives.

4. Grace - The Causitive Agent: Having Christ, Crucified, In Us

"Grace" is the causative agent, that which brings about our "salvation". But what is "grace", and what is the full basis for you and I having it appropriated to ourselves individually? An "unmerited favor or gift", yes. But does that merely mean God feels sorry for us or is nice to us? Far, far from it!

The words in the original languages that are translated "grace" are "Charis" in the New Testament Greek, and "ChN" in the Old Testament Hebrew. "Charis" conveys the meaning of an "act of bestowing", "imparting", or "implanting". But it is a word with the added meaning that the receiver benefits from the giver in a *dynamic* way through the gift or impartation. "ChN" in turn is from the Hebrew verb root "ChNH" that means "to recline, encamp, dwell".

"Charis", the *grace* of God, when all is said and done, is the *impartation* of the Holy Spirit of Christ Jesus to *dwell* within us. The fuller concept behind these two words translated "grace" is therefore Christ (technically, His Holy Spirit) *dwelling* or *abiding* in a believer! He does not give us *gifts or talents per se;* He imparts *Himself* unto us, and He *is* those things in and through us unto others! "... it is no longer I that lives, ... but Christ lives in me; and the life I now live in the flesh I live by faith in the Son of God ...", as Paul shouts in Galatians 2:20.

Since the Holy Spirit is in total oneness with the rest of the Holy Trinity, and since the Holy Spirit's function on Earth in this eon or age is to reveal Christ Jesus to us in our human experience, it is to us as if Christ Jesus Himself indwells us, even though technically Christ Jesus is now "physically" in the "Heavenlies" (Acts 3:21). This is the essence of the difference between the Old Testament (Covenant) and the New Testament (Covenant) relationship between man and God: Christ indwelling! Grace is this highly dynamic relationship with God.

Grace is therefore a strong concept of a gift, whereby the giver imparts of *himself*, of his very nature and *essence*, to the receiver; and the receiver responds dynamically by taking that very nature of the giver into his own nature, assimilating it, and being imbued by it. Grace describes Christ, *via* His Holy Spirit coming to ***dwell in us, and we containing Him.***

An Old Testament type of grace is milk, as imparted to an infant baby from its mother's breast. One of the names by which God called Himself, e.g. in Genesis 17:1, is "El Shaddai" (Hebrew El ShDI), that literally means "your Almighty Nursing-Breast". A very essence of God is imparted to us, as we remain in a *relationship* with Him that is compared to the most intimate of all human love-relationships: a relationship of total love, total protection, total provision, and a relationship through which we are nourished so that we can grow and mature. (Provided, that is, if we totally *yield* ourselves to Him in that relationship; a baby can't drink milk while having a temper tantrum!) Indeed, the "promised land", that to us is described in Romans 8, is called the "land flowing in milk and honey" - grace (milk) and Koininea fellowship (honey).

Just *how* are we "saved by grace"? Exactly *how* does this impartation to us of the Holy Spirit of Christ Jesus come to dwell in us, nullify the Adamic Curse we are under, and restore us to the full personal relationship with God that Adam had in the Garden before the Fall?

There is no way we can escape the Adamic Curse *except* through Christ Himself *living* within us. "Salvation" is much more than merely a "gift" that Christ gives us for us to simply receive from Him; it is a dynamic living **relationship** with Him, to be worked out in actual practice through our yielding to His Lordship moment by moment (Philippians 2:12-13). In the meantime, if we proceed to grow unto maturity in Christ, moment by moment, attitude by attitude, thought by thought, Christ permeates and replaces us; just as the imperishable and beautiful quartz of jasper, molecule by molecule, slowly over a period of time under heat and pressure, permeates and replaces the original, perishable substance of "petrified wood", but in a way that preserves the outward form. Salvation is a *process* of several milestone events plus a continuing growth; but all aspects involve the Holy Spirit of Christ Jesus in us, and we yielding to His control over the many facets of our thoughts and actions.

5. Faith: Total Abandonment

"For by grace we are saved through *faith"* (Ephesians 2:8). We'd like to define "faith", since much misunderstanding abounds on this concept even as an abstract term. Since this concept is so foundational to being a Christian, I can think of nothing more important than clearly knowing what it means. What is "faith" and where does it fit in?

But before we attempt to define such a very basic and foundational Christian concept, we need to first define what we mean by "define". Being an engineer, statistician and amateur physicist, I think of "definitions" as consisting of "So-and-so is:" followed by a list of ***propositional statements*** that apply to it. So, I study the scriptures to find just such "definitions".

Only one problem: such ***definitions*** of "faith" do ***not exist*** in God's Word!

I first became aware of this several years ago while reading Tozer[1]:

> "In the Scriptures there is practically no effort made to define faith. Outside of a brief fourteen-word definition in Hebrews 11:1, I know of no Biblical definition, and even there faith is defined functionally, not philosophically; that is, it is a statement of what faith is ***in operation, not*** what it is ***in essence***. It assumes the presence of faith and shows what it results in, rather than what it is....

I asked the Lord about this. There's a fine line, sometimes, between carrying on a temper tantrum with God and wrestling with Him all night at our Penuel's (PhNWAhL). You be the judge as to which category the following dialogue (that I actually had with our Lord Christ Jesus) belongs:

"Lord, what's going on, here? Are you playing games with us? Why don't you give us clear definitions of these most important Christian concepts? You say we can't please You without *faith*, but how do we know how to walk in *faith* when we don't clearly know what *faith* is and how it differs from *presumption?* Also with *grace*, and so forth."

"I don't think the same way you do."

"Yeah, Lord, I know that. Your Word says in Isaiah 55:8 that 'Your thoughts are not my thoughts, neither are Your ways my ways'. That's why I'm coming to you seeking answers, rather than trying to figure them out myself. Your Word also says in Isaiah 1:18 'Come let us reason together'. So, again, why are clear logical definitions of these basic concepts lacking in Your Word?"

"You think *propositionally;* I think *relationally.*"

"Huh?"

"Those concepts do not exist as separate entities, and hence cannot be defined in terms of sets of true propositions. Rather, they are *attributes* of My *personal relationship* with you, and exist only during those times when our relationship is being exercised. Furthermore, most aspects of our relationship are in *spirit*, and hence require a much deeper understanding of things of *spirit* before you can fully grasp them. I therefore do not require you to *understand* these concepts with your *mind;* rather I

desire that you *live* them out of love-motivated *choice*. My Spirit within you will empower you to so live when you choose for Him to."

"Aaaaauuuugh!"

In other words, the most significant aspect of Biblical faith is that it has no meaning whatsoever apart from our personal relationship with our Lord Christ Jesus. Faith is not a "thing" *per se*, but an aspect of our personal walk with Him. All Scriptural references to "faith" (or its verb form "believe") are not *definitions*. What we find in the Scriptures of these concepts are *operational* aspects of them. That is, the Scriptures give us glimpses not of the concepts *per se*, but rather of what they ***result in*** while being ***exercised***.

Nevertheless, being the human equivalent of a stubborn old mule, I want some propositional forms of these definitions. So, against these warnings from our Lord Christ Jesus, I have made such attempts. Of course, such attempts fall far short. Jesus is right: they will have meaning to us not as separate entities but only as operational aspects of our ***spiritual*** walk with Him. Nevertheless, such feeble attempts have helped me ***get started*** in my walk with Him, and I offer them to you that they may likewise help you.

First of all, "believe" is not a command of verbal actions of our ***minds*** nor ***intellect***, as is commonly assumed. Rather, it is an action of our ***will, volition;*** it is a matter of ***choices*** we must determine to make and abide by.

The Old Testament Hebrew word for "faith" is AhMWN, meaning "steadfastness, faithfulness, perseverance in one's commitments"; the New Testament Greek word for "faith" is Pistis, meaning "trusting, depending intimately upon". *Neither* of these words involve a *mental* determination to believe a statement in the face of apparently conflicting evidence.

"Believe" (Pisteuo) and its noun form "belief" or "faith" (Pistis) require determined self-discipline; "to be *faithful*", i.e., to a *person* (God *via* Christ Jesus). That in turn implies determined self-discipline to *depend* upon or trust in Him and in all He is and does and promises, and to *obey* Him! Operationally, our thinking and/or acting in faith requires apprehending our Lord Christ Jesus in His *spiritual* reality to some extent!

Our faith must be *initiated* by God in the first place. But even if He puts this urge within us to pursue Him, we still cannot trust in one of whose *existence* we have *doubts*. Hence, a major aspect of our sanctification process, particularly during the early stages, is our learning to apprehend the *reality* of God and His spiritual domain. In other words, it is a matter of "being near to God." "Being near to God" is a matter not of distance but of *awareness* of Him and being *spiritually receptive* to Him, as were the great men of God in the Bible. The bottom line in our growing in faith, then, is our learning to *see* God, to *gaze* upon Him. Faith is a matter of our *seeing* our Lord Christ Jesus in His *Spiritual* reality, of our soul *gazing* upon His reality.

A working definition of faith that reflects how Pistis and its verb form (Pisteuo - "to believe") are used throughout the New Testament is: "our inner response to God's initiative". That is, faith is an act of human *will* whereby we, in the present moment, respond inwardly to some initiative of God -

something He has done, said, promised, or revealed to us. That inner response, to be "faith" (Pistis), must be in three forms: we must: (1) *see* Him in His *Spiritual* reality; (2) be dynamically *dependent* upon Him (as a *Person*, not just as a source of truth); and (3) be sensitively *obedient* to Him. Faith involves the human *will*, not just our minds, logic, nor emotions.

For this we must *trust* God totally. Allender[2] addresses this quite succinctly:

> "Most assume that trust is quiet, serene, selfless dependence on God. Though there is an element of truth to that view of trust, more often than not such serene faith is [just] a byproduct of wanting very little from God. ...
>
> "Genuine trust involves allowing another to matter and have an impact in our lives. For that reason, many who hate and do battle with God trust Him more deeply than those whose complacent faith permits an abstract and motionless stance before Him. Those who trust God most are those whose faith permits them to risk wrestling with Him over the deepest questions of life. Good hearts are captured in a divine wrestling match; fearful, doubting hearts stay clear of the mat.
>
> "The commitment to wrestle will be honored by a God who will not only break but bless. Jacob [believed] ... [in Genesis 33] the freedom in his heart was worth the price of his shattered limb. The price of soul freedom is the loss of what has been deemed most secure [the tight grip over one's soul, the commitment to be one's sole

provider and protector] but is intuitively known as no security at all."

Hebrews 11:1 starts with "Now faith is ...". That links faith to the present tense. Faith only exists or applies to the *present moment*. We never have to exercise faith for past events; nor even for **future** promises (the word "hope" applies there). Hebrews 11:1 then continues with "... faith is the *substance* of things hoped for, the *evidence* of things not seen ...." The meaning here in the Greek is not that faith is a "thing", but rather an *action:* namely the substantiat*ing*, or mak*ing* of real effect, or physically manifest*ing* in real life, that which God has said.

6. Passover And The Lord's Supper: His Crucifixion Into Us

What has God said of the most essential aspect of our personal relationship with Him? It is Christ living within us!

A most beautiful way of depicting the concept of Christ coming to dwell *in* us, is the Biblical description of "Passover" in Exodus Chapter 12. In this account the Israelite's household is a type of a Christian believer's heart or inner person. The account speaks of the Lord, Christ Jesus in type, "passing over" us.

Exodus 12 is commonly misunderstood by Christians today. We must very carefully note exactly *who* actually did *what* on that first Passover night? First, note verses 12 and 29 of Exodus 12: we are clearly told that *God* will smite the first-born. But then note verse 23, that says just as clearly that it is the *destroyer* who will enter the houses to kill. Conclusion:

satan is merely God's *agent* to enforce the Adamic Curse. We note in Job 2:1-7, Luke 22:31-32, and Ephesians 1:19-23, that satan can do absolutely *nothing* except by the expressed permission of the Godhead (and/or by human will). As *God* allows (if we choose to reject Him), it is *satan*, not God Himself, who enters our hearts to enforce the Adamic Curse of death.

Just what does the *Lord* do? Actually, "pass over" is a misleading translation of the Hebrew word PhSCh. PhSCh does *not* mean to skip over or pass by (like "superman") and ignore, nor to not kill, nor to refrain from interfering, nor to remotely bless in some sense; rather, it means to take a *step* in order to *enter!* PhSCh in the Hebrew in verse 23 means that the Lord will *step* through the doorway (PhThCh or "entrance-way" in the Hebrew, not DLTh or "door") in order to *enter* the house. Once in, He will not let the destroyer enter to destroy.

The Blood on the lintel and posts of the doorway is seen not by man but by the *Lord*, who sees it as a *welcome* sign to Him. The *Lord* sees the blood and enters; the destroyer, seeing the *Lord* inside, does not enter. It is not the blood, nor the religious ritual, but the Lord's *presence* in the house, that keeps the destroyer out. In Revelations 3:20, our resurrected Christ Jesus says to us, "Behold I stand at the door (of your heart) and knock; if any one hears My voice and opens the door, I will come into him, and will dine with him, and he with Me." Passover denotes Christ *indwelling* us, not merely leaving us unmolested!

One or the other (satan or Christ) entered every house in the land. One or the other enters every one of us! Beware, all who ignore God's provisions for redemption!

7. The Shed Blood Of Christ Jesus

The **Blood** of the PhSCh sacrificial lamb of Passover played a key role. There were actually five specific ways in which the sprinkled blood was involved in keeping the destroyer out:

(1) It was seen by the Lord. Each man (the Israelites) had to *apply* the Blood to the doorway of *his own* home. That typifies our *inviting* Him into individual hearts. Though the Blood was of Earthly origin (as was the Blood of Jesus our substitutionary *man*), it was not to be seen by men but rather by the *Lord* (YHWH).

(2) The Lord sees it as attitudes on our part of *obeying* His word (even when it sounds foolish) and *desiring/welcoming* Him into our lives and hearts.

(3) The Blood is proof to satan that Christ has *purchased* us from him, and hence satan no longer has any *legal* right over us (except if/when/as *we* momentarily give him *permission)*.

(4) Christ, through His Blood, has rendered satan powerless. He (Christ Jesus) rendered powerless the devil (the death angel) by His death (outpouring of His Blood) - Hebrews 2:14.

(5) Through that, Christ is our PhSCh: His shedding or outpouring of His Blood or life-fluid *into* our hearts does this. His *presence* in us keeps satan out. Demonic exorcism is not the *ultimate* way, although in some cases that may also be necessary. It is rather flooding our hearts with Jesus!

Letting *Christ* be our PhSCh is not a simple nor trivial step. First of all, it must be done in accordance with these God-ordained principles. Note that our Lord PhSCh'ing us is *conditional*. There were *four* things each Israelite head-of-household had to do:
   (1) *hear* the Word of God - Exodus 12:3ff and 12:21ff;
   (2) *slay* a lamb - Exodus 12:3b-6 & 21;
   (3) *apply* the Blood to his doorway - Exodus 12:7 & 22; and
   (4) *eat* the sacrificial lamb - Exodus 12:8-11 & 43-46.

These are types of four ways in which *we* must change our thinking (repent):
   (1) *learn* of God's ways for our salvation, i.e., read the Bible and listen to the Holy Spirit as He draws us
   (2) *offer* Christ on the Cross of Calvary as our "burnt" offering;
   (3) *earnestly seek* to deepen our personal relationship with our Lord Christ Jesus; and
   (4) *allow* Christ in us to permeate every thought and motive and activity of our beings (by assimilating Christ in our being, as typified by "eating" His flesh and "drinking" His blood).

Applying the Blood typifies our saying to God, "Yes, that covenant You offer to us *via* Your Son dying on the Cross, applies to me, and I welcome You into my heart".

Coming to Christ is *not* the simple thing many evangelists represent it to be. He is ever willing, as He "would that all be saved" (1 Timothy 2:4); but He waits until we *seek* Him to enter us. It is utterly *impossible* to a fallen and depraved man

What Does Christ's Crucifixion Mean To Us?

unless and until Divine power is brought to bear upon him, his understanding is supernaturally enlightened, his heart is supernaturally changed, and his will is supernaturally broken. John 6:37 & 44 say "All who the Father gives to Christ, shall come to Christ and He will always accept; but no one can come to Jesus unless the Father draws him". This is why intercessory prayer is as important an ingredient of evangelistic outreach as are preaching the Gospel message and being a witness of Christ.

Nevertheless, once one does this, Christ is faithful to His Word and *does* enter into our hearts, no matter how black and long be our backlog of sins. *"All* whoosoever ...."

8. This Cup Is My Covenant

As we mentioned in point (4) above, we must partake of His flesh, i.e., receive it into us, or assimilate Him so that He *indwells* us. John 6:53-56 says:
> "Unless you eat the flesh of the Son of Man and drink His Blood, you have no life in you. Whosoever eats My flesh and drinks My Blood has eternal life, and I will raise him up at the last day. For My flesh is food indeed, and My Blood is drink indeed. He who eats My flesh and drinks My Blood abides in Me, and I in him."

1 Corinthians 10:16 says:
> "The cup of blessing which we bless, is it not the communion of the Blood of Christ? The bread which we break, is it not the communion of the Body of Christ?"

This full meaning of the Lord's Supper is rarely apprehended by Christian believers today. The Eucharist points to

Pentecost and beyond, *not* to Calvary! The word "death" in "Do this in remembrance of My *death* until I return" (1 Corinthians 11:26) does not refer in the Greek to the *act* of His dying (that would be the Greek word Nekros), but rather refers to His *absence* due to death (the Greek word used is Thanatos) until He returns. And "remembrance" (the Greek word used is Kataggellete) does not mean merely to keep in our memory, but to "announce" Him, to provide a *tangible* reminder of Him, to *be or comprise* a (living) *memorial* of Him, to *manifest* Him, to *represent* Him, during His absence. This we do as His Body.

The phrase "His Blood *shed for* us" (Matthew 26:28, Mark 14:24, Luke 22:20 and Romans 5:5) is a somewhat misleading translation. The Greek words used are Ekchuno Uper, which in the Septuagint is a frequent translation of the Hebrew word ShPhK. These words do not just refer to the removal (of blood or some other fluid) *from* Him but also emphasize the *bestowing* (Ekchuno in the Greek) of it liberally, and *unto* (Uper in the Greek) a *receiver* (us while still in this world). These words carry the strong implication that this shedding of His Blood *into* us is our becoming Christ-like and our representing Him on Earth as His Body "for the fullness of" or "to bring to a fuller measure or higher degree".

The phrase "*broken for* us" (i.e., the bread representing His Body) is also a misleading translation. In 1 Corinthians 11:24 and Luke 22:19, "broken" and "given" mean that His body is "propagated" among us. In 1 Corinthians 11:24 the Greek words used for "broken for" are Klaomai Uper. They do not mean physical separation on our behalf (the Greek word for that would have been Schizomai), but rather mean a *dispersal among* us, (again in a sense of "fullness"). This dispersal is in the sense of a horticulturist taking many cuttings from a single stock plant and planting those cuttings, each of which grows roots and becomes one of many "reproductions" of that common source. Jesus imparts to each of us some part of Himself, that we each are to become reproductions of Him (though each of us is imperfect and incomplete by ourself).

Summary:

In conclusion, our personal Passover goes beyond our regeneration. It involves our becoming *containers* of Christ.

The Eucharist or Lord's Supper delineates Christ as our Passover (PhSCh), living in and through us. An outpouring of His Blood and life through us is denoted by wine, that is to *transform* our behaviour as well as our thoughts; we drink of it even though it be bittersweet to our flesh.

Christ's life (Blood) is poured into us. John 19:34-35 tells us that out of Jesus' side, on the Cross, poured His Blood (and water), as astonishing as that was to man's observation. In Acts 2:27b and Psalm 16:10b we see that Jesus was not to undergo decay; His Blood was not to become coagulated, but to be *poured* out unto mankind (the "ground" or "world"), both in *substitution for* us, and as *life-fluid into* us.

Christ's life (Blood) *transforms us* to Christ-likeness. By Jesus' Blood (life) being poured *into* us, we are sanctified or brought into maturity. 1 Peter says, "By the sanctifying work of the Spirit, that you may obey Jesus Christ and be sprinkled with His Blood ...." In terms of Old Testament types, His Blood enabled *us* to be the Ark of the Covenant or container of the Presence of God on Earth.

Another way of saying this is that in Christ we become *overcomers*. 1 John 5:4-8 says, "For whoever is born of God overcomes the world, ... he who believes that Jesus is the Son of God. This is the One Who came by water and Blood, Jesus Christ. ... and it is the Spirit Who bears witness, the (Holy) Spirit and the water (Rhema Word of God) and the Blood (fluid of eternal life); and the three are in agreement."

Assimilating Christ (eating His flesh as typified by bread along with drinking the wine) means becoming Christ's physical manifestation (Body) on Earth. He is "dispersed" among us. To have Christ propagated through us means that each of us is to *contain* Christ and that He be *released* through us, so that He lives and ministers unto the world *through* us (*not* us doing it *for* Him!) Collectively we are a complete manifestation of Jesus on Earth. Until His Parousia return, we *collectively* manifest His Presence on Earth, we being a dispersing or propagating or multiplying of Him and His ministries here on Earth.

9. Crucifixion Stages Of The Salvation Process

As we mentioned above, "salvation is a *process* whereby the Adamic curse we are under is nullified and we are restored to the full personal relationship with God that Adam had in the Garden before the Fall. Salvation involves many stages, such as: first being brought into a child-of-God relationship (through becoming "born-again"); then maturing in the righteousness of Christ; and finally, upon physical (bodily) redemption, being fully established ("adopted" - Romans 8:11) as God's *sons* and joint heirs with Christ Jesus (Romans 8:23, Philippians 3:20-21, and Ephesians 1:5).

It is this multi-stage *process* of salvation that is the underling theme of this entire book. The salvation *process* is of *three* stages in time. First, I *have been* saved - an act or process that has been completed in the *past* (see for example Ephesians 2:5, 8, 13; 2 Timothy 1:9; and Titus 3:5). Second, I *am being* saved - a process that is taking place in the *present* time (see for example 1 Corinthians 15:2 and Philippians 2:12). And third, I *shall be* saved - an event that will occur in the *future*, if I "endure until then" (see for example Matthew 10:22 & 24:13; Mark 13:13; and Romans 5:9 & 10).

In each of these stages, what is important is not what I do *per se;* it is how my *personal relationship* with Christ Jesus deepens! As my personal relationship with Him deepens, so also does my *personal identification* with His crucifixion. At first, Calvary is simply a historical event that involved *Him*. But then it becomes *my* personal death *with* Him. And finally, and as a consequence of that, it becomes my personal *abandonment* unto Him, so that His *life is released* unto others through me!

The *Substitution* Work Of The Cross: *For* Me

At first, I acknowledge that He, Christ Jesus, was crucified *for* me (i.e., on my behalf to undo the Adamic curse on me). Through *repentance* (transformation of my thought life, my very mentality), I receive "His eternal life" (regeneration), and through my human *spirit* I begin true communication with Him Who is Spirit.

The *Identification* Work Of The Cross: *As* Me

However, we are commanded also to be *baptized* (Acts 2:38). Even John the Baptist linked baptism with repentance (Matthew 3:11, Mark 1:4, Luke 3:3, Acts 13:24 & 19:4). Romans 6:3-11 strongly emphasizes that *our* baptism is a profound and all-pervasive *personal* identification of us with *His* crucifixion. The water of baptism is a watery *grave* in which *our* body of self and sin, the life and power of our fleshly appetites, is *buried*. So, not only was Christ Jesus crucified for me, but He was crucified *as* me, and I *with* Him!

This is strongly implied in the meaning of water baptism by John the Baptist that was under the Old Covenant (Christ not yet having been crucified-resurrected-ascended). Then water baptism was a required part of the procedure whereby a gentile, who chose to, became an Israelite. It signified a cleansing (by water immersion) from all of the pollution of the "Goyem" (Hebrew GWIM) or "gentile-ness". But John the Baptist was exhorting people who were *already* Israelites to be baptized. Why? What he had the audacity (under the Holy Spirit's anointing) to say to Israelites, was: "although you are of Israel through birth, your life-style and attitudes and behaviour patterns - your very characters - are as if you are gentiles. Repent; become Israelites indeed in your character, and outwardly testify to your inner change through the ritual of water baptism".

Is that situation any different than that of us Christians? Although we are of Christ through birth (i.e., the new birth into eternal life), our *characters* are still as if we were not. Therefore repent; let His Holy Spirit, who is indeed in us from regeneration, help us transform our minds (Romans 12:1) and change our characters to that which is truly Christ-like.

His crucifixion *for* me dealt with my *legal or positional* relationship with God in Christ Jesus - that which is meant by the theological term "justification". But His crucifixion *as* me and I *with* Him deals with my life-style, my attitudes, my behaviour patterns - in short, with my *character*.

The *Release* Work Of The Cross: *Into* Me

Our existence does not end in the watery grave of baptism. For we are also raised up out of that grave in a resurrection into the new life! We not only have been crucified with Him; we are also to be *resurrected* with Him! We are now to *live* the life of Christ.

How?

We can't! In no way can you or I *ever*, in this physical world, live His life. Only *He* can! It is He *in us* living His life *through* us. Only in that way can we ever manifest His life to others in this world. So, He must yet further deal with us, that we can *truly* say with Paul in Galatians 2:20: "... though I have been crucified with Christ; it is no longer I who live, but Christ lives in me; and the life which I now live in the flesh [physical] I live by faith in the Son of God ...."

This is why we say that Christ Jesus must also be crucified *into* us. His life-fluid (Blood) is shed *into* us. By He being crucified into us, He is no longer constrained by (our) flesh, but is fully *released* to truly be all He is, in and through us. It means that we must enthrone Him as *Lord* of our entire beings!

But He has chosen to not override our human wills. He ever strives to mold our wills by His dealings in our lives, by both His love for us and His chastisements of us (Hebrews 12:2, 5 & 6). So, if He is to be Lord of our lives in actual fact, then our human *will* must yield, our human *soul* must be cleansed of all of self and be fully consecrated unto Him. Only by our *willful* yielding is He truly *released* to will and work His good purposes in and through us (Philippians 2:13).

10. How: The Effectual Power Of The Cross

All this theology is nice, perhaps very interesting. But what about our actually *living* it? How do we actually, physically, live the Christ-crucified-in-us life in this sin-plagued world? How do I *experientially* die to sin and live only the resurrected life in Christ? How?

We die to sin by fully apprehending a simple, but profound and astonishing, fact: when Christ was crucified, I was crucified! Period! Past tense! Fact accomplished! No ifs, ands nor buts; no maybe's, no I-hope-so's; but accomplished fact! When I became born-again, I was *born* crucified! And when I was water baptized, I acknowledged that fact by symbolizing my *burial* (i.e., in a watery grave) and *my resurrection* into the new life in Christ.

Romans 6 admonishes us unto this *determined mental attitude*, with such strong words as these. Verses 1 and 2: "... shall we continue in sin ...? Certainly not! How shall we who *died* to sin, ...?" Verse 4: "... we *were* buried with Him though baptism into death, that ... we also should walk in newness of life." Verse 5: "... we *have been* united together in the likeness of His death, certainly also ... of His resurrection." Verse 6: "*knowing* this, that our old self was crucified with Him, that the body of sin might be done away with ...." Verse 8: "We *have died* with Christ, we *believe* that we shall also live with Him." Verse 11: "... *reckon* (consider) yourselves to be dead indeed to sin, but alive to God in Christ Jesus." Verse 18: "... having *been* set free from sin, you became slaves of righteousness." And verse 22: "... having been set free from sin, and having become slave of God, you have your fruit to holiness, and the end, *everlasting life*. Hallelujah!

I do not need to crucify myself (in fact, I can't), but only to learn to *walk* in the Christ-crucified life! *My* crucifixion is a work already finished by the Lord Himself, and it is available to me, if/as I reckon it to be so (like salvation itself) by faith. The crucifixion of Jesus Christ on Calvary 1970 years ago was so powerful and effectual that it extends fully to this very day, and it can reach into the most profound depravity of *every* human soul!

If this be actually so, then what about the manifold temptations to sin, yea the sins that still so *easily* beset us? What *we* need to do, in the face of our many tormenting temptations, in order to apprehend the effectual power of the cross, is three-fold: (1) ever *focus* our attitudes and praises upon Him in worship and union; (2) have a *determined* mental attitude of rejecting the sin-area involved; and (3) *depend* upon Him to provide us victory.

1 Corinthians 10:13 directly tells us of the certain victory that will be ours as a consequence of our taking a determined attitude of renouncing the sins, if we but depend upon *Him* and not upon our own strengths or wisdom: "No temptation

has overtaken you except such as is common to man; but God is faithful, Who will not allow you to be tempted beyond what you are able [to withstand], but with the temptation will also make the way of escape, that you may be able to bear it."

It is in this area of determined mental attitude, that we all fail so often. There are usually several reasons for this. For example: (1) we don't *really* believe the Bible, except to the extent to which we have personally experienced it! That is tantamount to believing our experiences rather than the Word of God - a guaranteed route to failure. (2) We are out of the habit of disciplining our thought life (thanks to TV, etc.)! We let our thoughts rule us, rather than us ruling them - another guaranteed route to failure. (3) We do not realize how much our lives are driven by our self-seeking and self-protecting goals and strategies and their dysfunctional roots in our lives. (4) We don't really want to *forsake* the sin area involved in the temptations. No matter how distorted, even masochistic, may be the "pleasures" that our "little" sins give us for a season, we don't really *want* to forsake them. (5) This is tantamount to the real root to our failures: we don't desire the Lord and union with Him *desperately* enough!

Is Christ *really* crucified in you? Or more properly worded, to what *extent* do you, right now, apprehend His crucifixion in you? And even more elementary, how *strongly* do you care?

We live only the resurrected life in Christ actually by *releasing* His life from within us, i.e., from the *indwelling* Christ. In specific situations, this faith-release of His life within us involves three elements: (a) we *will* or *choose* to release His life; (b) we *declare* it being done or becoming so; and (c) we *anticipate* its completion. Perhaps our greatest stumbling block is not whether God *can* do it, but rather *will* He? He will, *if* we will Him to, so that stumbling block really is will *we*?

Underlying all of this, is our *ever* concentrating on Him, Christ Jesus, and on Him alone. "Turn your eyes upon Jesus: look forth into His wonderful face; and the things on earth will grow strangely dim, in the light of His Glory and Grace." This, incidentally, is the *full* meaning of "repentance" (Metanoia) - a total transformation of our mind, our thought patterns (Romans 12:1) unto a total orientation toward Him. The "poise of our soul" is to be one of "gazing upon Him".

End Notes: Chapter Two

[1.] A. W. Tozer, *The Pursuit of God*, (Harrisburg, Pa.: Christian Publications, Inc., 1948), pp. 87. Copyright © 1982 by Christian Publications Inc. All rights reserved.

[2.] Allender, Dan B. *The Wounded Heart - Hope For Adult Victims Of Childhood Sexual Abuse* (Colorado Springs, Co.: Navpress, 1990), p. 176. Copyright © 1990 by Dan B. Allender. Used by permission of NavPress. All rights reserved. For copies, call 1-800-366-7788.

Chapter Three

Our Qualifying Paradigm: That We Intensely Desire Him!

Do you *care* to grow in your personal relationship with the Lord Christ Jesus, and care ***strongly*** enough to endure the temptations, trials, disciplinings, and refining fires that lie along the way? Or are you simply hoping that the Lord will tolerate your current thought-patterns and ways, while you continue to enjoy the "pleasures" (even if masochistic) of your "little" sins? Are you clinging to Christianity mainly for the temporary relief it gives to the stresses of life? What are your ***real*** motives?

For that matter, why ***should*** you care? If all we can expect in this life are temptations, trials, disciplinings, and purifying fires - and yes, persecution - why ***should*** we care? What difference does it really make, anyhow, as long as we're going to "make it to heaven"?

1. Qualifications For Grace

As we studied in the preceding chapter, "grace", a key to salvation, is the gift *of God into* us: the gift of the indwelling Holy Spirit of Christ Jesus. It is a gift that we can never deserve, earn, merit, nor purchase. It comes to us, *free*, according to the promises of God.

But, we must nevertheless *qualify* for it!

How? By God's principle: "***Earnestly desire*** the greater gifts" (1 Corinthians 12:31). "***Pursue*** love, yet *desire earnestly* spiritual ...." (1 Corinthians 14:1). "Earnestly desire" here is a strong verb: "desire with white-hot passion and zealous intensity!"

Our *motivation* is the key issue here: we can't grow in our relationship with God in Christ Jesus unless we *strongly desire* to! That's right: *all* of the promises of God, though *freely* offered to "*all* whosoever ...", must be *sought* after by us in order for us to appropriate them. We must be one of those *whosoevers.* They do *not* come to us passively! They do not come to us simply because God loves us and wants to give us good things (although He does). We must *seek* them. "And you will *seek* Me and find Me, when you *search* for Me *with all your* heart", says Jeremiah in 29:13. We must cry as David cries, "As the deer pants (longs) for the water brooks, so my soul *pants* for Thee, O God. My soul thirsts for God, for the living God...." (Psalms 42:1-2a).

That We Intensely Desire Him!

Tozer[1] states this qualification for all of the promises of God including basic salvation and grace, in terms of four propositions:

(1) "We will get nothing unless we *go after* it. God will not force anything on us."
(2) "We may have as much as we *insist upon having*. When our requests are such as to honor God, we may ask as largely as we will."
(3) "We will have [only] as little as we are *satisfied with*. God will not make any man more godly than he wants to be. It is disheartening ... and surely a great grief to the [Holy] Spirit, to see how many Christians (alas the vast majority) are content to settle for less than the best."
(4) "You [right now] have [only] as much as you *really want*. Every man is as close to God as he *wants* to be; he is as holy and as full of the Spirit as he *wills* to be. ... by 'want' I mean *wholehearted* desire."

Why should we care? In order to possess even the most basic aspects of salvation. God loves us, but if we don't *care* enough for Him, we will fail to *know* Him. Dear believer, never take any of the promised blessings of God for granted; you must *earnestly seek* them in order to have them!

2. Qualifications For Ministry

Another reason why we should care: to qualify for *ministry*.

In Chapter Four and Appendix One of Volume V[2] of this series, we delineate 20 of the many distinct callings or ministries in the Body of Christ. We point out therein that one will never be completely fulfilled in life until he/she *knowingly* flows in his/her basic calling in the Lord, and also is *knowingly* receiving Christ through the callings of other members of the Body of Christ. Since one's calling represents the Lord's specific purpose for our lives, only in *it* will all that He has created in us (individually) be flowing as He intended.

But our Lord Christ Jesus *never* makes it easy for any of us to enter into our calling or ministry! To ascertain and flow into our appointed callings or ministries, is a most difficult and frustrating path to be trod. This is deliberately so by the sovereign wisdom and will of our Lord Christ Jesus Who appoints us unto those callings in the first place.

Why?

He has, no doubt, many reasons for this. Here we briefly discuss three.

First, and perhaps most obvious, is the necessity for careful *preparation.* Our callings bear an awesome responsibility. He will seldom establish any of us into functioning in our calling/ministry until *He* knows we are sufficiently prepared. We must be prepared not only in the sense of *competence* in the areas of our individual callings/ministries; we must also be prepared to fully accept, and never renege on, the obligations of *responsible steadfastness* in our callings/ministries in the face of all obstacles.

We must have *deeply* ingrained in our hearts - in our very guts - what Paul cries in 2 Corinthians 4:1: "Therefore, since we have our ministry, as we received mercy (from the Lord - 1

Corinthians 3:18), we *do not lose heart*." A large majority of God's servants today have "lost heart" due to insufficiently *intense* desire for the calling, an intensity calling for radical and total abandonment! There is no place in the Body of Christ for "armchair" ministries. For "knee-pad" ministries, yes! For "blood-sweat-tears" ministries, yes! For "bond-slave" ministries, yes! *All* true callings are of these types. And even for "pulpit-microphone" ministries, to which *only a very few* believers are called. But no "armchair" ministries.

Secondly, the warfare we *all* face in our individual callings/ministries will be intense. We *have* the power and authority of Christ to *withstand;* but withstand we *must* do if we are to "overcome". The attacks on us will always be in our areas of greatest *weaknesses*, whatever those happen to be: weaknesses mainly of flesh and soul, the "little sins" we have not yet fully abandoned, the things *we* still desire whether also of His will or not. (The most common area of such weaknesses among most of God's servants appears to be the marriage relationship!)

But unless we desire the will of our Lord Christ Jesus above all else, and desire it *intensely* enough to *abandon* all else, it is only a matter of time when we will be torn by the attacks and will falter, by burnout if not also by falling into overt sins. Not only will we then suffer personally. We will then also both: (1) *disappoint* the rest of the Body of Christ who need Christ to minister through us unto them according to our calling; and (2) bring *shame* to the Holy Name of our Lord Christ Jesus and our fellow believers!

A third reason for the Lord making it so difficult for us to enter into our callings/ministries, is the need for yet *deeper trials* He must put us through, if *His* purposes and glories behind our callings/ministries are to be effected. That is because Agape love is the essence of all ministries, and it is only through emptying trials that we grow in Agape love.

Christ gives us our ministries, yes. Nevertheless, His will is not that *we* minister according to our ministry, but rather that *He* do the ministering *through* us. As long as it is *our* ministry that He has given us, then *we* do the doing - and thus restrain Him from flowing freely through us as He wills. Also, to think we have a calling from God to some ministry tends to acerbate our spiritual *pride*, particularly when we try to function in that ministry by our own wisdom and strength.

Eventually we must become broken to the point where we, *willingly*, lay down our very *ministry* to Him, and do so without any expectation of Him *ever* giving it back to us. This is part of dying to self; but it is so much deeper a working of the Lord in our souls that few willingly allow Him to accomplish it.

A clear typical illustration of this is Abraham sacrificing Isaac on Mt. Moriah (Genesis 22:2-17). Isaac was the physical embodiment of God's full *purpose* for Abraham's life; just as our ministry is the physical embodiment of God's purpose for our life. But did Isaac *truly* belong to the Lord YHWH, or did Isaac actually belong to Abraham? That is the issue. Is my ministry in reality the Lord's who dwells in me? Or is it truly just mine?

If we would dare be totally abandoned to our Lord Christ Jesus, then He will, sooner or later, call us to *utterly surrender* our very *ministry*. And if we don't *willingly* lay it down, then He will *remove* it from us. Some of His ways of doing that are: (1) false accusations by a close friend who betrays us; (2) humiliating failures in our marriage or other family relationships; (3) humiliating errors we make, inadvertently, in our ministries; or (4) "natural" disasters involving our finances, health, homes, etc.

Both the state of being (sanctification) and of doing (ministry) that He is working to bring each of us unto, are to be dominated by an attitude of love-motivated and (Holy) Spirit-empowered *servanthood.* Servanthood? That we be unclogged vessels/channels through whom He pours Himself, both unto us personally and through us unto others. And in all cases it is to be He Who does the pouring, when, how and to whom He determines, often beyond our understandings and emotional preferences. In Chapters Five through Ten of Volume I[3] of this series, we studied in depth the many common self-seeking and self-protecting strategies we all have in us which hinder that. But God is sufficient to sanctify and unclog us unto that, if we would have the qualifying paradigm of intense *seeking* and *yielding to* Him in all things.

3. His Vested Interest In Us

Why does Christ Jesus offer to send His Holy Spirit to abide in us and transform us into Christ-likeness? Because He loves us? So that we will be blessed? So that we will share in His great inheritance?

Yes, but *not primarily!* Rather, the issue is this: so that *His* vested interest in us be effected! He has a *purpose* to accomplish through His redeemed and sanctified and matured people: if not through us, then through others; if not of our generation, then of some later generation. It is not our prayers nor cries nor bleatings that primarily motivate Him toward us, although He *does* hear us and *is* merciful toward us, and our prayers are necessary to "release" Him through us. Rather, it is our *value* to Him that primarily motivates Him toward us, value in terms of His purposes and objectives and plans.

He, Christ Jesus, is zealous for His vested interest in us! What is His vested interest in us, His purpose through us? That Christ be presented, be made available, to this world.

Ezekiel 36:21-38 graphically brings this point out. The context is that Israel had become subjected to the cruel taskmasters of Edom. Edom in Hebrew means "man", and this typifies how the philosophic religion of *Scientistic Humanism*, together with secular psychology, have all but subdued Christianity today. The religious leaders of Israel had compromised with the Edomite leaders. This also typifies most leaders of Christiandom today in their compromise with humanism; hence our Lord's sharp words against "fat shepherds" over lean sheep in Ezekiel Chapter 34. In Ezekiel Chapter 35 the Lord prophecies that in spite of Israel's terrible apostasy, He would destroy the Edomites, and He would restore His people as the rulers of Israel (Ezekiel 36:6-15).

Then in Ezekiel 36:22-23, 32, 36 & 38, in the context of prophecies of rich spiritual restoration and sanctification of Israel and His pouring of His blessings upon His people, He states bluntly: "I do this not for *your* sake, but for *My Holy Name's* sake, ... that the world will know that I am the Lord!" He sanctifies us, makes us Holy, and abides in us, *not* to bless us, but so that He can glorify *Himself* in the world *through* us. To glorify Himself means to make His Presence on Earth physically manifest; and He has chosen to do that through us, His people.

Another serious section of Scripture along this theme is Ezekiel Chapter 20. There God recounts many times during the history of the Israelites, when because they fell into gross national sin, He allowed them to be brought into captivity by a conquering people. Yet each time, He later called out of captivity a remnant people (a Biblical type is no more than one-sixth of those in captivity) to start over. In Ezekiel Chapter 20 God makes it very clear *why* He works that way: again, *for His Holy Name's sake!* What does that say to us? When we, who are called by His Name (i.e., ***Christ**ians*), fall into obvious worldliness and/or public sin, we shame His Holy Name. Yet He is always seeking a remnant people, who intensely seek Him and His righteousness, to start over. Those of us who have ears, let us hear!

He "would that all be saved", but the unsaved will only see Him through and in the midst of *us*, His redeemed men and women in Whom He lives and through whom He pours Himself out (to those unsaved ones). We are but His chosen vessels. No big deal for us in this life! It is for us to *die*, that *He* may live and glorify *Himself.* That is only our reasonable service, not any reason for us to boast. Any blessings that we get now are only for Him to *glorify Himself* through our lives. Most of us will also experience trials and tribulations and persecutions instead, just as He did, while still in this life. *Our* real rich blessings will come after this life.

He purposes to be presented to the world through each of us. Three aspects of Him as He pours Himself out (through us) unto the world: (1) His guiding *light (word);* (2) His delivering *life (power);* and (3) His enticing *love.* Each of us individually is to be used by Him in part. But collectively as His Body or Blood-covenant congregation, we are to be used by Him to present His *fullness* to the world. Since He pours Himself out of each of us only partially, it requires all of us, together and *in unison*, to present His complete Person to the world.

Are *you* willing to be sanctified? Do you care? Why *should* we care? Because He and His ways are worthy of all. That's why. If all we seek are our own ways and desires, then we *shouldn't* care.

4. The Impact Of Our Thoughts And Motives

Although we are seldom aware of it, our *thoughts* - good and bad, prayerful and mundane - have considerable *power!* They radiate into the spiritual world about us!

To emphasize that, the Bible uses the concept of odor to typify our thoughts. Our "spiritual fragrance" is that "spiritual aura" about us, *discernible* in *subtle* ways by God, by the Holy Spirit, by other human spirits if sensitive and discerning enough, and by evil spirits. Odor in the Bible refers to our *thought* life: our goals and aspirations, our framework of thinking, our true inner thought life, what we actually are, our personal paradigm. It does *not* refer primarily to what we *say* verbally or *do* in actions; those things only *follow* our thoughts.

As we pray or worship (or, negatively, murmur or complain or despair), God hears our *thoughts* and not our actual audible spoken sounds. Throughout the Law of Offerings in Leviticus

Chapters 1 through 9, for example, the concept is frequently repeated of our offerings being of a "sweet savor" or "fragrant odor" unto the Lord. Ephesians 5:2 and 2 Corinthians 2:14-17 tell us that Christ, and knowledge of Him, is a "sweet aroma".

1 Corinthians 12:17 lists "smelling" (i.e., discerning of spirits) as one of the manifestations of the Holy Spirit in the Body of Christ ministries. Romans 12:1-2 links our offering ourselves, as a living and "sweet-savor" *offering*, to: (1) our *worship;* (2) our *separation from worldliness* in our *thinking;* and (3) our being transformed by the *renewing of our mind* or patterns of thinking.

Many fragrances are mentioned in the Scriptures that are described as "sweet fragrances" unto God. Many are related to specific fruit and spices. Although most fruit and spices are to be tasted, 90% of our physical sense of taste is really our sense of smell. So also with our spiritual interpersonal relationships, in which our spiritual flavors play an important role.

The significances of the flavor characteristics of the love-fruit of the Holy Spirit in our hearts (Galatians 5:22-23) and the holy spices in the Lord's gardens of our hearts (Song of Songs 4:13-14) are separate and enlightening studies. We illustrate the parallels between these two lists of nine fruits and spices in Table One following The nine fruit-spice parallels also have a logical grouping into three categories: (1) the *beauty* that attracts others to Christ living within us and radiating through our *outward behavior;* (2) the *flavor* of Christ in us as reflected in our *inner emotions and thought patterns;* and (3) the *effects* of He in us working through us in our *interpersonal relationships.* We discuss these "holy Spices" in Chapter Ten later in this volume.

TABLE ONE

FRUIT AND SPICES OF THE HOLY SPIRIT IN OUR HEARTS

TYPE/QUALITY	Galatians 5:22-23 FRUIT OF THE (HOLY) SPIRIT IN US	Song Of Songs 4:13-14 PLANTS OF SPICES IN LORD'S GARDEN
BEAUTY Attracting Beauty & Radiance Of God In us	AGAPE: LOVE - The Greatest Of These Never Seek Anything But The Highest Good Of Others (An Attitude Totally Impossible Without Christ Indwelling)	RMWN: POMEGRANETES - To Be Tasted Important Fruit Related To Citrus Hot, Dry Weather Important For Ripening (Root Meaning: To Be High, Lofty)
	CHARA: JOY - Joy Of Living Radiance Being Bright Rejoicing	KPhR: CAMPHIRE (HENNA/MIGNONETTE) - To Be Seen Used As An Ornamental Shrub Also For Cosmetic Dyes (Hair, Fingernails, etc.) (Root Meaning: To Cover, Overlay)
OUTWARD APPEARANCE	EIRENE: PEACE - Life At Its Best: Perfect Contentment In Security Peaceful Perfection In Personal Relationships	NRD: SPIKENARD - To Be Smelled A Perfume Used As Oil For Anointing The Head (Root Meaning: To Descend, Come Down, Flow Out)
FLAVOR Character Of God In Us	MAKROTHUMIA: LONGSUFFERING - Patience Long Holding Out Of Mind Before Venting Feelings Never Losing Patience/Hope For People Never Losing Hope/Faith In Events	KRKM: SAFFRON - To Improve General Atmosphere Air-Sweetener In Public Places Perfume, Coloring, Food Flavoring (Root Meaning: To Surround, Wrap Around)
	CHRESTOTES: GENTLENESS - Divine Kindness Kindness Which Draws Men With Cords Of Love Kindness, Goodness, Benign-ness	QNH: CALAMUS - To Captivate By Fragrance Costly Fragrance (Scent, Not Taste) An Ingredient Of Holy Anointing Oil (Root Meaning: To Form, Acquire, Purchase)
INNER ATTITUDES	AGATHOSUNE: GOODNESS - Generous Goodness CHRESTOTES In Action Generosity Which Wishes The Well-Being Of Others	QNMWN: CINNAMON (CASSIA?) - To Transform Food Flavoring; Also Medicinal Also A Perfume Used In Holy Anointing Oil (Root Meaning: To Form In Likeness [i.e., Of God])
	PISTIS: FAITHFULNESS - Reliability Ethical Virtue Of Faithfulness, Fidelity, Loyalty, Reliability, Trustworthiness	LBWNH: FRANKINCENSE - God's Cleansing Through Heat/Fire - Aromatic Gum Obtained By Incision Burns Incense, White, Cleansing Odor By Heat (Root Meaning: To Be White, Clean)
EFFECTS Outflowing Of God Through Us To Others	PRAUTES: MEEKNESS - Strength & Gentleness Having Strength But Being Gentle In Its Exercise Soothing, Peace-Making In Midst Of Conflicts (A Form Of Mind Self-Control; Linked With Agape)	MR: MYRRH - God's Circumcising Through Death Bitter Gum Resin, Obtained By Incision Of Tree Costly Incense; Perfume Used For Embalming (Root Meaning: To Be Bitter, Grevious, Tearful)
INTER-PERSONAL BEHAVIOUR	EGKRATEIA: TEMPERANCE - Victory Over Desire Chastity; Exercise Of Self-Control Flesh Dominated By Soul, Soul By Spirit (Root Meaning: To Possess, Take Hold Of)	AhhLWTh: ALOES - God's Outpouring Fragrant Wood (Used As We Might Use Cedar) From Heartwood, When Outer Layers Are Decayed (Root Meaning: To Sojourn, Be Exposed)

In contrast, our *mundane* thoughts can and do hinder the Holy Spirit working through us, and through others near us. This is true not just of our sin-thoughts, but also of our fears and anxieties and dreams and worldly concerns. Such thoughts on our part during a worship service, for example, will hinder the abilities of others present to worship.

An extreme example of the negative influence our thoughts can have on others is ESP. ESP is a manifestation of this between people who are particularly sensitive in their human spirit in consciously discerning radiated thoughts. The phenomenon is real, and it applies to people whether regenerated in Christ or not. For Christians, it is the Holy Spirit of Christ in us Who sensitizes our human spirits, primarily to receive intelligent communication from *Him*, and also to "discern the spirits" (1 Corinthians 12:10). But for unregenerated people, it is *satan* who sensitizes their human spirits. *That* is the power behind ESP: a satanic exploitation of human desires for "mystic" experiences. It is *identical* to the mechanism that satan uses to entice people into all other forms of mysticism, ranging from transcendental meditation, occult experiences, and false prophecies on one hand, to outright satan worship on the other hand.

For us to constitute a "sweet savor" offering to God, means that our thought life must be in *harmony* with, and pleasing to, God. That in turn means that the very core of our thought life must be fused into oneness with Christ in *holiness*. "Come let us reason (think) together, says the Lord" - Isaiah 1:18. So, disciplining our thoughts, to be ever centered on Christ Jesus and on His will for our lives, is extremely *vital* in all aspects of a Christian's walk.

So we must be careful how we pray for others: our very thoughts during prayer, if not consistent with God's will for that person, can and usually do bring *soulish pressure* on that person, even though perhaps unintentionally. On the other hand, when our thoughts/wills are aligned with God's, then our prayers release Him to accomplish much!

5. The Necessary Vision And Perspective For Motivation

Staining a positive motive on our part is a key issue! The vast majority of believers today are far too *under*-motivated to be *able* to walk the path of total abandonment unto Christ Jesus and yield to His perfect will in their daily lives. And the few who are highly motivated are often so for *wrong* reasons (i.e., self-seeking and/or self-protecting goals and strategies)! Yes, it is in the area of our *motives* that He must deal most deeply.

We cannot remain stationary in our personal relationships with Christ Jesus. Either we *grow* in our relationship, or we *slip back*. His will is that we be disciplined and sanctified unto a mature union with Him and unto a yielding to Him indwelling, as He flows through us unto others as He sovereignly wills. But if we do not allow Him to thus mature us, He will not force Himself on us. His Holy Spirit in us will allow us to go our own ways. And the result of *that*, if continued to its conclusion, is deception and idolatry (Romans 1:21, 24, 26, 28 & 32)! Oh how *vital* it is that we allow *Him* in us to *mature* us!

Such positive motivation begins by *seeing* Jesus! It does *not* begin by imposing pressure on people through church programs, discipleship meetings, etc. Faith is our very walking in His will: depending upon Him in total trust and worship; and obeying His very will. Yet, as Proverbs 29:18 says, "Where there is no vision, the people perish" (i.e., become confounded, abandon their faith, and hence become vulnerable to satan's destroying them through deception). Without a vivid vision of Him, in no way could we trust in Him nor be obedient to Him.

Christians need to walk in proper balance between two diametric and conflicting truths: (a) our utter depravity - *all* of us have sinned; but (b) the depth of His love for us and the value *He* places on us.

The New Testament's emphasis is on how the Holy Spirit of Christ Jesus, Who indwells *every* true believer, works continually in us to blend into one these two opposite tendencies in our thinking. He works in us to bring us unto proper balance between our immediate concerns and God's "ultimate" concerns. He in us is both our pattern for daily living and our source of enlightenment of God's principles.

6. Christ Must Be Central To Our Thinking

He establishes Christ Jesus in us to be a central point of reference or coordination that unifies all of our concerns into one pattern of thinking. And that central pattern of thinking is essential if we are to ever sort out all of God's dealings in our lives and to be brought unto His true peace. For without such an all-encompassing sense of purpose or meaning or direction in our lives, we cannot fully know our calling in Christ. And if we do not clearly see and function in our calling in Christ, we cannot hope to fulfill God's highest expectations in us!

Our starting point therefore must be a *vivid* positive vision of Christ Jesus:
> (1) of Who He really *is;*
> (2) of His *love and acceptance* of us and of others;
> (3) of our total *security* in Him;
> (4) of His full *glory*, both now and to come;
> (5) of His purposes and *will* for our lives, individually as well as collectively; and
> (6) of His need to *discipline and sanctify* us, according to His will, and in His timing!

It has been said that the longest path in a Christian believer's walk is the path from his mind to his heart! There is a *vast* difference between mentally knowing *about* God's plans and will for our lives, and our actually *living* them. The Holy Spirit of our Lord Christ Jesus has been sent unto us to bring us along that long path, to work out that vast difference in our lives.

Nevertheless, He cannot bring us very far along this route, without us having a proper mental perspective. We do not mean to imply here that one needs comprehensive and detailed mental knowledge of the Scriptures nor a complete systematic theology of God's ways; that may follow but never precede the initial step of salvation. But we must have a proper *orientation* of our thinking, a correct *Weltanschauung* ("world-view"), a clear perspective of our relationship with God, a proper philosophy underlying our thinking patterns and attitudes and life-styles. "Be ye transformed by the renewing of your mind ..." (Romans 12:2).

The various orientations of thinking or personal philosophies that characterize believing Christians lie along a wide spectrum, and are various shades of "gray" rather than either "black" or "white". However, that spectrum can be defined by its two extremes:

At one extreme are those who are only concerned with immediately practical concerns and in meeting only present needs in their daily lives. To the extent that God plays a role, it is primarily that He answers our prayers for our immediate worldly needs and/or such needs of others. Most Christian ***religious*** structures and institutions are directed almost entirely toward such ***human*** needs. That can be called a "philosophy after the needs and traditions of men".

At the other extreme are those who long for knowing "truth", even if not immediately related to the daily problems of living. Such believers grasp at remarkable insights on Who God Is in His Fullness and Glory and who we are In Him. That can be called a "philosophy after the Will of Christ".

But alas some believers may also regard such "truth" as an end in itself, seldom allowing it to become operational in their daily walk in this world, and they may use it as an excuse to avoid the real repentance and practical sense of responsibility that the Scriptures call all Christians to.

One consistent and sad observation: the personal philosophies and mental perspectives that underlie many branches of Christianity are man-centered rather than God-centered! That God loves *me;* that Christ died for *me;* that God promises rich blessings for *me* in this life; that *I* will make it to heaven. Such thinking borders on the very essence of the original sin! "What's in it for me?" "How can I benefit most from God's promises?" "I, ..., me, ..." Note that the centrality of s*i*n is pride, and the central character in both is *I*.

We were created by God to live a certain *other* kind of life, and every fiber of our being has been designed to that end! We have been created so that *He* would live *His* life in and through us, in this world as well as in the next. Not a life centered on "I", but a life centered around King Jesus enthroned on our hearts.

He has created us with an insatiable spiritual/soulical hunger to have an integrated heart-understanding of how all details of all that we see and feel and know fit into God's overall plans and intentions. He created into each of our human spirits a deep yearning for knowing the meaning and purpose for our lives. And the object of that yearning can be found *only* in Him. It is only as we see all things as properly related to Him and His overall purposes, that that hunger or yearning can be satisfied. In order for us to be fully that which satisfies and which truly brings us inner peace, our personal philosophy must be God-centered and not man-centered.

When it is not, then everything in our thinking is out of kilter with reality. It is strained. Most Christians observe the *acts* of God, but few indeed come to know the *ways* of God (Psalm 103:7). If we only see the *acts* of God and how things pertain to our personal lives, how *narrow* is our vision and framework of thinking. We are confounded and disoriented. We find no peace. Profound loneliness awaits us in the midst of exhausting busyness. Priorities out of order. Unsatisfying religious and social involvements. Undependable personal relationships. Where, oh where, is the peace that Christ Jesus promises to all who believe in Him?

That We Intensely Desire Him!

Yes, He has created into each of us a deep yearning to experience all things relating to Him and to His overall purposes. We each sense that we have a role to play in God's overall purposes - a personal "sense of destiny". This yearning is a major function of our (human) spirit.

There is *no* possibility whatsoever for any of us to be living in God's promised fullness for us[4] without Christ Jesus being totally central in our lives, being the focus of our every goal and desire, and hence satisfying that yearning. For only *He* can satisfy it. And He can satisfy it *only* when we allow Him *reign* internally.

But the unfulfilled needs of our human spirit work havoc in our lives when we try to live by the "Tree of Knowledge ...", i.e., by self-seeking and self-protecting goals and strategies. Even atheistic psychologists recognize it and call a distortion of it by the word "id"; and liberal theologians steeped in higher criticism but with experience in ministerial counseling recognize it and refer to a distortion of it as our "existential condition".

It is interesting to note that even liberal theologians of recent years, without clear testimony of personal *companionship* knowledge of Christ Jesus, still recognize this. For example, Jackson[5] in summarizing Soren Kierkegaard's conclusions, says:

> "... One can only become a complete person when one seeks to be completely responsive to the highest goals for life. Values are nourished not through a selfish quest for personal satisfactions but rather through an intimate commitment to the highest one can know...."

Conversely the strain, disorientation, frustration and impotence we experience when we do not live our lives with Christ truly central, is also recognized by them. Jackson[6], in commenting on Ignace Lepp's *The Depths Of The Soul*, expressed it in these words:

> "... when the conscious direction of life is in conflict with its deep source of psychic energy, the person is sentenced to live in ... darkness .... But when the two realms are in harmony there is a new sense of peace within that can tolerate the light. (Hence) it is essential ... to understand that the deep inner loneliness that characterizes our existential condition is not resolved by some simple procedure such as joining a group or playing games with oneself, no matter how pleasant and temporarily diverting that may be." [To this list of diversions, we would add religious activities.]

High-sounding words, perhaps, but true nevertheless.

Christ central in our hearts, and Christ alone, can fulfill and satisfy our God-established deep spirit-yearning. Christ the **Person**, Whom we *experientially* know and *consciously* enthrone as Lord of our lives. And He living ***His life through*** us as He wills, as He calls us as His vessels and instruments. He cannot be our saviour without also being our indwelling Lord.

But to what extent is He actually our center and our indwelling Lord. Few of us, indeed, are actually seeking to live and function in Christ and in the role or calling He designates for us. Why? Why do the vast majority of us manifest such *indifference* toward really fulfilling God's purposes and callings for our lives?

We suggest four fairly common and closely related causes: unconcern, intimidation, religion, and lack of vision of Christ in His Glory.

Unconcern among Christians is basically rooted in a passive acceptance of one's life circumstances as being about the best one can achieve in this life. This in turn stems from such sources as: love for the pleasures of this world; cares and worries borne out of our earthly responsibilities (Matthew 13:22, Mark 4:19 and Luke 8:14); and fear that if we indeed fully yield to Christ we would lose much that we now have and are (Matthew 19:21-22, Mark 10:21-22, and Luke 18:22-23). Are not these the all putting secular concerns above Christ? Unwillingness to trust Him for our worldly problems and needs? Unbelief in Him? We have an innate aversion against Him, and we don't really believe that He is sufficient to meet our deep needs.

Intimidation within the Body of Christ has two forms: that which is intrinsic to our particular level of immaturity in Christ; and that which is imposed upon us by our Christian (religious) leaders. Intimidation is when we think we can not be useful to Christ: "We have no training; we have no talents; we are still only babes in Christ. How can we therefore have a calling?" Or, "All of my efforts so far have had little lasting results and have only left me burned out." All of these are various forms of unbelief.

Intimidation is also often imposed upon us by our church. Should any of us truly apprehend our personal calling in Christ Jesus, we will quickly find that our present church structures make no allowances for it. So, we must either forget it, or modify it and compromise it to fit some established church role for us, regardless of whether Christ is with us in that role or not. Also, should any of us truly seek a deeper relationship with Christ Jesus than that which our particular church teaches and emphasizes, we often soon get the "left foot of fellowship".

Religion is a major stumbling-block in other ways as well to our truly placing Christ central. I do not mean here some pagan religion, nor even the modern atheistic religion of scientistic humanism. I mean here our *christian* religion, our churches, our denominations, our familiar christian traditions. Denominational religion[7] fosters two *soulish* reactions on our part that oppose the workings of the Holy Spirit of Christ Jesus in our midst and in our individual hearts: complacency and zealousness. Complacency makes us comfortable when He would rouse us unto concern and offers false hopes of "victory in Christ" through our Church rather than truly through Christ Himself. Zealousness is when we strive to serve Christ, not a wrong motive in itself, but to meet needs as *we* conceive them through our *own* efforts, rather than allowing Him in us to minister to others *through* us.

Once again we emphasize a major underlying factor in our indifference to Christ's fullness for our lives: a lack of *vision* of Who Christ really is in His Glory, and who we are in Him! We ignore Him because we do not really *know* Him. We remain oblivious to His plans and intentions for us, for we remain ignorant in our hearts as to whether He even *has* plans and intentions for us.

Except in the "bye and bye". Yes, we have faith for the future - that He will get us to Heaven when we die. But, brothers and sisters, we are in Heaven with Him right *now* (Ephesians 1:3)! Not future hope, but present fact! Not a mystery to be accepted mentally by "faith", but a present *reality* to be experienced, to be grown into. He indeed has overall plans and intentions, to be worked out among His people in this life. He indeed has a specific calling for each of us here and now. And He ever seeks that we would *know it, understand it, experience it, grow* in it, *walk* in it (Ephesians 1:18-19). Now, in *this* life!

End Notes: Chapter Three

[1] Tozer, A. W., *That Incredible Christian*, (Harrisburg, PA: Christian Publishers, Inc., 1964, Assigned 1977 to Horizon House Publishers), pp. 62-67, emphasis added.

[2] Sherrerd, Chris S., *Social Dynamics In The Body Of Christ*, Volume V of the series "Where Do You Fit In? Practical Commitments In The Body of Christ", to be published.

[3] Sherrerd, Chris S., *The Christian Marriage - A Six-Fold Covenant Of Love-Motivated Servanthood*, Volume I of the series "Where Do You Fit In? Practical Commitments In The Body Of Christ" (Shippensburg, PA: Treasure House, Destiny Image Publishing Group, 1994). Copyright © 1994 by Shulemite Christian Crusade.

4. This is what is really meant by God's promise of "peace" - the Hebrew word ShLWM literally means "wholeness of living".

5. Jackson, Edgar N., *Understanding Loneliness*, (Philadelphia PA: Fortress Press, 1980), p. 69. Copyright © 1980 by Edgar N. Jackson.

6. *Ibid.* p. 112.

7. We define "denominationalism" as a paradigm or mentality of Christian religions wherein: (1) the **person** of Christ indwelling has been replaced by philosophy and theology based on **doctrines** about Him; (2) the social structure of the **Body of Christ** has been replaced by a religious organization; and (3) the social dynamics of Body members ministering to one another has been replaced by a preisthood-*vs*-laity order in which one or a few elite "priests" or "ministers" do all the ministering, and the people provide the context and logistics for him/her. This error began to encrust Christianity before the end of the first century AD, and by the mid-300's fully characterized the "visible" Christian church. The Protestant reformation over the past 450 years has not yet completely weaned us from it.

Chapter Four

God's Ultimate Intention[a]

Before we study God's *patterns* of sanctifying us, we further emphasize the extremely important point of view that our personal thinking and motives be totally God-centered. We need to fully understand the current human condition, but we must understand it from *God's perspective*. God's dealings in our lives cannot be understood apart from understanding God's goals and plans and purposes from His point of view. God did *not* create us to redeem us, but to bring us unto far deeper and more wonderful purposes than just "being saved" and getting to Heaven! Sanctification is the next step, *after* basic salvation, toward those deeper and far more wonderful purposes!

This cannot be emphasized too strongly. Sanctification simply cannot be fully understood when viewed from *our* human perspective. It is then but a deep mystery, a baffling set of experiences, a confusing path to walk. Yet 99.44% of

---

[a] *WARNING:* The Eternal General has determined that reading this chapter may be hazardous to your self (that is, to your Christian soulish *self-centeredness*)!

Christian believers today view salvation and God's dealings in our lives almost solely from the human perspective - what it does for *us*.

That is why we had to lead up to this point in this book the way we did: we had to *start* this study with three introductory chapters on believers' motivation. We specifically emphasized in Chapter Three, that a vital starting point for our maturing in our personal relationships with our Lord Christ Jesus is our acquiring a *vivid* positive vision of Christ, Who He is, and who we are in Him. If you are *not* hungering for that, then for your sake we urge you to read no further; the rest of this book (and quite possibly the rest of your life here on Earth) will be at best a waste of time.

1. Our Oneness With God's Overall Plan

What are God's overall plans and intentions, with which we are to be in harmony?

God's overall plans and intentions have in times past been a secret (Greek: Musterion) - a secret known only to certain persons (i.e., initiates - Ephesians 1:9). But now it is available to us all: that *all* things be summed up, culminated in, centered around, Christ Jesus (Ephesians 1:8-10, 19-23)! That *every* thing, in Heaven and on Earth, has meaning and purpose *only* as related to Christ Jesus our Lord, our Head, our All in All.

The mid-1960's saw the publication of perhaps the clearest books up to then on this subject. One of those, *The Ultimate Intention* by DeVern Fromke[1], is in my opinion a most significant foundational treatise. It should be prerequisite reading for any serious study in sanctification. Reprints of it and some associated publications by Fromke (See Fromke[2], Fromke[3], Fromke[4], and Swindoll[5]) are still available. We also recommend more recent publications by Billheimer[6] and Edwards[7] as excellent parallel treatises. Since these resources cover such a foundational and necessary basis for the rest of this book, we devote this chapter to summarizing their main points, with a few comments and interpretations of our own.

Our individual purposes for living - and all other spiritual riches of life - are impossible to fully apprehend outside of our ultimate standing as the *Bride* in the *Sonship* of Christ under the *Fatherhood* of God! That is the one theme of our study of God's Word and Ways: the ultimate Fatherhood of God, ever underlying *all* of human history (and before), and now culminating in the Sonship of Christ Jesus, with each of us a vital extension of that Sonship in this 4-dimensional space-time domain. Under the ultimate Fatherhood of God, we see ourselves: first as His *creation;* then as His *redeemed;* then as His *sons* and *daughters;* then as His *heirs;* finally as His *Bride!* How far along in it are, *you* right now?

Being in Christ and apprehending God's purposes for us in Christ - the *key* to which is our choosing out of a pure motive of love to *do* His will - is an entirely *new* way of living for most of us. Each of us, born in sin, comes from total deception and hopeless separation from God (Ephesians 2:1-3 and 11-12). Saved through faith in Christ Jesus, we have been raised up by Him in new life *now* with Him in Heavenly places (Ephesians 2:4-10; Romans 8:10-11). Everything we *now* are derives from our ever-deepening personal relationships with Him. That is what Paul really means by our putting on the "new man" (Romans 6:4-6, 2 Corinthians 4:16, Ephesians 4:22-24, and Colossians 3:9-10). Not just "being saved", but *living* in the Spirit, that is, totally under the control of and enlightenment by the indwelling Holy Spirit of Christ Jesus.

This is also the true meaning of "repentance" - Metanoia: that our total ways of thinking, attitudes, motives and personal philosophies, be completely *changed* to that which is consistent with our having been raised up in Christ. Not "I", but Him. All things be of God in Christ Jesus, unto Him, through Him, and Him living and doing His will though us.

What does it mean to be "all things in Christ" in actual personal experience? To relate all our thoughts and goals to Him. To associate all our experiences to His will, even though we lack full understandings of His detailed workings in our lives. To *yield* to Him in full willful obedience - not just out of a sense of legal obligation, but out of *love* for Him. If/as we love Him, we will *want* to obey Him. And to live in joy in the sense of anticipation of all things being right and righteous.

It also means being privileged to partake of His *sufferings* (2 Corinthians 1:5, Philippians 3:10, and 1 Peter 4:13)! Sufferings borne out of heart-break over seeing so many people around us, who need Him and His love and salvation so desperately, but who continue to reject Him. Sufferings directly resulting from persecution of His people in the wake of that rejection. Suffering from the intense spiritual warfare into which we are continually plunged. Sufferings of the continual temptations and worldly trivia that constantly beset us to divert our attention and our intentions. And sufferings out of chastisement as He, our loving Father, disciplines and corrects us to perfect our souls' spiritual orientations.

Even more: it means fully accepting *every* fellow true believer in Christ as our brother or sister in Him. For every true believer in Christ has been born in the *family* of God and is a "member" or "extension" of the very Godhead itself, even though we are now for a season still here on Earth. As members of the Godhead, we are "expected" to adopt the same *modus operandum* toward every other member, as do the Three of the Trinity: each related to each other in harmony borne out of total sacrificial and supportive love! Hence, it means that we think and walk in love-motivated and Spirit-empowered servanthood!

We must be willing even to lose our very (physical) lives if/when that be a consequence of obeying Him (Matthew 10:39 & 16:25, Mark 8:35, Luke 9:24 & 17:33, and John 12:25)! For as He pours His Light, Life and Love unto others in this world *through* us, He does so in the demographic context of those other people. Since that demographic context is presently that of satan's Kosmos or organized domain, satan inevitably becomes intensely stirred up against us who are Christ's vessels and instruments. He (satan) not only counterattacks us directly through our thoughts; he also counterattacks us physically through his deceived human agents.

Now, remember: our Lord Christ Jesus has, right *now, all* authority in Heaven and on Earth and in hell (Ephesians 4:21 and Philippians 2:10)! So, we have to obey *Him*. But we must learn to be strong in spiritual defense and offense (Ephesians 6:10-18), and to leave the *consequences* of our obedience also to our Lord Christ Jesus in *His* hands, even if those consequences be unto death. Yet it is as we do so that we actually experience victories and the joy of being utterly *abandoned* in Christ.

2. Were We Created To Be Redeemed?

For the majority of Christian believers, a quite difficult area of our thinking or mentality or personal philosophy to be changed over to that of *God's* perspective, is our basic view of redemption through the shed blood of Christ Jesus at Calvary.

Becoming redeemed and born-again totally affects us and is a powerful, complete, dynamic, overwhelming change in our status and destiny. But even though redemption through the blood of Christ Jesus is so dramatic an event in my life and in yours, we nevertheless need to seek understanding of it from *His*, not our, perspective!

When we view the entire Gospel of God's dealings and promises purely from the *human* point of view, God's work falsely *appears* to be *totally* redemptive. But in God's plans, redemption is *not* His *primary* objective; it is only a necessary *prerequisite* to *enable* Him to fulfill His original *purposes* in spite of the Fall. He did not create us in order to redeem us, but to realize His purposes through us. God's objectives are *not* to deliver mankind from sin *per se*, but rather (after having done that) to *expand* Himself through His thus-redeemed people! It is not for our redemption, but rather for His purposes, for which we were created (Revelation 4:11). It is not just redemption, but His *good pleasure* (Godly intentions - Rev. 4:11) that He is now working into us.

The principle is this: He has a *purpose* to accomplish through His redeemed and sanctified and matured people. He does

God's Ultimate Intention 91

love us, yes. We do get blessed, yes. But any blessings that we get now are only for Him to glorify Himself through our lives; they are otherwise *not* His main *purpose.* "Not for your sake, Oh Israel, but for My Holy Name's sake, ...", saith the Lord (Ezekiel 36:22). It is not our cries nor bleatings that primarily motivate Him toward us (although He does hear us and is merciful toward us), but rather our *value* to Him, value in terms of His purposes and objectives and plans.

God's very essence is His *Eternal Fatherhood,* first to have been fully realized through the *Eternal Sonship* of His Firstborn Son Christ Jesus (that was fully accomplished 1970 years ago), and second through us as we expand and complete that Eternal Sonship in Christ (Ephesians 1:3-10) by being the *Eternal Brideship* of the believers! "Fatherhood" and "Sonship" are terms of interpersonal relationship, not terms of theology nor religion. It is *relationship* with Him that He desires, and redemption and subsequent sanctification are parts of the experiential process that He brings us through for that purpose.

He (the Father) did not will for Him (the Son) to die on the cross only, nor even primarily, for *our* benefit, but rather so that He (the Father) may expand and multiply His Fatherhood (through us in Christ). It was not for *my* benefit that He purchased me from satan my former slave-owner (Ephesians 2:2 & 12-13) *via* His Son's Shed Blood, but rather for *His* benefit: that as you and I (through redemption) come into Christ, He would complete the Eternal Sonship of Christ and thus His Eternal Fatherhood. His purposes unfold not by my being *redeemed,* but through my *yielding* to Him and *only* to Him, by my becoming part of the completion of the Body of Christ and hence of His Eternal Sonship.

What does "expanding His Eternal Fatherhood through us in the Eternal Sonship of Christ Jesus" really mean?

In the present age and space-time domain, it is to *present* Himself to the world (i.e., glorify Himself) *through* us! To "glorify" Himself means to make His Presence on Earth *physically* manifest. He has chosen to do that through His people. He "would that all be saved" (1 Timothy 2:4). But for the most part the unsaved will only see Him through and in the midst of God's redeemed men and women, in Whom He lives and through whom He pours Himself out to those yet-unsaved ones. We are but His chosen vessels for that purpose.

We should expect no great blessings for us *in this life*. We are not promised prosperity in this life. On the contrary; only suffering (John 16:33, Acts 14:22 and Romans 5:3)! It is for us to *die*, that *He* may live and glorify *Himself*. That is only our reasonable service (Romans 12:1), not reason for us to rejoice! We will actually experience trials and tribulations and persecutions (as Christ Jesus did) while still in this life; our real, rich blessings will come only in our resurrection life.

More specifically, He purposes to present Himself to the world through each of us in several important ways. First, He purposes to use each of us *individually* to pour out to the world through us His guiding *Light (Word),* His delivering *Life (Power),* His enticing *Love*. Second, He wills to use us *ethnically* (i.e., as a sub-culture in the world about us) to present to the world the peace and beauty of the life-style of love-motivated servanthood that He offers to all people who will enter into union with Him and hence with each other in Him! 2 Chronicles 7:14 is a typical promise of this. And

God's Ultimate Intention

third, He works to present His *fullness* to the world through us *collectively*, as His Blood Covenant congregation or Body-of-Christ or church ("called-out ones"). Since He pours Himself out through each of us only partially, it requires all of us, together and in Holy-Spirit-directed *unison*, to present His *complete* Person and Presence to the world.

Yet the fullness of the Eternal Sonship of Christ Jesus, involving us in Christ, goes even beyond His presenting Himself to the world through us here and now. Ephesians 1:3-10: "... blessed us ... *in Christ*" (*vs* 3); "... chosen us *in Him* before the foundation ..." (*vs* 4); "... predestined unto adoption ... *by Jesus Christ* ..." (*vs* 5); "... accepted *in the Beloved* ..." (*vs* 6); and "... gathered together all things ... *in Christ* ..." (*vs* 10).

Note that this has nothing to do with the Fall of mankind into sin, nor the Blood of Christ to redeem man from sin. This was purposed *before* the foundation of the world was laid, and hence before the Fall. It starts not with the Fall but with God Himself. He determined it not because of the Fall (although He foreknew that would happen), but as part of His very purposes for *creating* us. These purposes of God are to be effected through the Son Christ Jesus and centered in Him. The Eternal Fatherhood of God did not originate with His creating the world, but was a very part of the triune-ness of the Godhead before the beginning. The Eternal Sonship of Christ, and the Eternal Brideship of His people, began *then*, before the beginning; indeed it was the key element in creation itself (John 1:1-3)!

So, even if sin had never entered the world, these Eternal purposes of God would still prevail. Therefore, we must see the proper context of sin in God's purposes, and not make our redemption from it the *main* element of our walk with Him. Sin *did* enter, and of course our redemption from sin *is* necessary. But it is only *part* of His means for bringing us unto those marvelous Eternal relationships.

In order to see how the Fall of mankind into sin and God's plan for our redemption from it fit into His plans, we briefly review His overriding objective behind the Creation of mankind in the first place.

Genesis 1:26-28 reads: "... after Our '*image* ...'" That means much more than "of the same physical form and appearance", since God is Spirit (i.e., John 4:24). It means of the same mentality, interests, personal objectives, desires, goals, and emphases of operation. The *modus operandum* of the Godhead is: each member chooses by *free choice* to live and function totally for the *other* members.

God's single overall objective in His creating mankind has been to obtain and have a family of *sons* (mature agents), each of whom, by *free choice*, lives and functions solely to effect and further His (God's) interests and the interests of all other members of the Godhead (including other believers), and whom God can trust to be responsible over other portions of His creation as His agents. This is what is meant by "expanding His Eternal Fatherhood".

How could God obtain such a family who by *free choice* would so choose such total oneness with Him and His objectives? God could *create* man: being omnipotent, He could create man *anyway* He chose. He could create them as *puppets* to be automatically in oneness with Him. He already

God's Ultimate Intention

did just that with the hierarchy of angels; but angels are in oneness with God by *nature,* not by *free* choice. (Satan as a high-ranking angel was apparently an exception to this, but all other angels under him by their nature went with him.)

How could He create men to *freely choose* His ways? We were created by God such that oneness with Him is the most "natural" way of life for us. But that is the extent to which He has created into us a nature of obedience to Him. So, what God did was this: (a) create man with a free choice in his nature; (b) confront man with a real, practicable (though depraved) choice of self-seeking (amplified by satan's temptations) and challenge him by it; (c) allow man to try that alternative; (d) show man by experience that His (God's) way (being a way of love-motivated and Spirit-empowered servanthood) is so much more desirable a way (even for man) than man's self-seeking ways; and (e) by a tremendous practical display of that Love on His part, redeem men and women from their depraved state into oneness with Him. Through this, individual by individual, moment by moment, we will see that God's way for us is so much better for us. By that process, redeemed man, out of *gratitude*, would want to *freely choose* His (God's) way of self-abandoning Love as their (man's) *modus operandum* as well.

Hence, even if sin had never actually entered into the human experience, God had to *allow* for the possibility of sin, and to somehow reveal to mankind the awful consequences of sin. For only then would His *sons* be able to truly and *freely choose* Him out of love. The Fall, having occurred, indeed gives every man and woman that contrast, that choice, that opportunity.

God is now working to bring men to see this contrast, and the people called "Israel" in the Bible are His primary instrument to that purpose. Oneness with Him requires our living the *"Way"* of the *Cross!* All "whosoever" of *true* "Israel" - including gentiles who are grafted into His people by appropriating Christ's death on the Cross (Romans 9:6-8 & 24-29 and 11:17-29) - are being brought into the *Way* of the *Cross* by the blood covenant relationship with God in Christ Jesus.

So the incarnation, Christ becoming flesh, was not just for redemption: it was centered in the *Eternal* purposes of God, purposed before the creation itself. Sin and the Fall did not alter God's Eternal plan; it only made redemption an *additional* requirement. Yes, the incarnation's purpose *included* our redemption; but it had first and foremost a far more reaching purpose in God's Ultimate Intention: to establish a blending of the human and the divine so that mankind can grow in relationship with Him. The Father originally purposed for everything to be accomplished *through* and *centered in* His Son. Hence, Christ Jesus was to become our very life, even if we had never sinned and required redemption in addition.

God of course foreknew man would sin, and hence He planned for it through Christ. So, not only is God's glorious Ultimate Purpose being realized through His Son Christ Jesus and our expanding Christ's Sonship in Him; when redemption became necessary Christ was central to that also. But that in no way changed His original purpose: Christ being our total life and we being embedded with Him in His Sonship.

We are being brought into the *Way* now in this life, albeit in an imperfect sense until the final stage of our redemption, (i.e., of our bodies: Romans 8:23 and Philippians 3:21). We are, that is, *if* we are willing to move from our state of being in Israel under the *Old* Covenant to being in Israel under the *New* Covenant, and to seek the Kingship of Christ Jesus over *all* aspects of our lives.

We of course do not treat lightly the destiny of those who do not choose God. Those who do not choose His way and the advantage of His great redemption, can never in this eon be brought to the point of being useful to Him for His Eternal Purposes. Hence they must be "discarded". This is suggested by one of the New Testament Greek transliterations of the Hebrew name for "hell": Geenna was the name of the Jerusalem town dump or rubbish heap and incinerator.

But those who *do* choose His ways, He can use, and He will do all that He must to prepare them for that use.

God is drawing us into this Blood Covenant relationship so that He can use us to show the contrast, to others of the world, not by our *words* but by our *lives* (*being* witnesses, not *doing* witnessing). Thus it was in the early New Testament church. That is what God is now trying to accomplish: by our *lives,* joyously radiating Christ Jesus in the midst of utter chaos. Those are the characteristics of the church of Christ as the "Bride of Christ" when she becomes matured. And that is the very essence of what our Lord Christ Jesus is effecting in His people today: bringing His Bride into that maturity!

Christ's dealings to adjust us to maturity, to sanctify us unto His Lordship, comprise a life-long process over time, whereby He works into us His very Holiness. This personal holiness in character and action is a holiness ***unto*** Christ, not just a holiness *from* the world. Holiness is not a legalistic obedience to certain laws and taboos. Holiness is first and foremost an ***inner union with Him***, Christ Jesus the Person. ***Only*** as we are growing or choose to grow into that union with Him, shall His Holiness (as well as all other aspects of His Person) be manifested in us and through us unto the world about us. We were created with the ***potential*** to grow unto that full relationship with Him. And redemption merely brings us, once again, to what Adam was upon creation: a vessel with that growth potential.

At this time, His children are at widely differing stages in their personal relationships with Him. So, our Lord Christ Jesus is working in many ways with individual believers and groups, each way diverse from all others. He carefully tailors His dealings with each of us according to His knowledge of our current state and needs. He has the blueprints for each of our lives.

His Holy Temple, His Body, His Bride, is at this time far from mature and complete! Not a single ***present*** structure of local manifestations of His Body even remotely represents what He is bringing us ultimately unto. All present religious and demographic structures and contexts of His children are but ***momentary, interim*** steps in His Bride-perfecting process. He is now building and perfecting His church on Earth! During this process, He also deals with us ***collectively***: (1) first to build us as living stones into His Holy Temple (dwelling place on Earth); and (2) second to order us as members of His Body (physical manifestation on Earth). This first form of adjustment emphasizes our *relationships* with one another, and that we become fitted and adjusted to one another; the second form of adjustment emphasizes our *functioning* in ministries and service to one another and to the world.

It is possible for us to be redeemed unto that state and yet never grow into that Ultimate Intention of God. When we (falsely) view redemption as the *primary* purpose of God for our lives, we do not expect, let alone *seek,* anything further from Him in this life. The Biblical promises of full relationship with Him are then put off to the future - in the "heavenlies bye and bye". So we barely cooperate with what He wants to work into us *here* and *now*. Yes, we have great glories from our *position* in Christ; but to experientially mature in His Sonship is another matter.

3. Historical Unfolding Of God's Ultimate Intention

In Figure One, following, we briefly sketch God's ultimate intention for us, how He started to unfold it, how it was interrupted by the Fall of mankind, how He redeems us unto it through the "Work of the Cross", and how He now is effecting it among His redeemed people in the "Way of the Cross". It indicates some key aspects of that Ultimate Intention that still apply and in which we, once redeemed from sin, are purposed by Him to walk.

The horizontal line at the top of Figure One, that curves gently upward to the right, symbolizes God's plan for us if sin had not entered into the world. Note that He still purposes it for us, with our fall into sin and His redeeming us from it

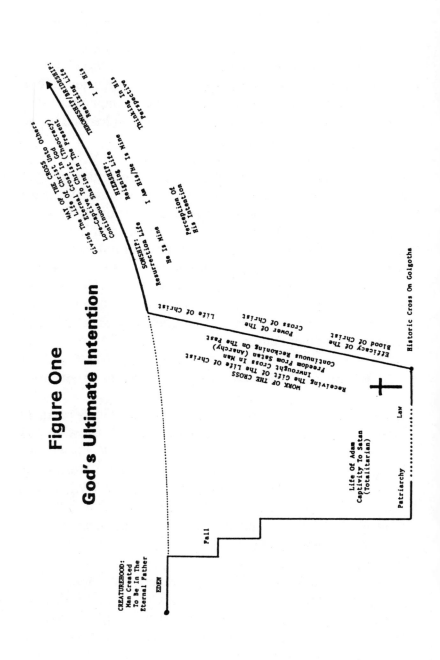

being but a "temporary" interruption in God's timing. Note also how the key details of His redeeming us from sin are distinct from, yet intimately related to, the key details of His subsequently sanctifying us unto His Ultimately-Intended walk in relationship with Him.

During the four millennia between the Fall and Calvary, God allowed (indeed ordained) mankind to try several schemes for redemption, other than Calvary, only for us to know experientially the vacuity and intrinsic futility of any other way. Law, religion, prophetic revelation, patriarchy, human government, covenants - they all failed. Yet they *did* succeed in preserving the righteous remnant *until faith came at last* (Galatians 3:22-26) through Calvary.

For each of us today, our starting position is the condition described in Ephesians 2:1-3 & 11-12: hopelessly cut off from God and slaves to the spirit of sin - satan our slave-master. Only through the historic cross on Golgotha can we ever escape such a state; only the Work of the Cross will be efficacious in restoring us to the point where that Ultimately-Intended relationship with Him can begin.

The historic Cross on Golgotha, and the *Work* of that cross, is dynamically effective in our lives. But let us first be reminded of some of the details of how we reached such a "hopeless" state of bondage. The Fall of mankind occurred not all at once, but in *three* distinct steps (and the *Work* of the Cross to restore us does so also in three distinct corresponding steps in reverse order)!

We know that man *did* exercise his free choice to disobey God and determine his own way. But, look carefully at just what that first choice was, as distinct from its awful consequences. "The fruit of the tree of knowledge of good and evil..." is the knowledge and wisdom that gives us the false "ability" to live our lives by our own strength, by self-seeking and self-protecting. It includes what we today call theology and philosophy, even if "God-oriented". What is so evil about that? Simply this: it made it possible for man to live "on his own", to function *apart* from God, at least ostensibly.

Except, the hooker is this: *never* do we *really* have the freedom to control our own lives. Whether we like it or not, whether we know it or not, we are always slaves of *some* slave-master! Our only choice today is *who* shall be our *slave-owner*: satan or YHWH/Christ (Ephesians 2:2 and 13 etc.)

Back to the awful consequences of man's choice to disobey God. "And the day ye partake thereof, ye shall surely die" (Genesis 2:17 and 3:3). Just what did God mean by that? "Spiritual" death? "Spiritual" death is *not* a Biblical phrase, and its use does not *answer* the question, only confuses it! Rather, a meaningful clue is found in Genesis 2:7. The word translated "life", that God breathed into us to make us living beings, is in the *plural* in the original Hebrew (ChYYM). Hence, it implies that God originally imparted into us *two* or more forms of life.

And in the Fall we died in more than one way. We here consider *three* aspects, two initially and the third a few hundred years later. These three aspects pertain separately to the three parts of our nature as God created us: flesh, soul and spirit.

First, the flesh. Did Adam and Eve actually die *physically*, i.e., in the flesh, "in the day they partook thereof"? It was physical *immortality* that mankind *immediately* lost in the Garden of Eden! Furthermore, it is physical immortality that we who abide in Christ Jesus will finally regain (1 Corinthians 15:51-56 and Philippians 3:21). So, loss of "physical" life was involved in the Fall, the *first* to be lost, and the *last* to be regained in Christ!

Second, the *soul*. God delegated His authority over all of the earth and all created life on it; mankind was to be His *agent* on earth (Genesis 1:29-30 and 2:19-20). Also, it is implied that God visited Adam with face-to-face fellowship, speaking directly to him (Genesis 2:16-17 and 3:8). How the Adamic curse changed all that: toil, difficulties, and eviction from the Garden (Genesis 3:17-24). It is this form of life we regain *secondly* in Christ.

And third, the *human* spirit. Our human spirit is that capability God created into us to communicate (both ways) with Him and to know Him. Now, certainly *direct* communication with God was lost; loss of a face-to-face walk with God did occur in the Fall. But those forms of communication involved the human soul more than spirit. However, in Genesis 6:3, that pertains to a time about 1400 years after the Fall of mankind, we see strong implications that God's Spirit still abode in and dealt with men. That implies that man still had the capacity to know God and to communicate with Him for some years after the Fall under the Adamic curse, that is, *via* his spirit. We did then finally die spiritually. But note that this was not *immediately* after the Fall. And it is this form of life that we *first* regain in Christ.

4. Constraints Under The Adamic Curse

Even though death came under the Adamic curse, nevertheless God never gave up on mankind nor forsook him. Even though mankind chose satan by default as his slave-master, God placed many *constraints* on mankind: constraints against which we tend to balk, but constraints that He placed on us out of His *love* for us; constraints for *our* sake; constraints that tend to *preserve* us from *total destruction* by satan until we each, individually, are able to choose YHWH/Christ Jesus. Those constraints included: (1) flesh-dominance; (2) law; (3) prophetic revelation; (4) patriarchy; (5) covenants; and (6) husband-wife tensions.

(1) *Flesh-dominance?* In Chapter 1 of this book, we discussed the triparte psychological makeup of human nature: human spirit or center of our God-consciousness; soul or center of our self-consciousness, and flesh or the appetites and drives of the physical body. Before the Fall, YHWH our God and the souls of Adam and Eve were in union and perfect rapport *via* their human spirits, and their spirits ruled their souls and bodies. But through the Great Transgression, satan also gained the capability of influencing mankind through our human *spirits*. We see that today in false religions, the occult, demon worship, etc.

It is through the human *spirit* that God intends us to be related to Him, and though which He rules us. Likewise, it is through our human *spirit* that satan desires to rule us. Now that satan had gained that potential, God our loving father had to suppress the role of our human spirits for our benefit: in order to hinder that spiritual rule over us by satan from fully developing. How did God do that? By allowing us to become fleshly, carnal - reducing our souls to be dominated by our flesh!

This meant that satan had to now work to influence us primarily through our *flesh*, rather than through our spirits. So, satan's main evil influences on mankind since the Garden has been through our carnal drives and passions. Of course, he also continues to try to directly influence our souls; but with our souls now under dominance of our flesh and our spirits now under dominance of our souls, he is greatly hindered.

That also hinders *God* Himself from influencing us. But our human spirits are not dead, simply suppressed by our flesh-dominated souls. God must first lead us to exercise the will functions of our souls so that we *listen* to Him, and only to Him, through our *spirits*. That is the full meaning of repentance. God's workings in our lives, through Christ and the workings of His Holy Spirit in us, is to reverse us to the God-through-human-spirit-to-soul-to-body order of control. (We revisit this in detail in Chapters Eight and following.)

(2) *Law?* Law is God's standards of righteousness for our lives on earth. That has always been the case, and still is so today. What has changed during the several "dispensations" or eras of God's dealings with mankind, is not the "law" *per se*, but the *form* in which that law is presented to mankind.

God's law, applicable to each era, has always been presented to mankind in *some* form. In the earliest days it was a set of orally transmitted precepts. Genesis 4:3, "... in the course of time ..." strongly implies that some form of God's law, at least as pertains to offerings unto Him, was clearly known to both Cain and Abel. Genesis 6:22, 7:9 & 16, and 8:20 likewise imply that God's law was available in some form to Noah. And similarly, *re* Genesis 12:7, to Abraham. After Moses, God's law was extensively delineated in **written** form. In the New Covenant, God's law is presented to us in the form of the Holy Spirit of Christ Jesus "written", i.e. **indwelling**, into the hearts of the believers in Christ (Proverbs 3:3 and Romans 2:15 & 28).

For each era prior to Calvary, God's law was given to His children to **channel** and **preserve** them. The Mosaic law, for example, really consists of three sets of precepts and commandments: civil, religious, and moral. The "civil law" was to protect God's children from civil and social anarchy and its concomitant physical/political destruction. The "ceremonial or religious law" was to channel the **spiritual** quests of His children toward Him rather than toward enslaving (really satanic) spiritual sources. The "moral law" was to protect God's children from being destroyed by carnality and sin until they each laid hold of faith in their Lord YHYH/Christ Jesus (Galatians 3:22-24)!

(3) **Prophetic revelation?** Perhaps the most dramatic signs of God's faithfulness throughout the Old Testament were the prophets that He sent among His children, so that they would know the current directives of God for them, both of exhortation and of guidance. By this means God constantly channeled the **soulish** quests of His children.

(4) **Patriarchy?** This was God's form of government for His people until they insisted on an earthly king (i.e., Saul - 1 Samuel 8:5-9). Until the Mosaic law, and throughout the

period of the Judges, this was God's way of perpetuating social *order* among His children, and of continuing their heritage in Him.

(5) *Covenant?* Noah. Abraham. Moses and Joshua. God's way of giving His children *hope* for the future and *assurance* and security for the present. Hallelujah!

(6) *Husband-wife tensions to protect us?* Yes, to *protect* us: to preserve the family unit outside of the Lordship of Yahweh/Christ Jesus, while we are under the Adamic curse and outside of fellowship with God!

God's ordering of the husband-wife relationship, both before and after the Fall, is widely misunderstood, even among "Spirit-filled" Christians today. Adam and Eve at the time (before the Fall) were both *mature* as adults and *complete* as sons/daughters of God. They were created equal but different. Adam, the human male, tends to concentrate on logic, to deal with "physical things", and to deal with physical "facts", apart from immediate human needs. But when it comes to knowing the subtle needs of people, of children, and the innuendoes of social interactions, men are usually less sensitive than women (though by no means zero in those areas). God created Eve, the human female, on the other hand, to be particularly sensitive to human social needs, to the practical needs of not only bearing children but in *maturing* them. Where he's weak, she's strong, and *vice versa*, so that together as a coordinating team they will raise spiritually mature sons and daughters of God.

Now let's look at God's description of the husband-wife relationship *after* the Fall: Genesis 3:16(b). "Your *desire* shall be for your husband, and (but) he shall *rule* over you." "Desire" here is the Hebrew word ThShWQH, that literally means "clutch to possess". The sense here is that the wife continually strives to manipulate, control and dominate her husband for personal satisfaction, such as in the sense that a lion clutches its prey. And "rule" here is the Hebrew word MShL, that means "to rule or dominate with power and authority" as a king rules his subjects, or a slave-master rules his slaves.

Wow! What an explosive situation! Each with the intrinsic nature to strive to dominate and control the other: she over him with her prowess and wile and *social* wisdom; and he over her with his logical and *physical* force. Talk about tensions!

Why would God order the husband-wife relationship in such a way, for 4000 years until the Holy Spirit of Christ Jesus works in the hearts of believers to undo the Adamic curse and restore the relationship of *cooperative* harmony? Because if each were not so obsessed with dominating the other, no marriage outside of the actual Lordship of YHWH/Christ Jesus could ever survive. And without the resulting *tensions*, each would destroy the other's spirit if they *did* stay together! Men and women are so different in mentality, in ways of thinking, that without such obsessions, they could never tolerate each other for more than a few years at most, resulting in total family breakdown and its concomitant social chaos - as indeed we are seeing increasingly so in the world about us today.

These examples illustrate that God never gave up on us nor forsook us, but rather constrained and preserved us until

Calvary.

5. The *Work* Of The Cross

We now turn to studying the *Work* of the Historic Cross of Calvary, and how it *restores* the sincere seeking believer, *step by step*, to the fellowship mankind had with God before the Fall. But in reverse order of how the three aspects of our relationship with God were lost: *spiritual* relationship, last lost, first restored; *soulish* relationship, second lost, second restored; and *physical* relationship, first lost, last restored.

After nearly 4000 years of God constraining mankind to preserve him, came Calvary! At long last, "faith came" (Galatians 3:25), as it now still comes to "all whosoever" will embrace the Cross of Christ Jesus so that It can begin Its work in us.

The first time mankind received the new life after having lost it hundreds of years before, was after Christ's resurrection. Just as God originally "in-breathed" or "inspired" life into mankind upon Creation (Genesis 2:7), Jesus did likewise to the disciples in John 20:22. Later, as a consequence of Pentecost (Acts 2:41 and 47), "thousands" followed in receiving. At last, "faith came" to all whosoever .... "Spiritual life", meaning the "eternal life" of knowing God the Father and Christ the Son through our (human) spirits was the *last* form of life *lost* to mankind in the Fall and is the *first* to be *restored* in the New Covenant.

In Chapter Two we studied the "Work of the Cross of Calvary" by outlining its *three* stages in the life of a believer: (1) the *substitutionary* work - Christ crucified *for* us, undoing the Adamic curse of hopeless separation from God, bringing us *via* "eternal life" unto having personal *relationship* with God through Christ Jesus; (2) the *identification* work - we being crucified *with* Christ, which is depicted by baptism (Romans 6) brings to us the power of the Cross to put to death the life of sin, thus deepening our personal relationship with God in Christ Jesus; and (3) the *releasing* work - Christ being crucified *into* us and He in us being released to flow through us unto others as He wills.

Through these three stages, we are transformed first into little children of God ("born" into His Family *via* receiving "eternal life"), then into bond-slaves of Christ Jesus, and finally into love-slaves of Him. We are freed: (1) first from satan's *ownership* of us, as Christ purchases us from him our former slave-owner and becomes our new Slave-owner (Ephesians 2:13); (2) second from satan's *power* over us, as we die to the sin-nature that gave him that power; and (3) third from our *desire* for sin, as Christ increasingly lives *His* life though us. We obtain: (1) forgiveness *by* God; (2) cleansing *for* God; and (3) empowerment, direction and other revelation *from* God. This is the multi-stage *process* whereby the Work of the Cross fully undoes the Adamic Curse in us. Yes, we go from "glory to glory" (2 Corinthians 3:18), as we experience: (1) new "life"; (2) victory; and (3) ministry. We grow from being: (1) "little children"; to (2) "young men"; and finally to (3) "elders" (1 John 2:12-14). The Holy Spirit of Christ Jesus effects these in us as He first enters and indwells our (human) spirit, then as we allow Him to control our souls, and finally, as He gains total control over our entire beings - the full Lordship of Christ.

The essence of the ***Work*** of the Cross of Calvary, which He effects in us, is ***life,*** His life, full personal ***relationship*** with Him. It is that His ***life*** be fully wrought ***into*** us, so that He can ***disperse*** it through us unto others, when and as He sovereignly chooses.

That dispersal, we now call the "***Way*** of the Cross".

6. The *Way* Of The Cross

The "Way Of The Cross" is a life-style unto which the Holy Spirit of our Lord Christ Jesus works to bring us: a life-style, a way of living, a state of being, through which the full and perfect will of God our Eternal Father is ever to be accomplished. It is not a "pie in the sky bye and bye" dream, but a reality to be experienced in ***this*** life here and now. Granted, we now experience it only partially, as "through a mirror, darkly" (1 Corinthians 13:12); its full expression is in the next life after our Lord's return. But it is a goal for ***this*** life in which He wills that we ***start*** to walk.

What is that life-style? The issue again is ***life,*** divine life, the life of Christ Himself: that we fully partake of it. It is a walk of ***exchanged*** life, that we live not of ourselves, but by the life of Another within us: the indwelling Holy Spirit of Christ Jesus. It is a way of existence whereby He, sovereignly and at all times, does exactly as ***He*** chooses in, of and through us. It is what is fully meant by the "Kingdom of God": the full Lordship of Christ Jesus in us, effected ***via*** His indwelling Holy Spirit!

This "exchanged life", this "divine life", was the issue behind creation. Adam had "created" life, the life of the physical body, including full capabilities of the human soul. But he had much more than that. He also had the capacity to *grow* in "divine life", to *become* full *sons* of God our Father, to *share* in His (God's) *reign*, all according to God's plan. And as long as he (Adam) continued to partake of the fruit of that "Tree Of *Life"*, he would continue to grow therein!

So also do *we* have that capacity today, because of the accomplished *Work* of the Cross of Calvary. But so also with us, that *capacity* will become reality in our lives *only* as we continue to partake of the fruit of that "Tree of Life".

What *is* that "Tree of Life" for us today? "Tree" here in Hebrew (ITs) means a source of fulfillment of our needs, a source which is readily available to us, but of which we must take initiatives to partake thereof. None other than Christ Jesus Himself! And what does it mean to *partake* of the *fruit* of Him - our Tree of Life? No less than to *fully allow and depend upon* Him to live *His* life through us! Only this way will the *fruit* of Him be made manifest in this world: the divine power to minister His will, in love-motivated and Spirit-empowered servanthood, to "all whosoever". And only as It is made manifest through us can it be said that we truly *partake* of It. Otherwise we are merely "armchair spectators" of It, not "participants" fully involved in It!

But to "fully allow" Him to live His life through us, means our enduring the Cross as a *continual* way of life - to be ever and always reckoning our own self, our own wills, *dead* unto *our* ways and living only in Him (Romans 6:4, 8 and 11, again).

Will we live our lives by our *soul*, or by our *spirit?* One or the other! To live by our soul means *we* do the living, as *we* think and feel and choose to be appropriate. Such is not fully allowing Him to live His life through us, no matter how "pure" our motives may be in Him. At its very best it *restricts* Him tremendously to only that which we can understand and feel and choose. It totally restricts our ministry to the natural plane. It is our *self,* the intrinsic sin-nature within us, that is *de facto* enthroned.

But to live by the *spirit* means our living in *life-union* with Him, and doing all we do by *His* life and strength. It is totally free of our human restraints. It also means that we have absolutely no rights of our own to exercise control over what we do!

It is that total life-union with Him that is really meant by the Hebrew word ShLWM for "peace". It means "wholeness, entireness", all of that for which we were created.

If *He* is going to live His life through us as He chooses, then His life (with love-motivated servanthood as its fruit) will be shared to others *via* us, continually and in the present human context, just as He shared His life, light and love to each of *us via* other servant-vessels of His to bring *us* unto "so great salvation". That also involves us continually *embracing* of the Cross. It is not (just) His *words*, but His *life*, that He shares through us: it is not necessarily (nor even primarily) *preaching* of the Gospel, but by us *being* witnesses - through personal *demonstration* - of His Life. It means we exposing ourselves to those who need His love, we consequently being in utter vulnerability to their rejecting it (and us) just as He also was rejected.

It also involves a deeper working of crucifixion of our self by His hands! For even if we be truly "reckoning ourselves crucified with Him", our *motives* for doing so may be wrong, or more commonly be such as to exercise the very self that is being crucified. He works "dark nights in our souls", wherein we learn *experientially* that *no* motive of ours is ever pure, and that our *only* recourse is to "let go and let God". Nothing less than total abandonment unto Him will bring about His full glory (manifestation) through us.

That is why we call this the "Way of the *Cross*". Calvary is ever before us in a continually deepening sense. But so is *He Himself* and His life and His fullness!

The issue may seem subtle, but it is monumental: the difference between *doing* and *being* in our calling or ministry. Am I to concentrate on *doing* His will for me, or in *being* what he wants me to be. Job is an excellent illustration of this. The basic issue in Job was: did Job belong to God for God, or only to Job for Job? What God intended to realize through Job was to *flow* through him unto the world. But Job was initially blind to his *deepest* need. He tried so hard to please God through his *human* efforts. That was the trouble; he (Job) was still doing the doing, rather than God doing the doing *through* Job.

This is the conflict between soulish living *vs* spiritual living. So easy it is for Christians to be living by the soul and yet think they are living by the spirit. For example, a most prominent indicator of being soulish is an obsession with mental search, acceptance and propagation of *truth*. Also is how often we mistake *emotion* for spirituality: to "feel" the presence of God *via* our senses and emotions.

We ask, "What wrong is there for us to live by our own natural (soulish) abilities as long as we avoid sinning?" To the extent that what the Bible says about living by the soul does not lead us astray, we are not in sin. But we could not distinguish the truly spiritual from the soulical: we would not yet have received those insights from the Holy Spirit that convict us of the intrinsic *evil* of our natural or soulical activity. Also, our actions would not only be *by* our own efforts but also primarily *for* our own glory. (For example, for many years I personally coveted becoming a "big shot" in the Body of Christ.) We are not disposed to obey God on *His* terms or by His guidance and strength. At best we restrict God's workings through us to only that which we can understand and with which we agree! A horrible restriction that is, since His ways are far above ours (Isaiah 55:8 and 9). Though we use our God-instilled "gifts", we do so on *our* terms, and often lose sight of the Giver of those "gifts". In fact, we lose sight of the fact that He does not give us gifts *per se*, but rather He *is* the gift, He *is* those abilities through us.

So few of us are so possessed of the Lord's mind as to be amenable to fully yielding to Him voluntarily. We need to allow the Holy Spirit of Christ Jesus to impart such insight to us *via* personal revelation. Often He cannot until we are subjected to disciplinings by our Father's Hand (Hebrews 12:5-15) or sufferings (1 Peter 5:10). Only He can point out to us the utter corruption of our natural hearts (Isaiah 64:6). And if/when He does, our human souls are so deceitful that we still resist denying our natural life.

What is also painfully disturbing is that the more "spiritual" we become, the more ***difficult*** it is for us to detect the degree with which our soulical efforts and thoughts pollute those of the Holy Spirit of Christ Jesus through us. All of us operate under *mixture* to some extent, and the more "pure" be our mixture, the harder it is to detect the *remaining* soul-pollution in our mixture!

How can we ever become *that* spiritual, *that* pure in our walk by the spirit and not by our soul? How can we ever become *that* utterly yielded to Him and His will in *all* things?

We *grow* into it. Not overnight; often it takes many years. And the growth may at times seem imperceptible to us. But we indeed do grow in it! It is so like the grain of wheat, a seed planted. How does it grow? First is the *crisis* of dying to self and to its old nature; it cannot retain its seed-nature if it is to grow! Then the slow growing process itself, by ever *yielding* peacefully to its total environment - both the warmth and the cold, both the rain and the dry seasons. Note that it never grows by *striving* to grow. Finally it forms buds that lead to *fruit*. Fruit of love-motivated and Spirit-empowered servanthood: the goal, the full purpose of our lives in Christ!

It can be described as growing into three levels of partaking of His divine Life (although in actual practice the points of demarcation between these three are not always precise). We first learn to *participate* in His Life and purposes for us, that brings us unto sonship and ministry. Then we learn to *appropriate* Him in us and all that He desires to share with us, that brings us to being heirs of so great an inheritance in Christ (Ephesians 1:11 and 18). And finally, we *actualize*, by discipline, His life and what it is to reign with Him (Ephesians 1:19)!

Participation means ministry in the spirit as He ministers through us. He determines two callings for each of us: (1) a general calling to become His love-slave and to grow in this Way of the Cross; and (2) a specific ministry in which our Lord does the working as He chooses. As the Body of Christ, we *collectively* manifest His *fullness;* but each of us individually only in part. Our ministry is to be *He* flowing through us unto others in the world as *He* determines, and *not* us doing the doing "for" Him!

For it to be He in us (Galatians 2:20) and not we ourselves, we must appropriate three essential principles. First is *honesty and openness in all of our relationships,* not only with Him but also with one another. By this, we not only remain humble and pliable in His hands, but we also be vessels of His love to be poured out through us unto others. Second is to *ever give the Lord Christ Jesus in us full centrality.* "Seek the Lord while He may be found ..." (Isaiah 55:6). Where may He be found? *In us,* that we be vessels or containers of Him Himself. He in us should be ever in our thoughts and attention. And third, that we *continually experience the flow of grace through us;* that we not offer Him resistance. The "anointing" on us as He ministers through us is at whatever level He knows is needed for the moment, and hence reflects the state at the moment of the heart(s) of the *receiver(s)* of the ministry. But the *flow* of that anointing depends upon how pure we are, as His *pipes* or *channels* for that flow. God is ever seeking for a people (Isaiah 6:8) to stand in the gap between Him and our fellow men. Only such people as these can He send and use.

The end result of our being love-slaves, voluntarily ever giving up our freedom in order to become fully what He wills, is

adoption. Romans 8:15 uses the Greek word Uiothesia, that means to be fully established as recognized and responsible agents (of God on Earth). Established unto what? To be fellow heirs with Christ (*vs* 17), that we glorify Him. To glorify Him: to make Him manifest in this physical space-time world. To fill the entire earth with His Presence. That the "Lord shall arise upon us, and His glory shall be seen upon us" (Isaiah 60:2). That is His Intention for us now: that we present Him, in His fullness, to this world.

7. Kids, Grow Up!

The exhortation unto partaking of the divine life of Christ Jesus means our maturing in our personal relationship with Him. "Therefore leaving the discussion of the elementary principles of Christ, let us go on to perfection *(maturity)*, not laying again the foundation .... This we will do, if God permits" (Hebrews 6:1 & 3).

The "elementary principles of Christ" that we are to leave behind once we fully accept them, are those concerning His ***redeeming*** us. The maturity for which we are to press are "all things summed in Christ"! We are to leave behind us a purely human-oriented view of the Cross, and to press on to embracing a God-oriented view of His full purposes.

Why must we earnestly seek to grow unto spiritual maturity? Because we are ***commanded*** to. The Word of God condemns attitudes of complacency on our part, and strongly admonishes us to grow up in our knowledge of Christ Jesus!

8. Maturing In Our Personal Relationship With Christ Jesus

The New Testament actually uses two distinct Greek words for maturity: Teleiosis and Katartismos. Both of these words are often somewhat misleadingly translated as "perfecting". Teleiosis carries the meaning of "bringing near that which was far off". It is usually applied to the spiritual maturity of *individual* believers. Katartismos, on the other hand, bears the idea of "properly being knit or woven together", as a fishing net or a piece of embroidery. It is usually used for maturity of the body of believers as a *corporate* unit. In this Volume we explore the full ramifications of an *individual* believer's Teleiosis. We delineate the process of *corporate* Body-Of-Christ Katartismos in Volume III[8] of this series.

First of all, a Biblical principle of major importance is that Christian spiritual maturity is a matter of deepening one's *personal relationship* with Christ Jesus. It has no *meaning* whatsoever outside of personal relationship with Him. It is not a matter of increasing one's mind knowledge *about* God, about Christ Jesus, about the Bible. It is not a matter of theology. Nor is it a matter of being "religious" nor moral. It is a matter of knowing *Him* personally!

Note how the apostle John defines spiritual maturity in terms of knowing God the Father, God the Holy Spirit, and Christ Jesus: "I write to you, little children, because your sins are forgiven you for His name's sake. I write to you, fathers, because you know Him Who is from the beginning (Christ Jesus - John 1:1-2). I write to you, young men, because you have overcome the wicked one. I write to you, (little) children, because you have known the (Heavenly) Father. I have written to you, fathers, because you have known Him Who is from the beginning. I have written to you, young men, because you are strong, and the Word of God abides in you, and you have overcome the wicked." (1 John 2:12-14).

One of the many Biblical descriptions of us Christians is "children of God" or "members of the family of God". The New Testament Greek word Teknon (and the Old Testament Hebrew word BN) mean any son, any descendant of the father; however, the words are frequently used, not only genealogically, but also to denote *immaturity*.

They are distinct from the Greek and Hebrew words Uios and BR, respectively, which mean a son *matured* and in a position of *responsibility*. "For you did not received the spirit of bondage again to fear, but you received the spirit of adoption by whom we cry out, 'Abba, Father!'" - Romans 8:15. "Adoption" here does not mean becoming children of God - that comes through regeneration. Rather, the Greek word Uiothesia means "to be *established* as sons (Uios) or agents in positions of responsibility." We indeed share that in our rich inheritance in Christ Jesus (Ephesians 1:11-12). It is one of the purposes or goals of spiritual maturity. But note that even here it is couched in terms of having an intimate personal relationship with God!

As with children in the natural, we are expected to grow up. And growing up involves going through several stages of maturing over time. The nursing stage, the toddler stage, the pre-school years, grammar school years, junior and senior high school adolescence stages, college years, young adulthood, middle age, and elderly - these are examples. We are to start in total dependence upon Him in all things, and from there grow in becoming mature and responsible agents attending to our Father's business in this world.

The Bible speaks, in many places and in many ways, of the corresponding maturing process of Christians. Much has been written on this, variously denoted as consisting of 3, 4, 5, 6, 12, 15, or even 40 "stages", depending upon the point of view one takes of the maturing process. I myself have taught on each of these Biblical points of view at various times; each is valid and gives its unique understanding of how our personal relationships with Christ Jesus are to unfold and develop. We touch upon each of these many points of view later in Chapters Eight and following. Here we first briefly discuss what such maturity is to lead us *to* and what it *entails*.

9. Chastened As Sons

Maturing in our relationship with Him is a process of *adjustment* in our lives. Our sins are not the *primary* issue. Rather, the primary issue is the *sin-nature* behind our thinking, our mentality, our understandings of reality that up to now are heavily influenced by our worldly experiences. Our concepts of Christ Jesus and His ways and His will for our lives are at best greatly distorted and limited, if not actually erroneous in many aspects. So, our patterns of thinking, our attitudes, our motives, our perspectives, all must be adjusted.

That comes not primarily through mind-knowledge or didactic education. Rather it comes through a process of interaction between His dealings in the circumstances in our lives, the guidance and direction we daily receive from the Holy Spirit of Christ Jesus in our hearts, and our responses thereto in the midst of those dealings.

It is not a matter of being "zapped" by the Holy Spirit in a single "altar call" experience or singular event, such as laying on of hands and/or receiving the Baptism into the Holy Spirit. We study the "Baptism Into The Holy Spirit" and "speaking in tongues" later in Chapters Six and Seven. But here in passing we emphasize that the *primary* function of the Holy Spirit in us as Christians is to lead us unto maturity in our personal relationships with our Lord Christ Jesus.

It is not the Baptism into the Holy Spirit *per se* that matures us for ministry or for God's will for our lives. The route to spiritual maturity is *trial and error* while being dealt with by the hand of God *via* the Holy Spirit of Christ living in us. Among the Biblical references to God's process of adjusting us is the concept of the "wilderness experience". It is that process which prepares us, as it did our Lord (Matthew 4:1-11, Mark 1:12-13, Luke 4:1-13, Romans 5:3-4, and Hebrews 12:5-11). It prepares us by refining and strengthening our faith, as we discuss in the following section. The Baptism into the Holy Spirit is to enable us to *endure* those "wilderness experiences" and to respond to them positively and constructively rather than with bitterness and discouragement.

In Hebrews 12:5-11 the writer speaks of the adjusting process as *chastening* by a loving Heavenly Father. Yes, the maturing process is painful at times. But the love of our Lord Christ Jesus toward us is ever more real during the chastening tribulations, and it is that love that ever deepens our union with Him. And we become settled and stable through it all - 1 Peter 5:10.

10. Purification Of Our Faith Through Fire

God's dealings in our lives to adjust us unto maturity in Him are also referred to in the Bible as *fire:* "My God is a consuming fire" - Deuteronomy 4:24.

1 Peter 1:6-9 has these powerful words:

> "In this you greatly rejoice, though now for a little while, if need be, you have been grieved by various trials, that the genuiness of your *faith*, being more precious than gold that perishes, though it is tested by *fire*, may be found to praise, honor, and glory at the revelation of Jesus Christ; whom having not seen you love. Though now you do not see Him, yet believing, you rejoice with joy inexpressible and full of glory, receiving the end of your *faith* - the salvation of your souls."

"That our *faith* be refined, as gold from ore, in a refiner's fire...." What is faith, that it must be refined and strengthened through *fire?* Faith, again, is our inner *response* to God and His initiatives in our lives. Our response, though, must involve three aspects: *seeing* Christ Jesus in the spirit; dynamic *dependence* upon Him in the "now"; and sensitive *obedience* to His Will.

Our dependence upon the Person of Christ Jesus alone, and our obedience to His will alone, is compared to the gold in the ore. The dross is our dependence upon everything else: for example our dependence upon the pastor or priest of our local church, upon our spouse, our jobs, our bank account, our abilities and talents. The dross is also our obedience to all other voices than that of Christ Jesus alone: for example the voices of our loved ones, those in the world whom we try to impress, those who admire us, and most tyrannical of all, the voice of our hideous *self!* **We must learn to depend utterly on Him alone,** and to *yield* to His will, alone.

This learning and yielding process is also typified in the Bible by such concepts as: (1) heart circumcision; (2) wheat being ground into fine flour in the crucible of testings; and (3) clay being kneaded and smoothed by the Master Potter to remove the lumps and unevenness and resistances in our wills.

Our dependence upon Him needs to be beyond our mind understanding; otherwise our ministries and our Christian walk are in human strength or soulishness rather than in His wisdom and power. So, our dependence upon our many idols, tangible and intangible, and our obedience to the demands they make on our time and efforts, must be transferred to Him alone. That takes many "wilderness experiences", over time, for most of us. It is not the suffering of those trials, but our learning to trust and obey Him through them, that adjusts us to true spiritual maturity in Him and that refine and strengthen our faith.

Later in Chapter Nine we study one aspect of these wilderness experiences or trials by fire, under the subject "Maturing Through Soul Affliction". For the final phases of our process of being adjusted unto maturity entail an emptying of our self, so that we become *completely* yielded to the Holy Spirit of Christ Jesus in us - that we become completely fused into Him. It is a matter of *internal* holiness, holiness *into* Him, our losing ourselves in Him. Holiness *from* the world, even pious religiousness, are not the issue.

God's Ultimate Intention

The process of *purifying our faith* is yet another way of viewing the sanctification process. Therefore, let us pause to discuss purification of our faith in a bit more detail before we study the sanctification process *per se*.

First of all, purification of our faith involves our growing in experiential *trust* in God. *Trust* is one of the pivotal aspects of *faith*. Indeed Hebrews Chapter 11 is devoted to many examples of mighty men and women of God who were mighty because of their totally abandoned *trust* in God. Trust is *active* and *dynamic*, not passive!

Allender[9], page 176), reflecting on Genesis 23, addresses this:

> "Most assume that trust is quiet, serene, selfless dependence on God. Though there is an element of truth to that view of trust, more often than not such serene faith is a byproduct of wanting very little from God. ...
>
> "Genuine trust involves allowing another to matter and have an impact in our lives. For that reason, many who hate [God] and do battle with God trust Him more deeply than those whose complacent faith permits an abstract and motionless stance before Him. Those who trust God most are those whose faith permits them to risk wrestling with Him over the deepest questions of life. Good hearts are captured in a divine wrestling match; fearful, doubting hearts stay clear of the mat.
>
> "The commitment to wrestle will be honored by a God who will not only break but bless. Jacob ... the freedom in his heart was worth the price of his shattered limb.

The price of soul freedom is the loss of what has been deemed most secure (the tight grip over one's soul, the commitment to be one's sole provider and protector) but is intuitively known as no security at all."

Allender[10] also enlightens us as to the role of *suffering* in maturing our trust/faith in God:

"... personal suffering ... can lead us to place our trust where it ultimately belongs. Suffering of any sort points to the fact that something terrible, unnatural, and wrong has occurred, and that something better, more fitting to beauty, righteousness, and justice must await. ... Christ's suffering was in bearing the disgrace and shame of the Cross; our suffering is in losing ourselves and taking up His Cross so that we can find who we are really made to be.

"The path of the valley [of the shadow of death] of the Cross requires biblical expressions of honesty, repentance, and bold love. *Honesty* removes the pleasant, antiseptic blandness of denial. *Repentance* strips away self-contempt and other-centered hatred and replaces it with humility, grief, and tenderness. *Bold love* increases power and freedom through the exhilaration of loving as we were made to love. ..."

How do we *begin* this route of learning to trust in God enough to be determined to wrestle with Him? The process begins by God Himself: "faith is a gift of God" (Ephesians 2:8) along with "eternal life" (Romans 6:23) and grace - the impartation of the Holy Spirit (Acts 2:38). Our faith is *initiated* by God in the first place.

Tozer[11] illustrates that as follows:

> "We pursue God because, and only because, He has first put an urge within us that spurs us to the pursuit. 'No man can come to me,' said our Lord, 'except the Father that hath sent me draw him,' and it is by this very prevenient *drawing* that God takes from us every vestige of credit for the act of coming. The impulse to pursue God originates with God, but the out-working of that impulse is our following hard after Him; and all the time we are pursuing Him we are already in His hand...."

But even if He puts this urge within us to pursue Him, we still cannot trust in one of whose existence we have **doubts**. Hence, a major aspect of our sanctification process, particularly during the early stages, is our learning to apprehend the *reality* of God and His *spiritual domain*. Listen again to Tozer[12]:

> "Faith enables our spiritual sense to function.... God Himself is here waiting our response to His Presence. This eternal world will come alive to us the moment we begin to reckon upon its reality....
>
> "What do I mean by *reality?* I mean that which has existence apart from any idea any mind may have of it, and which would exist if there were no mind anywhere to entertain a thought of it. That which is real has being in itself. It does not depend upon the observer for its validity....

"Another word that must be cleared up is the word *reckon*. This does not mean to visualize or imagine. Imagination is not faith. The two are not only different from, but stand in sharp opposition to, each other. Imagination projects unreal images out of the mind and seeks to attach reality to them. Faith creates nothing; it simply reckons upon that which is already *there*.

"God and the spiritual world are real. We can reckon upon them with as much assurance as we reckon upon the familiar world around us. Spiritual things are there (or rather we should say *here*) inviting our attention and challenging our trust.

"Our trouble is that we have established bad thought habits. We habitually think of the visible world as real and doubt the reality of any other. We do not deny the existence of the spiritual world but we doubt that it is real in the accepted meaning of the word....

"At the root of the Christian life lies a belief in the invisible. The object of the Christian's faith is unseen reality. The spiritual *is* real."

"Being near to God" is a matter not of distance but of *awareness* of Him and being *spiritually receptive* to Him, being in personal relationship with Him, as were the great men of God in the Bible.

Along this line, we further quote Tozer[13]:

"To speak of being near to or far from God is to use language in a sense always understood when applied to our ordinary human relationships. ... Obviously ... speaking of *experience* ... coming to know him more intimately and with deeper understanding ... the barriers of thought and feeling between the two are disappearing, that father and son are becoming more closely united in mind and heart.

"So when we sing 'Draw me nearer, nearer, blessed Lord,' we are not thinking of the nearness of place, but of the nearness of relationship. It is for increasing degrees of awareness that we pray, for a more perfect consciousness of the divine Presence. We need never shout across the spaces to an absent God. He is nearer [in relationship] than our own soul, closer than our most secret thoughts."

The bottom line in our growing in faith is our learning to *see* God, to *gaze* upon Him. Here are Tozer's comments on faith being our *seeing* God, on our soul *gazing* upon His reality[14]:

"In the New Testament ... [The serpent of brass lifted up, in Numbers 21:4-9] is interpreted for us by ... Jesus Christ Himself. He is explaining to His hearers how they may be saved. He tells them that it is by believing. Then to make it clear He refers to this incident in the Book of Numbers. 'As Moses lifted up the serpent in the wilderness, even so must the Son of man be lifted up: that whosoever believeth in him should not perish, but have eternal life' [John 3:14-15].

"...[A] plain man in reading this would ... notice that 'look' and 'believe' were synonymous terms. 'Looking' on the Old Testament serpent is identical with 'believing' on the New Testament Christ. That is, the *looking* and the *believing* are the same thing. And he would understand that while Israel looked with their external eyes, believing is done with the heart. I think he would conclude that *faith is the gaze of a soul upon a saving God."*

But oh how often we fail in the sin of unbelief! Our sin of unbelief is rooted in desire for the honor of fellow Christians and refusal to honor God at one's personal expense. Tozer[15] counters this as follows:

"... The man of God set[s] his heart to exalt God above all; God accept[s] his intention as fact and act[s] accordingly. Not perfection, but holy intention make[s] the difference.

"In our Lord Jesus Christ this law was seen in simple perfection. In His lowly manhood He humbled Himself and gladly gave all glory to His Father in heaven. He sought not His own honor, but the honor of God who sent Him. ... far had the proud Pharisees departed from this law that they could not understand one who honored God at his own expense. ....

"Another saying of Jesus, and a most disturbing one, was put in the form of a question, 'How can ye believe, which receive honour one of another, and seek not the honour that cometh from God alone?' [John 5:44]. If I understand this correctly, Christ taught here the alarming doctrine that the desire for honor among men made belief *impossible*. Is this [the] sin at the root of religious unbelief? Could it be that those 'intellectual difficulties' which men blame for their inability to believe are but smoke screens to conceal the real cause that lies behind them? Was it this greedy desire for honor from man that made men into Pharisees and Pharisees into Deicides? Is this the secret back of religious self-righteousness and empty worship? I believe it may be. The whole course of the life is upset by failure to put God where He belongs. We exalt ourselves instead of God and the curse follows."

11. Meekness, Honesty And Love

Our faith has not been purified, has not been perfected, until we are *also* walking and serving in *meekness, honesty* and *love*. Remember our Lord's goal for us: that we be love-motivated and Spirit-empowered servants, unclogged vessels through whom He will pour out His light, life and love unto others.

Tozer comments on how through *meekness* we can obtain deliverance from burdens of pride, pretense and artificiality[16]:

"The burden borne by mankind is a heavy and a crushing thing. The word [load/burden] Jesus used [Matthew 11:28] means a load carried or toil borne to the point of *exhaustion*. Rest is simply release from that burden. It is not something we do; it is what comes to us when we cease to do. His own meekness, that is the rest.

"Let us examine our burden. It is altogether an interior one. It attacks the heart and the mind and reaches the body only from within. First, there is the burden of *pride*. The labor of self-love is a heavy one indeed. ...

Such a burden as this is not necessary to bear. Jesus calls us to His rest, and meekness is His method. The meek man cares not at all who is greater than he, for he has long ago decided that the esteem of the world is not worth the effort. ... The meek man ... has stopped being fooled about himself. He has accepted God's estimate of his own life. He knows he is weak and helpless as God has declared him to be, but paradoxically, he knows at the same time that he is in the sight of God of more importance than angels. In himself, nothing; in God, everything. ... The old struggle to defend himself is over.

"Then also he will get deliverance from the burden of *pretense*. By this I mean not hypocrisy, but the common human desire to put the best foot forward and hide from the world our real inward poverty. For sin has ... infus[ed] into us a false sense of shame. There is hardly a man or woman who dares to be just what he or she is without doctoring up the impression. ... Let no one smile this off. These burdens are real, and little by little they kill the victims of this evil and unnatural way of life.

"Another source of burden is *artificiality*. I am sure that most people live in secret fear that some day they will be careless and by chance an enemy or friend will be allowed to peep into their poor empty souls. So they are never relaxed. ... This unnatural condition is part of our sad heritage of sin... [But] artificiality is one curse that will drop away the moment we kneel at Jesus' feet and surrender ourselves to His meekness. Then we will not care what people think of us so long as God is pleased. Then *what we are* will be everything; what we appear will take its place far down the scale of interest for us. ..."

Honesty and openness with God and with self are the next necessary steps. Allender[17] gives us some very practical suggestions in making that step of honesty, namely ***prayer, fasting***, and ***absorbing God's word:***

"... Honesty [and openness] does not bring forth its benefits unless it is active and purposeful. 'Priming the pump' involves the spiritual disciplines of prayer, fasting, and reading the Bible. Prayer expresses the deep hunger for intimate relationship with God; fasting exposes the soul to its emptiness and the temporal shallowness of all earthly satisfaction; the Word of God feeds the soul and satisfies the hunger like no other bread can do. The pursuit of honesty without active openness will set the heart on a path that may evoke honest reflection, but will not carry it toward the deepest issues of the self.

"... prayer is conversation - a human-divine interaction that is our opportunity to face God as a son or daughter whose presence is welcome and desired. Prayer begins with the assumption that the infinite, all-knowing God knows every thought and intent of the heart before it is conceived or spoken. Prayer does not inform God; rather, it draws us into His presence and invites Him into our life. Prayer is involvement through the [inwardly] spoken word. In that sense, prayer of any kind and about any subject delights God's heart. ... Prayer opens the door to the unacknowledged anger, sorrow, and hunger of our soul.

"Fasting is the choice to put aside legitimate satisfaction, for a time, to concentrate on a more pressing spiritual pursuit. It is not merely an abstaining from pleasure, though the absence sets into play an awareness of our gnawing dependence on temporal satisfaction. It is not simply an exercise in self-control, though it does solidify our resolve to pursue a calling higher than comfort. Fasting is an expression of single-minded intention to pursue experiential knowledge of God.

"While prayer invites exposure and fasting intensifies hunger, study of the Word exposes, awakens, and ultimately satisfies the heart by taking it into the mind of God. The Scriptures orient the heart to ask the questions that are of greatest concern to God [for us to ask]. ..."

Also significant: we must *love* those who might, or have, hurt us. But what does that mean in actual practice? Allender[18] addresses this as a balance between respecting personal dignity and confronting self-ness and need of repentance:

"The objective must be to bless the other person rather than to ... [protect ourselves from him/her hurting us again]. We are to draw a boundary [of respecting personal dignity in righteousness] in order to better love the one to whom we are relating. We cannot wholeheartedly give if we live in fear of another. Most boundaries are allowed to be violated because we are afraid to offend or lose the paltry relationship that currently exists. *To love is to be more committed to the other than we are to the relationship, to be more concerned about his walk with God [and his well-being] than the comfort or benefits of his walk with us. ...*

"Is it possible that love implies and requires its own boundaries? In order to love, we must both honor the dignity and expose the depravity of the person with whom we are in relationship. We cannot love if we distance ourselves or overlook the damage of another's sin; neither can we love if we fail to move into another's world to offer a taste of life. In both cases, the lover often is a martyr for the sake of the gospel, sacrificing personal comfort for the sake of helping the other experience his own longings and need for grace.

"Love has boundaries, but often boundary setting is a means of fleeing the requirements of love. A good heart will always feel unsettled by any path that does not offer the opportunity of sacrifice for the sake of the gospel. The common route of self-discovery, self-expression, and self-protection seems reasonable, but the byproducts are often not true strength, tenderness, or faithfulness."

The ultimate step we must take, therefore, is *repentance* of all in us, both intrinsically and that resulting from past hurts, that hinder us from serving God *today* in our inter-personal relationships through love-motivated and Spirit-empowered servanthood.

12. Pleading The Shed Blood Of Christ Jesus

"Old-Time Pentecostalism" had an interesting expression: "Pleading the Shed Blood of Christ Jesus." When fully understood, it is an apt descriptor for plunging of our soul into the Spiritual reality of Christ Jesus. Let us therefore study it, since it means far more than "mere salvation."

The Biblical roots of this expression are in the Passover story in Exodus Chapter 12. Each home was destined to have a destroying angel enter at a specified time, who would destroy the "first born" or most precious resident. The only way a household could escape this terrible curse was by the head of that household killing a spotless lamb, collecting its blood in a basin, and sprinkling that blood on the entrance-way of the house. On the specified night, the Lord went through the land, and of those houses on which He saw that sprinkled blood, He *entered*, and by His *Presence* kept the destroying angel out.

Revelation 3:20 explains this Old Testament typology. Christ says to each of us today: "Behold, I stand at the door (of your heart) and knock; if any one hears My voice and opens the door, I will come in to him, and will dine with him (i.e., dwell in him), and he with Me." The blood in the Passover typology is a *sign* that the head of the household *desires* the Lord to enter, a sign that the Lord is *welcome* therein, or in the Revelation 3:20 sense, "hears the Lord and opens the door for Him". When we, by an act of our human *will*, seek and desire Him to enter, He does, and His indwelling Presence keeps the "destroying angel" (satan and his demon spirits) from destroying us.

But if we don't, then the Adamic curse of death follows according to the Law of God (Genesis 3:17-19, Romans 3:23 and Romans 6:23a). Although His love and mercy toward us is great, the Lord chooses to honor our human will; hence it requires a decisive act of our human will toward Him to release Him to fulfill this marvelous promise. This "so great salvation" requires the supernatural miracle of His indwelling Presence, and we are not worthy of it; it requires the shed blood of a "sinless" Paschal Lamb. But He, Christ Jesus, was that Paschal Lamb for us on Calvary. So, what is required of us is simply to acknowledge that fact and seek/desire Him to become our *indwelling Lord*. This is what is really meant by the phrase "accepting Christ as your saviour", although that phrase is a careless over-simplification that belittles its full meaning. He cannot be our savior unless He is also our indwelling Lord!

His shed blood is His *"life fluid"*; it speaks of His full *power* and *authority* for us to dynamically and creatively interact within the spirit world. That is the true meaning of "eternal life". When we yield to Him as saviour, He comes as the indwelling Holy Spirit of Christ Jesus, and with Him is His full power and authority. This involves far more than mere assurance that we'll get to heaven when we die; it involves deliverance, victory, and fulfillment here and now!

In the New Testament Greek, the word translated "shed" is Ekcheo. It literally means to "pour [out] *unto*". It takes an *object*; it speaks not only of a *source* of the fluid, but also a *receiver*. We, each of us who seek/desire His indwelling presence and who covenant to yield to His Lordship, are the receiver: of His life-fluid, of His power and authority, of His love. Us *receiving* It is what is really symbolized by our "drinking of the cup" in communion. And since receivers, we are also to be transmitters.

"Plead" is a legal term: to plead a cause or argue for one's position. Here it means that the full power and authority of our Lord Christ Jesus is at our disposal, *via* the indwelling Holy Spirit of Christ Jesus, in our "legal" contentions against satan the accuser of the brethren. How do we deploy that power and authority against satan? In meditation on God's Word, prayer, intercession, body ministries, etc. But all this works for us only under His *Lordship*, only through our *yielding* to His will in *obedience* and *trust*. Only as we exercise our will to choose His will, is He released to work in us. Hence, our yielding to His Lordship is a prerequisite for His subsequent workings of sanctifying and using us.

Redemption and propitiation, entering into *fellowship* with God, comes this way (Romans 3:24-25, Romans 5:8-9, Ephesians 1:7, Ephesians 2:13 and Hebrews 10:19). Also: becoming His *possession* (Revelation 5:9); receiving *forgiveness* (Hebrews 9:22): and being cleansed, purged, sanctified (Hebrews 9:22, Hebrews 13:12, 1 John 1:7 and Revelation 1:5).

For Christians, "pleading the shed blood of Christ Jesus" has many practical applications. Here we mention two particular applications in passing: first, to become delivered from some sin area or carnal habit or failure in mental discipline for prayer and worship; and secondly, when seeking resolution of some question we may have about His will in some matter (i.e., a pending decision) or some spiritual pressure or oppression we may be under. We plead the shed blood of Christ Jesus over that sin or habit or failure, or over our need for revelatory wisdom and/or knowledge.

In all such situations, however, the primary issue is our will: we openly *choose* whatever be the will of our Lord Christ Jesus in the matter. In areas of sin or habits or failures, we choose to *renounce* it, knowing full well that the sin area is contrary to His will, and depend upon Him to give us the power to actually do that renouncing - to stand on 1 Corinthians 10:13, for example. (It is at this point that most of us fail most frequently; we do not hate and detest the sin area or habit or failure intensely enough, to remain sufficiently faithful in our renouncing it.) In matters of ascertaining His will, "pleading the shed blood of Christ Jesus" over the matter will cause whatever element(s) of our burden that *are* in His will to be considerably strengthened, and whatever elements that are *not* in His will to be abated. Hence, if we are not yet fully ready to embrace whatever His will turns out to be, "Pleading His shed blood" in the matter might actually *increase* the pain of our burden!

The breaking is unto the humiliating realization that we, *each* of us, need an inner healing of our (human) spirit, a healing that we cannot do on our own. This healing is like the breaking of horses during their early training; the goal is not that our will be *destroyed*, but rather that it be *channeled* unto the will of another. When we are truly plunged into the Lordship of Christ Jesus, our will ever yields to the indwelling Holy Spirit of Christ Jesus, Who sanctifies us over time. The first step of that sanctification process, after we receive the baptism into the Holy Spirit, involves inner healing of our spirit. Sanctification is truly a dynamic, fully interactive cybernetic *process*.

How will this take place? Remember our definition of "Charismatic Cybernetics": how the indwelling Holy Spirit of Christ Jesus, and our human *soul*, work "together" to attain and maintain a Christ-glorifying countenance in our lives, thoughts and behaviour patterns *via* a dynamic interaction. The key element or "channel" of this dynamic interaction is our human *spirit*. That dynamic interaction between the indwelling Holy Spirit of Christ Jesus and our human soul, under the direction of our Lord Christ Jesus, involves these many things: (1) again, inner spiritual healings both of us and though us of others, to purify us; (2) spiritual release of us unto effective prayer, worship and intercession; and (3) a dynamic flow of the Word, Power and Love of our Lord Christ Jesus unto others. In *all* aspects, the bottom line is that we increasingly yield to our Lord Christ Jesus, ever real to us *via* the indwelling Holy Spirit.

End Notes: Chapter Four

[1] Fromke, DeVern F., *The Ultimate Intention*, (Indianapolis, Indiana: Sure Foundation, 3rd Edition 1968).

[2] Fromke, DeVern F., *Unto Full Stature*, (Indianapolis, Indiana: Ministry Of Life Inc., 3rd Edition 1967).

[3] Fromke, DeVern F., *No Other Foundation*, (Indianapolis, Indiana: Sure Foundation, 1965 Edition).

[4] Fromke, DeVern F., *Discerning Things That Differ*, (Indianapolis, Indiana: Sure Foundation, 1966 Edition).

5. Swindoll, Orville, *Destined To Express His Life*, (Indianapolis, Indiana: Sure Foundation, 1965 Edition).

6. Billheimer, Paul E., *Destined For The Throne*, (Fort Washington, PA: Christian Literature Crusade, 1975).

7. Edwards, Gene, *The Divine Romance*, 1984 (Available through *SeedSowers*, P.O. Box 285, Sargent, GA 30275).

8. Sherrerd, Chris S., *From Sheepfold To Bride: Christ Maturing His Church*, Volume III of the series "Where Do You Fit In? Practical Commitments In The Body of Christ", to be published.

9. Dr. Dan B. Allender, *The Wounded Heart - Hope For Adult Victims Of Childhood Sexual Abuse*, (Colorado Springs, Co.: Navpress, 1990), p. 176. Copyright © 1990 by Dan B. Allender. Used by permission of NavPress. All rights reserved. For copies, call 1-800-366-7788.

10. *Ibid.* p. 181.

11. A. W. Tozer, *The Pursuit of God*, (Harrisburg, Pa.: Christian Publications, Inc., 1948), pp. 11-12. Copyright © 1982 by Christian Publications Inc. All rights reserved.

12. *Ibid*, pp. 52 & 55-56.

13. *Ibid*, pp. 65-69.

14. *Ibid*, pp. 88-89.

15. *Ibid*, pp. 106-107.

16. *Ibid*, pp. 111-115.

17. Dr. Dan B. Allender *The Wounded Heart*, pp. 193-195.

18. *Ibid*, pp. 179-180.

Part II

The Holy Spirit Our Sanctifier

The overarching role of the Holy Spirit in this age is to search out a bride for Christ, reveal Christ to her, and prepare her for Him.

The role of the Holy Spirit to reveal Christ (God's Son) to us (His Bride), is seen in type in Genesis Chapter 24. This is the story of Abraham (a type of God the Father) sending His servant (a type of the Holy Spirit) back to the city of Nahor (a type of this world) to search out a bride (Rebekah, Hebrew RBQH, means "captivating; enticing") for Isaac (a type of Christ, God's Son), and on the trip back (a type of the time of the "church age" until the "Marriage Convocation of the Lamb) to describe Isaac (the Son) to Rebekah (the bride) so that when they met, they immediately recognize each other.

We are that Bride of Christ, now being made ready for that day, as we yield to Him in us working us unto "full stature in Christ". Hallelujah!

The Holy Spirit of Christ Jesus dwells in our hearts, and ever works to make us increasingly cognizant of, and into deeper inner union with, our Lord Christ Jesus. It is in this sense that the Scriptures, particularly the writings of Paul, talk about "Christ indwelling". That "indwelling" is the real meaning of "grace". Grace is the inward workings of the indwelling Holy Spirit in our hearts to bring us unto *intimacy* with Christ Jesus.

We start this study in this chapter, and expand on it considerably in the following two chapters on the Baptism into the Holy Spirit.

Chapter Five

Roles Of The Holy Spirit In Believers

Acts 3:20-21 clearly says that right now, until the "time of restitution of all things" (whenever that will be), Jesus Christ is "in *heaven*." On the other hand, Galatians 2:20 indeed talks about "Christ living *in us*". How therefore can He be living in our hearts here on earth?

It is actually the Holy Spirit of Christ Jesus who lives in us. The *Holy Spirit* lives within us from the moment we became "born again" (i.e., received "eternal life"). His role is to reveal Christ Jesus to us, both inwardly and outwardly. So *to us* it is as if it be *Christ* in us.

How is it possible *in this life* to know Christ indwelling with *certainty*? By the Holy Spirit Who ever works to reveal Christ Jesus to our soul-awareness and to bring our soul unto obedience/dependence.

So, we need to lay hold of the inner workings of the indwelling Holy Spirit of Christ Jesus, before we can understand the New Covenant release of our soul unto Christ.

So, to understand more fully what it means to know Him experientially, we start with a brief review of the functions of the Holy Spirit as revealed to us in the Scriptures.

1. Specific Workings Of The Holy Spirit

"Holy Spirit" is not just some abstract concept. He is a dynamic Person, a member of the Godhead, a servant of Christ Jesus. The Holy Spirit seeks out "all whosoever" would receive "so great salvation" *via* Christ's shed blood on Calvary, and to impart that salvation to those who respond. He:

> (a) Convicts us of our sin;
> (b) Imparts our salvation, resurrection life and truth;
> (c) Bears witness that we are children of God;
> (d) Pours out the love of Christ into and through us;
> (e) Enables us to walk in faith believing;
> (f) Intercedes for us where we can't ourselves;
> (g) Gives Us Joy In The Lord;
> (h) Sanctifies us and gives us victory over sin nature;
> (i) Deploys the authority of the Name of Christ; and
> (j) Is the very essence of "Eternal Life".

(a) *Convicts Us Of Our Sin:* In John 16:8-11, Jesus makes it plain that it is the Holy Spirit Who will convict us of our sin, of our lack of righteousness (by His personal example), and of our coming judgment.

That is for *Him* to do, not for *us* to do; our job is to *love* Christ and one another. How often we Christians try to reverse those roles, we trying to convict the world of their sins and leaving it up to the Holy Spirit to do the loving.

(b) *Imparts Our Salvation, Resurrection Life and Truth:*

We see the role of the indwelling Holy Spirit of Christ Jesus in bringing us unto salvation in Ephesians 2:8: "For by grace you have been *saved* through faith ...."

This role of the indwelling Holy Spirit of Christ Jesus is typified by the Passover story in Exodus 12, esp. vs. 13, 23 and 27. When the Lord *stepped through* the entrance way of the homes (our hearts, see Revelation 3:20), His *presence* in the home (our hearts) on that night (the time of our regeneration) kept the destroying angel (satan) out!

Romans 8:11: "But if the Spirit of Him who raised Jesus from the dead dwells in you, He who raised Christ Jesus from the dead will also give life to your mortal bodies through His Spirit who indwells you."

John 14:17 calls Him "the Spirit of Truth" Who now (since Christ's resurrection) is *in* us. In John 14:26 Jesus then says "But the Helper, the Holy Spirit, whom the Father will send in My name, He will teach you *all things*, and bring to your remembrance *all things* that I said to you."

What "all things"? Ephesians Chapter 1 lists some examples: our pre-destined inheritance (Eph. 1:5-12); assurance of His riches and power being available to us (Eph. 1:18-19); and Who He is, i.e., with all power and authority (Eph. 1:22-23).

First, we are brought unto a *basic* "salvation" relationship with God *via* the shed blood of Christ on Calvary and the impartation of "eternal life" (the indwelling *presence* of the Holy Spirit). Then that Holy Spirit begins in earnest to prepare us unto Christ-likeness, ultimately to be His corporate Bride. That is the full meaning of "salvation".

(c) *Bears Witness That We Are Children of God:* Romans 8:14-17: "For as many as are led by the Spirit of God, these are sons of God. For you did not receive the spirit of bondage again to fear, but you received the spirit of adoption by whom we cry out, 'Abba! Father!' The Spirit Himself bears witness with our [human] spirit that we are children of God, and if children, heirs also, heirs of God and joint heirs with Christ, if indeed we suffer with Him, that we may also be glorified together [with Him]."

(d) *Pours Out The Love Of Christ Into And Through Us:* He manifests Christ in and through us, that we be the communication channels of Christ's Light, Life and Love to one another (John 16:13-14). Romans 5:5: "Now hope does not disappoint, because the love of God has been poured out in our hearts by the Holy Spirit Who was given to us."

(e) *Enables Us To Walk In Faith Believing:* Walking and praying "in faith believing" is not determining if some statement is true, but rather is our first determining God's will in each specific situation, and then responding accordingly, certainly in prayer and intercession, plus personal ministry if/when appropriate. We determine God's will from the Holy Spirit, who also empowers us to respond accordingly. This ties in with the following:

(f) *Intercedes For Us Where We Can't:* Romans 8:26-27: "Likewise the Spirit also helps in our weaknesses. For we do not know what we should to pray for as we ought, but the Spirit Himself makes intercession for us with groanings which cannot be uttered. Now He who searches the hearts knows what the mind of the Spirit is, because He makes intercession for the saints according to the will of God."

(g) *Gives Us Joy In The Lord:*

The Holy Spirit is the essence of the *joy* of interpersonal relationships within the Godhead, and He enables us also to exude joy in our relationships. It is a matter of trusting in our new *life* unto "Godheadism".

The Greek word for "joy", Charo, is related to the word "grace" and has the meaning of "radiating". The Holy Spirit is to radiate the Light, Life and Love of Christ into us and through us unto others. This beautiful grasp of the role of the Holy Spirit in the lives of Christians is given to us to enable us to delight in Him, enjoy Him, and worship Him.

Piper[1] introduces this concept with these words:

> "... the Holy Spirit is the delight that the Father and the Son have in each other.

> "... the Holy Spirit is the divine Workman Who gives us a new heart of faith, and is Himself the personification of the *joy* that the Father and the Son have in each other. ... the change that must occur in the human heart to make saving faith possible is permeation by the Holy Spirit, that is nothing less than a permeation by the very *joy* that God the Father and God the Son have in each other's beauty."

Maturity in the Christian life is manifested when that life *radiates* to others the *presence* and *preciousness* of the Lord. That indicates a total abandonment and yieldedness unto Christ indwelling.

(h) *Sanctifies Us And Gives Us Victory Over Sin Nature:* He sanctifies us by leading us to *choose* true and deep repentance, area by area; and as we so choose He *empowers* the results. Romans 6:14: "For sin shall not have dominion over you, for you are not under law but under grace." And 1 John 1:9: "If we confess our sins, He is faithful and just to forgive us our sins and *to cleanse us from all unrighteousness.*"

(i) *Deploys The Authority Of The Name Of Christ:* He deploys, through us, the authority of the Name of Christ; also the Power of His shed blood (life) in spiritual warfare when/as needed. He provides its spiritual power, i.e., He *empowers* us. This is closely tied with enabling us to walk in faith believing (see (e) above).

(j) *Is The Very Essence Of 'Eternal Life':* The indwelling Holy Spirit of Christ Jesus is the very essence of *eternal life*. John 17:3: "This is eternal life, that they [you and I] may know [intimate, intrinsic, inner knowledge] You, the only true God, and Jesus Christ whom You have sent." That life enables us to fully and dynamically interact, two-ways, with God the Father, Christ the Son, and the rest of the "spiritual domain".

But even more, the indwelling Holy Spirit of Christ Jesus is the very same Spirit of God behind creation, of the "Tree of Life", and of God's purpose for creation. We were created to live according to the life of God's righteousness, not according to the life of self-seeking. He is now redeeming us back to that original life in Eden, by empowering us to focus onto the full reality of eternal life in Him and His life.

It *is* possible *in this life* to know Christ indwelling with *certainty*. Yes! That is the by far most significant role of His indwelling Holy Spirit in our lives! How? Initially through our being baptized into that Holy Spirit. (That we discuss thoroughly in the following two chapters of this volume.)

We now turn our attention to the role the Holy Spirit plays concerning the Word of God.

2. A Word On The Word's Word "Word"

Huh?

The word "word" obviously has many meanings. In the above:
>(1) message
>(2) the Bible
>(3) a group of letters which means something
>(4) the Biblical phrase "the Word of God"

Just what does the Bible mean by "the Word of God"?

John 1:1-5 & 14:
> "In the beginning was the ***Word***, and the ***Word*** was with God, and the ***Word*** was God. He was in the beginning with God. All things were made through Him, and without Him nothing was made that was made. In Him was life; and the life was the light of men. And the light

shines in the darkness; and the darkness did not comprehend it.

"And the *Word* became flesh and dwelt among us, and we beheld His glory, glory as of the Only Begotten of the Father, full of grace and truth."

Obviously, here "Word" refers to Jesus Christ.

But then, Romans 10:17:
"So then faith comes by hearing, and hearing by the *Word* of God."

And Ephesians 5:26:
"... that He might sanctify and cleanse her [the church] with the washing of water by the *Word* ..."

And Hebrews 1:3:
"... and [He] upholding all things by the *Word* of His power ..."

Two different Greek words are used here. In the first (John 1:1-5 & 14) the word is ***Logos***. In the next three, the word is ***Rhema***. But Greek lexicons have both words meaning "speech, word, matter, reason, ...". So, that's not much help. Or is it?

What are we doing when ever we use words, either spoken or written? We are ***communicating!*** What is communicating? It is the implanting of insights, thoughts, etc., from one's mind into insights, thoughts into another's mind.

Roles Of The Holy Spirit In Believers

Logos refers to the *content* of what is being communicated. *Rhema* refers to the *process* of that communication.

So when the Bible talks about the "Word of God" it's refering to God-to-man communication. But *how? Of what?*

God is *spirit* - John 4:24. What is *spirit?* A domain of tremendous power and incredible intelligence - God spoke and creation was created, etc. And *we*, having been created in the "image of God", have a *spirit* - Hebrew 4:12, 1 Thess. 5:23, etc.

What is our *human* spirit? Our ability for 2-way communication with that spiritual domain (prayer, praise, worship, intuition, conscience, love, etc.). It is distinct from our human soul: The seat of self - mind/reason (conscious and unconscious), emotions (feelings) and will (choice/volition).

Again, the "Word of God" implies God-to-man *spiritual* communication. Not just to our mind or emotions as doctrinal truths or emotional "highs". In John 4:24 we see that God-man communication is in spirit *and* truth.

What is it that God, as the Holy Spirit, desires to communicate/transmit into us *via* our human spirits? Logos: ***Christ Himself!*** Intimate, personal knowing of Christ Jesus! When you became born again, Christ Himself (as His Holy Spirit) came to dwell in your Human Spirit. Again, eternal life is that we intimately, intrinsically, inwardly ***know*** God and Jesus Christ. That's the full meaning of *grace* - Christ Indwelling!

Some references of "Word", Logos, as Jesus Christ indwelling, are:
> John 5:38 - "... have His ***Word abiding in*** you ...".
> Gal. 2:20 - "... but ***Christ lives in*** me; and the life which I now live in the flesh I live by faith in the Son of God ...".
> Col. 3:16 - "Let the ***Word of Christ dwell in*** you richly in all wisdom ...".

But He (in us) chooses to honor our human will. So, He (by His choice) is powerless in us until our will is aligned with his! But our soul is seat of self. It (our self) must yield (we must die to self). Then He can work in/through us. His Rhema Word (process of His communicating Christ to us) is that working of Him *via* His indwelling Holy Spirit.

3. Charismatic Cybernetics: Me *vs* Christ In Me

Just how does the indwelling Holy Spirit of Christ Jesus ***interact*** with me and with you, i.e. with our human spirit-soul combination, to bring us to deep repentance and to effect sanctification unto Christ-likeness?

To capture the essence of this highly dynamic interaction, we use the phrase "Charismatic Cybernetics". "Charismatic" means "pertaining to charisma." "Charisma" is the Biblical term "grace" whose full meaning is the Holy Spirit of Christ Jesus dwelling/living *in* each of us. The role of that indwelling Holy Spirit of Christ Jesus is to reveal Christ Jesus, first unto us in whom He dwells, and through us unto others by our lifestyles. And the main aspects of that revealing of Christ Jesus are of His Light (Word), Life (Power) and Love.

Roles Of The Holy Spirit In Believers

"Cybernetics" is a modern term of communication theory that refers to a system wherein two "units" dynamically interact with each other over a communication channel in order to accomplish a certain task. A common example is how the furnace in our homes, and the thermostat on the wall, linked by electric wires, work "together" to attain and maintain a desired temperature level.

"Charismatic cybernetics" therefore refers to how the indwelling Holy Spirit of Christ Jesus, and our human *soul* (especially the will/choice function of our soul), work "together" to attain and maintain a Christ-glorifying countenance in our lives, thoughts and behaviour patterns. The key element or "channel" of this dynamic interaction is our *human* spirit.

This dynamic interaction is a little understood Biblical concept. Foremost is required a change in the framework, orientation, basis of our thinking, mentality, "world-view", even of "Spirit-filled" Christians. For most of us, our current starting point mentality, *from* which the indwelling Holy Spirit of Christ Jesus must bring us, is that of "churchianity" or *denominationalism*, the present context of Christian living for most of us. The new mentality, *to* which the indwelling Holy Spirit of Christ Jesus is to bring us, is that of *full spiritual reality*. The transforming process, called "sanctification", is varied but extensive for all of us: we must be *plunged* head-first into spiritual reality, and *broken* of our self-will.

Just what will the *plunging* of us into full dynamic Spiritual reality, the *breaking* of our wills, entail in our lives? First and foremost, the *plunging* is unto Christ's Lordship over our *total* self. Secondly, the *breaking* is unto the humiliating realization that we, *each* of us, *need* an inner healing of our human spirits.

Once we each take that plunge, we discover the awesome power and authority we have in Christ to be victorious. But it has to be a personal experiential discovery, not an intellectual or doctrinal one, for our natural minds cannot grasp spiritual truths.

Charismatic cybernetics is the indwelling Holy Spirit of Christ Jesus bringing us along this route. How do we get to the state of His indwelling presence being fully acknowledged and expressed? It does not happen automatically in a believer's life. It requires God's sovereign workings in our lives, yes; but at every painful step, the soul must also choose to yield. And that is the problem: our soul's grip or domination over the spirit must be broken!

The basic issue is the orientation or poise of our soul, the goals and interests and desires and world-view of our hearts. What do we *really* seek, desire, expect in our Christian walk? Do we seek security in comfortable and righteous religion? Do we seek fulfillment "in Christ" through our ministry? Or do we seek to allow Christ indwelling to fully have His way, at any cost? Are we actually self-seeking, or are we really seeking only to please and glorify Him? We must desire *Him*, not things of Him. Only by seeking to give Christ indwelling full reign, are we partaking of the "Tree of Life". All else is really us partaking of the "Tree of Knowledge of Good and Evil" - albeit the "good" part, but which nevertheless ultimately brings death and in the meantime brings bitter frustration.

Our soul's grip must be broken; we must stop seeking things of Him by our own efforts, and learn to truly "let go and let God" in us do the willing and doing (Philippians 2:13).

Hebrews 4:12 introduces us to that in a context of contrasting our *resting* in God *vs* our hearts becoming hardened. "For the Word of God (Logos - Christ indwelling) is powerful and active and sharper than any two-edged sword, piercing even to the division of soul and spirit, and of joints and marrow, and is a discerner of the thoughts and intents of the heart."

Note this comparison. Marrow is the soft pithy part inside a bone. It reproduces the red corpuscles that carry oxygen (which is the main life-sustaining substance) to all cells of the body and remove the waste (byproducts of life functions). The bone is the outer hard structure that encases, protects, and hides the marrow. This bone-marrow relationship is used as an example of the barrier of our soul-spirit relationship. In the natural, our soul (mind, emotions, will, and self-consciousness) fully controls and dominates our behaviour, whereas it is in our human spirit that the Holy Spirit of Christ Jesus lives and works. He ever seeks to disperse eternal life through us to others. The idea is that the bone structure, the hard outer crust (typifying the human soul) that *protects* the marrow (typifying the human spirit) from being exposed, *hinders* it and must be broken. Our soul (our will in particular) has to ever *yield* to what Christ through His Holy Spirit is seeking to work in or through us.

Another type of His sanctifying dealings in our lives is the pruning of a fruit tree. It is not just *dead* wood that is removed, but *living* branches. Left to itself, a fruit tree tends to grow far more branches than it can fully bear fruit on. So a husbandman cuts off those branches that do not bear fruit or do so most poorly, so that the tree will concentrate its strength into maturing fruit on the branches that are left. So also in our soul-lives. The fruitless branches that He, Christ our Husbandman, must remove, are those tendencies we have of doing things *for* Him without His Holy Spirit's instigation: all those "good" Christian activities that are only peripheral to His primary purpose in our lives; those emphases and activities that are based on our understandings rather than on His initiatives; and those things that *we* love to do most, whether they be His will or not.

His prunings are painful but inevitable. They come in ways we least expect (so that we cannot easily circumvent them). But they are God's sovereign disciplining of us (Hebrews 12:4-13). The power of Christ's death in me - my death of flesh and self - is the ruling principle through which the power of His life, His Holy Spirit, can be released in me.

4. Cleanses Our Kidneys As Well As Our Hearts

The Old and New Testaments use the words LB (Hebrew) and Cardia (Greek), translated ***heart***. It does not of course refer to the physical organ that pumps our blood, but to the central "core" of our consciousness or psychological nature. It refers to the seat of all emotional, intellectual, volitional and moral functions. Our "heart" expresses our personality, our outward expressions of thinking, feeling and behavior. And much is said in the scriptures about the Holy Spirit cleansing our "hearts".

Less known, however, are two other words used in the Old and New Testaments using another inner organ of the body as

Roles Of The Holy Spirit In Believers

a type. These are the words KLYWTh (Hebrew) and Nephros (Greek), often translated "reins". They are the words for our *kidneys*. And many of the passages in the scriptures refering to our "heart" also refer to our "kidneys" in the same vein:

Psalm 7:9 - "For the righteous God tests the *hearts* and the *kidneys.*"

Psalm 16:7 - "My *kidneys* instruct me in the night seasons."

Psalm 26:2 - "Prove me; try my *kidneys* and my *heart.*"

Psalm 73:21 - "Thus my *heart* was grieved, and I was vexed in my *kidneys* [over destruction of the wicked]."

Jeremiah 11:20 - "O Lord ... You judge righteousness, testing the *kidneys* and the *heart.*"

Jeremiah 12:2 - "[O Lord] ... you are near in their mouth [what they speak] but far from their *kidneys.*"

Jeremiah 17:10 - "I the Lord search the *heart;* I test the *kidneys.*"

Jeremiah 20:12 - "O Lord ... You who test the righteous and see the *kidneys* and *heart.*"

Revelation 2:23 - "... all the churches shall know that I am He Who searches the *kidneys* and *hearts.*"

Also, in Leviticus Chapter 3 on the "Peace" offering, the two *kidneys* are to be offered by fire unto God along with the fat

In that offering, *we* are the offering unto our "wholeness"; it is *our* kidneys being referred to there. Our "kidneys", as smoke, are to rise as a sweet savor pleasing to God.

Now, our physical kidneys are internal organs which purify our blood, removing toxins and maintaining a proper level of sodium in our blood plasma. But what do they typify in these scripture uses?

Our secret most thoughts and motives and desires and intents! Our foundational belief system!

Whereas our *heart* typifies the outward functions of our souls, our *kidneys* typify the inner functions, the very things we try most to hide from others (often also from ourselves). It refers to our level of both (a) God-awareness (to what extent we are intimate with Who He is and where He is - in us); and (b) our self-awareness (to what extent we realize who we are in Him).

Our *kidneys* determine our *heart!* Our kidneys "rein" our heart.

So, for the Holy Spirit to sanctify us, He must sanctify our *kidneys* as well as our *heart.* He must plough deep, very deep, to accomplish His purposes in us.

Later in Chapter Nine we study in detail His deep ploughing to sanctify our inner most parts. We now refer to that ploughing as He effecting "inner heart healing" in us by bringing us unto deep repentance.

5. Holy Spirit Empowerment Of Healing Repentance

Victory can and will come as we learn to totally depend upon and obey Christ indwelling in all things. That is a *process* over time. It requires the *discipline of deep repentance*. But even that discipline is impossible without absolute assurance that *Christ indeed dwells within us*, and without our being *focused unto Him*. He Himself must even help us in our basic sin of unbelief, for even our faith ultimately comes from God.

In Chapter 5 of Volume I[2] of this series, we introduced the need for the indwelling Holy Spirit of Christ Jesus to lead us through this discipline of deep repentance unto "inner heart healing". In Chapters 5 through 10 of that Volume I we delineate both the exegetical and experiential aspects of that inner heart healing process, including many aspects of transferring repentance, as we are led and enabled by the indwelling Holy Spirit.

Victory over dysfunctionally-rooted traumas and our grievous reactions thereto out of self-protection, comes not from one merely choosing to repent from the inappropriate and destructive *behavior*. One must understand the basic choice he/she has made at the heart's deepest level to avoid the pain of sense of emptiness and worthlessness. That in turn requires understanding of the particular detailed forms of pain he/she is choosing to avoid, and the strategies he/she has formed to avoid them. For it is those strategies which are the force behind the inappropriate and destructive behavior. But all of those basic choices of pain-avoidance goals and strategies, resulting from *our failure* to truly trust that Christ actually exists inwardly and is sufficient, are usually far below the conscious awareness of the person himself/herself. Hence, final victory requires a painful confrontation with *why* he/she feels those deep-seated pains, plus a difficult struggle to replace those senses of emptiness and worthlessness, not with self-seeking and self-protecting efforts, but with genuine and profound faith in Christ indwelling. Gaining that understanding, enduring that confrontation, and persisting in that repentance, requires an active working of the indwelling Holy Spirit as we yield to Him.

How do we repent? How do we do the self-discipline? By a totally-involved ***surrender*** of the darknesses to Christ, specifically *to **Christ on the Cross when He died to remove our sins!*** Repentance is far more than merely "accepting Christ as our personal Saviour"; it is a total yielding unto Him the areas of darkness in our thoughts, a surrendering that requires our total involvement. By ***totally-involved surrender*** we mean just that. It is not merely a mental exercise, though mental ***discipline*** is the heart of it. Nor is it an emotional exercise, though the power of our emotions that are locked into our dysfunctionally-rooted darknesses must be broken. It is an act of our will, wherein our entire being intensely seeks Christ to release us, a seeking of Him that involves every resource, every thought, every feeling, at our disposal. The Bible refers to that as our being "broken". It is a ***choice*** we make, and that we make with our entire being. It is a choice we make as an act of faith. It is a releasing of ***life*** within us: ***His*** life! It is our consciously and deliberately ***choosing*** to ***transfer*** the many aspects of our sin-nature, our weaknesses, illnesses, sins, self-seeking and self-protecting ways, onto Him on the Cross.

6. Is It Actually Possible?

It is not just *difficult* to live the Holy-Spirit-filled life; it is *impossible!* Only He, Himself in us, can live it (Galatians 2:20). Amen! But I have found that it is also very difficult to achieve the state where even He does that living through us. For, try as we may to totally yield to Him in us, the obstacles in our path are so numerous, so nearly-overwhelming, that very few indeed are the believers who truly overcome in this life. Rather, the vast majority who start out sincerely seeking, sooner or later reach some point, to go beyond which they lose the motivation to even try. Our Lord Christ Jesus does *not* make it easy.

The most common stumbling block to us is our innate tendency to do our Lord's will *for* Him. That is what "religion" is all about: human organizations to meet human (albeit "spiritual") needs by *human* methods. This is borne out of impatience and *soulical* ambition (though we often erroneously think it to be "spiritual"), which in turn is but a form of our sin-nature of pride. Our natural talents in ministry are most often our greatest enemies.

Another common stumbling block to most of us, is our striving to overcome the *carnality* in our lives by our own efforts! It is indeed very right when we are *grieved* over our sin nature to the point of being *willing* to do whatever is necessary to effect its crucifixion. For Christ in us cannot effectively work His perfect will through us in those areas in which we choose our sin-nature and carnality to be still active. But crucifixion is *never* something we can do of/to ourselves: that is simply impossible! Our very *striving* for being crucified of self hinders that working; for *as* we strive, the center of our attention is on *our* being crucified, rather than on *His* will that we be totally abandoned unto Him. When the me in me is striving to become not-me, it is that very me in me that is doing the doing, and hence by its very activity far from becoming not-me. When the very center of self that is to be crucified strives to do the crucifixion, it becomes *more* active rather than *less*. It is the effectual power of the cross of Christ that works that, once we *determine* to *allow* it to.

How do we determine to allow Him to crucify us? Under what circumstances does the effectual power of the cross of Christ work crucifixion in our lives? It is only when and as we lose ourselves in Christ, when and as we saturate our mind - our attention, our motives, our entire thinking process - unto Him and His purposes and will, and depend upon the power of that cross to do the work.

But in actual practice, that is a most difficult thing for us to do. For the pressures of our life-styles, the legitimate and "right" responsibilities we have, *overwhelmingly* tend to squeeze Christ out of our thinking for most of our waking hours. It requires intense determination and severe *mental discipline* to forcefully set aside time to spend with Him in prayer and praise and meditation; and even then it is so difficult to discipline our thoughts to keep those (even legitimate) worldly concerns from blocking our flow in Christ! True worship is *extremely* rare in *each* of our lives!

Over and over again in our lives we fail to flow in Him to any significant and effective degree. We cry out to Him to help us. He then encourages us, lifts our heads (Psalm 3:3) as our loving Father and High Priest and Shepherd and Advocate. So, we try again. Yet too often the cycle merely repeats itself.

And after the 7*th* or 17*th* or 70*th* time of 1 John 1:9, we finally give up in disillusionment.

What, then, can we do? Fast? Pray? "Let go and let God"? Yes. But those things we *have* been doing, for so long now, in our striving. What, yet, is missing?

It comes down to one thing: *total*, absolute, complete commitment to and *abandonment* unto Christ Himself. Total, absolute, and complete! Anything short, and it cannot be a *lasting* walk in Him. That slightest holding back, that slightest self-centeredness, is the mole hill that quickly becomes that mountain, that sin that so often besets us (Hebrews 12:1), and dissipates our *experiential* power over our self-seeking nature and its inevitable reinforcement by satan.

I consistently observe that such a total, absolute, complete commitment to and abandonment unto Christ Jesus, is more particularly difficult for believers who come to Christ out of a pseudo-Christian cultural background (such as in "Bible belt" America), than it is for Christian converts from a totally heathen, godless and pagan sub-culture. For to simply *become* a Christian out of a totally anti-Christian sub-culture requires that total, absolute, complete commitment and abandonment in the first place. On the other hand, in a pseudo-Christian sub-culture we almost never see the need for so *radical* a change. Indeed, we are seldom able to see how non-Christian our pseudo-Christian sub-culture here in America really is.

Certain intrinsically pagan aspects of our pseudo-Christian sub-culture are as a rule very ensnaring. Those include our holiday customs. Also the deeply-ingrained drive in our socially **matriarchical** sub-culture for women to be the ***religious*** leaders of the family and local community. Virtually all aspects of the Christian ***religion***, the Christian religious structures, rituals, traditions, holidays, cultural practices, practices of Christian ministries, and its supporting doctrinal mentality, has come down to us not from Christ Jesus or His Holy Spirit, nor from the Bible, but from the ancient religious system of Baal! That is not speculation, but a raw historical fact. We study that in detail in Volume VII[3] of this series.

Such a total, absolute, complete commitment to and abandonment unto Christ, I observe, is also much more difficult for believers from a materialistically affluent cultural background (such as here in America) than for believers from a destitute cultural heritage. That is true even for those believers whose personal lives have always been in poverty; for it is not material affluence *per se* that trips us up, but rather our ***dreams*** of personally acquiring material affluence, and our willingness to devote so much of our personal time and effort and resources toward that dream, that so squeezes Christ out of our thinking. But, again, what are one's highest priorities, sources of motivation, causes for dedication of our time and efforts and talents and other resources? We all tend to commit ***far*** more to legitimate concerns than is really necessary!

And so it goes. There is always that one area of our lives, that one legitimate, right and proper responsibility, that one area of enticing non-evil pleasure, to soothe our hectic feelings of loneliness or frustrations. Off of Christ, and on to it, goes our attention. For hours or days on end. And when we wake up to it, and allow Christ to give us victory within that area, up pops another stumbling block in our attention. And another.

It seems there is no end to it.

Are we making any progress at all? Yes, but it's like the bumper jack we use on our automobiles. At each step, we go up two notches of the ratchet and then down one notch. When we tend to focus on our failures (the one-notch downward steps), it's hard to feel that we *are* overall growing in Christ-likeness.

But yes, in *His* sight, we *are* making progress! For such is the "dark night of the soul" to which He must subject every Spirit-filled believer who is honestly desiring to be totally in His will. (That we study in detail later in Chapter Nine of this volume.) Our "dark night of the soul" has a definite pattern of progression to it. We ourselves might not be able to see that pattern, that progression, while we are in it. But in His sight we indeed remain in His will and in His timing.

Providing, that is, that we never lose our sensitivity, imputed to us solely by Him, for His will for our lives. Providing, that is, that we *desire* Him above all else, *seek* Him, *search* for Him. "... and you shall seek Me, and (indeed) find Me, when you search for Me *with your whole heart*" (Jeremiah 29:13)!

End Notes: Chapter Five

[1.] Piper, John *Desiring God - Meditations Of A Christian Hedonist* (Portland, OR: Multnomah Press, 1986). Copyright

© 1986 by Multnomah Press. Pp. 39 Note 5 and p. 59 Note 13.

2. Sherrerd, Chris S., *The Christian Marriage - A Six-Fold Covenant Of Love-Motivated Servanthood*, Volume I of the series "Where Do You Fit In? Practical Commitments In The Body Of Christ" (Shippensburg, PA: Treasure House, Destiny Image Publishing Group, 1994). Copyright © 1994 by Shulemite Christian Crusade.

3. Sherrerd, Chris S., *The Deceit Of Baal - Religious And Intellectual Deceptions In The Body Of Christ*, Volume VII of the series "Where Do You Fit In? Practical Commitments In The Body Of Christ", to be published.

Chapter Six

Receive Ye The Holy Spirit In His Fulness

In the preceding chapters of this volume we have studied some of the basic issues of the workings of the Holy Spirit of Christ living in us. Our primary emphasis has been the *indwelling* of that Holy Spirit of Christ Jesus: "Nevertheless I live, not I, but Christ lives in me..." says Paul in Galatians 2:20, referring to the *Spirit* of Christ in us. And the main goal of He in us is to bring us unto love-motivated and Spirit-empowered servanthood, that His good will and purposes be effected (Philippians 2:13), not by us *for Him* but by *Him through* us.

Yet since we start from a condition so depraved and removed from that, He must work a deep work within us, not only of basic *redemption*, but also of *sanctification*. Furthermore, since He chooses to not override our human wills, we must *repent* before each step of His sanctifying work in us can occur. Repentance means a change in our thought life and appropriating the Lordship of Christ Jesus in all areas of our lives. That change of thinking must be unto one of *surrendering* unto Christ all of our self that hinders our relationship with Him.

None of this is possible without our *knowing* Christ in some experiential way. Faith is not a mental activity, but a choice to abandon ourselves unto the person of Christ Jesus in dynamic dependence and sensitive obedience. Faith is *knowing and seeing* He Whom we sensitively *obey* and upon Whom we are dynamically *dependent*.

This ability to *know* and *see* our Lord Christ Jesus comes to us as we invite and welcome Him and yield to Him. More specifically, to *know* and *see* our Lord Christ Jesus requires His baptizing us into His Holy Spirit; *knowing* and *seeing Him* is the *primary* purpose and effect of our receiving His Baptism into the Holy Spirit! The Baptism into the Holy Spirit is the *vital key*, a key that we must obtain if we are to make the necessary transition in repentance unto inner heart healing, and from there unto the rest of our sanctification. That key is so vital, we devote this and the following chapter to it.

1. Baptism Into The Holy Spirit?

The Baptism into the Holy Spirit, although taught and experienced by many Christians today, is a *poorly understood* New Testament truth. Much confusion reigns in the minds of sincere, Bible-taught believers: is it a "second work of grace" beyond regeneration? Does it always involve speaking in tongues. If so, why? The Baptism into the Holy Spirit is at the root of much controversy and division in Christiandom. Many a pastor has lost his pulpit, and many a believer has been forced to leave his church, because of it.

Furthermore, disillusionment exists among many believers, both who *have* received the Baptism but still seem to be so incomplete and unfulfilled, and also those who have been seeking it without success for so long. Why should a truth that is so intrinsic to the New Testament be so often accompanied by such confusion, controversy, and disillusionment? Why do so many who testify of the Baptism, seem so powerless in their lives, so lacking in love in their dealings with other believers, or so uninterested in personal evangelism?

Part of the answer is the fact that almost all of us, even those of us who have "received" this Baptism by Jesus, still are grossly lacking in its *fullness*. Because so much misunderstanding exists (both Biblical and experiential), those who seek the Baptism into the Holy Spirit are seldom taught to seek or expect its fullness. Since we receive according to our seeking and to our faith, most of us who have received it are missing certain Biblical aspects of it. That does not mean that our experience has not been valid; it means that it is time, now, for us to go back and look at the *fullness* of it, and encourage one another to seek and to flow into it in those areas where we are still lacking.

Let us first set aside our pet doctrinal golden calves and our favorite spiritual jargon and cliches, and seek what the Bible really says and does not say about it. Then in the following chapter we explore in more practical terms what its *full* appropriation entails in lives.

The Word of God presents four concepts of the Baptism into the Holy Spirit:
- (1) God's Law *inscribed* **on our hearts;**
- **(2)** *Circumcision* of our hearts;
- (3) Us being *Baptized* (immersed) into the Holy Spirit;

(4) and Us being *"filled"* with the Holy Spirit.

In all four of these cases, the essential or root meaning of the New Testament Greek words is that we be brought under the *influence* and *control* of the indwelling Holy Spirit of Christ Jesus. In this study we show that that involves: (1) a "releasing" of our human soul unto the Holy Spirit indwelling, Who is God's standard of righteousness for us today; (2) not an *initial* receiving of the Holy Spirit, but a deeper *yielding* to Him who dwells within us from regeneration; (3) not a *"thing"* nor an "experience" as such, but a deeper dimension of our *relationship* with Christ Jesus as a *Person;* and (4) not an *instant* maturity of us in Christ, but rather an *enablement* for us to *endure* the "wilderness" trials, it being our growing in faith through our *trials* that matures us.

It is impossible to fully understand the Baptism into the Holy Spirit without understanding how the Bible describes the human psychological make-up. This we summarized in Chapter 1 of this volume above. Our human *spirit* is our seat of *God*-consciousness: *intuition*, our ability to know things of God and spiritual truths in a way other than by what we've learned; *conscience*, our ability to know moral truths and to know God's Will for us in specific situations; our ability to feel and express *love*; our spiritual *yearning*, our ability to seek, *praise and worship* God. Our *soul* is our seat of *self*-consciousness: our *mind*, our ability to consciously and logically think and reason; our *emotions*, our ability to consciously feel and emote; and our *will or volition*, our ability to deliberately determine and choose our course of behaviour. And our *body* is our *world*-consciousness: all of our abilities to know the physical context of our lives and being.

The Baptism into the Holy Spirit does not primarily involve our human spirit nor our flesh (as do regeneration and water baptism, respectively), but rather is an *immersion* of our *soul* into the Holy Spirit. This enables us to grow in vivid **awareness of Christ Jesus**, since the Holy Spirit's total mission is to reveal and manifest the *Person* of Christ Jesus to us, and through us to others, experientially.

We use the preposition "into" rather than simply "in" or "of" the Holy Spirit. We do this deliberately for two reasons. First, the word "baptize" is a Greek verb meaning to immerse or dip into a fluid; hence the very verbal action implies a dynamic, *new* encounter *into*, rather than a passive rest *in*. Second, throughout the New Testament as one proceeds from the Gospels through the Pauline Epistles, etc., one notes an advancing development of the concepts conveyed by the Holy Writer to a maturing Body of Christ. This advancing development of concepts is accompanied by a shift from the use of the Greek preposition En (in, of) to Eis (into, unto, toward, with motion to). In our earthly relationship with Christ, we first learn to rest *in* Him, and we (our human spirits) are indeed "in" His indwelling Holy Spirit. But as He brings us to maturity in our relationship with Him, we (our human souls) must learn to increasingly come *"unto"* the full influence and control of that indwelling Holy Spirit.

The Baptism into the Holy Spirit is not a matter of "altar call emotionalism", but a decisive ***determination*** on our part that Christ Jesus, Himself, truly be *Lord* of our entire beings. Concerning the subjective experience of entering this new dimension of knowing Christ Jesus, the key to both our entering into it and growing in it is ***worship:*** that is, our losing our*self* in His Presence.

2. Old *vs* New Covenant Baptisms

Our starting point in examining the Biblical meaning of the Baptism into the Holy Spirit is to look at the first place in the New Testament where it is referenced, and to note carefully both the content and the context of that reference.

The first explicit reference to it in the New Testament is Matthew 3:11, and this reference is repeated 6 times, the other 5 being Mark 1:8, Luke 3:16, John 1:33, Acts 1:5, and Acts 11:16. The context is John the Baptist, at the Jordan River, administering *water* baptism within a strictly Old Covenant framework. He said prophetically, "Someone is coming whose shoes I am unworthy to tie or untie; and when He comes He will Baptize into the Holy Spirit. I baptize into water; He will Baptize into the Holy Spirit." John the Baptist was prophesying about Jesus, but the significance of this is that John was making a comparison: "John the Baptist baptized into water, but Jesus will baptize into the Holy Spirit." He was in essence saying "This water baptism that we're doing is a type of a New Testament baptism that will be into the Holy Spirit; this water baptism will be *replaced* by a better covenant baptism by the Messiah Jesus."

What was the meaning of water baptism in the Old Covenant sense? Much light has been shed on this in recent years through scholarship with the Dead Sea Scrolls and other ancient writings. Under the late Old Covenant Law, water baptism was a necessary part of the procedure whereby a *gentile*, who chose to, became an Israelite. It signified a cleansing (by water immersion) from all of the pollution of the "goyem" (GWYM) or being gentiles.

John the Baptist was in essence saying to Israelites, "Although you are of Israel through birth, your life style is as if you were of the gentiles. *Repent;* become Israelites indeed in your *thought life and life style,* and outwardly testify to your change through this ritual of water baptism."

Symbolically through John's prophetic comparison, the word of God is saying to *us* today, "Although you are Christians through the new birth, your life style is as if you are not; therefore *repent* and be Baptized into the Holy Spirit, so that you can become truly *Christ-like.*"

This New Testament's first reference to the Baptism into the Holy Spirit depicts it as a separate experience that *enables* us to transform our thought life and life style to that of Christ, even though our human *spirit* is *already* in union with Him through our having been "born again". Repentance is of our *soul;* the Baptism into the Holy Spirit affects not our human spirit but our self-consciousness, i.e., our thoughts, emotions and will. Christians, although genuinely born-again, are not Christians in thought-life until *humbled beyond self!*

3. Baptism Unto The Presence-Glory Of God

The first church had a lesson in this as early as Acts Chapter 15. We never have any Biblical account of Jesus *water* baptizing, but we know the disciples continued John-The-Baptist's water baptism among Israelites until then. Although they were very dynamic Spirit-filled Christians who had known the Master, they at first continued to follow several of the Old Covenant traditional ways. Acts 15 is a very pivotal chapter. The disciples had a council at Jerusalem because they had a fight (the wording is more polite than that, but they had a knock-down, drag-out doctrinal battle): Peter and Paul were saying that God was anointing the gentiles with the Baptism into the Holy Spirit just as He had done to themselves as Israelites; and the other disciples were saying that that couldn't be, since God's blessings were only for Israelites, and gentiles would first have to become Israelites (as denoted, for example, by first being circumcised and *water* baptized) before God would Baptize them into His Holy Spirit.

James, inspired by the Holy Spirit, quoted from Amos a verse that at first seems almost irrelevant to the issue. He read Amos' prophecy that the Tabernacle of David would be restored. That is a prophecy of praise and worship. The Tabernacle of David is where the Ark of the Covenant was on Mt. Zion (after David became King and put it there), and where the "Shekinah" (ShKNYH) or "presence" glory of God abided and was *accessible to all people* of all backgrounds *who desired* to come unto Him. It was before that where David, during praise and worship, received much of the inspiration for some of the Psalms he wrote. So this lesson taught the early church that the Baptism into the Holy Spirit involves bringing *all* (of any background) who repent, into the power and the glory of the *presence* of God in their lives through praise and worship.

4. Regeneration *vs* Baptism Into The Holy Spirit

Much of the confusion between regeneration and the Baptism into the Holy Spirit, and the controversy over whether it is or is not a "second work of grace", stems from the limitations of our understanding of what it means to become "born again".

Receive Ye The Holy Spirit In His Fulness

To be "born" of course means to receive life, or to manifest of a form of life, that was not previously possessed or manifested. To be *"born again"* means to begin to manifest an *additional* form of life. It is typified in the Bible by God (Christ) "breathing the breath of life" into us (Genesis 2:7). The parallel Biblical account of when the disciples became "born again" is John 20:22. After Jesus was resurrected and glorified, He appeared to the disciples, commissioned them, "breathed on them", and imparted the Holy Spirit to them.

That this was regeneration, and not Holy Spirit Baptism, is seen in two ways. First, it took place before Jesus' ascension, and Acts 2 (when the disciples received the Holy Spirit Baptism) took place 10 days after His ascension; hence, in the disciple's lives, these two events took place at least 10 days apart. Both were clearly singular or "crisis" experiences, not gradual processes. Second, we see in Genesis 2:7 that God's "breathing" on man is an impartation of *life* to man. The Hebrew word for "life" in Genesis 2:7 (CHYYM) is in the plural; God initially imparted *two* forms of life to man: natural or physical life, and "eternal" life. The "eternal life", lost by man as a result of the Transgression, is linked with having direct experiential knowledge of God the Father and Christ Jesus the Son (John 17:3). Hence, *regeneration* is linked to receiving the Holy Spirit in order that we become able to know and experience God through Christ Jesus. We *receive* the Holy Spirit (in our *human spirit*) upon becoming "born again"; and since we receive a Person, we then receive *all* of Him.

The Acts account speaks of something else. Acts 1:8 speaks of the Holy Spirit "coming upon" *us* (that is a dynamic action involving our *soul* or seat of our self-awareness or "us-ness", not our human spirit), and links that with receiving *power*. Indeed that occurred in the disciple's lives in Acts 2:1-4,6,14-36,40-44, etc. Later in this chapter we further discuss this distinction between we "receiving" the Holy Spirit (in our *human spirits*) and the Holy Spirit "coming upon" us (our *souls*), when we study "heart circumcision". But here we note simply that *both* are a work of the Holy Spirit, regeneration bringing us into a *"communicating"* relationship with God through Christ Jesus, and the Baptism into the Holy Spirit bringing us into *experiential* knowledge of Him along with concommitant abilities to minister His word in power.

We also note three accompanying phenomena stated in Acts 2: *wind*, denoting the Holy Spirit Himself moving as He wills (usually invisibly to human consciousness); *speaking* in tongues, denoting His reality and manifestations of Himself through us in ways beyond our rational intellect as we respond in faith to Him; and *fire*, that denotes God *purifying* us. This latter involves removing the dross of self-will and self-dependence (1 Peter 1:6-7) from us, and disciplining us (Hebrews 12:4-11) in the subsequent "wilderness" adjusting processes He puts us through.

5. Mount Sinai A Type

A very illustrative type of the Baptism into the Holy Spirit and the distinction between it and regeneration is found in the story of the escapades of the Israelites in the Exodus events. The entire books of Exodus through Joshua describe the full deliverance/salvation plan and pattern in type, with several distinct stages involved: deliverance from the *consequence* of sin (death - Passover of Exodus 12:12-30 and Romans 6:23); deliverance from the *bondage* (slavery) to sin (Red Sea crossing of Exodus 14:1-31); deliverance from the *thought patterns* of sin (Exodus 19-31 and 33-34); deliverance from the (Adamic) *nature* of sin (40 years of wanderings in the Wilderness); deliverance from the *self* of sin (Joshua 3-4); and *conquering* the promised land (rest of Joshua). Our New Testament "promised land" is described in Romans Chapter 8. The first two of these stages (Passover and Red Sea crossing) typify regeneration and water baptism, and the remainder typify the Baptism into the Holy Spirit and His subsequent sanctifying of us.

To the Israelites, the term "Pentecost" simply meant "50 days", and it recalled to them that it was 50 days after leaving Egypt (i.e., after the Passover festival of First Fruits) when the Israelites in Exodus came to Mount Sinai. There God descended on the mountain with physical manifestations of power, including consuming *fire*. The power of the presence of God overwhelmed Moses ("I exceedingly feared and quaked"). For 40 days Moses remained in that awesome presence of God, during which time God revealed to Moses His standards for *righteousness* - the Old Testament law - and engraved it on permanent tablets (of stone). The Israelites were very uncomfortable with this and desired that the voice of God never come to them again. But the Holy Day of Pentecost was kept by Israel to perpetually remind them of the day God inscribed His standards in stone so that all nations could be held accountable before God, could see their unholiness, and have a tutor-master that would bring them to justification through faith in Christ (Galatians 3:24).

Hebrews Chapter 8 tells us that many of the details in Exodus are types of corresponding details of our walk and maturing in Christ in the New Covenant. So as a type of the Baptism into the Holy Spirit, the Mt. Sinai events shed light on the following aspect of it. On Mt. Sinai, God engraved His commandments on tablets of stone; 'He also imparted to Moses much of His law, that Moses in turn inscribed on tablets of paper (i.e., the Books of Exodus, Numbers, Leviticus, and Deuteronomy). God's law is His standard of *righteousness*, and that is secondary only to His *love* as the most essential aspect of living in the Kingdom of God (Lordship of Christ). But, specifically pertaining to the Baptism into the Holy Spirit in our day, He said "I will engrave My laws upon your hearts" (Jeremiah 31:33, Hebrews 8:10 and 10:16). Hence, in the Baptism into the Holy Spirit, He implants or "engraves" (i.e., makes us *consciously* aware of) His standards of righteousness inwardly in our hearts. Since the Holy Spirit's function today is to manifest Christ Jesus in the world though His Body, the righteousness of Christ in our behaviour and thought life is a natural consequence of that manifestation. His law, His standard of righteousness, is a *Person*, dwelling in us!

6. That The Body Of Christ Be Matured

Paul's most direct teachings on the manifestations of the gift of the Holy Spirit though our behaviour is in Chapters 11 through 14 of 1 Corinthians. 1 Corinthians Chapters 11 though 14 is a single discourse (with many exhortations) on the theme of the Body of Christ (local groups of believers) *maturing* in their relationship with Christ. Paul makes it clear that that can be possible *only* as we allow the Holy Spirit to direct our ways, thoughts, motives, desires and behaviour. The Baptism into the Holy Spirit is a mandatory prerequisite for the maturing of the Body of Christ!

7. The Charisma Of Our Callings

Maturing of the Body of Christ and edification of the believers, are also linked to the "gift" of the Holy Spirit and His diverse manifestations though the attitudes and behaviour of the believers.

To understand this, we study the words for "gift" in the New Testament Greek. In Ephesians 4:11-13, where certain **men** with certain ministries are **given** to the Body for edification thereof, the Greek word is Edoken. That has much of the meaning of the verb "to give" in modern conversational English. But whenever "gift" is used in conjunction with the Holy Spirit and His manifestations, the word is Charisma or Charismatos. That is closely related to the word Charin (translated "grace"). These are strong words for us today, for they speak not just of a gift of unmerited favor, but that the gift is an *impartation* of a *Person* indwelling Who manifests Himself to others through us *as* we yield to Him! Charin always speaks of the *one* gift of the Holy Spirit imparted into us and working through our self as we release our self unto Him. He "gives" (imparts) *Himself* to us to the extent to which we "give" (yield) ourselves to Him.

1 Corinthians 12:4-13 clearly speaks of *one* gift - the Holy Spirit - with various manifestations distributed among us as He wills for the common good, for effecting unity among us, and for bringing the Body to corporate maturity. These manifestations are called "spirituals" or "spirit-manifestations" (Greek word Pneumatika) in 1 Corinthians 12:1, 14:1 and 14:12. Romans 12:3-8 also addresses this theme, going into more detail. Romans 12:3 & 6 speak of a measure or *specific* delegation of faith (Pisteos) and grace (Charin) that He has

divided/dispersed among us. Romans 12 then lists specific examples of types of ministries within the Body. He (Christ Jesus) imparts to us His Holy Spirit to dwell within us, and when we willfully yield to Him in us, we manifest Him as He wills us to.

8. Heart Circumcision And Soul Release

But, although He imparts His Holy Spirit to us fully at regeneration, we (our self, our soul's functioning) must *yield* to Him indwelling in simple dependence and obedience. And we must yield beyond our soul's ability to interfere. That requires a *release* of our soul, an immersion of our center-of-self, into that indwelling Holy Spirit. That release, that immersion of self, is the essence of the Baptism into the Holy Spirit.

A type used in the Bible for this soul release is "heart circumcision". Circumcision involved a cutting or an inscribing of the "foreskin" of the male organ of dispersal of the seed of life (Leviticus 1:12 & 3:4, etc.). The knife of Hebrews 4:12 is the word of God as wielded by our High Priest Christ Jesus, as He inscribes the soul's grip over our human spirit. Our human spirit is the male organ that He uses to disperse the seed of eternal life: both RWCh and Pneuma ("spirit") are words of masculine gender in the Hebrew and Greek (in contrast to the feminine gender used for the words for soul and flesh); and the human spirit is our seat of God-consciousness.

Note the following Scriptures on this:

Deuteronomy 30:6: "... God will circumcise your heart and the heart of your descendants, to love the Lord yourGod with all your heart and with all your soul, that you may live."

Jeremiah 4:4: "Circumcise yourselves to the Lord, and take away the foreskins of your hearts ...."

Romans 2:28-29: "For he is not a Jew who is one outwardly, nor is circumcision that which is outward in the flesh; but he is a Jew who is one inwardly; and circumcision is that of the heart, in the Spirit not in the letter, whose praise is not from men but from God."

Romans 4:11: "... the sign of circumcision, a seal of the righteousness of the faith which he had while still uncircumcised ...."

Romans 15:8: "... Jesus Christ has become a servant to the circumcision for the truth of God, to confirm the promises made to the fathers."

Philippians 3:3: "We are the circumcision, who worship God in the Spirit, rejoice in Christ Jesus, and have no confidence in the flesh."

Colossians 2:11: "In Him [Christ] you were also circumcised with the circumcision made without hands, by putting off the body of sins of the flesh, by the circumcision of Christ."

In the Old Testament history of the Israelites, there were *two* circumcisions: the circumcision of the covenant of Passover (Genesis 17:4-16 and Exodus 12:43-48); and that of embarking on conquering the promised land (Joshua 5:2-7). The first, associated with deliverance, typifies regeneration, when through our human spirit we become in *communication* with God and *learn of* Him. The second, associated with the start of a *walk* in the power of the presence of God, typifies our being "filled" with the Holy Spirit.

Before this second circumcision of our heart, the human spirit (although filled with the Holy Spirit and containing Him and the righteousness of God) is totally impotent as long as we, our self, our soul, *dominates* that spiritual organ. Christ chooses to not override our will; He *allows* our soul to dominate. But when *we choose* to yield and to release our self (our soul) unto Him, *then* He allows His Holy Spirit to function through our behaviour and attitudes (to manifest Himself) as He wills. We then become people of the true circumcision, the true children of the Abrahamic promise, the true Israel, "man in relationship with God." Our "promised land" of Romans Chapter 8 can then become a reality; we can then enter in and possess it step-by-step. But only when, though the Baptism into the Holy Spirit, we take a plunge totally beyond our selves into Him and His marvelous Person!

9. Cutting Asunder The Soul-Spirit Barrier

What do we mean by the necessity of our soul being *released* unto the Holy Spirit of Christ Jesus in a Baptism into the Holy Spirit? Hebrews 4:12 introduces us to that necessity: in a context of contrasting our *resting* in God *vs* our hearts becoming *hardened*, the author says "... the word of God is living and efficient, like a two-edged sword but sharper, that penetrates unto dividing the soul-spirit barrier, like separating bone from marrow, in discerning among the thoughts and intents of the heart" (Sherrerd's translation). The Greek word used here for "word" is Logos or "content" or "absoluteness" of God's truths: the indwelling presence of the Holy Spirit of Christ Jesus.

Note this comparison. Marrow is the soft pithy part inside a bone. It reproduces the red corpuscles, which carry oxygen (that is the main life-sustaining substance) to all cells of the body and remove the waste (byproducts of life functions). The bone is the outer hard structure, that encases, protects and hides the marrow.

This bone-marrow relationship is used as an example of the barrier in our soul-spirit relationship. In the natural, our soul (mind, emotions, will, and self-consciousness) fully controls and dominates our behaviour. Christ, through the Holy Spirit through our human spirit, ever seeks to disperse eternal life though us to others. But this soul-dominance, this soul-spirit barrier, hinders it; and that dominance, that barrier must be shattered. The idea is that in the bone structure, the hard outer crust (typifying the human soul) that *protects* the marrow (typifying the human spirit) from being exposed, also *hinders* it and must be broken. Our soul (especially our *thought* patterns and our *will*) has to yield to what Christ through His Holy Spirit is seeking to do through us. This *releasing*, this breaking of the soul's dominance, is the essence of the Baptism into the Holy Spirit.

This releasing must involve spiritual *phenomena* that the soul cannot dominate (that the mind cannot understand, and is outside our emotions) but which is recognized as real and Christ-centered. It involves a walk with and dependence upon the **Person** of Christ Jesus, *beyond* what our *soul* can apprehend. That is one reason (not the main reason, but one of several) why *tongues* is of value: because: (1) our soul (self, mind) cannot *understand* either what's being said nor the mechanism; (2) it by itself is unemotional; (3) but it is ***Christ***-oriented; and (4) it is phenomenologically *real* and verifiable at our will. The fact that we can't understand it is an important aspect of it. It forces us to *trust* in Jesus *beyond* our understandings or feelings *about* Him. Otherwise we are *limiting* Christ to our understandings and feelings; that would be a severe restricting of Christ working through us.

What happens to us in the Baptism into the Holy Spirit, then, is basically a *releasing* of He Who is in us (His Holy Spirit in our human spirit) to manifest Himself though us (our soul). Why do we call this Baptism a "releasing" when the word "baptism" is Greek for "immersion"? The Baptism into the Holy Spirit is a submerging of our human *soul* unto control of the Holy Spirit. The human soul (self-consciousness, hence "me") is *immersed* into the Holy Spirit, as He is released from my human spirit when my soul-spirit barrier is broken. It is our soul, our *self*-nature, that is immersed; our spirit had already been immersed into the Holy Spirit upon our regeneration. Since our soul is the means of *expressing* the spirit, our soul must be *released* unto Him in order for God's power and physical Presence to flow through and become manifest by us.

10. Unto The Kingdom Of God

God's direct goal of our redemption is that in the throne of my heart, king *self* must abdicate to King Jesus. But as long as my *soul* can apprehend my walk with Jesus, king self reigns in actuality. Hence, my walk with Jesus must be beyond my reason and feelings, yet real and verifiable (and, of course, Biblical).

John the Baptist and Jesus both preached that "the Kingdom of God can at last be grasped by you" (i.e., is "at hand"). The Israelites had been waiting, for a few hundred years, for the Kingdom to be established. But they misunderstood it. The Kingdom of God is first and foremost the Kingship/Lordship of Christ Jesus. It is a personal relationship of mutual servanthood: we serve Him by total obedience and dependence (faith); He in turn serves us by providing us with all the peace and well-being of economic, social and political harmony. We can acquire *that* now in the Spirit, at least partially, through repentance and submission to Him. It is for the Kingdom as a world-wide *physical* thing that we wait these 1970 and more years.

What *we* are to do is *repent* (change our ways of thinking). Becoming born-again (acquiring the ability to know God and Christ) is a first consequence of our repenting, and is an obvious prerequisite of us living under the Kingship/Lordship of Christ in our lives. Yielding to the actual *control* of the Holy Spirit of Christ Jesus in us, *via* the Baptism into the Holy Spirit and a subsequent walk in His Spirit, is the subsequent prerequisite for us to *live* in (and hence experience the promised *power* and other blessings of) the Kingdom of God.

It is this *power* that eludes so many believers who have received the Baptism into the Holy Spirit or have sought it in vain for so long. Why? Because our yielding to Him is *incomplete*. Our soul still retains some of its tenacious grip over our spirit; we still insist upon *understanding* what we're getting into, or upon *seeing* the object of our trust and *proof* of His trustworthiness, or upon *feeling* His presence. We live in *mixture:* some manifestations of His presence as we *partially* yield to Him in some things yet with also much flesh and soulishness, hesitation and doubt.

When Jesus told the disciples to wait in Jerusalem, He did not command them to wait for some physical manifestation such as speaking in tongues or flames of fire or mighty rushing wind; rather, it was that they should wait until they were imbued with *power* from God. We must clear the clutter of self from our heart, and then wait; and wait beyond self, beyond feelings, beyond our intense urge to be doing and accomplishing something in the mean-time. This waiting was not passive: they met in unity and prayer for several days in the upper room, and then went to Solomon's Portico of the temple at the appointed time of the Feast of First Fruits, where the Holy Spirit actually came. And there, being public, that brought ridicule (i.e., "they're drunk", etc.). This is the very death of self, the very antithesis of our soul's dominance. But it brought the *power* of the presence of God.

11. Forgiveness Unto Regeneration *vs* Purity By Fire

1 Peter 3:21 tells us that Baptism (into the Holy Spirit), corresponding in type to God's salvation of Noah and His family in His ark, does not involve removal of dirt from the flesh.

Rather, it involves an appeal to God for a good conscience, a godly life style, a righteous walk in the world: unto full resurrection, of which His indwelling presence is an "earnest" or a "down payment" or an "advance foretaste" (Ephesians 1:14 and 2 Corinthians 1:22 & 5:5).

But as we go from regeneration unto power, then we meet the requirement of *purity*. Since the Holy Spirit is now God's standard of righteousness for our behaviour and attitudes, inscribed on our hearts (rather than law on stone tablets or paper), we must yield to that *righteousness* as we yield to His *power*. Yes, we are "saved"; yes, we are forgiven; yes, our redemption is secure. But as we talk to Him asking for the power of His presence and glory in our lives; **then** at that point He talks to *us* asking for purity in our lives:

> (1) purity in our desires and *motives*, for He alone is worthy of our desires, to be desired above all else;

> (2) purity in our *thoughts*, for our thoughts radiate much power, evil thoughts unto evil, and good thoughts unto good;

> (3) purity from bondage to *flesh*, for no flesh can be subject to His Kingship;

> (4) purity in our *worship* and our choice of objects of worship, for He is a jealous God, and He would have us worship no other gods or obsessions before Him;

> (5) purity in our *ethics* and *morals*; and

(6) purity in our *life style*.

The symbol of God's subsequent dealings in our lives to work purity into us, is *fire*. In the six passages of Scripture in which John the Baptist prophesied of Christ Baptizing into the Holy Spirit, he also said "...Baptizing you in ... *fire*."

God's fire does not speak of *destruction*, but of *cleansing:* of a complete removal from us of all that is not of Him, of not depending upon Him alone, of not yielding to His Will alone (i.e., wood, hay, stubble and chaff: 1 Corinthians 3:12-15 and Matthew 3:12 & Luke 3:17).

Fire denotes God's purifying us, removing the dross and self-will in the subsequent adjusting process He puts us through. In the Old Testament type of Pentecost, Moses encountered God's *fire* on Mt. Sinai. The three Hebrew children (Daniel 3:23-28) went through a Baptism in fire in order to experience the *physical* experiential power of the presence of Christ.

How does the Holy Spirit actually cleanse us through fire? What actually happens in our lives? It requires an adjusting *process*, because the adjusting of our thought patterns that He has to put us through is very involved. It's not that we are deliberately, willfully, calculatingly rebelling against the Lord Christ Jesus; it's just that He knows that our thought patterns have to be changed, that our nature has to be cleansed, that our own self and our own ideas must be crucified. Yet, for our sake and because of His love for us, He must do it in a way that does not destroy, but edifies, us. So, subsequently to our being Baptized into the Holy Spirit He confronts us with situations where there's no way out except for us to cry unto Him for help. He *does* help us, and as He does, we learn not to depend upon our own ideas and thinking and abilities, but upon Him and upon Him alone. We learn this step-by-step, first in little things, and eventually in matters of our very survival.

We study in depth two types of this adjusting process. We studied the process, *via* deep repentance, of inner heart healing from self-seeking and self-protecting goals, strategies and behavior patterns, in Chapters 5 through 10 of Volume I[1] of this series. In Chapter 10 later in this volume we introduce how He matures us through soul afflictions, i.e., by what we call "emptying cycles" of loss-struggle-surrender-revisitation-consummation.

End Notes: Chapter Six

[1] Sherrerd, Chris S. *The Christian Marriage - A Six-Fold Covenant Of Love-Motivated Servanthood,* Volume I of the series "Where Do You Fit In? Practical Commitments In The Body Of Christ" (Shippensburg, PA: Treasure House, Destiny Image Publishing Group, 1994). Copyright © 1994 by Shulemite Christian Crusade.

Chapter Seven

The Experience Of The Baptism Into The Holy Spirit

Most of our living in the purity and power and presence and glory of Christ only *begins* upon our being Baptized into the Holy Spirit, and it *develops* during our subsequent walk in him and in the wilderness adjusting process He then subjects us to. But how do we know when the *initial* step of the Baptism actually takes place?

1. First We Must Be Born Again

Many Bible scholars, aware of the "in-abiding" or indwelling of the Holy Spirit in our human *spirit* upon regeneration, find it quite controversial to talk of the Baptism into the Holy Spirit as a separate, distinct "crisis experience" or "work of grace" in a believer's life. Regeneration is indeed a "crisis experience" to which they personally testify, but Holy Spirit Baptism is beyond the experiential knowledge of many. What is the distinction between them with respect to our inner consciousness of God?

Regeneration enables us to mentally grasp the existence and word of God as truth. We knowingly become the immature children of God, although immature at first. We have an inner consciousness of *being forgiven*, accepted, appointed inheritors of eternal life, and of living in covenant relationship with God the Father through the shed Blood of Christ Jesus. Because we are logical and emotional people, we respond by being "religious" Christians, with a definite social life style commensurate therewith. We say that we *have* the light of the Gospel, and indeed we do.

Did that acquisition require a definite "crisis experience", a specific "conversion experience" to which we could point a specific time and place? Not necessarily! Each of us has a different testimony of it. In my personal experience, because I lacked the Biblical understanding about being "born again", I had actually been regenerated several years before I knew it as such. The Scriptures only require that we truly testify that it is an *accomplished* fact, even if we cannot pinpoint the exact time of acquisition. Yet most of us require a *specific* starting point for a new consciousness. So we rightfully stress that regeneration is a specific "crisis experience" for the *majority* of believers.

2. The Experience Of The Baptism Into The Holy Spirit

But on the other hand, the Baptism into the Holy Spirit involves a far more dramatic change in our inner consciousness of God than does regeneration! Here, it is not only a matter of having a *mental grasp* of God's word, but also a matter of a life *lived* spontaneously as part of it. Jesus is no longer only an *historical* figure who purchased our salvation *via* His shed Blood; He is now my *vivid "companion"*. The Holy Spirit is no longer a remote voice or source of guidance to us when we listen; He has replaced *us* at (and as) the core and center of our being. He does not *give* us light; rather He *is* that light in us.

This level of consciousness, regardless of what we call it and regardless of what outer signs that may or may not accompany it, is dramatically different from the mere truth-level of our awareness of Him. No step of our entry into this new dimension can possibly escape our awareness as a distinct event or experience or point of departure. How this takes place we briefly discuss in subsequent paragraphs. But such an *experiential* union with God so permanently affects our consciousness and our walk with Him, that it most certainly *does* involve a definite "crisis experience".

The difference between these two levels of our inner consciousness of God through Christ Jesus has been compared to such contrasts as dew *vs* rain, or drinking *vs* swimming in water, or a vessel containing a few drops of a precious fluid *vs* being filled to overflowing. But bear in mind that these comparisons refer not to the *quantity* or measure of the Holy Spirit in us (He is a Person, and we obtain *all* of Him upon regeneration); but rather to the extent or measure to which we allow Him to be in our *consciousness*, the extent or measure to which our self (soul) *yields* to Him and deliberately allows Him to live His life through us. Only in this sense is the Baptism into the Holy Spirit a new "filling". The Greek word translated "filled" (i.e., with the Holy Spirit) means us being under His *control*. The command given to us (Ephesians 5:18) is not that we *be* filled, but that we "continuously *be being* filled", i.e., that we *continue* to allow Him to flood our soul.

Our *holiness* depends on that, for the true secret of deliverance from sin and self is to be filled with God and to have Him fully run our lives. The way to get out of darkness is not to rebuke and cast out the darkness but rather to turn on the light. Our ability to *distinguish* truth from error is at stake, for only He indwelling is wisdom and knowledge and truth and can "properly divide and interpret the word of God" (2 Timothy 2:15). Our service *and testimony* requires His full control, for otherwise it is only us and *our* own righteousness, and in His sight we are but "filthy rags" (Isaiah 64:6 and Titus 3:5).

One particular form of confusion between these two "crisis" experiences was almost unique to the "Charismatic Movement": mistaking the born-again experience for the Baptism into the Holy Spirit. This can occur in cases where the Charismata has penetrated traditional churches where the need for being born-again had not been taught. People who had always believed in God and have been faithful to their Church for years, but now sought Jesus in a new dimension, were exposed to teachings on the Baptism into the Holy Spirit through tapes, books and home prayer meetings of the "Charismatic Movement". Jesus met them marvelously at their needs, and they became "born-again". But because they had always "believed", they assumed they were born-again all along and that this new experience was the Baptism into the Holy Spirit, albeit without "tongues". This misunderstanding was devastating to those persons involved, because in subsequent months without the power and stability in Christ that they were expecting from the Baptism, they became disillusioned and stopped seeking further. "Is that *all* there is to it?" The result was much heartache.

3. A Person, *Not* An "Experience"

The *experience* of the Baptism into the Holy Spirit is not that of a physical or emotional event (though it is *accompanied* by such, often with outward signs); it is rather an increase in our *awareness* of a Person and a "walking-with" relationship with Him. That Person, of course, is Christ Jesus, since the function of the Holy Spirit is to reveal and manifest Christ Jesus to us and through us unto the world. Although it is theologically, or technically, the Holy Spirit Who dwells in us, we say it is Christ Jesus in us, because as far as our consciousness is concerned, it is the reality of Christ with which we are saturated. So, what we are most conscious of during the Baptism into the Holy Spirit is not the function of the working of the Holy Spirit *per se*, but the working of Christ Jesus in us. He uses the Holy Spirit, but it is the reality of Jesus that is flowing upon us and through us.

Until I received the Baptism into the Holy Spirit, I believed *in* (i.e., *about*) Jesus; I lived in a continuous real or subjective or emotional experiencing of Him, whereby or wherein I knew of His existence, His reality, and His forgiveness of my sins. But it wasn't until then that I had a *vivid awareness* of Him as a personal Presence in my life.

So frequently believers are encouraged to receive the Baptism into the Holy Spirit as an experience, or as an ability to speak in tongues, and are often frustrated. I assert that such practices, though common throughout "Charismatic" and Pentecostal circles, give the wrong emphasis and actually often do more to *hinder* than to help true seekers in flowing with Him in this new dimension.

In October of 1967 I was so hungry for the Baptism into the Holy Spirit, I would have given anything for it. One night I went to a national convention of the FBGMFI in New York City, and I was *determined* to receive it. Through the meeting I just waited for them to call us into a little room for ministry. But when we finally went into that side room to receive, I just sat there, while other people about me were receiving the Baptism and praising in new tongues. It didn't turn me off: I wanted it, I believed totally in it; but I didn't receive it. I was so deflated. A month later, the Lord told me "the trouble was, you were seeking an *experience;* you should seek *Me"*.

Receiving the Baptism into the Holy Spirit, and also growing in it, involves not "experiencing" something *per se,* but rather earnestly seeking to allow the Holy Spirit of Christ Jesus, Who already indwells our human spirit since regeneration, to *control* our actions, even our very lives.

The key to both our entering into it, and growing in it, is *worship:* that is, our "losing ourselves in His presence"; and the greatest hindrance to both our entering it and growing in it can be *anxiety*, that is, our earnest desires to receive a blessing and our fears that we won't. Again, we get out of darkness by simply turning on the light. Since the very essence of the Baptism into the Holy Spirit is a new dimension of knowing King Christ Jesus, it is only by allowing Him to indeed become central in our thoughts and attentions that we can *walk* in that new dimension.

Since that new dimension involves death of our self, any and all *seeking* on our part to receive or experience something, or to be able to *do* something, or to still our fears that we not be full citizens of the Kingdom of God if we don't thus receive, merely concentrate our attention on (and encourage) that very *self* that must be set aside. Hence, such attentions on self *hinder* us from that receiving or entering. It is very rare, indeed, that a seeker can receive under such emphasis. The Baptism into the Holy Spirit is not a matter of "altar call emotionalism", but a decisive determination on our part that Christ Jesus, Himself, truly be Lord of our entire beings. Granted, however, such practices may be warranted in cases where laying on of hands is necessary to assist a seeker in his faith and his yielding to Christ Jesus.

4. That We *Know* Him

It *is* possible *in this life* to know Christ indwelling with *certainty*. Yes! That is the by far most significant role of His indwelling Holy Spirit in our lives!

Lloyd-Jones[1] points out in a careful and thorough exegesis on the subject, that that is the ***primary purpose and essence***, above all else, of our being Baptized into the Holy Spirit by our Lord Christ Jesus. Here are several excerpts of Lloyd-Jones on this emphasis[2]:

> "... a deeper knowledge of and relationship with Jesus Christ [indwelling] was at the heart of the baptism with the [Holy] Spirit.
>
> "... one of the main effects and results of the baptism with the Holy Spirit is to give us an unusual ***assurance*** of our salvation....
>
> "The thing that was so obvious about the New Testament Christians, as seen in Acts 2 or anywhere

else, was their spirit of joy and of happiness and assurance, their confidence; they were so certain, that they were ready to be thrown to the lions in the arena or [otherwise] put to death. And this has always characterized every great period of reformation and revival in the history of the church.

"... the primary purpose and function of the baptism with the [Holy] Spirit is beyond any question to enable us to be witnesses to the Lord Jesus Christ and to His great salvation.

"... the personal, subjective, experimental consciousness of the individual. What is it that inevitably happens when one is baptized by the Lord Jesus Christ with the Holy Spirit? Well, first and foremost I think we must put this - a sense of the glory of God, an unusual sense of the *presence* of God. ... What the Holy Spirit does is make *real* to us the things which we have believed by faith, the things of which we have had but a kind of indirect certainty only. The Holy Spirit makes these things *immediately real*.

"... This is what happens when a man is baptized with the Holy Spirit - this immediacy. This is not reason, or faith; but action taking place upon us and to us. It is a manifestation, God - Father, Son, and Holy Spirit - making themselves real to us and living in our very experiences.

"Another pronounced characteristic that always accompanies it is an assurance of the *love* of God to us in Jesus Christ. This is most important and remarkable.

> On the one hand you have such a conception of the glory and the greatness and the majesty of God, and of your own vileness and filthiness and foulness and unworthiness. ... [But] ... at the same time you have an overwhelming knowledge given to you of God's love to you in our Lord and Savior Jesus Christ. ... This is the greatest and most essential characteristic of the baptism with the [Holy] Spirit. He makes us witnesses because of our assurance."

This was indeed this author's personal experience with the Baptism into the Holy Spirit: not tongues (though I indeed was a "gusher"), not gifts, and certainly not holiness; but an ***absolute certainty of the reality and presence of our Lord Christ Jesus!***

We do our fellow Christians a great disservice by emphasizing all these "peripherals" of the Baptism. Perhaps that is why the vast majority of those who claim to have been Spirit baptized in the Pentecostal and Charismatic movements still lacked in holiness and power and discernment: their focus was on "things" more than on Him. It is not an "experience" we seek and obtain, nor "abilities"; it is a ***person!*** To ***know Him***, experientially, and with ***certainty.*** For only through that can we be His witnesses, His servants, His vessels.

5. Some External Evidence

What ***should be*** the characteristics of a Holy Spirit Baptized believer that are recognizable to others? Since the real essence of the Baptism into the Holy Spirit is a vivid awareness of and a new dimension of fellowship with the ***Person*** of Christ Jesus, the characteristics that ***always*** mark a

Holy Spirit Baptized believer are *internal and subjective.* Here are a few ways in which that new reality should always be manifest in *outward behaviour:*

(1) A deep hunger for God's word, and a perpetual tendency to search the Scriptures and to learn the precepts of God.

(2) Gladness and thanksgiving in the heart, not only for Christ's salvation, but for He Himself. This gladness is not dependent upon nor related to external circumstances, that are often adverse.

(3) Love, not merely the Philea or "common-interest" love so prevalent in most Christian groups with like-minded believers, but a deep and constant concern and compassion for others, particularly for those who are yet unsaved and for those Christians who have not yet received the Baptism. The closer we actually get to Jesus, the *less* we view ourselves and the more we desire to exalt others.

(4) An unquenchable desire to be used by God, and to apprehend and walk in His Will for our lives.

(5) A willingness to submit to the Body of Christ and to be rightly related to one another as He directs.

6. What Does It Mean To Be *"Filled"* With The Holy Spirit?

An expression that is widely used throughout traditional Pentecostal Christian circles to refer to the Baptism into the Holy Spirit is that of "being *filled* of the Holy Spirit".

The Baptism into the Holy Spirit is *not*, Biblically, a "filling" in the sense of *initially* containing Him. Upon *regeneration* we receive all we can of the Holy Spirit, because He is a Person and can't be divided (although He divides His various *manifestations* among us severally as He wills).

The misunderstanding that being "filled" means *receiving* Him initially, comes from an inaccurate translation of the Greek in Luke 1:15, Acts 2:4, 4:8, 4:31, 9:17 & 13:9 and Ephesians 5:18. In these passages, the Greek word translated "filled" is Pletho, that means "to be filled *mentally"* or "to be under the full influence or control of". Its fuller root meaning is "to **saturate**", "to take possession of", or "to fulfill". Ephesians 5:18 uses the related Greek word Pleroo, that means "to cause to abound" or "to furnish liberally". It does not imply an *initial* indwelling of the Holy Spirit, but rather our yielding to the full *control* of He Who (already) indwells us, that He abound in or saturate our seat-of-self (soul)!

A further common misinterpretation of the Greek in the Ephesians reference has also caused much confusion. It is a matter of the tense used. Ephesians 5:18 uses a continuing or imperfect present tense in the Greek, and is more accurately translated "... be continuously *being* filled". The context of Ephesians 5:18 is not referring to the initial Baptism into the Holy Spirit, but rather to our *walk* after the Baptism. It means that our subsequent walk should be one of a constant *flowing* under the *control* of Christ Jesus *via* His Holy Spirit in us. A parallel passage on this is 2 Timothy 1:6-7, wherein Paul advises Timothy to keep the life-flowing work of the Holy Spirit in him "rekindled" or "stirred up" as the embers of a slow fire.

Once again we emphasize that the Baptism into the Holy Spirit is the *beginning* of a *process* wherein we learn to give the indwelling Holy Spirit of Christ Jesus increasing *control* over our lives as He Wills.

7. "Peace Offering": QRBN Of ShLM

Yet another important set of truths on the Baptism into the Holy Spirit is found in the "Law of Offerings" in Leviticus Chapters 1 through 9, particularly in Chapter 3. We must look carefully at some of the original Hebrew words here, since the English words "offering" and "sacrifice" are among the most misleading and understated translations in our modern versions of the Bible. Many different types of "offerings" are described, with important distinctions between them that are utterly lost in the English.

We start with Leviticus 1:2: "When any man of you brings an *offering* to the Lord...." The Hebrew word for "offering" here is QRBN, that has the basic meaning, not of what we give up or sacrifice, but rather of something we do to improve our personal *relationship* with another person (in this case with God).

Leviticus Chapters 1 through 9 speak to those who desire to improve their personal relationship with God. We are not *commanded* to do this out of duty; rather, God wants and waits for us to *desire* and *seek* Him, before He will work in our lives. For those who *do* seek to QRBN God, He states in Leviticus Chapters 1 through 9 several things we can do that He will consider acceptable in His sight. Chapter 1 describes the ILH or "ascending" offering (mistranslated "burnt" offering). This typifies our offering Christ crucified as our substitute to pay the death penalty for our sins, thus improving our personal relationship with God from *zero* (Romans 3:23 & 6:23 and Ephesians 2:1-3), to a *covenant* relationship of regeneration. Chapter 2 then describes our MNChH or "grain" or "meat" offering, and typifies both Christ's completed work at Calvary, and *our* service *for* God as part of the Body of Christ on Earth, and of His preparation of us for that service.

Leviticus Chapters 3 and 7 then describe the ShLM or "wholeness" offering (mistranslated "peace" offering), and its ThWDH or "thanksgiving" variation. This is an offering wherein *we*, our self or soul-life, is the offering (Leviticus 3:2). It typifies our yielding to the Holy Spirit of Christ Jesus indwelling, which begins upon our Baptism into the Holy Spirit. Chapters 4 and 5 then describe the ChTAhH or *"sin nature"* offering and the AhShM or "transgression against our neighbor" offering, that typify God's subsequent dealings in our lives (that are *impossible* for any of us to endure until after we "offer" our ShLM), those dealings being to bridge the holiness gap between He and us, and through which we acquire His holiness and righteousness fully assimilated in us: Not us, but He living *fully* through us (Galatians 2:20).

These types are a subject of separate study, and we only mention them here in passing. Nevertheless, the Baptism into the Holy Spirit is in no way the *end* goal for us, nor even any particular blessing *per se*, but is rather a necessary stage of our yielding to Him, to *enable* us to endure the adjusting process that God subsequently puts us through. It is that subsequent *adjusting process* (with "fire") that brings us unto the *power* of the presence and glory of Christ in our lives.

8. Necessity And Commitment, Not Option Nor Luxury

Although we have the free will to reject this Baptism into the Holy Spirit and its plunge into Him, and we would probably still "make it to Heaven" if we don't, nevertheless God desires us to seek and want Him. To not earnestly *seek* Him is to *reject* Him. To think "If it is His will for me to receive this Baptism, then OK" but to not intensely *desire* Him, is to guarantee (for *your* sake) that He will *not* Baptize you into the Holy Spirit. It *is* His will for you, but only if you desire it "with white-hot passion": "earnestly desire" (Greek Zeloo) in 1 Corinthians 14:1 means "desire with fervent heat".

But *if* we seek to have His power and presence and glory in our lives, then this is *not* an option nor a luxury, but a necessity. And it is a life-long commitment, not something we enter into lightly nor only temporarily on a trial-and-error basis. For it is the beginning of a purging *process* whereupon we learn to walk in Him, love one another, and manifest His glory on Earth. This requires us encountering both the *grace* and the *awesomeness* of God. Without His grace, we cannot encounter His awesomeness, or we will be destroyed by It! But it is the power of His love alone that bears fruit.

Furthermore, the power of His presence will increasingly be an utter necessity for our very *physical* survival in the days to come as we enter the "Mountain Pass" days (See Volume VI[3] of this series). We will require *maturity* in our walk with Jesus in order to *endure* the days to come and to fulfill *His* purposes for our lives.

9. Point Of No Return

One very sobering aspect of the Baptism into the Holy Spirit, and of which we should "count the cost" (Luke 14:28-30) before seeking it, is that it is a "point of no return" in the life of a Christian. The "point of no return" is a real concern to trans-oceanic aircraft flights; it is the point where you know

The Experience Of The Baptism Into Holy Spirit

you don't have enough fuel to get back to where you just started from, and so you have to count on having enough fuel to get to where you're going. Once we receive the Baptism into the Holy Spirit, we *must* go on unto *intimacy* with Christ indwelling, or we will be destroyed by either deception or atrophy. For we will have "too much of Jesus to ever be satisfied with this world", even if we still have "too much of this world to fully apprehend Jesus". At that point, we're at a point of no return. When we receive the Baptism into the Holy Spirit, we *must* continue on in Jesus, or we'll be *worse* off than before.

There is no other time in a believer's life when we are more vulnerable to spiritual deception, and in more need of in-depth Bible teachings, than the moment we have received the Baptism into the Holy Spirit. Once we receive the Baptism, we are consciously opened up to Spiritual influences. Unless we are mature at that point in our mental or doctrinal understanding of the Scriptural teachings, *or* under firm discipline of a mature Body of Christ fellowship, we are open to one of two routes: either falling ultimately into spiritual deception; or falling back into worldliness (that will be even more unpleasant than it was before). This is why it is usually *unwise* for us to be flippant in seeking the Baptism, or to urge young children to seek it.

Why is it so easy for a Holy Spirit Baptized believer to be deceived? Hear this: in the *natural* it is virtually *humanly* impossible for any of us to distinguish the difference between the Holy Spirit speaking to us and satanic spirits speaking to us. It is only through a conscious and deliberate dependence, first of all upon the written word of God, and then upon the Lord Christ Jesus, that we have assurance of being kept from being deceived. He is faithful and will not allow those who depend upon Him to be deceived (1 Corinthians 1:8-9 & 10:13; 1 Thessalonians 5:23-24; and 2 Thessalonians 3:3); so we *do* have assurance that if we consciously depend upon Him, we will be kept from destruction. But only through that route.

But if we lose our awareness of the Person of Christ Jesus, and we're only conscious of "God" or the "Holy Spirit" separated from a conscious awareness of the Person of Christ Jesus, we can be led down into deception. Many mature Holy Spirit Baptized believers have been led astray by satan literally appearing to them as an "angel of light" (2 Corinthians 11:14-15). We need to know the Bible; we need the Body of Christ; we need one another to protect each other from this and to encourage one another to keep our thoughts concentrated onto the Person of Christ Jesus. This is a very important point that most of us are not aware of. For this reason, I do not believe it is ever wise to ***worship*** the ***Holy Spirit*** or to pray to Him; but keep the Person of ***Christ Jesus*** foremost in our mind when we're praying and praising and worshiping, and also as we meditate on God's word.

10. Not Instant Maturity

Many believers, when encountering the Baptism into the Holy Spirit either in others or in their own lives, become shocked when they realize that it has ***not*** effected complete sanctification or perfection in the person's life. There are basically two reasons for that: first, it is not intended to; and secondly, we never enter into its fullness all at once.

The Experience Of The Baptism Into Holy Spirit

What does the *full* experiential appropriation of the Baptism into the Holy Spirit entail in our lives? We now discuss some aspects that it is *not* but that are commonly associated with it. We then discuss what it *should* entail in its Biblical fullness, and how we can proceed from our present incompleteness to that fullness.

Kids *vs* Grown-Ups

One of the many Biblical descriptions of us Christians is "children of God" or "members of the family of God". The New Testament Greek word Teknon (and the Old Testament Hebrew word BN) mean any son, any descendant of the father; these words are frequently used not only genealogically but also to denote *immaturity*. This is distinct from the Greek and Hebrew words Uios and BR, respectively, which mean a son *matured* and in a position of responsibility.

As with children in the natural, we are expected to grow up. And growing up involves going through several stages of maturing over time: for example, the nursing stage, the toddler stage, the pre-school years, grammar school years, junior and senior high school adolescence stages, college years, young adulthood, middle age, and elderly.

The Bible speaks in many places and in many ways of the corresponding maturing process of Christians. And much has been written on this, variously denoted by 3, 4, 5, 6, 12, 15 or even 40 "stages", depending on the point of view one takes of Christian maturing. Each of these Biblical points of view is valid and gives its unique understanding of how our personal relationships with Christ Jesus are to unfold and develop. We mention these here to point out that in all points of view, the

Baptism into the Holy Spirit is of an *early* stage or level, and it is far from being the end goal or the mark of a *mature* Christian.

An example is the 12-stage model of His process of adjusting us *corporately,* that we study in detail in Volume III[4] of this series. Our Lord Christ Jesus desires to subject His *willing* Children through to fully mature them, are: (1) Children of the Blood Covenant; (2) Sheepfold; (3) Fishers of men; (4) Wineskins; (5) Ore in the refiner's fire; (6) Children of Heart Circumcision; (7) Body of Christ; (8) Branches of the Vine; (9) Holy Priesthood; (10) Army of God; (11) Pilgrims; and (12) The Lord's Fiancee. In this context, the Baptism into the Holy Spirit is at level 4, with levels 5 through 8 being the main subsequent levels of adjusting wherein we grow in the manifestations of the Holy Spirit in us, and in the outpouring of the *love* of God through us to others.

Not Yet Maturity For Ministry

A common misunderstanding about the Baptism into the Holy Spirit is a widespread expectation that it *instantly* prepares us for ministry. The disciples' experiences in Acts 2 is the usual basis for that assumption. But not so! It does *not,* by itself, prepare us for the ministries to which we associate the power of Christ through His Holy Spirit. The Baptism into the Holy Spirit does involve power in some ways, but Spirit-empowered ministries involve other things as well.

In actual practice, we grow in empowered ministries *as* we *grow* in maturity in faith. When we receive the Baptism into the Holy Spirit, we *do* usually enter into some form of power ministry almost immediately; it is very specifically directed by

The Experience Of The Baptism Into Holy Spirit 211

the sovereignty of God. But at that point we are far from the fulness of it, nor are we stable in what we have. To become settled and stable therein, we are also brought through subsequent wilderness trials (1 Peter 5:10).

Let us briefly study Jesus' promise to the disciples in Acts 1:8. "But ye shall receive power when the Holy Spirit is come upon you, and ye shall be My witnesses, both in Jerusalem and in all of Judea and Samaria and even unto the remotest parts of the Earth." At first reading this verse gives one the impression that the moment we receive the Baptism into the Holy Spirit, we're going to have all the power we need to do all the ministering the Lord's going to send us into. But take a closer look. There is a *time sequence* here. This passage has an inverted sentence structure, but the time sequence is: (1) when the Holy Spirit is come upon us ("has come", past tense, although it's the second in order because of the inverted sentence structure); (2) you shall receive power ("shall receive", future tense, the second step although the first listed); and (3) you shall be His witnesses ("shall be", future tense, the third step). Luke throughout the Book of Acts emphasizes the power of witnessing, so it's understandable that Luke would write it in just this way, glossing over the importance of the time sequence.

But there's much that must normally take place in an individual believer's life between the first and second steps. It is not the Baptism into the Holy Spirit *per se* that matures us for ministry or for God's will for our lives; rather, it is the subsequent "wilderness" experiences that prepare us. God's adjusting process in our lives is indicated in such Scripture passages as Matthew 4:1-11, Mark 1:12-13, & Luke 4:1-13; Romans 5:3-4; and Hebrews 12:5-11). They prepare us by refining and strengthening our faith. The Baptism into the Holy Spirit is to enable us to *endure* those "wilderness" experiences and to *respond* to them *positively* rather than with bitterness. Although the disciples experienced power for specific ministry *immediately* in Acts 2, they went through many wilderness trials: first during the three and one-half years with Jesus, then during the 50 days preceding Pentecost, and finally during the several years following it. Indeed they required many dealings in their individual lives, including a severe doctrinal controversy (Acts Chapter 15), before they left Jerusalem to obey the "great commandment" of Mark 16:15-20.

What is faith? Why must it be refined and strengthened? We discussed this in Chapter 2 earlier in this volume. Faith is essentially our "seeing" Christ in the Spirit and then our *inner response* to Him, that response on our part being a yielding which involves both dynamic dependence upon Christ Jesus in the "now", and sensitive obedience to His Will. Our learning to be willing to *yield* to His Will is typified by: (1) heart circumcision as we discussed above; (2) wheat being ground into fine flour in the crucible of testings; and (3) clay being kneaded by the Master Potter to remove the lumps and unevenness and resistances in our wills.

Our dependence upon Him needs to be total and beyond our mind understanding; otherwise our ministries are in human strength (soulical) rather than of His wisdom and power (spiritual). Hence our dependence upon our many idols, and our obedience to the demands they make on our time and efforts, must be transferred to Him alone. That takes many wilderness experiences, over time, for most of us. It is not the suffering of those trials, but our learning to trust and obey

Him through them, that matures us and refines and strengthens our faith.

We Must Grow In Unity And Love

The Scriptures call for *unity* within the Body of Christ. In Ephesians 4:3 & 13, Paul speaks of *two* kinds of unity: (1) unity "in the Spirit"; and (2) unity "in the faith". Unity in the Spirit is an inner and subtle unity of all Christians that the Holy Spirit of Christ Jesus brings about simply by indwelling all who seek Him, of all backgrounds and levels of maturity. But unity in the faith, as we see in 1 Corinthians 1:10-11, is that we "all speak the same thing, and there be no schisms among us, and we be united in the same mind and in the same judgment". Unity in the Spirit comes first; afterward that we grow in unity in the faith. We manifest unity in the Spirit when we recognize what He has done, and that it truly exists even when unity in the faith has not yet begun to exist among us. But Christ, not us, brings about unity in the faith as part of His building His Body.

We need to distinguish between these two in terms of our relationships with one another. Unity in the Spirit is God's basis for our *fellowship* with one another, whereas unity in the faith is God's basis for his *building* His Body/House/Temple. Most of us have experienced unity in the Spirit to *some* extent. But our walk in Christ, to be built into unity in the faith and to jointly contain and manifest Christ and His presence and glory on Earth, is an entirely different matter.

11. Have We Two Natures Or One?

A common experience of Christians, but that is often made quite acute *after* one has received the Baptism into the Holy Spirit, is deep frustration and confusion over manifestations of our "old nature" or the "old man" (Ephesians 2:2-3), that should have been put to death when, upon regeneration, we "became new creatures in Christ", and upon water baptism we buried it. If I am a partaker of the divine life and nature of Christ, why does so much of my old sinful nature still remain in practical effect?

The issue here is to whom we are in bondage, satan our former slave owner (Ephesians 2:2 & 12), or Christ our Lord. When we acknowledge Christ as our divine redeemer and ask Him to be Lord, He purchases us from satan (the ransom payment having been His shed Blood at Calvary), and He then becomes our new owner or master. He replaces satan at the center of our nature; and we are no longer in *bondage* to the spirit of sin.

But until our *self*-nature (soul) fully yields to Christ our new owner, though He fully "possesses" us, because He chooses to honor our will He does not have full control over our thoughts and actions. As wicks in a lamp, when the flow of the oil (Christ *via* His Holy Spirit in us) through us is hindered, we (the wick itself) start to burn and give off much offensive smoke and stink (un-Christlike self-attitudes and thoughts).

So, when our "old man" seems to be still alive, some aspect of our heart is not yet fully circumcised and hence hinders Him flowing through us. It is not that we intend nor desire to hinder Him; it is that His process of sanctifying us has not yet been completed. It is our self-consciousness, our soulishness, that still expresses its own will, or still insists upon both understanding (mind) and feeling (emotions) the will of God before we choose (will) to yield and obey. Not just in big "spiritual" matters, but in the millions of small mundane things that occupy our attention day in and day out. But the more we walk in the Holy Spirit's guidance, the more habitual it becomes and the less aware we become that it is Him. Yet it still really *is* Him; and we indeed live more and more as Children of the new nature.

12. The Biblical *Fulness* Of The Baptism Into The Holy Spirit

The lackings and imperfections in the lives and thoughts of Holy Spirit Baptized Christians, then, are due to a lack in our yielding to the Holy Spirit in His *fulness*.

What would His fulness involve, if we were fully yielded to Him? By comparing the lives of the disciples and other mature Christians before and after they received the Baptism into the Holy Spirit, we see that in its Biblical fulness there are at least five aspects of our behaviour (or of the reality of Christ in us) that **should** be effective:
    (a) Faith;
    (b) Personal holiness in thinking patterns;
    (c) Love;
    (d) Worship; and
    (e) Ministry.

In His Biblical fulness, the Holy Spirit in us works *faith* in us in the sense discussed above: *seeing* Him in His Spiritual reality; ***dynamically depending*** upon the Person of Christ Jesus (and He alone), and ***sensitively obeying*** His will. His will is revealed to us *via* His Holy Spirit indwelling and enabling us to assimilate His Word (John 16:13 and 1 Corinthians 2:10 & 12), as we inwardly respond to His initiatives. Walking and/or praying "in faith believing" is first our determining God's sovereign will in the specific situation(s), and then our responding with our ***will*** accordingly, certainly by prayer and/or intercession, and often also by other specific acts of personal ministry.

The Holy Spirit also works in us to produce His ***fruit*** of ***holiness*** in our thoughts and behaviour patterns. As we discussed in Chapter 3 earlier in this volume, the nine fruit of the Holy Spirit (Galatians 5:22-23) and the nine spices in the Lord's Garden of our hearts (Song of Songs 4:13-14) speak of three groups of behaviour characteristics of Christ manifested in us: ***beauty*** of outward appearance (the ***attractive*** beauty and radiance of Christ in us); ***flavor*** of inner attitudes (the ***character*** of Christ in us); and effects of interpersonal ***behaviour*** (the ***outflowing*** of Christ and His love through us to others). Trustworthiness, or ***faithfulness***, is when we flow in faith in response to His faithfulness toward us (1 Thessalonians 5:23-24, Hebrews 10:22-23, and 1 John 1:9).

Love here is Agape love, not Philea nor Eros nor Storge love. Agape love is humanly totally impossible for any of us to produce. Agape is manifested through us ***only*** by Christ in us (*via* His Holy Spirit abiding) loving His love through us (Romans 5:5); hence it requires us fully yielding to the Holy Spirit, not us struggling to do it ourselves. And that love is always ***specifically*** directed: to God the Father Himself, and

The Experience Of The Baptism Into Holy Spirit 217

to one another as specific individuals with specific needs and contributions.

So often we confuse a "general compassion" we have for people, such as to "save souls" or to "preach the Gospel", for this. Rather, those are forms of Philea love for our ministries. Though perhaps linked to our special callings (Romans 12:3-8), they are *not per se* the Agape love-fruit of the Holy Spirit of Christ Jesus.

Worship, either public or private, is, like Agape love, a humanly impossible act; only Christ in us can bring us into it. And, like Agape love, true worship is very rare and very little understood. Worship is *not* praise! Praise and thanksgiving are our appreciating and enjoying God because of our relationship with Him: our response of appreciation for His marvelousness and our gratitude for what He has done (and will do) for us. But worship is our totally *abandoning* ourselves unto Him! Worship is ministry unto God. And only for God's sake. We enter into it because God is worthy of praise and worship, not because of what He means to us and/or does for us. We put aside all consideration of our *self*, and acknowledge God for Who He is. It is both awesome respect for Him, and our totally losing ourself in Him. We worship only because He is worthy of our worship and because we were created to.

All form of *ministry* are forms of Agape-love-motivated servanthood. Hence ministry consists of the manifestations of the Holy Spirit as He wills through us to edify the Body of Christ.

13. What About Speaking In Tongues?

What about *tongues* as a sign of the Baptism into the Holy Spirit? Are tongues a necessary manifestation of it?

Note first that of the five aspects listed above of the Biblical fulness of the Holy Spirit in us, only *two* (worship, and some of the power ministries) involve tongues, and the other three do *not*. Yet more importantly, *all five* of these aspects result if we fully yield to the Holy Spirit.

But again, almost none of us, when we initially receive the Baptism into the Holy Spirit, yield to Him in all five nor fully in any one. The Baptism into the Holy Spirit initially brings us into *only* what we have been taught to expect when we seek it: as our faith, so shall it be unto us (Matthew 9:29, Galatians 3:14, Ephesians 3:17 and James 1:6). Many have been taught to seek and expect tongues; so they speak in tongues, even if love and personal holiness be missing in their lives. And others are taught to seek personal holiness or "entire sanctification" but to avoid tongues; they manifest the love and peace of Christ in their personal lives in beautiful ways, but lack tongues and are weak in power ministries and in worship. Each has, indeed, received the Baptism into the Holy Spirit; each has indeed a valid testimony of the Holy Spirit Baptism. But also, each has no right to judge or criticize the other. For we are instructed to mature in our yielding to Him in *all five* areas, and only then will we have the Holy Spirit in His fulness.

Is tongues then a *necessary* manifestation of the Baptism into the Holy Spirit? No. Is love? No. Is personal holiness? No. Are power ministries? No. Is worship? No. But *all five* are manifestations of the Baptism into the Holy Spirit in His *fulness*.

Nevertheless, speaking in tongues is Biblical, is a viable aspect of our personal relationship with Christ Jesus, and is of great value to the believer!

The Principle Of Worship

It is impossible to discuss that manifestation of the Holy Spirit in us that is known as "glossolalia" or "speaking in tongues", apart from *worship*. This is because there is a basic principle of God involved in worship, and tongues plays a vital role in one aspect of that principle. The principle behind worship, both public (i.e., leading a group into corporate worship) and individual (i.e., in our private devotions) is this: *as* we minister *first* unto God, *then* He ministers to us. It's as we minister to God, that God ministers to our needs. As long as we minister to ourself or to others, we are not going to get the blessings of God on us, because we're not worshiping Him even though we may be encouraging and teaching one another. We worship God because He's worthy of our worship. Worship is an act we choose to do: it is something we *do*, not say; it is our utterly abandoning ourselves unto Him; and it is the highest act for which we were created.

Tongues plays a major role in the operation of this principle in *private* worship. When we desire to truly worship God, we need His help; we can't adequately worship Him on our own. The best of our efforts are woefully inadequate, and anything we say to Him is unworthy of Him. The only way we can worship Him in a manner that is worthy of Him, is for His Spirit in us to worship Him through us.

Hence we need the ability to speak in tongues. Tongues *is* an essential part of the Baptism into the Holy Spirit, because it enables us to go from praise into true worship. But it is not *all*, as we discussed above: love and personal holiness are even *more important* aspects.

In Order That We Prophecy

Look carefully at 1 Corinthians 14:1 & 5. Much misunderstanding exists on the priority Paul gives to speaking in tongues. A first glance at these two verses in most of our English translations gives the impression that Paul is saying "tongues is nice, but it's more important to be able to prophecy"; i.e., a statement merely of *priority*. It seems logical that prophesying, that edifies the whole Body of Christ, is of much higher priority than speaking in tongues that merely edifies the individual (1 Corinthians 14:4).

However, that is not Paul's meaning. The Greek is much stronger than our English translations imply. The actual Greek for "but especially that you may prophecy" is "Mallon De Ina Propheteuete". Note the preposition "Ina", that is virtually left out of the English translations. "Ina" is a preposition used to denote a strong linkage between words, almost of the force of a cause-effect relationship; it has the meaning of "in order that (it become possible) for" or "as a prerequisite for". Therefore, Paul's meaning is that true prophecy, though of higher *importance* than speaking in tongues, *requires* the ability to speak in tongues as a *prerequisite* or enablement!

Tongues Will Cease?

Another common misunderstanding of the Biblical teachings on speaking in tongues, that comes from the weaknesses of our English translation of the original Greek, is found in 1 Corinthians 13:8-10. The thrust of most English versions of verse 10 is "when that which is perfect has come, tongues will cease". This verse is used by many Christians to argue that speaking in tongues ceased with the New Testament Church in the first century AD.

The Greek for "that which is perfect" is the single word "Teleion". That is a pronoun of neuter gender from the verb "Teleo" that means "to be brought near, brought to maturity or fulness or completeness". It is significant to note that in this verse it is of the *neuter* gender. As a pronoun, it must agree in gender with the noun it refers to, unless we allow grammatical errors by the Holy Spirit as He "breathed" or inspired the writing of God's Word (2 Timothy 3:16). So, to find Paul's meaning, we must find a neuter noun in the preceding (or possibly immediately following) verses that can grammatically be that to which Teleion refers. It certainly does not refer to the coming of our Perfect Lord Christ Jesus, for He is masculine, and the Greek word for "Lord" ("Kurios") is of masculine gender. In fact, every noun we encounter in 1 Corinthians 13 as we go backwards from Teleion in verse 10 is either of masculine or feminine gender, until we encounter the noun "Soma" or "Body" (of Christ) back in 1 Corinthians chapter 12 (verses 27, 25, 24, 23, 22, 17, 15, 14, 13, etc.).

1 Corinthians chapters 11 through 14 are a single discourse by Paul on the subject of the maturing of the Body of Christ, the

corporate body of Christians in any given locality. He discusses many aspects of that maturing, including not depending upon traditions nor rituals (Chapter 11), avoiding cliquishness and properly regarding the Body as the corporate and unified manifestation of Christ on Earth (Chapter 11), manifesting the Gift of the Holy Spirit in our midst as He wills (Chapter 12), demonstrating Agape love (Chapter 13), and properly exercising the "spirituals" or Holy-Spirit-directed ministries in the Body for the edification of all members (Chapter 14). Although he emphasizes that Agape love is the most important ("more excellent") way in Chapter 13, in verses 8-10 he does not *exclude* speaking in tongues but merely subjugates it to that exercising of love.

In this reference, Paul emphasizes that speaking in tongues is of use only during the maturing *process* of the Body of Christ, and once the Body becomes mature, it will no longer be needed and hence will cease. Such a maturity would involve *all* of us having acquired full Christ-likeness in our thoughts, attitudes, motives, behaviour, etc. That has never been reached yet during the history of the Church, and we are *far* from it as of now. Even in the New Testament Church, by AD 90 much *immaturity* was still apparent (and was increasing), as we know from Paul's several epistles, and also from Revelations Chapters 2 and 3. So, valid Holy-Spirit-inspired speaking in tongues did not cease then, nor has it ceased yet as of now.

Tongues And Spiritual Pride

One primary reason why speaking in tongues is so opposed by a large segment of Christianity today and is so divisive in many established Churches, is not exegetical but experiential:

a strong element of spiritual pride on the part of tongues-speaking Christians has been frequently apparent to non-tongues-speaking Christians. My own personal experience proves how easy it is to give *valid* cause for others to make that accusation. The attitude, however subtly implied, is "I speak in tongues and you don't; therefore you're not as mature in Christ as I". This is both totally contrary to the Holy Spirit of Christ in us and factually untrue in most cases. We need not openly *express* such an attitude; it becomes apparent to others, particularly born-again (and hence Spirit-indwelling) Christian believers, during the normal course of our social interactions. Many Christians have been hurt (some quite deeply) by tongues-speaking Christians because of that attitude.

In subsequent years after I received the Baptism, I *did* believe myself to be more mature than other Christians. I placed more emphasis on God's *means* for maturing me than on the goal of maturity Himself. And, in sincerity, I did believe that I had strong convictions of truth, real truth, that many other Christians lacked. Perhaps indeed I did. But Agape love, the Philippians 2:3-7 attitude, and personal holiness, are what He seeks to bring us into, and not "truth" *per se*. He seeks compassion, not systematic theology nor our enthusiasm over a special "truth" or experience. "Truth" is never something He imparts to me, but is something He *is*, in me (John 14:6). I never *have* truth; I only manifest truth when I yield to He, who *is* truth in me, to dominate my thoughts and actions as He wills. And He never does that without love, for He also is love. Although I speak in tongues, if I do not manifest His love, I am of no consequence (1 Corinthians 13:1-3); for I have not yet learned to allow Christ in me to manifest Himself through me to others in His more important ways.

We mentioned above that tongues is only one of several manifestations of having received the Baptism into the Holy Spirit, and by no means *the* manifestation, nor the most important one. It is part of it in its Biblical *fulness*, but so are the more important other aspects, such as faith, personal holiness, love and worship. But regardless of whatever outer manifestations we may display, the essence of receiving the Baptism into the Holy Spirit is the *centrality of Christ Jesus* in our very being, and a yielding of our soulishness to the free flow of Him, as He wills, through our thoughts and actions to others. Spiritual pride, in any form, is the very *antithesis* of this! *If* we indeed allow Christ to reign central and supreme in our lives, then we will be growing in the attitude of Philippians 2:3-7 instead.

Strengthening Our Faith

On the other hand, speaking in tongues *does* greatly assist the faith of weak Christians, and it must not be *spurned* either. "Theology that is slanted in the direction of attempting to justify a *lack* of personal experience" is *also* a form of spiritual pride!

Speaking in tongues is not only an ability to worship God in a form worthy of Him, it is also a means by which the Holy Spirit gives a convincing, supernatural, and glory-filling inward confirmation of the union of our human spirit with His Spirit, and of the indwelling of God. Most of us in the natural find it hard to develop a strong faith: we *need* definite crisis experiences, points of departure in our experience, or some *physical* manifestations, in order to retain the faith we have.

I was a weak believer before my Baptism, having been exposed to the philosophy of Scientistic Humanism through many years in contemporary American public education! *Only* through my speaking in tongues, that was to me both so overwhelmingly Christ-oriented and also phenomenologically reproducible at any time at my will, were *all* doubts on the existence of our Living Christ and of the truth of the Bible, finally and totally dispelled! And the fact that it was *intelligent* communication and not psychological gibberish was proven to me when, a few years later, I was able to identify the language of my first words spoken in tongues (and tape-recorded at the time) as Hebrew, and was able to translate it:

"This cluster of blessings is not a vague or turbid dream or mere mental concept held by men, but a very energizing fountain or source of drink to be slowly and persistently sipped or partaken of."

14. Our Present Condition: Saved But Immature

99.44% of those who receive the Baptism into the Holy Spirit do *not* receive it in its Biblical *fulness* initially. We receive what we *seek* (i.e., to the extent we *yield* to Him); and what we actually seek is conditioned by what we've been taught to expect, by our cultural and church backgrounds, etc. But we never receive from Christ Jesus anything unless we seek and *respect* it. We must take the initiative of *seeking* this closer walk with Christ. Unfortunately, many do *not* really seek a deeper walk with Christ, but rather just to be blessed, and they use "church" (even Spirit-filled "Charismatic" groups) as a means of escaping anything deeper than that.

It is both possible and common to be still lacking in some aspect of yieldedness to the Holy Spirit of Christ Jesus after receiving the Baptism into the Holy Spirit, even many years after. It is only in this sense that we say it *is* possible to receive a Baptism into the Holy Spirit without tongues or without love or without personal holiness or without true worship; but it is not possible in anything even approaching its Biblical *fulness* without *all* of these. Those who lack in love tend to be harsh and zealous in ministry. Those who lack in the power of ministry tend to be weak in faith (i.e., in their *now* dependence upon Christ) and are easily discouraged. Those who lack in worship tend to have their soul not poised toward Christ, they are still much of this world in their patterns of thinking, and they are weak in their desire to glorify Christ. So each of us are still lacking in some areas of the Biblical fulness of the Holy Spirit of Christ Jesus in us.

The Hebrew word for "peace" (ShLM) means "to be entire" or "to be completely and fully that for which we were created". That does not mean being tranquil nor passive; rather, it refers to the very subject of our concern in this chapter: to manifest Christ Jesus in us, and to be yielded and cleansed vessels through whom He will pour Himself out to this love-starved world.

What shall we do, then, to be full? Where do we start, then, if we would reach our ShLM? Through faith? Unity? Love? Ministry?

We start by *realizing* that we are *not* yet complete, and that we are *far* from it. We must overcome the natural tendency to think ourselves to be more mature than we actually are. It starts also by realizing that only *He* can mature us. But the key to it all is to ever *desire* and seek to make Christ central and supreme. Again and again we say, the way to get from darkness to light is not to fight (nor exorcise) the darkness, but to turn on the light: to supersaturate ourselves with Christ Jesus.

The Baptism into the Holy Spirit is a breakthrough in our consciousness of our *union* with God through Christ Jesus. Period! All other aspects are *results* of that *union*, not results of our *experiences*. And that union is the only true reality. As in all things of the Spirit, we enter and grow in Him by the "law of faith": the outworking in us of a specific desire (in this case the specific desire that Christ alone abide and reign at the deep central core of our being and that He replace us in us) comes as we dynamically depend upon Him as a Person, and be sensitively obedient to His will in our lives.

This requires a blind leap, a total commitment, to that which repels our "natural" (physical and soulish) instincts. Yet we must act upon our desire for Him by totally abandoning ourselves unto Him without looking back on the ground just plowed (Luke 9:62). Then, little by little, His manifestations of Himself through us to others increase. And since our self now takes a back seat, it no longer matters to us just how or where He leads. We can never satisfactorily run our own lives; when we try, we always make a mess of things. But when He, who created us, and for whose pleasure every fiber of our being has been designed, runs our lives for us, then and only then is true ShLM an experiential reality, and our faith becomes fact.

End Notes: Chapter Seven

[1.] Lloyd-Jones, Martyn, *Joy Unspeakable - Power & Renewal in the Holy Spirit* (1984) Published by special permission with Kingsway Publication, Ltd., Susses, England. Used by permission of Howard Shaw Publishers, Wheaton, IL.

[2.] *Ibid.* pp. 13, 38, 39, 81, 83, 85, 89 and 90.

[3.] Sherrerd, Chris S., *Unto The Mountain Pass - A Theology Of The End-Time Purposes Of God*, Volume VI of the series "Where Do You Fit In? Practical Commitments In The Body Of Christ", to be published.

[4.] Sherrerd, Chris S., *From Sheepfold To Bride: Christ Maturing His Church*, Volume III of the series "Where Do You Fit In? Practical Commitments In The Body of Christ", to be published.

Part III

Profiles In Sanctification

In earlier chapters in this volume, we have studied the human condition with both its tremendous potential for love-motivated servanthood and its current deeply penetrating depravity. We have emphasized the role of the Holy Spirit of Christ Who lives within us since regeneration. His ever working to sanctify is closely linked in the Scriptures to three powerful concepts: (1) deep *repentance unto* Christ; (2) reckoning our sin-*nature* (intrinsic to our soul) *crucified* with Christ; and (3) our being *sanctified* unto *Christ-likeness* by the indwelling Holy Spirit of Christ Jesus.

Up to now we mainly emphasized the first two of these three and only introduced the third. We now focus our full attention onto the third, i.e. *sanctification*, for the remainder of this volume. We start that with various *experiential* aspects of His sanctifying us, and follow with several further chapters on direct Biblical portraits of three general stages.

Chapter Eight

Experiencing Sanctification

Our understanding and discernment of spiritual things comes by a ***growing process***, as we are led by the indwelling Holy Spirit of Christ Jesus. This growing process is called **sanctification**. It does not come to us suddenly in some experience in which we get spiritually "zapped". The Baptism into the Holy Spirit does not effect *full* spiritual understandings; it only makes it possible for us to ***begin***.

How He sanctifies us is different for each of us - the process is tailor-fitted by Him to each of us. However, it does have some common elements. For example, it involves stages described by the Apostle John as "little children", "young men" and "fathers" (1 John 2:12-14), whose spiritual "food" is "milk", "bread" and "meat" or "solid food", respectively (1 Corinthians 3:2 and Hebrews 5:12-14).

1. The Sanctification Process Takes Time

Each of the three components of our psychological make-up - the human spirit, soul and carnality - must be dealt with, and each in a totally different way, by the indwelling Holy Spirit of Christ Jesus. If we would proceed to nearly full maturity during this life, each of these three components must be dealt with in turn, and each in a different way according to an explicit Biblical pattern. In Chapters Nine and following, we discuss the three-fold process of sanctification in detail: regeneration of the human spirit, crucifixion of the flesh, and circumcision of the soul.

That process involves several distinct phases with sub-phases of growth between, and it is discussed in this book as three general stages of spiritual maturing. The human *spirit*, with its functions of intuition, conscience, worship and love, is fully sanctified upon *regeneration*. The *flesh*, the power of the appetites of the physiological, can *never* be sanctified; it must be put to *death*, now in our disciplined mental *attitudes*, and ultimately in *physical* fact. And the *soul*, with its functions of mental activity, emotions and will/volition, must be broken and *yielded* to the Holy Spirit through the human spirit.

The most difficult of these three components to be brought to full yieldedness to the Lord Jesus Christ is the human *soul*. It is the seat of the self, the "I", the Adamic Nature. No matter how strongly we desire (and pray for) being yielded to the Lord, the soul will continue to dominate our behaviour and to suppress the human spirit until we *force* it to yield. The human mind demands understandings; the human will demands that understanding *precede* commitment; and our emotions confuse and deceive us.

Experiencing Sanctification

The human soul-spirit combination, as God has created us, and even now after the Fall, has an awesome and incredible potential. But the Lord has chosen to never *force* us into anything against our will: He *draws* us unto entire soul sanctification through a combination of: (1) enticing us by His *Love* (to soften our emotions); (2) physical *miracles* (that our mind can *not* understand) such as tongues and healings (to weaken our *mind's* dominance); and (3) trials and tribulations in the circumstances of our daily lives (to redirect our *will*.

The bottom line of *our* responsibility in this process by which the indwelling Holy Spirit of Christ Jesus sanctifies is, is illustrated in Isaiah 40:31: "Yet those who wait upon the Lord will gain new strength; they will mount up with wings like eagles, they will run and not get tired, they will walk and not become weary." The Hebrew word for "wait" here is QWH, a very *dynamic* verb which means basically to be closely *involved* with: "those who *entwine* their life with our Lord Christ Jesus, shall...." We use the English word "yield" as more closely capturing the original meaning: "those who choose to yield their wills to the indwelling Holy Spirit of Christ Jesus, shall...."

Another Biblical concept that pertains to the *results* of that waiting/entwining/yielding is *fruit* of the Holy Spirit. They are various forms of the Agape love of our Lord Christ Jesus (Galatians 6:22-25). How does a fruit tree produce fruit? By zealous efforts to "serve"? By anxiously seeking? No, but rather by yielding to its environment, dynamically, in all seasons. That means yielding with *patience*. So also with us.

Guyon[1] relates insights gained through her own deep, painful, life-long sanctification, in these words:

"I saw ... or rather experienced the ground on which God rejects sinners from His bosom. All the cause of God's rejection is in the *will* of the sinner. If that will submits [yields], how horrible so ever he be, God purifies him in His love, and receives him into his grace; but while that will rebels, the rejection continues. .... if the sinner comes to die truly penitent, then the cause, which is the wrong will, being taken away, there remains only the effect or impurity caused by it. He is then in a condition to be purified. God of His infinite mercy has provided a laver[2] of love and of justice, a painful laver indeed, to purify this soul. And as the defilement is greater or less, so is the pain; but when the cause is utterly taken away, the pain entirely ceases. Souls are received into grace, as soon as the cause of sin ceases; but they do not pass into the Lord Himself, till all its effects are washed away. If they have not courage to let Him, in His own way and will, thoroughly cleanse and purify them, they never enter into the pure divinity in this life."

The early step of spiritual growth in Christ (i.e., basic regeneration) is "easy" - wide is the way and easy the path. But Truth - and *He* is The Truth - is expensive. it costs us our *everything*. Narrow and steep is the way to discipleship and the Kingship of Christ Jesus.

2. Sanctification Ladders?

The classical concept of the several distinct *levels* or *stages* of sanctification of all believers is not accepted by many serious, anointed and highly respectable Bible scholars. Such scholars, very correctly, point out that God is sovereign, all aspects of

Experiencing Sanctification

our salvation are sovereign acts by Him, and He deals with every believer differently and uniquely.

For example, Lovelace[3] explains some of the difficulties with the "classical model" of sanctification:

> "Ladders are always intimidating, and it is my suspicion that Christians should always assume that they start each day at the top of the ladder in contact with God and renew this assumption whenever they appear to have slipped a rung. The Triple Way of classical mysticism, which moves from the stage of cleansing one's life through illumination toward union with God, seems to reverse the biblical order, which starts from union with Christ claimed by faith, leading to the illumination of the Holy Spirit and consequent cleansing through the process of sanctification. Doubtless there is a valid place for both models in promoting Christian experience - some Christians need to work at one end of the series, some at the other - but it is my assumption that growth in *faith* is the root of all spiritual growth and is prior to all disciplines of works. True spirituality is not a superhuman religiosity; it is simply true humanity released from bondage to sin and renewed by the Holy Spirit. This is given to us as we grasp by faith the full content of Christ's redemptive work: freedom from the guilt and power of sin, and newness of life through the indwelling and outpouring of his Spirit...."

We agree with this as an appropriate ***guiding attitude*** for us to have during our sanctification. A salvation union with Christ, claimed by faith, is indeed our starting point. And illumination by the Holy Spirit and consequent cleansing by

Him indwelling are a subsequent, continuous and *iterative* process that ever deepens our union with Christ. None of this occurs except to the extent that we *yield* to that indwelling Holy Spirit of Christ: what the Bible calls *repentance* by us. Even that repentance is something we *grow* in during that iterative process.

Lovelace does not fault that *per se;* he is simply and correctly faulting the often observed efforts by some to obtain sanctification by self-strivngs rather than by yielding to the indwelling Holy Spirit of Christ Jesus.

The sovereignty of God in our sanctification process must be balanced with the fact that in this "Church age" our Lord Christ Jesus has chosen to not override human will. All aspects of our salvation are indeed sovereign acts of God as He wills; but our human wills also play a key role, at least in us choosing to yield to His sovereign acts in our lives. This yielding of our wills to Christ our Lord is a *process* that takes place in each of us in unique ways and according to unique time schedules. That yielding involves repentance at increasing depth, and it results in our apprehending God in faith at correspondingly increasing depth.

This yielding in repentance has at least three main components: (1) repentance *from* our intrinsic aversion against God due to our shame/guilt over our sin nature, and *unto* full appreciation of God's continual forgiveness and apprehension of God's grace; (2) repentance *from* our sin of unbelief that thinks Christ is not really sufficient, or willing, to provide all our needs and protection against all that is not in His will for us, *unto* a deep-seated trust in Him in all things at all times; and (3) repentance *from* self, specifically from our self-protecting strategies that distance us from God and from one another, and *unto* full enjoyment of Christ both in us and in one another.

Along these lines, at least three "stages" of Christian sanctification are clearly identified in the Bible. Paul talks about "carnal", "natural" and "spiritual" Christians. 1 John 2:12-14 talks about "little children", "young men" and "elders". Etc. We reflect on three bases for living the Christian life: (1) by *law;* (2) by Spiritual *light;* and 3) by *true faith* in the Lord. This is the New Covenant typological counterpart of the Old Testament three "classes" of God's people: (1) the eleven and two half-tribes of Israel; (2) the tribe of Levi among them; and (3) the tabernacle/temple priests among the Levites.

3. Shifts In Influences During Sanctification

We now proceed with a delineation of the three general stages of our sanctification model. We do this from several points of view and with explanations of what each stage entails for us. We start with a technical exegetical study of the sanctification process itself; in this and the following chapter we look at some key *theological* aspects of how the Holy Spirit in us works to deepen our personal relationship with Christ. In the three chapters then following, we present many Biblical concepts that enable us to *understand* the sanctification process, including examples in the lives of some Biblical individuals.

As our Lord draws us unto maturing in Him, each of the three aspects of our triparte psychological nature must be dealt with separately, and in totally different ways. We introduced that in Chapter 1 beginning this volume. Briefly, our human spirit is sanctified upon *regeneration*. The Holy Spirit of Christ Jesus comes in His entirety to dwell in our (human) spirit, placing us in two-way communication with God and hence enabling us to "know" Him and possess "eternal life" as defined in John 17:3. Our soul is *sanctified* by the process of our increasingly yielding our soul-functions of mind and emotions and will to that Holy Spirit Who already indwells our spirit. Our soul is the totality of our consciousness; hence this is when we become *experientially aware* of He Who has already been dwelling in us. And our bodies are sanctified upon final redemption in conjunction with Christ's Parousia return when we become established fully in Him. In the meantime, our carnality (Sarx) can *never* be sanctified; it must be *reckoned as crucified!*

The spiritual and psychological interactions and influences that occur during these stages of sanctification of the human triparte nature are illustrated in Figure Two, albeit in over-simplified form.

First of all, note the labels used in Figure Two. The **"UNREGENERATE"**, of course, refers to us prior to our becoming "born-again", prior to our having any personal relationship with God at all. (Ephesians 2:1-3 and 11-12 refer to us in that state.)

The labels **"CARNAL"**, **"NATURAL"** and **"SPIRITUAL"** believer are terms used by the Apostle Paul in Romans 7:14 & 1 Corinthians 3:1-4, 1 Corinthians 2:14, and 1 Corinthians 2:15 & 3:1, respectively. These terms reflect that aspect of our human triparte nature that has the most dominating influence on our thoughts, actions and behavior at the time. The Greek words used for "carnal", "natural" and "spiritual"

Experiencing Sanctification 239

Figure Two

Influences On Our Hearts

⟶ Dominating Control
----→ Occasional Influence

(1) THE UNREGENERATE: **(2) CARNAL BELIEVER:**

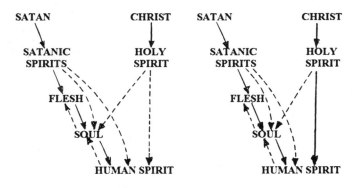

(3) NATURAL BELIEVER: **(4) SPIRITUAL BELIEVER:**

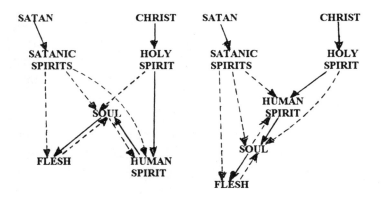

are Sarkikos, Psuchikos and Pneumatikos. Since Psuchikos means "soulical", we use that term as well as "natural" throughout the rest of this volume.

The key role is played by our *soul*. It is the seat of our volition/will; it is in actual control of our thoughts, feelings, actions and behavior. It is the battleground to be won or lost. Either satan or Christ will have control of our soul and have his/His way with us. But God has so ordained that neither can *directly force* our will; both must honor the capability of free will that God created in us. Hence each must use indirect means of influencing us to the point of our choosing his/His will.

Note the case of the "**SPIRITUAL**" believer in Figure Two (4). This was the human condition prior to the Fall, and it is the goal of our salvation/sanctification: Christ *via* His Holy Spirit indwelling our human spirit, being given total control *via* our soul so choosing - our soul *yielding* to Him in us.

While still in this world, even the most "spiritual" of believers is still capable of being influenced by the subtle deceptions of satan. Also our soul is still vulnerable to yielding to fleshly desires, and the soul still has the capability to suppress our human spirit and hence Christ in us. These we show by dotted arrows in the Figure. But as we increasingly yield to Christ indwelling, He replaces such evil temptations and deceptions, and we do not yield to them in our thoughts.

But satan would *like* to have total control of us: like the pattern shown in Figure Two (4) but with *SATAN--->SATANIC SPIRITS* and *CHRIST---->HOLY SPIRIT* reversed in roles: satan dominant and Christ at most only occasional. Toward that goal, satan primarily uses *religion* with its icon and idol worship. Many today are indeed caught up in that to some extent by Eastern mysticism, New Ageism, satanism, etc. - even by some forms of "Christianity"!

In either case, however, our starting condition, as a result of the Adamic curse, is that illustrated in Figure Two (1).

The issue in the Fall was the ***Tree of Knowledge of Good and Evil.*** The human soul uses its *knowledge* as the source/basis for living, rather than the Tree of Life (Christ) as the source. We (our soul) tries to control all of our living independently of Christ. Of course, we usually do not *deliberately* choose to live under satan's control. But satan is too crafty and deceptive for us, and as a result, we all ***by default if not deliberately*** early in life fall under his control. As Ephesians 2:1-3 & 11-12 expresses it: we are ***bond-slaves*** of satan our *slave-master*, totally cut off from God. This is a hard but real truth - satan was our slave-owner whether we knew it or not, whether we deliberately chose him to be or not!

But in specifying the conditions of the Adamic curse, God in His mercy nevertheless placed constraints on satan's exercising his slave-mastership over us. Satanic spirits are able to control our human spirits *only* to the extent that our soul - volition/will/choice - chooses to allow them to. By placing us first under a Patriarchical governmental environment, and later under (Mosaic) law, God gave us a reason to choose to not allow satan to directly control us through our human *spirit.* In the unregenerate man, the human spirit is so suppressed by the soul-flesh combination that it loses its distinction in manifestations from the soul. Hence he (satan) must primarily control us through our fleshly and soulish desires. That, however, he is quick to do *via* his demonic spirits - when/as we allow them to do by default and/or out of ignorance.

Where do satan's spirits dwell? In ***darkness!*** Wherever there is darkness! What is darkness? By "darkness" we mean all aspects of our hearts - our desires, our patterns of thinking, our personal philosophies of life - *that are not of God.* How do we dispel darkness and all who dwell in it? By rebuking that darkness? No! By turning on the light! By repentance; by focusing our thoughts and intents upon our Lord Christ Jesus!

When we start out apart from God (Ephesians 2:1-3 & 11-12), all of our mind is in darkness; hence, satan "has a ball" with us, he being constrained only by our "common sense" and/or cultural influences. His means of influencing us are: (a) temptations of the flesh (indicated by a solid line in Figure Two (1)); (b) lying deceptions of the soul (dotted line); and (c) spiritual influences (dotted line) as we ***religiously*** "worship" icons and/or idols.

But Christ, our "hound of heaven", is also trying to gain our attention. Not shown in Figure Two (1-4) are His workings in the *circumstances* of our lives. But at times when we discover (fleetingly, perhaps) that we can't actually control our lives anyhow and our ways lead at best to frustration, He also plants thoughts in us: by our conscience and intuition (dotted line *via* human spirit), or by the direct witness of His written Word and by the testimonies of Christians (dotted line *via* soul). That requires the Holy Spirit working in our hearts to (1) lift the veil so that we see Christ for Who He is, and our need for Him (2 Cor. 3:14); and (2) demolish our strongholds of thinking patterns and belief systems that are not of God, and pride-thoughts which rise up against God, and put all of

Experiencing Sanctification

our thoughts under Christ (2 Cor. 10:5).

Once we "see the truth" of our need for a saviour and that He is Christ, and we choose to allow Him to indwell us and run our lives, He indeed sends His Holy Spirit to live in our human spirit. This we illustrate by a solid line in Figure Two (2). But although He dwells in our human spirit in full reality, our *soul* is still in control, and we do not yet feel anything different. Although our "accepting Christ as our saviour" is real, it is at best mental and/or emotional to us - to our soul - since we have not yet learned to discern what is actually happening in the "spiritual" domain. Christ, *via* His Holy Spirit dwelling in our human spirit, is lord ***only to the extent*** that our soul allows Him to be, only to the extent that we consciously and deliberately *yield* to Him and His will and word. This we illustrate by a dotted line in Figure Two(2). Yet carnal ways still dominate us by habit if not by actual desire for sin.

Since the soul is still in control and is controlling by its own distorted knowledge and desires, this is a quite precarious condition for the believer to be in. For unless the believer concentrates on obeying the insights of conscience and intuition *via* the indwelling Holy Spirit and by the Word of God, he/she will be overwhelmed by carnal and worldly influences, to his/her continued depravation. He/she is in great danger of being one of the seeds fallen on rocky places or among thorns (Matthew 13:5-7 and 20-22).

We have yet far to go at this point, to both bring our carnality under control and to learn to fully yield our self - our soul in its entirety - to Him. Bringing carnality under control requires discipline. Fully yielding to Him requires our dying to self -

Romans 6 applied to our flesh and sin **nature**. In the meantime, the only differences between Figures Two (1) and Two (2) are the direct and dominant control of the human spirit by the indwelling Holy Spirit of Christ Jesus, with satanic influences on the human spirit considerably less (but still significant) and with the human spirit's influence on the soul considerably more (as the soul allows).

The "transition" from being a carnal believer (Figure Two (2)) to a natural or soulical believer (Figure Two (3)) is both a crisis event and a slow process. The crisis event, called "Baptism into the Holy Spirit, opens our soul to an experiential *awareness* of the Spiritual reality of Christ and His indwelling Holy Spirit. That awareness brings with it a great increase in both our faith and in our love-desire for Him and for other believers. Our soul therefore *seeks* to be controlled by Christ *via* His Holy Spirit in our human spirit, as illustrated by a solid upward arrow in Figure Two (3).

Once our soul chooses to seek Him and His righteousness as is now clearly being communicated to us, we learn to control our flesh and carnality, rather than allowing our flesh and carnality to control us. Of course, satan still tries to tempt, deceive and divert us, but we listen less and less to him and more and more to our Lord Christ Jesus. By this means we become less and less influenced by the "evil" of the Tree of Knowledge of Good and Evil.

Although the Law of the Lord is now written on our hearts (*via* His indwelling Holy Spirit in our human spirit), it is still more a matter of living by His *Law* than by Him Himself. This is a very subtle, but important, point. It is still we doing the

Experiencing Sanctification

doing. Our soul is still controlling all things, albeit under Christ's directions. Our self is now oriented toward Him most of the time, but it is still our self doing the doing. The tragic consequence of this is that what we end up doing (and being) *in Christ* is limited by our understandings of His Law/Will and by our willingness to be obedient. That, being a tremendous limitation on what our Infinite Lord would be and do in and through us, is far from all He would have us be and do.

Even though we be a "Spirit-filled believer" in an indeed valid sense, we are still not a truly "spiritual believer" as Paul uses the term. To see this, study carefully the differences between Figures Two (3) and Two (4). At first glance, note that the arrow arrangements and emphases are identical. The difference is now the *extent* to which we, our soul, actually yields to Him. Our heart - our soul - is so utterly deceitful and has yet many usually hidden habits of thinking, self-seeking goals, self-protecting strategies, etc., that present considerable impedance to His controlling us. Hence it yet needs to be dealt with before we become all that Christ works for us to become. So our *self* must die, must be reckoned as crucified with Christ.

This is a great enigma. For we cannot crucify ourselves. Only He can do it. We are not to *seek* being crucified: He does not call us to be masochists or ascetics, but rather that we desire Him and *rejoice* in Him. What enables us to grow in being the "spiritual believer", is us (our soul) becoming so caught up in Love of Him and in experiencing His wonderful Presence and Life, that nothing else matters to us. As we do this, we no longer struggle under law but find life ever rejoicing. Then we become impedance-free channels of His Light, Life and Love unto others totally when and as He wills. Then we become pliable vessels of His life and power unto salvation and edification of others. Then we truly be a member of His Body, manifesting His life and ministry here on earth. Then we truly glorify Him. We are no longer His *servants;* now we are His *sons/agents!* Trials and tribulations are our lot here on earth, as were His while He was here on earth. But His burden is easy and light, for He is everything to us.

The challenge before us is to allow Him to bring us all the way. This is what is meant by "be ye perfect" (Matthew 5:48, 1 Corinthians 2:6, 2 Corinthians 7:1 & 13:11, Galatians 3:3, Ephesians 4:13, Philippians 3:15, Colossians 1:28 & 4:12, 1 Thessalonians 3:10, Hebrews 13:21, James 2:22, 1 Peter 5:10, 1 John 4:17, etc.) "Perfect" in the Greek, Teleios, means "to reach the goal, to be completed". This indeed is the end goal of His perfect Will for each of us in this life!

4. The *Process* Of Sanctification

The sanctification process is a process over time wherein the indwelling Holy Spirit of Christ Jesus, in conjunction with cooperation with the volition/will function of our soul, effects a shift of control of our thoughts, feelings, goals and behavior: from satan *via* our flesh/carnality, unto Christ *via* our human spirit. And that shift progresses along a specific course, although the details of that course vary considerably from believer to believer.

The first thing the indwelling Holy Spirit of Christ Jesus accomplishes is to establish a two-way communication link between our Lord Christ Jesus and our human spirit. Once that has occurred, then the indwelling Holy Spirit of Christ Jesus strives for our soul to increasingly exercise that two-way

Experiencing Sanctification

communication link. That is, us communicating to Him through thanksgiving, praise, prayer, worship and intercession; and He communicating to us through our *listening* and responding to His Word.

The indwelling Holy Spirit of Christ Jesus then works to become *dominant* in that two-way communication to the goal of Christ *controlling* our soul functions. That is, that we choose His full Lordship. These second and third aspects of His workings are *iterative* sub-processes, involving both singular "crisis events" and "wilderness wanderings." The bottom line issue is we, *via* our soul function of volition/will/choice, *yielding* to Him.

Does this involve "crisis events"? A "crisis event" is any moment when we become increasingly *consciously aware* of Him and His indwelling reality: any time we observe a specific answer to our prayers; any time we sense His dynamic presence; any time we significantly increase in our desire for Him; any time we consciously choose to appreciate Him and yield to Him. How many such "crisis events" are there to be in a believer's life: one? two? three? About ten zillion in this author's life so far, and I have yet a long way to go!

So, the "sanctification process" is a continuous sequence of workings of the indwelling Holy Spirit of Christ Jesus, with many crisis events intertwined with many emptying iterative loops.

Nevertheless, the general *direction* of that sequence is well defined in the Scriptures. We discuss that *general direction* in terms of *three* "stages" as Biblically identified. We do this in order to better understand it, even though the inevitable result is over-simplification with the danger of our losing sight of the iterative loops that painfully characterize the specific workings of the sanctification process in each of our lives.

In the remainder of this chapter, we study these three general Biblically-identified stages from several theological perspectives. We discuss in Chapter Nine the *emptying* aspects of the process in more detail. Then in Chapters Ten and Eleven we then add to our understandings of the three general stages through use of Biblical typology. In closing Chapter Twelve we cite examples of the specific workings of the sanctification process in the lives of individual believers.

Throughout the subsequent discussion, we use a tabulation of many viewpoints of these three general stages of the sanctification process as portrayed in Sanctification Stages Charts One through Three in this chapter with its subsequent continuations as Sanctification Stages Charts Four through Twelve discussed later in Chapters Ten, Eleven and Twelve. We use the same labels for the general stages as used above: the "carnal" or "fleshly" (Greek: Sarkikos) stage; the "soulical" or "natural" (Greek: Psuchikos) stage; and the "spiritual" (Greek: Pneumatikos) stage

We start with Sanctification Stages Chart One, following.

Rows [1] and [2] of Sanctification Stages Chart One summarize our discussion so far. Row [1] lists the aspect of our "heart" or human triparte nature that others about us would observe to be most dominant in our actual *behavior* at that stage of our lives, even though we are genuinely "born-again": our flesh/carnality, our soul, and our spirit, respectively. Row [2] summarizes the discussion in Chapter

Sanctification Stages Chart One

Row #	Three "Types" Of Believer	CARNAL/FLESHLY [SARKIKOS]	SOULICAL/NATURAL [PSUCHIKOS]	SPIRITUAL [PNEUMATIKOS]
[1]	Aspect Of Our +Heart+ Most Dominant In Our **Behaviour**	Flesh	Soul	**Human Spirit** By Holy Spirit Indwelling
[2]	Three Aspects Of Human **Psychology** Being Sanctified (I Thessalonians 5:23 & Hebrews 4:12)	**SPIRIT** [RUACH/PNEUMA] (Intuition, Conscience Yearning, Worship) Receives New Life (John 3:2,5,16 etc.)	**FLESH** [BASAR/SARX] (Power Of Needs & Drives Of Physical Senses) Reckoned Crucified With Christ (Romans 6:2-14 etc)	**SOUL** [NEPHESH/PSUCHE] (Mind, Emotions, Will) Broken (Hebrews 4:12 etc.) Denied (Matthew 16:24-26) Refined (1 Peter 1:6-77)
[3]	**Steps** Being Taken Daily (Matthew 16:24)	Take Up Your Cross: Reckon Flesh Crucified	Deny Yourself: Soul Yielding	**Follow** Christ Jesus: Holy Spirit In **Control**
[4]	Three Levels Of **Maturity** (1 John 2:12-14)	Little Children	Young Men	Elders
[5]	Member Of **Godhead** Most Real To Believer (I John 2:12-14)	God The **Father**	God The **Holy Spirit**	God The **Son** Christ Jesus
[6]	**Victory** Of Believer (I John 2:12-14)	Sins **Forgiven**	**Defeat** Of Evil One (Satan)	**Oneness** With God's Plan Of All Things In Christ
[7]	Level Of **Food** From Heaven (Hebrews 5:12-14)	Milk (**Grace**)	Bread (**Body Ministry**)	Meat (Mature **Word** Of God)
[8]	We **Obtain**	Forgiveness **By** God	Sanctification **For** God's Use	Enablement **From** God
[9]	How We Live Christian Life	By **Law**	With **Light**	True **Faith: Intimacy** With Christ
[10]	O.T. Type Of **God's People**	**Israelite**	Levite	Tabernacle/Temple **Priest**

One beginning this volume and in this chapter above: the aspect of our human triparte nature that has been most dealt with by the indwelling Holy Spirit of Christ Jesus to bring us into this stage - our spirit, our flesh, and our soul, respectively.

Row [3] associates to each stage the step we take daily in obedience to our Lord's command in Matthew 16:24, as discussed above: taking up our cross and reckoning our flesh crucified; denying our self and yielding to the indwelling Holy Spirit of Christ Jesus; and following Christ Jesus as He exercises His Lordship *via* His indwelling Holy Spirit.

One of the most illustrative Scripture passages on these three general stages of the sanctification process is 1 John 2:12-14. We discussed this in Chapter Four earlier in this volume.

> "I write to you, little children, because your sins are forgiven you for His name's sake. I write to you, fathers, because you have known Him Who is from the beginning. I write to you, young men, because you have overcome the wicked one. I write to you, little children, because you have known the Father. I have written to you, fathers, because you know Him Who is from the beginning. I have written to you, young men, because you are strong, and the Word of God abides in you, and you have overcome the wicked one."

Here the apostle lists three types of believers to whom he writes his epistles, and gives a few attributes of each type. The three types of believers, corresponding to our first, third and second general stage of the sanctification process, are indicated in Row [4] of Sanctification Stages Chart One: little children (the most immature); fathers or elders (the most mature); and young men (the intermediate stage of maturity). One significant attribute of these stages is the member of the Godhead which is "known" by the believer, i.e. of which the believer is *most aware*. As Row [5] of Sanctification Stages Chart One lists them in order of who is most vivid to us. They are: God the Father initially; the indwelling Holy Spirit of Christ Jesus during our spiritual warfare; and finally the *Person* of God the Son, our Lord Christ Jesus. Another significant attribute of these stages that the apostle identifies, is the maturity level itself, or the victory obtained by the believer in each stage. As Row [6] of Sanctification Stages Chart One lists them in increasing order, they are: Forgiveness of our sins; Defeat of the evil one (satan); and Oneness with God's plan (that is all things in Christ according to Ephesians 1:10-11).

Two other passages of Scripture that identify believers by their level of maturity are 1 Corinthians 3:1-3 and Hebrews 5:12-14. Here the least mature and the most mature levels are contrasted: "little babes" *vs* "spiritual men". Both passages talk about those levels in terms of how they are fed the Word of God: little babes can only receive "milk"; "solid food" or "meat" can be assimilated by the mature believer, by the "spiritual man". We include this contrast in Row [7] of Sanctification Stages Chart One, wherein we have added the intermediate stage of maturity, wherein we feed on "bread". What are the meanings of these Biblical types of "spiritual food"? Simply stated: "milk" refers to grace, the indwelling presence of the Holy Spirit of Christ Jesus; "bread" refers to the Body of Christ, and the brethren ministering one to another; and "meat" refers to the mature Word of God, "Word" being the Rhema or dynamic dealings of God in our lives (i.e., the *act* of God "speaking" to us).

Three other viewpoints of these three general stages of the sanctification process, that were mentioned previously in this volume, are summarized in Rows [8], [9] and [10] of Sanctification Stages Chart One. Three things we obtain at the beginning or during each stage (see Row [8]) are: forgiveness of our sins *by* God as Christ on Calvary; sanctification *for* God's use by the workings of the indwelling Holy Spirit of Christ Jesus; and revelation and enablement *from* God to walk as sons/agents of Christ or Lord. The three stages of believers we also indicate by the basis upon which we live (Row [9]). How we live is: by *law;* by *Spiritual light;* and by *true faith* in intimately knowing Him, respectively.

We further contrast our stages of maturity by Old Testament typology of corresponding Old Testament believers (Row [10]): *Israelite*, i.e., anyone born of any one of the 11-½ tribes of Israel; *Levite*, i.e., anyone born of the specific tribe of Levi; and tabernacle/temple *priest*, i.e., those of the tribe of Levi who were called and trained to minister in the house of God. These three types have strong parallels in the Body of Christ today. The "Israelites" are all born-again Christians, "children of the promise", in covenant relationship with God through Christ on Calvary, as Paul argues for example in Romans 9 through 12. They live according the Law, albeit interpreted according to the New Testament. They are witnesses of God's glory to unbelievers, the "gentiles" of the world, by their *testimony* of salvation according to God's Word. The Levites are the "spirit-filled" believers among all Christians. They demonstrate by their *lifestyles* their dependence upon and obedience to the *person* of our Lord Christ Jesus. They minister the word of God to the other Christians, by being witnesses of the present dynamic *presence*

Experiencing Sanctification 253

and *reality* of Christ. And the priests are the more mature among the "spirit-filled" believers. They live as directed by the Rhema Word of God, and radiate a joy of being in intimate *union* with Him. They minister the present-day purposes and directives of God, primarily to other "spirit-filled" Christians, through such callings in the Body of Christ as the prophet and apostle.

5. Reconciliation *vs* Consecration *vs* Sanctification

How are these three generic "stages" of our sanctification process related to the "basics" of salvation? In Chapter Two earlier in this volume, we outlined some of those "basics" of salvation in the context of our Lord Christ Jesus *enabling* us to be, and to function as, members of His Body: salvation, eternal life, faith, grace, and baptisms. In Chapters Five, Six and Seven earlier in this volume we discussed the practical meaning of "grace" in some depth, along with one of those "baptisms": "baptism into the Holy Spirit".

How does all of that tie into our generic model of the sanctification "process"? That tie-in is summarized in Rows [11] through [18] of Sanctification Stages Chart Two, following, as a continuation of Sanctification Stages Chart One.

Reconciled Stage

First, we summarize some of our former discussions on this first stage of sanctification. As we initially repent of our sins and turn to Christ on Calvary for our forgiveness and initial stages of our salvation, we are "born again" into the "family of God". This brings us into the first stage, where we are "little

Sanctification Stages Chart Two

Row #	Three "Types" Of Believer →	CARNAL/FLESHLY [SARKIKOS]	SOULICAL/NATURAL [PSUCHIKOS]	SPIRITUAL [PNEUMATIKOS]
[11]	Believer's **Status/Position**	Justified/Reconciled	Consecrated & Empowered	Sanctified & Humbled
[12]	Our **Attitude** To The Gospel	Acceptance	Involvement	Commitment
[13]	"**Crisis**" Experience Of Entering Into This Stage	Repentance Experience: Reversal Of Attitude Unto Seeking God With Whole Heart (Jeremiah 29:13)	Supernatural Experience: Encounter Of Vivid Awareness Of The Presence Of The Person Christ Jesus	Emptying Experience: Realizing That We Are Nothing: Utter Abandonment In Christ Let Go And Let God
[14]	"**Pre-Occupation**" Of Believer During This Stage	Sin-Forgiveness: Grateful Acceptance Of Fact Christ Died For My Sins Immersion In Word: Bible Study & Prayer Victory Over Carnality: Reckon It Crucified	Body Of Christ Ministries: Word & Healing Gifts Of Holy Spirit; Victory Over Demonic Forces Heart-Circumcision: Yielding To Will Of Christ's Indwelling Spirit	Offensiveness Of Our Residual Sin-Nature Resurrection Life Of Christ Indwelling (Galatians 2:20) Abandonment In Christ Companionship Walk In Him
[15]	**Baptisms** Involved in Entrance Into This Stage (Hebrews 6:2a)	Into Body Of Christ via New Covenant: Rom. 6:3, 1 Cor. 12:13	Into Holy Spirit: Matt. 3:11, Mark 1:8, Luke 3:16, John 1:33, Acts 1:5 & 11:16	Into Sufferings: Matthew 20:22 & Mark 10:39
[16]	**Deliverance** By Christ	Delivered From Wages (Consequences) Of Sin (i.e., Death)	Delivered From Presence Of Sin (i.e., From Living In Flesh)	Delivered From Desire For Sin (Romans Chapter 8)
[17]	We Are **Freed** From	Satan's Ownership Of Us	Satan's Power Over Us	Our Desire For Sin
[18]	We **Experience**	New Life	Victory	Ministry As His Love-Vessels

Experiencing Sanctification

children" (Row [4]) of God the Father (Row [5]). We receive forgiveness of our sins (Row [8]) by the milk of God's grace (Row [7]), are grafted into the "Israel" of God (Row [10]), and we live according to law (Row [9]).

What does it mean for us to having been "born again"? We discussed this in Chapter Two earlier in this volume: to receive "eternal life", a quality of life that enables us to dynamically and creatively interact with the godhead in the "spiritual domain". Hence, as noted in Row [2], our human *spirit* is made alive in Christ.

This gives us a status before God that is described in the Scriptures by the words "justified" and "reconciled" (see Row [11]). "Justified" here means our former sins are forgotten by God, and we are *positionally* reconciled or restored to being a member of the Godhead, no longer under satan's slave-ownership (Row [17]). (See our discussion of the *work* of the Cross in Chapter Four of this volume above.) By our *acceptance* of that truth (Row [12]) *via* a crisis experience involving a choice on our part to "repent" or to change our attitude to that of seeking God (Row [13]), we are delivered from the consequences of our former sins by His forgiveness (Row 16]). As Row [14] mentions, our pre-occupation during this period of our Christian walk is on our sins having been forgiven, on learning God's Word, and on subduing our carnality. We are freshly grateful for the great forgiveness of our sins by Christ on Calvary; we can't seem to spend enough time in the Bible; we are growing in the habit of daily devotions and prayer; and we are deeply concerned with the sinful desires of our flesh. We are initiated into the Body of Christ (Row [15]) to manifest Him here on earth, when receive that new "eternal" life (Row [18]).

Consecrated Stage

Summarizing our previous discussion on the second stage of sanctification, as illustrated in Sanctification Stages Charts One and Two: It is by the Holy Spirit in us (Row [5]) that we learn to minister to one another as fellow members of the Body of Christ (Row [7]) as we are sanctified for His use (Row [8]) as New Testament Levites or priests (Row [10]). We increasingly grow in light of God's Word (Row [9]) as we begin to mature as "young men" in our relationship with Christ (Row [4]).

By this He *consecrates and empowers* us (Row [11]). We become much more *involved* with Him (Row [12]) in the "spiritual domain" as we grow in mental and experiential awareness of the presence of the person of Christ Jesus (Row [13]). We also grow stronger in victory over our satan's residual influences (Rows [2], [6], [17] and [18]) through our flesh and sin-nature that is being purged (Row [16]). (See or discussion of the *way* of the Cross in Chapter Four earlier in this volume.

The milk of Grace (the Holy Spirit of Christ Jesus living within us) now begins His workings within us, that our soul increasingly yield to Him through our human spirit as we grow in faith through repentance. How this is explosively enhanced by our being "Baptized into His Holy Spirit" (Row [15]) by Christ is discussed in Chapter Seven earlier in this volume. This is indicated in Row [14]: our pre-occupation is now with growing in exercising our callings in the Body of Christ. Heart *circumcision*, a Biblical concept that applies here, refers to our choosing to ever *yield* to those workings of the indwelling Holy Spirit of Christ Jesus, so that He in us does the doings of these Body of Christ ministries rather than we trying to do the doings *for* Him.

Sanctified Stage

Summarizing our discussion above on the third stage of sanctification: Oneness with God's plan (Row [6]), through tighter union with Christ the Son as a dynamic ***Person*** (Row [5]), enables us to receive revelation much more purely from God (Row [8]). That is the meaning of the type of "meat" (Row [7]), as we function as elders (Row [4]) and priests to fellow believers (Row [10]). Our relationship with Christ is now one of joy, the most mature form of faith (Row [9]).

Our self, our soul, still controls, and whatever He seeks to effect through us is subject to our "veto", i.e., is constrained by our human wisdom and choice. Hence, our soul yet requires a more complete *emptying* (Row [13]) in order that the indwelling Holy Spirit of Christ Jesus is more fully in control (Rows [1] through [3]).

But the emptying experience of Row [13] (otherwise known as our being "broken") through which He must bring us in order for us to reach this stage, humbles us as well as sanctifies us (Row [11]). As indicated in Row [14], we are shockingly pre-occupied with increasing discoveries of various residual aspects of our sin-nature that still hinder us from being pure vessels of the Light, Life and Love of Christ both unto us and through us unto others. We are led to ever seek to more deeply abandon ourselves unto Christ our Sabbath Rest, and to flow with Him in deeper companionship-union. These disciplining dealings by Him in our lives (Hebrews 12:5-11, etc.) have been referred to by some as a "dark night of our soul" or "maturing through soul affliction". We discuss these purging experiences in depth in the following Chapter Nine.

Only by a *total* commitment on our part (Row [12]) would we persist during these dealings. We are baptized into the *sufferings* of Christ (Row [15]) by virtue of our close union with Him and in accordance with His use of us in ministry (Row [18]) as vessels of His love and life to the world and instruments in His hand as the High Priest. But through this we are delivered from even our desire for sin (Row [17]), and we begin to indeed realize in our lives the "Promised land" of Romans Chapter Eight (Row [16]). Hallelujah!

7. Take Up Your Cross

Note the emphasis upon our increasing personal relationship with Christ Jesus: He first being a "remote" savior Who forgives us of our sins but Who also becomes our slave-master; He then being Who *empowers* us but Who also purges us; and ultimately to He being One in Whom we are so embedded, so in union with, so close to, that He is all and nothing whatsoever else matters to us.

That ever deepening of our personal relationship with Him involves two sub-processes that must occur *simultaneously*, and through which He brings us, step by step, *iteratively:* dying to self; and trusting and depending upon Him alone. The first process is known as *crucifixion;* the second as *following Him.*

The concept of our being crucified with Christ we introduced in depth in Chapter Two earlier in this volume. This is also tied to the differences between the *work* of the Cross and the

Experiencing Sanctification

way of the Cross, as we discussed in Chapter Four earlier in this volume. We summarize those discussions in Rows [19] and [20] of Sanctification Stages Chart Three following, a continuation of Sanctification Stages Charts One and Two.

In each of these stages, what is important is not what I am or do *per se;* it is how my ***personal relationship*** with Christ Jesus deepens! As my personal relationship with Him deepens, so also does my ***personal identification*** with His crucifixion. At first, Calvary is simply a historical event that involved ***Him***. But then it becomes ***my*** personal death ***with*** Him. And finally, and as a consequence of that, it becomes my personal abandonment unto Him, so that His ***life is released*** unto others through me!

At first, I acknowledge that He, Christ Jesus, was crucified *for* me (i.e., on my behalf to undo the Adamic curse on me). Through ***repentance*** (transformation of my thought life, my very mentality), I receive "eternal life" (regeneration), and through my human ***spirit*** I begin true communication with Him Who is Spirit.

However, we are commanded not only to repent, but also to be ***baptized*** (Acts 2:38). Romans 6:3-11 strongly emphasizes that ***our*** baptism is a profound and all-pervasive ***personal*** identification of us with ***His*** crucifixion. The water of John's baptism is a watery ***grave*** in which ***our*** body of sin, the life and power of our fleshly appetites, is ***buried***. So, not only was Christ Jesus crucified for me, but He was crucified ***as*** me, and I ***with*** Him!

His crucifixion *for* me deals with my ***legal or positional*** relationship with God in Christ Jesus - that which is meant by

Sanctification Stages Chart Three

Row #	Three "Types" Of Believer	CARNAL/FLESHLY [SARKIKOS]	SOULICAL/NATURAL [PSUCHIKOS]	SPIRITUAL [PNEUMATIKOS]
[19]	Christ Is **Crucified**:	**For** Us	**As** Us	**Into** Us
[20]	"Working" Of **Cross** For Entering Into This Stage	**Substitution**: Christ's Death **For** Me	**Identification**: My Death (Flesh) With Christ	**Release**: Christ's Life Poured Out Through Us
[21]	The **Righteousness** Of Christ **In** Us Is:	**Imputed** (Legal State With God)	**Imparted** (Our Behaviour)	**Impregnated** (Our Character)
[22]	Christ Is **In** Us As:	**Mental** Awareness	His Spiritual **Presence**	Total **Pre-Eminence**
[23]	**Growth** In The Spirit-Led Walk	We **Serve** Him As Bond-Slaves	We **Appropriate** Him In Us	We **Actualize** He Himself

Experiencing Sanctification   261

the theological term "justification". His crucifixion *as* me and I with Him deals with my life-style, my attitudes, my behaviour patterns - in short, with my *character*.

Our existence does not end in the watery grave of baptism. For we are also raised up out of that grave in a resurrection into the new life! We not only have been crucified with Him; we are also to be *resurrected* with Him! We are now to *live* the life of Christ.

How? We can't! In no way can you or I *ever*, in this physical world, live His life. Only *He* can! Only as He, in us, lives His life *through* us, can we ever manifest His life to others in this world. So, He must yet further deal with us, that we can *truly* say with Paul in Galatians 2:20: "... for (though) I have been crucified with Christ, ... it is no longer I who live, but Christ lives in me; and the life that I now live in the ... (physical) I live by faith in the Son of God ...."

This is why we say that Christ Jesus must also be crucified *into* us. He had to leave His own earthly body in order to abide in ours. By He being crucified into us, He is no longer constrained by (our) flesh, but is fully *released* to truly be all He is, in and through us. Only by our *willful* yielding is He truly *released* to will and work His good purposes in and through us (Philippians 2:13).

One way of depicting the concept of Christ being crucified *into* us, is the Biblical description of "Passover" in Exodus Chapter 12. "Passover" (PhSCh in the Hebrew) in verse 23 means that the Lord will *step* through the doorway in order to *enter* the house. The *Lord* sees the blood and enters. It is the Lord's *presence* in the house that keeps the destroyer out.

The Blood is seen by the *Lord* as a *welcome* sign to Him. Revelations 3:20 says, "Behold, I stand at the door and knock; if any one hears My voice and opens the door, I will come in to him, and will dine with him, and he with Me (in intimate fellowship!)." Passover denotes Christ *indwelling* us.

8. Follow Him

To "follow Him" means, of course, to live our lives in increasing identification with Christ in all He is and does.

In Row [21] of Sanctification Stages Chart Three we outline the corresponding increasing stages of our identification with the *righteousness* of Christ. First, it is legally *imputed* to us, just as my earthly father's name was imputed to me as his little child from the day of my birth, even though it would be years before I was sufficiently mature to live up to his name. But as we mature in identification with Him, His righteousness begins to influence our behavior, our actions, our thoughts and words. This we denote as His righteousness being *imparted* to us, slowly but increasingly over time. As that impartation of His righteousness continues, it slowly becomes an actual part of our very being, our very character - our entire soul becomes increasingly *saturated* or *impregnated* with Him as a Person, and hence with His righteousness.

Another way of saying this is summarized in Row [22]. At first, Christ is in us as His Holy Spirit indwelling and enlivening our human spirit, but our grasp of His reality is primarily only *intellectual,* that is, a *mental* awareness. As we grow, i.e. as our soul continues to yield to Him indwelling, we increase in seeing His *spiritual reality* and His indwelling *presence*. And the more mature stages are of His being

Experiencing Sanctification

prominent is described by Paul in Colossians 1:18 as He having the *pre-eminence* or "first place in all things" - in our individual hearts as well as in His Body collectively.

Since all of our growth is effected by His indwelling Holy Spirit, we can also summarize the process as stages in our Spirit-led walk, shown in Row [23]. At first, we only know to *serve* Him as His bond-slaves. Then we learn to increasingly *appropriate* Him, His strength, His life, His love, in ministry one to another. As our yielding to Him in us increases, others will increasingly see Christ Himself in us and in all we do and say. That we note as our *actualizing* Him, His Light (Word), His life, His love - He Himself.

In summary, salvation is a multi-stage *process*, with the significance of crucifixion related to each stage. For simplicity, we view the salvation *process* as also of three stages of sanctification. First, I *have been* saved - an act or process that has been completed in the *past* (see for example Ephesians 2:5, 8, 13; 2 Timothy 1:9; and Titus 3:5). Second, I *am being* saved - a process that is taking place in the *present* time (see for example 1 Corinthians 15:2 and Philippians 2:12). And third, I *shall be* saved - an event that will occur in the *future*, if I "endure until then" (see for example Matthew 10:22 & 24:13; Mark 13:13; and Romans 5:9 & 10).

End Notes: Chapter Eight

1. Madame Guyon, *Madame Guyon* (Autobiography), (Chicago, Ill.: Moody Press, c/o MLM), pp. 313-315.

2. Reference to the laver in the Tabernacle in the Wilderness. See for example Exodus 30:18, 38:8 and 40:30.

3. Richard F. Lovelace, *Dynamics Of Spiritual Life - An Evangelical Theology Of Renewal*, (Downers Grove, Illinois: Inter-Varsity Press, 1979), pp. 19-20. Copyright © 1979 by InterVarsity Christian Fellowship of the United States of America. Used by permission of InterVarsity Press, P.O. Box 1400, Downers Grove, IL 60515.

Chapter Nine
Maturing Through Soul Affliction

In the preceding chapter we briefly explored several Biblical depictions of the three general stages of the Holy Spirit's sanctifying us in our personal relationships with our Lord Christ Jesus. We have yet many additional typological depictions of the three general stages, which we explore in Chapters Ten, Eleven and Twelve following. But in this chapter we pause to study in more detail the role of suffering, i.e. emptying, in each stage.

There have been several missing gaps in our treatise so far, such as: (1) more details on just how does what we call "inner heart healing" fit into sanctification? (2) just how do we grow from freshly receiving the Baptism into the Holy Spirit unto full functioning in our ministry callings in the Body of Christ? (3) just how and when do we transverse from the *second* to the *third* stage? (4) how many believers actually transverse from stage to stage and how long in time does that usually take? and (5) just what does growing into and functioning during the *third* stage actually involve?

These questions are not new; they have been deeply searched out by many saints throughout church history. However, perhaps no one has addressed in writing the second and third general stages of sanctification more completely than has Madame Guyon in her late seventeenth-century treatise *Spiritual Torrents*[1]. Because of the timeliness and thoroughness of that classic, we basically follow her insights throughout this chapter. An excellent summary and interpretive discussion of Madame Guyon's *Spiritual Torrents* is found in Penn-Lewis's *Life Out Of Death*[2]. Madame Guyon's autobiography is currently available in English, published by Moody Press[3].

Mme. Jeanne Marie Bouvier Guyon (1648-1717) was one of a number of Roman Catholic "mystics" or "Pietists" of the 16*th* and 17*th* centuries. Others were Theresa de Cepeda y Ahumada (1515-1582), Juan de Yepes y Alvarez ("John of the Cross") (1542-1591), Michael Miguel de Molinos (1627?-1697), and Francois de Salignac Fenelon (1651-1715). While the Protestant Reformation of that period was predominantly intellectual and doctrinal, these mystics and their followers found genuine ***experiential Spiritual union*** with their Lord Christ Jesus. Had the movement not been stamped out by the Jesuit Inquisition during the 1680s, it could likely have been perhaps the greatest Spiritual revival in all of church history. Nevertheless, the movement was squelched, and it remained completely dormant for two centuries.

Edwards has recently published Molinos' *The Spiritual Guide*. In that reprint[4] he comments on the movement as follows:

"... a revival which, had it continued even just a few years more, might well have changed the entire Catholic mind.

"Thrown out by the Catholics, unknown by the Protestants, we could almost say that the deeper Christian walk has been looking for a home ever since.

"Certainly that deeper walk has never, since that day, made roots and spread its influence quite as deeply as during the later part of the seventeenth century. The Protestant church, born in intellectualism and in doctrinal disputes, an affair almost entirely of the mind, has left little room within its walls for emphasis on a deeper walk with Jesus Christ. Catholicism reigned in its tolerance and gave such practices a far smaller place of influence than previously. ..."

The writings of that movement were finally translated, interpreted, taught and published in English in the late nineteenth century. Since these works are still so valid and enlightening today, we quote from them throughout this chapter, especially from Penn-Lewis' above-cited interpretation of Guyon and Edward's above-cited interpretation of Molinos.

1. "Torrents", "Classes", "Planes" And "Degrees"

The original *Spiritual Torrents* is available in English today[5] and we highly recommend it to the serious reader. However, it is a bit too lengthy and tedious for general readership. Note Penn-Lewis[6] comments on "Spiritual Torrents":

"The book itself, *Spiritual Torrents*, is too analytical, too involved in expression, too overdrawn, too mystical, for general circulation; yet the deeply-taught writer had learnt to diagnose God's dealings in the deeper walk of faith as few modern writers can."

So we basically follow Penn-Lewis' summary and timeless insights of "Spiritual Torrents", interwoven of course with our current understandings of the general stages of sanctification. The original author (Guyon) and interpreter (Penn-Lewis) used quite different wording, expressions and semantics in many places than we do. Furthermore, they wrote primarily from their own *personal experiences* of their deep Spiritual walk with their Lord Christ Jesus; whereas in this volume we add considerable Biblical exegetical undergirding. Guyon's primary Biblical source, aside from the New Testament writings of Paul (esp. Romans, Ephesians and Philippians) was the Old Testament book Song of Songs (as we indeed also use in Chapter Ten following in this volume.)

Guyon uses the terms "torrents", "class", "ways", "planes" and "degrees" to describe the several stages or "levels" of sanctification, i.e., of the dealings of the indwelling Holy Spirit of Christ Jesus in our lives. By "torrents" she refers to the relative *intensity* with which the "soul" (believer) is longing for a deeper walk with the Lord at the time. By both "class" and "way" she means the same thing as our three general stages of sanctification (with one exception discussed below). In some sense she uses "torrents", "classes" and "ways" somewhat synonymously. And by "degree" she introduces several details of the inner workings of the indwelling Holy Spirit of Christ Jesus.

Here is Guyon's introduction of these terms[7]:

"As soon as a soul is touched of God, and its return to Him is true and sincere, He gives to it, after the first cleansing effected by confession and contrition, a certain instinct to return to Him more perfectly, so that it may be [entirely] united to Him. Then it feels that it is not created for the amusements and trifles of the world, but that it has a center and an end, whither it must endeavor to return, and out of which it can never find true repose.

"This instinct is communicated to the soul in a very high measure, though higher with some than with others, according to the designs which God has with them; but they all have a loving impatience to be purified, and to take the ways and means necessary to return to their source and origin. They may be compared to rivers, which, after issuing from their sources, flow with a perpetual course into the sea. Some of these rivers you see moving majestically and slowly, and others more rapidly. But there are some rivers and *torrents* which run with a frightful impetuosity that nothing can check. All the burdens you might put upon them, and all the dikes you might erect to hinder their course, would serve only to redouble its violence.

"It is thus with these souls. Some advance gently towards perfection, never arriving at the sea, or reaching it very late; being satisfied to lose themselves in some stronger and more rapid river, which hurries them along with itself to the sea. Others, of the second kind ["class"] proceed thither more decidedly and rapidly than the first. They even carry along with them to the sea a large number of smaller streams; but they are dull and sluggish in comparison with the last ["class"], who hurry on with so much impetuosity that they are fit for very few purposes. ... The second ["class"], on the other hand, are more agreeable and more useful. Their majesty is pleasing to behold; they are quite loaded with merchandise; and all persons venture upon them without fear or danger."

We illustrate Guyon's concepts, interleaved with ours, in Table Two following. We have the same three general stages of the sanctification process as are illustrated in Sanctification Stages Charts One through Twelve of the preceding and following chapters in this volume. In fact, we "peg" some of the rows of Table Two to corresponding rows in those Sanctification Stages Charts, as follows:

> Row [a] of Table Two --> Row [4] of Sanctification Stages Chart One.
> Row [b] of Table Two --> Row [16] of Sanctification Stages Chart Two.
> Row [d] of Table Two --> Row [9] of Sanctification Stages Chart One.
> Row [f] of Table Two --> Row [32] of Sanctification Stages Chart Four.
> Row [h] of Table Two --> Row [24] of Sanctification Stages Chart Four.
> Row [i] of Table Two --> Rows [13, 14 & 15] of Sanctification Stages Chart Two and Row [30] of Sanctification Stages Chart Four.

Note particularly how both the second and third general stages of sanctification are each sub-dived into two sub-stages. By this subdivision we note some important details of how the

Table Two
Maturing Through Soul Affliction

"Level" →	1	2a	2b	3a	3b
Stage of Believer's [a] Spiritual *Growth* In Christ	SARKIKOS/CARNAL "Babes In Christ" "Little Children"	PSUCHIKOS/NATURAL or SOULICAL "Young Men"		PNEUMATIKOS/SPIRITUAL "Elders"	
Effecting (Working-[b] Out) Of Cross To Which Our Lord Calls The Believer	*Remission* (Forgiveness) Of Sins	*Deliverance* From Appeal Of The World And Corruption Of Self		Profound *Emptying* And *Outpouring*: Experiencing With Christ His Spiritual Shame And The Full Mystery Of His Cross	
God's *Purpose* For Us [c] In This Stage	Apprehending The Totality Of *Forgiveness* Of Our Sins & Our *Freedom* To Come To God via Christ	Our Fully Apprehending *Spiritual Reality* And Our Becoming *Unimpeded Channels* Of The Spiritual Light, Life And Love Of Christ Flowing Into Us And Through Us As He Chooses		Our Fully Apprehending Our *Position With Christ In The Heavenlies, Here And Now;* To Function As His *Agents;* And To Prepare Ourselves For *Bridehood*	
[d] *"Way"* Of Walk	Way Of *Law*	Way Of *Light*		Way Of *Faith*	
[e] Soul/Torrent *"Class"*	Souls Of *"1st"* Class	Souls Of *"2nd"* Class		Souls Of *"3rd"* Class	
4 *"Planes"* Of The [f] Spiritual Life	*Evangelistic* ("Salvation")	*Revival* (by Holy Spirit Indwelling)		Path Of *Cross* *Emptying* Of Self-Nature	*Ascension* And Spiritual Warfare Standing In His *Presence*
Torrent Level And [g] *"Degree"*	Low, Erratic *Advance* By *Human* Strength	Saturated And Empowered By The *Holy Spirit* Initial Filling	1st Deg: *Inner Healing*	2nd Deg: *Powerlessness* 3rd Deg: *Loss/Burial*	4th Degree: *Posessed* By God In *Life Abundant*
[h] *Song Of Songs* Ref's	1:1 - 2:7	2:8 - 3:5	3:6 - 5:1	5:2 - 6:3	6:4 - 8:14
Major *Steps* In Our [i] Relationship In Christ	*Regeneration* via Repentance	Baptism Into Holy Spirit	Unto Mount Moriah Inner Heart Healing	Emptying - Baptism Into Suffering	Holiness In Walk And Victory Of Mt. Zion

indwelling Holy Spirit of Christ Jesus actually works in our hearts.

Guyon makes a different demarcation between our second and third general stages. In Rows [d] and [e] we see Guyon's "Way of Light" and "Souls of the Second Class of Torrents" refers only to the *initial* substage of receiving the Baptism into the Holy Spirit, and her "Way of Faith" and "Souls of the Third Class of Torrents" refers to all *subsequent* workings of Him in us. In Row [f] we reflect her use of the idea of "Plane" or level of our personal relationship with our Lord Christ Jesus, and note the two sub-stages of the third general stage, being first an *emptying* of all of our self-seeking, and then an *ascension* into a fuller union with our Lord Christ Jesus. In Rows [g], [h] and [i], we capture Guyon's concept of "degrees" of the Holy Spirit's actual workings.

2. The Repeated Cycle

Just what are these "degrees" of actual workings? Penn-Lewis[8] interprets Guyon in some vital areas for our edification:

> "Madame Guyon ... says that in every plane of the spiritual life there is a beginning, working out, and a consummation of the life in that degree, followed by a passage into the next plane, where there is again a beginning, a working out, a consummation. In each plane you appear to learn the very same lessons over again, but they are all being learned in a deeper degree. For instance, in the first plane you learn the way of faith in Christ as Saviour, and then you have to learn to exercise [that] faith again in the next plane, and again in the next. It is just as hard to learn the lesson of bare

faith in the fourth plane as in the first, and yet, as you look back, you can see the hard lessons of the first plane are now quite simple and easy.

"Furthermore, it is true that, speaking generally, it often takes years to get through each plane! When you pass into a new plane of the spiritual life, it is often with some great conscious 'blessing'. [It is] a God-given experience of fullness in Christ, which may be described as a 'taste' of what God has for you in that plane in its consummation. For instance:

[1] you get a ***revelation*** of the ascension life, seated with Christ in the heavenly places, and the joy and light of it is so real, that you think you will never come down again to the lower planes you now leave behind you; but

[2] in a brief while of weeks, or months, the 'conscious' blessing - lasting according to the extent of the revelation and its power - ***apparently disappears***; and

[3] you perhaps ***struggle to regain*** what you think you have lost. Now you have to fight by bare faith, to hold the ground you have taken. Then

[4] follows what may be called a 'tunnel' experience, when you go through test upon test; in which, perhaps, you may think you fail, but through all you find there is ***advancement;*** and

[5] final emergence into the ***full consummation*** of that specific plane of the spiritual life, where you understand the way of abiding; for in the working into you of that life by the 'tunnel' experience, God has removed what stands in the way of the permanent abiding in that stage of the knowledge of Him...."

"But let us remember, if God gives you a message which He means you to take hold of, *He holds you*, even when you appear to lose it. His Word given to you *lays hold of you*. That word has divine life and energy in it, and it can grip you, and hold you to it. God requires your co-operation, of course, and you must actively take the word by faith; but the power is in the Word itself when God has spoken it to you. If the Lord has given you the word 'power over the power of the enemy', you have to co-operate by saying in response, 'I *choose* and accept it, Lord, but I have no power to hold it; the Word must hold me.'

"And in truth you often apparently lose it, so that it goes right away from you, but if you go on steadily in bare faith, you come at last through the tunnel working of God, to the consummation point, and then what looked like a literal impossibility to you when God gave you the light, you find has been wrought into you as part of your very life; assimilated and incorporated into your spiritual being."

In summary, then, these emptying cycles consist of a sequence of six aspects:

(1) the *vision or initial possession* of a new truth or aspect of relationship with Christ, with faith to exercise new abilities thereof;

(2) a subsequent *loss of our awareness* of Christ's presence in this new relationship, and an apparent loss or diminution of our abilities to walk in the new vision;

(3) our vain *striving*, with human wisdom and strength, to regain Him and them;

(4) *surrender*, when we become "burned out" or

Maturing Through Soul Affliction

otherwise realize that our self-strivings are vain and useless;

(5) *revisitation*, when He restores our awareness of His presence, and also our faith to exercise the new abilities; and

(6) *consummation* of the stage, whereupon we actually walk in our new relationship with Christ with faith to exercise the new abilities, purely on His strength, by His wisdom, in His righteousness, and upon His initiatives.

One saint in the twentieth century whose life-story includes several vision-loss-struggle-surrender-revisitation-consummation cycles, but who as a result radiantly ministered the Presence and Word of Christ to many of the Lord's servants who came to her, was Martha Wing Robinson[9].

Also to this author's knowledge, the most recent servant of the Lord to teach on these emptying cycles (but not in those terms) is David Wilkerson[10].

When God gives us a specific personal promise, He also puts a *sentence of death* on that promise, and places us in circumstances in which there is no way that the promise's fulfillment is possible. Just before its fulfillment, is the darkest moment, when its fulfillment appears to be totally and utterly hopeless. His purpose for this is to get us to the point where we trust *only* in Him to bring it to pass, that He alone gets the glory, and that our faith in Him become purest (i.e., most refined).

It is natural, but a lack of faith, for us to doubt the promise in those times. How do we know that the promise was/is indeed of God and not of our vain imaginations? Two ways: (1) the promise keeps *repeating* itself in our spirit; He won't let us forget it. (2) *Many tiny blessings*, including micro-miracles, all *re* the promise but not its fulfillment, occur during those darkest and most hopeless moments.

So, we must not die in the winter (as Dr. Millicent Thompson[11] admonishes). There will come a window (of time) to exercise our faith. Again, that window occurs when things look darkest and most hopeless. Then, faith *alone* will see us through the trials and darkness. But also then, nothing whatsoever can withstand that faith. What is the evidence that our faith is pure and refined? *Rest.* Quiet assurance that God will do it. Freedom from anxiety about it. Deep-seated trust in the Lord.

Incidentally, there is a direct relationship between these loss-striving-surrender-revisitation-consummation aspects and the five stages of the "grieving process" as we discussed in Volume I[12] of this series. Elisabeth Kubler-Ross's[13] model of the grieving process has five phases: (1) denial and shock; (2) anger with both depression and hope; (3) emotional resistance, often also with attempts to "bargain" with God; (4) grief and emptying, often with deep depression; and (5) surrender and acceptance. We "combine" her 2nd ("anger") and $3rd$ ("bargaining") phases into what we call "striving". We do this since anger may or may not be present, but here the real issue is that we tend to blame ourselves for having "failed God", and instead of "bargaining" with Him we may try (harder) with our own efforts on our own strength.

3. Purging Of Self

Why this repeated cycle of vision-loss-struggle-surrender-revisitation-consummation? Is our Lord "playing games" with

Maturing Through Soul Affliction

us? Once the Lord blesses us with a fresh revelation of Him and His ways and we indeed respond with genuine and deep appreciation of Him, He then takes away from us our awareness of that. And even then, when we *intensely* seek Him afresh, He does not answer, until we stop our striving? Why? What is He trying to teach us?

There are several forms in which these questions are answered, but they all relate to this issue: our intrinsic tendencies to live our lives by our own efforts of self-seeking and self-protecting! He *must* break and purge us of that if His will is to be effected in our lives.

So one of the primary reasons for this repeated cycle is to force us to realize that *nothing whatsoever* that *we do* can bring His blessings; they come and come only by *His grace* given freely to us because of His love for us. We need to yield to Him, yes! We need to seek and desire Him, yes! It is *He* we seek, desire, and yield to. And our thus seeking and desiring and yielding to Him releases His grace unto us. But the bestowing comes from Him through grace, not through our striving to "earn" it (i.e., through ministry).

The general cycle is usually repeated one or more times in each of the three general stages of sanctification. Each general cycle may involve several local iterations. And each time the trials and sufferings, and the new discoveries of faith, are more intense than before.

In the first general stage of our sanctification, the cycle involves our: (1) laying hold of the *magnitude* of the forgiveness of our sins by the shed blood of Christ on Calvary; (2) sacrificing our *labors* in service to Christ; and (3) reckoning our *flesh* or carnality crucified with Christ. In the second stage, the cycle involves shifting from our *serving* Him by *our* ministries, to being vessels/channels of *Him* ministering *through* us, and inner heart healing to *release* the indwelling Holy Spirit to flow through us unto others with less impedance (i.e., a significant step in reckoning our *self* or soulishness crucified with Christ). In the third stage, the cycle is a more complete *emptying* of our *self*, of our sin-nature, of our soulishness, and a more complete walk in union with Him in *faith*, so that the outpouring of the indwelling Holy Spirit becomes *pure* in the holiness and righteousness of Christ Himself.

Each repetition of this vision-loss-struggle-surrender-revisitation-consummation cycle is yet a deeper yielding in the three main components of *repentance:* (1) repentance *from* our intrinsic aversion against God due to our shame/guilt over our sin nature, and *unto* total appreciation of God's continual forgiveness and full apprehension of God's grace; (2) repentance *from* our sin of unbelief that thinks Christ is not really in us and/or is not really sufficient or willing to provide all our needs and protection against all that is not in His will for us, *unto* a deep-seated trust in Him in all things at all times; and (3) repentance *from* self, specifically from our self-protecting strategies that distance us from God and from one another, *unto* full enjoyment of Christ both in us and in one another. In other words, these three main components of required deep repentance are not limited just to the inner heart healing processes of the second stage; they are involved in *all* stages of our sanctification to some extent.

The "new" blessings that we first get a "taste" for and finally appropriate, are totally unrelated to our *soulish* facilities: they are neither emotional nor intellectual. They are *spiritual*, and can be appropriated only *spiritually*. Yet how we insist that we be able to understand them, that we be able to feel them! That's so we can control and manipulate them in our self-seeking and self-protecting. But in this repeated cycle, we are forced to set aside our emotional desires and our intellectual/doctrinal quests, and to wait until we *experience* His reality, and experience Him in *depth*. It is *He*, and not things *from Him*, that is central.

Suffering is to be expected at every stage of our growth in our personal relationship with our Lord Christ Jesus. Edwards reflects on Molinos's "The Spiritual Guide"[14] on this:

> "Molinos says it again and again, a great deal of suffering awaits us if we follow the Lord as we should."

We need such trials and sufferings to discipline us, specifically our soul. Molinos strongly emphasizes this[15]:

> "It is the nature of each of us to be rather base, proud, ambitious, full of a great deal of appetite, judgments, rationalizations, and opinions. If something does not come into our lives to humiliate us then surely all these things will undo us. ... So, what does your Lord do? He allows your faith to be assaulted, even with suggestions of pride, gluttony, rage, perhaps blaspheming, cursing and yes, even despair. All of these serve to humble our natural pride, as a wholesome medicine within the midst of these assaults."

"At the time of your conversion, your Lord came to dwell within you ... in your spirit ... the inmost part of your being. ... Now for that celestial King to make even [particularly] your *soul* His habitation, it is necessary that changes be wrought in your soul. The Lord purifies our soul as gold is purified in a terrible furnace of fire.

"... the soul never really loves and believes [God] more than at those times when it is afflicted. Whether you believe it or not (and whether you consent to it or not), those doubtings and fears and tribulations that beset you ... are nothing else but the refinements of His love. ... If you need proof of this fact you need only look at the progress made in the soul when the conflagration is over. ... First, there is a growing distrust of the self nature and a profound acknowledgement of the greatness and omnificence [i.e., unlimited in creative power] of God[;] there is a greater confidence that the Lord will deliver you from all dangers. Furthermore, the mouth is more willing to confess with vigorous faith.

"There are two ways for the soul to be cleansed. The first is that of affliction, anguish, distress, and inward torment. The second is that of fire of a burning love, love impatient and hungry. ... It is true that sometimes the Lord uses both these ways to deal with our souls. *All* revelation and insight into God, all true experiential knowledge of God, *arises from suffering*, that is the truest proof of love."

In the soul being disciplined through trials and sufferings, the object is our seeing Christ not by our mind nor emotions but in our *spirit*. Molinos explains that[16]:

> "Believe that you *are* before the Lord, *and* in His presence; continue to come to Him with sweetness and quiet attention. Don't try to discover things. Don't try to understand. Don't particularly try to seek a way out of darkness, and most of all do *not* stop coming before Him as you did in the most faithful time of your life and in those times when spiritual riches and blessings were at their highest! ... Do not try to look for some emotion, or even a tender devotion, toward your Lord. Only express your desire to do His will and to be His pleasure. Otherwise you will simply go in circles throughout your life and take not even one step toward the inward goal. An emotional experience with Jesus Christ must not be your goal, for it is not His goal."

That is, we must *know* Him, not just know *about* Him with our reasoning minds nor just *feel* Him with our emotions[17]:

> "One of the healthiest things you can do in order to learn to walk in the inward way ... is to look upon reason and 'sound logic' as something that is created. The most *reasonable* conduct you can perform is to discard a great deal of your reasoning. Believe God. Believe that He permits grievances to fall into your life, for it is true. He *does* allow grievances into every life lived on earth. He does this so that we may be humbled, and so that certain aspects of our nature may be annihilated. He does these things so that we may live in complete resignation to His will. Your Lord *pays more attention* to *that* believer who lives in an internal resignation than He does to all those who work

miracles ... even to raising the dead.

"The understanding of spiritual truth is actually hidden and shut off from most men, even those of *theological* learning. ... Because theirs is a scholastic knowledge. But there is also a *science* of the *saints*. This science is known only to those who heartily love and those who seek the end of their self-nature. ...

"It is a maxim that will endure: To truly know the living God, *this* begets humility. To acquire learning, information, speculation, theory and theology and even Scripture, *this* begets pride. ..."

The basic issue in all of these inner dealings by the indwelling Holy Spirit of Christ Jesus, is that we set aside our self-seeking and our sin nature that empowers it. In Chapters Five through Ten of Volume I[18] of this series we delineate one type of the emptying cycles that are typical of the second general stage of sanctification, namely that pertaining to "inner heart healing" so that we be free to minister to others. So also with the cycles at other stages of our sanctification. Nothing of self-seeking, nothing based on our sin-nature, can be allowed to contribute to our obtaining the new blessing of His reality. Indeed, the very opposite, i.e. *servanthood*, must prevail.

4. Outward Prayers *vs* Inner Poise Of The Soul

Edwards[19] emphasizes Molinos' distinction between "outward" and "inner" prayer:

"The Roman Catholics speak of two kinds of prayer. One is outward and one is more subjective. One is called 'meditation' and the other is called 'contemplation'. Yet to a Protestant, to Scripture, the two words and the concepts behind them are utterly foreign. Molinos was saying, 'Once you lay aside the first kind of prayer - meditation - you should never return to it but continue only in the second kind of prayer, contemplation. ..."

He then quotes Molinos extensively on this[20]:

"Eventually you may come to a place where you find yourself unable to go on with an intelligent prayer life, *or*, at least, you will begin to *desire* to lay aside such prayer. This will not come to you by way of your natural inclinations nor because you are in a period of dryness, but rather it is provoked by the Lord Himself, deep within you. ... What you are longing for is something that only the Lord can give you. You will not fully know the inward life that I speak of until you know what it means for your own will to be conformed to that of the Divine will. If you, the believer, would have everything succeed, if you would have everything come to pass according to your own will, then you will never know the way of peace. Such a person will also lead a bitter and empty life, always restless and disturbed, never touching the way of peace. ... [When] we do not submit to the sweet yoke of the Divine will and ... we suffer many perturbing situations. ..."

"Throughout the ages it has been the common view of spiritual believers that the believer cannot attain to a deeper walk in relationship to his Lord by means of prayer that is mostly consideration, requests, meditation, reasoning and a great deal of objective discussion. At best such prayer is only of benefit *at the outset* of the spiritual quest. ... Why seek the Lord by means of straining the brain, in searching for some place to go to pray, in selecting points to discuss, and in straining to find a God without ... when you have Him within you?"

"Just as there are two *prayers,* there are also two devotions. One devotion is real, and one is quite tied to the senses. In devotion that is true there is not a particularly great *delight, nor* are there many *tears.* A devotion to the Lord which is based on the outward senses, the rational [or] the emotional, ... is actually an obstacle to progress and advancement in the internal way. ... You must realize that thing which is deepest within you is *pure spirit.* It does not feel in the same way that the emotions feel. That which goes on inside the [human] spirit is not outwardly perceptible as are those things which go on in the more outward portion of your being. Your spirit does not have to stand up and say that it *knows* what it loves, and *feels* what it loves; it does not *need* such things."

The central issue in our inner prayer and devotional life is that we *gaze* on our Lord Christ Jesus and that we desire *Him*; and not what He gives us or how we benefit by Him or what He does for us.

Edwards quotes Molinos on this point[21]:

"There are two kinds of spiritual man. And they are contrary to one another. Some tell us that the mysteries and the sufferings of Christ are always to be meditated upon. Others, to the other extreme, tell us that the only true prayer is an internal thing, offered up in quiet and silence, a *centering* [upon] the exaltation and supreme Deity of God. ...

"... we are certain we should *not* lay aside the redemption of our Lord. But neither should we tell a believer who has learned something of living within his spirit that he should *always* be reasoning, meditating and considering the suffering and death of our Lord. ... As long as an outward prayer nourishes and benefits, a believer should follow outward prayer. It is only when a longing for something more is sensed in the heart that the pilgrimage into the inward way should be considered. It is up to the Lord alone to take us from one to the other. ...

"[But] ... recognize the difference between the outer and the inner way. The difference is the presence of God. His presence, which you practice by faith, is entered by your collecting your center, and then waiting before the Lord. ...

"... *You should have no desire for what will come out of your having an inward walk with God.* ... Your desire must be to end *your* life for *His* sake. ... The believer who would be united with Christ must follow Him in the way of suffering. ...

"If you do begin to taste the sweetness of Divine love it will only be a matter of a very short time before the enemy comes to you and kindles in your heart a desire *to go to* the desert and there live before God in solitude.

... you will continually *delight* in prayer. This reflects a very *immature* understanding of the Lord's ways. And it shows that you wish to have the Lord for the reason of having the delights and thrills which result from living in His presence. ... There are many Christians abroad who have received from the Lord magnificent revelations, great visions and a great grasp of high mental truths. Yet for all of this they do *not* deeply understand those hidden secrets which come to those who have gone through great *temptations* and *trials*. ... What great fortune it is for your soul when it is subdued!"

5. Other Basic Lessons, Again And Again

At the core of our new blessings is the reality of our indwelling Lord Christ Jesus. It is not our intellectual/doctrinal nor emotional grasping. ***We must experience Him ourselves in order to teach others!*** It is therefore important for us to learn experientially that we cannot teach nor lead others into full appropriation of the new blessings until we ourself have thus attained.

Molinos emphasizes how we must personally experience the consummation of inner union with Christ before we can teach others accordingly[22]:

"It has become a maxim among those who follow the internal way: ***practice ought to be laid hold of before theory!*** This simply means that you should have some ***experiential*** exercise of having touched your Lord in a very real way before you start searching out knowledge and doing a great deal of inquiring about such matters.

... Any study, any seeking, any acquiring of information that is not for the purpose of getting to know the Lord is but a short road to hell. ... ***Because of the wind of pride*** which such pursuits beget. The greater part of the theological and learned men of our day are miserable because they only study to satisfy the insatiable curiosity of the human nature. ..."

Also, Penn-Lewis[23] interprets Guyon on this important point:

"When a believer has pressed on with God faithfully from plane to plane, and has reached the sphere of warfare and victory over the powers of the air, then he should be able to lead others into any of the degrees of blessing they need; but, usually, when the soul is in a certain stage, and not arrived at its full consummation, he can only help others in the same stage, speaking out of his present light and experience. It is not until the consummation point is reached that the believer has liberty and facility in dealing with others in planes which he himself has left behind. In the transitional stage of each plane, you can only give the *vision* you have, so that your ministry seems limited to those who are at the same stage. You interpret to them what you, *and they*, are experiencing. But when you are *through that plane*, it seems as if you are able to minister to souls at any degree as they may need it. ... Remember you cannot meet the needs of all until you have passed through the *stages* of all. ... When a believer has passed through these 'planes' - a matter of years, more or less - and he reaches the plane of power over the forces of darkness, in its fullest degree, then [and only then] he is in the 'apostolic' stage. We must as workers

> be able to lead souls back from point to point to the place of [their] need, and recognize the ... [several different] grades, or planes of growth in dealing with them."

Penn-Lewis[24] discusses a "lesson of bare faith" we must learn over again at each "plane" of spiritual life. What is it? It is simply the victory of Christ on Calvary over the powers of sin and evil, as we now further quote Penn-Lewis[25] on this:

> "What is also needed is that Christians should know that the victory of Calvary over the powers of darkness is required to be apprehended by them in every stage of the spiritual life, and every plane of experience. (1) ***The evangelist needs to know it***, because to win souls to Christ, he must learn how to bind the devil holding souls, and therefore the truth of victory over the powers of darkness as declared in the Word of God is part of the evangelist's armor and equipment. (2) Those who receive ***the baptism of the Holy Spirit*** need to know the victory over the powers of darkness, so as to be able to detect the counterfeits, and to refuse them. (3) Those who go on in the ***path of the cross*** equally need to know the devices of the deceiving spirits, because they will interfere with them at every step onward in their knowledge of the Cross and try to mix their workings with the work of God in every degree. In fact, the truths about the powers of darkness need to be known in every plane, and at each stage of the spiritual life, according to the measure and need."

6. Balance Between Two Conflicting Truths

In our progression from stage to stage, we must understand and teach others that we have *two* apparently conflicting truths: (1) the depths of our depravity, and (2) the heights of our domicility in the heavenlies. Edwards expresses that as follows[26]:

> "One of the great paradoxes of the Christian faith is the need of seeing *both* our deeply damaged state as totally *fallen* creatures and, at the same time, our *worth* in Christ. ...
>
> "We must often proclaim the absolute destitution and depravity of the fallen nature. On the other hand, there is that high and awesome proclamation of who we are in Christ. It is left to each of us, experientially, to lay hold of both these understandings. We may never reconcile them but if we are to go on with Christ we must come to a profound revelation of both."

7. How Many, How Long?

How long does each cycle take in time for most of us? That varies considerably from believer to believer. It depends upon many factors, such as: how desperately is our seeking to mature in our personal relationship with our Lord Christ Jesus, what we have been taught (i.e., through our church backgrounds) about what and how to seek, and the strength of our self-seeking and self-protecting strategies. But up until now throughout Church history the general answer has been *many years* for most believers.

For me personally, I was in the first general stage for 7 years (January 1961 through May 1968), and in the second general stage 26½ years (May 1968 through November 1994): (including 8 years until "Mt. Moriah"[27] and almost 16 years until having gone through a major phase of inner heart healing). I am now but 6 years into the third general stage, and have yet far to go. Since I personally have not yet reached consummation of the third stage, I can give you for the most part only the *vision* of it, which I do in Table Two and several sections of this chapter. But my discussions of the first two stages and the early part of the third stage are backed by considerable personal experience!

Actually, the vast majority of believers never proceed to the second and/or third stage at all during this life. Of all adults in the so-called "Christian nations" today (USA, Canada, New Zealand, etc.), only a small percent are truly "born-again" in the Biblical sense; that is because many "mainline" christians denominations teach that "being a Christian" and/or "being born-again" is an automatic result of being a member of that denomination, either by infant christening and/or by adult confession of faith. But of those who are truly born-again in the Biblical sense, I have what I call "Sherrerd's Seven Percent Observation":[28]

> *Only maybe 7% make it to the beginning of the second stage. Of those who do, maybe 7% make it to the beginning of the third stage. And maybe 7% of those few ever make it to the end of the third stage.*

Also, the actual such make-up of God's people is highly dynamic. The great healing and evangelical camp meeting ministries of the late 1940s and 1950s brought many men and women into the first stage. The so-called "Charismatic" or "neo-Pentecostal" movement of the 1960s and 1970s brought many of those men and women into the beginning of the second stage. The "back-burner" suppression of many of those during the late 1970s and the 1980s brought them through to the end of the second stage. And now, we see the Lord beginning a significant "new work" of bringing those into the third stage. Hence, any present "snap-shot", i.e. of who is how far along, is misleading. And perhaps in the future these percentages may be much higher.

8. The First Stage: Law And Labor

We now separately study the several "planes" or "stages", as illustrated in Table Two.

Guyon calls the first phase the "evangelistic plane". It is the "plane" of basic salvation, i.e., remission or forgiveness of our sins by Christ's shed blood on Calvary. It is the initial stage of our Christian life, entered upon regeneration or our becoming "born again".

Here is Penn-Lewis' interpretation of Guyon's definition of this "evangelistic plane"[29]:

> "Where the soul knows the new birth; knows that he has eternal life in Christ; where he becomes a soul winner, preaches salvation from the penalty of sin, and is used to lead others to Christ; where he is faithful in proclaiming the gospel of salvation in Christ."

In terms of the intensity of the "spiritual torrent" of the believer in this plane, it is slow, feeble, sluggish, and by human efforts (though enabled by grace). The believer lives by outward sources, since he/she has not yet learned to tap on the indwelling Holy Spirit of Christ Jesus in him/her. His/her prayer is mostly the "outward" or "meditation" form. He/she is always *doing* something for the Lord rather than seeking Him for Who He Is. He/she is concerned with growing in knowledge *about* Christ through God's Word.

But he/she yet needs to know *Him*, not just *about* Him. The general cycle of vision-loss-struggle-surrender-revisitation-consummation of this cycle, with many local iterations usually the case, involves our laying hold of the *magnitude* of the forgiveness of our sins by the shed blood of Christ on Calvary, of our sacrificing our labors in service to Christ, and of our reckoning our *flesh* or carnality crucified with Christ.

The characteristics of this stage or "plane are as follows. The believer: is 'saved' but still much under influences of fleshly habits *(carnality);* views God totally with *awe* at a distance (i.e., He will "get me to heaven bye and bye"); is *worldly* in patterns of thinking (i.e., works by human wisdom); is self-centered in view of salvation (i.e, *my* sins have been forgiven); is only able for service in conjunction with *others;* is very dependent upon *outside sources* for help. But he/she indeed *desires earnestly* to serve and obey God (which translates into a great desire to always *be doing* something for the Lord); yet is *easily discouraged;* tries to serve God and walk with Him, but by *own (human) strength* and efforts, fettered by own ways; tends to be *erratic* in emotions and motivations to serve Lord; and is zealous to defend and persuade others of his/her *doctrines*.

Maturing Through Soul Affliction

The struggles of this stage or "plane" involve dealing with two issues of distinguishing between the *fact* of having received eternal life and the *experience* of manifesting it. The first issue is the soul consciously choosing to yield to Christ now speaking through the (human) spirit; and the second issue is putting aside the sins of the flesh. God's purpose for us in this first general stage is to help us to apprehend (know deeply and experientially) the totality of the forgiveness of our sins by Christ's shed blood on Calvary, and the resulting full freedom we have to come before God the Father in Christ's Name. The vision-loss-struggle-surrender-revisitation-consummation cycles in this stage are to that end.

Since re-birth involves the human spirit, not soul, it is not something *of itself* of which we are *consciously* aware. What we mean by "born-again experience" might better be called a "repentance experience", since it involves other aspects of which we *are* vividly aware: conviction of our sinfulness and its consequences, desperate begging of Jesus for forgiveness, and release of our burden of *guilt.* If a believer is brought to Christ this way, then he will know he is born-again; but many *genuine* believers exist in non-evangelical environments who have never been taught John 3:3-8 and the words "born again". (That was the case for me personally: I had been "born again" for five years before I knew it as such.) John 3:3-8 is a statement of theological understanding, but not a practical guide for our striving - that we do by repenting of our sins and trusting in Christ on Calvary.

The key to *becoming* born again is belief (trust, dependence) on Christ Jesus as the resurrected Son of God. If we indeed thus trust in Christ, then we know with certainty by John 1:12 and 3:15-18 that somewhere along the line we became born again.

A newly regenerated Christian has new life in his *human spirit*, and his soul (mind and will) is learning to listen to God through his spirit. So, the first thing God does is place the believer into bondage to ***Law*** (Romans 7:5-22; Galatians 3:13 & 21-24) so that the believer learns in his mind (soul) both: (a) his flesh is utterly corrupt and sinful and incapable of being sanctified; and (b) Christ on the Cross not only paid his ransom, but also was an example to follow. By identifying himself/herself with Christ, he/she identifies the crucifixion of his/her flesh with Christ's crucifixion. Hence he/she learns mentally the *fact* that his flesh *has been* crucified (past tense, already completed) with Christ.

This defies common sense, and hence is very difficult for many people. So we must live under *law* (for protection) until that fact becomes a deeply settled and understood reality. In such key texts as Romans 6:1-21, Galatians 5:24, Philippians 3:3-4 and 1 Peter 3:21, we see that the words ***know, reckon, and yield*** - three acts of the *soul* - are involved in this process. Law or "churchianity" is necessary to make the "old man's" soul *aware* of its sinfulness of the flesh, so that he/she would *choose* to seek deliverance. The word "reckon" involves the soul's will: we *determine* decisively that our flesh has indeed been subdued or rendered ineffective, and under law we increasingly learn to actually live *as if that fact* is indeed true. We also start to learn to *yield* to the power of the indwelling Holy Spirit to empower us to thus live.

However, the full vision and outworking of that inner empowerment is characteristic of the next general stage of sanctification. Until then, we need all outside sources of help available, i.e. through *law* and "church".

In summary, the essence of the first general stage of the workings of the indwelling Holy Spirit to sanctify us, is our apprehending the fullness of forgiveness of our sins (and removal of our guilt) by Christ's atoning work on Calvary, and by that our freedom to approach God *via* Christ.

9. The Second Stage: Holy Spirit Empowerment

This second phase/stage Guyon calls the "revival plane". She also calls it the "Way of Light", *light* here referring not to mental Biblical understandings but to ***spiritual reality***. It is the stage of the Holy Spirit, dwelling within us (our human spirits), ***saturating*** us (our soul) and ***empowering*** us for ministries as members of the Body of Christ.

Here is Penn-Lewis' interpretation of Guyon's definition of this "revival plane"[30]:

> "The stage in personal experience [is] where the believer receives the fullness of the Holy Spirit, learns to know Him and to obey Him; to rely upon Him and to look to Him to work as he [the believer] co-operates with Him, and is used to lead others into the experience of the fullness of the Spirit."

According to Guyon,[31] the intensity of the "spiritual torrent" of the believer in this plane is like:

> "... a large river that moves with decision and rapidity, yet dull and sluggish compared with the impetuous torrent described later on. ... these souls are so full of

light and ardent love that they excite the admiration of others, for God seems to give them gifts upon gifts, graces, light, visions, revelations, ecstasies. Temptations are repelled with vigour; trials are borne with strength. Their hearts are enlarged, and they gladly make great sacrifices for God and souls. ... [But] these souls are often admired too much [i.e., by other believers], and their minds are thus diverted to themselves. They are caused to rest in the gifts of God, instead of being drawn to run after God through His gifts. ... These souls are beautiful as regards themselves, and greatly help others, yet they often exact too much from them and are 'tried' by their [others'] inconsistencies. *They are not able to help weak souls according to the degree they are in*, and consequently often put them [others] out of the right path, i.e., by expecting them to 'see' or 'accept' spiritual things that may be beyond their capacity at the time."

Once the believer (having received the Baptism into the Holy Spirit) initially walks in this stage or "plane", he/she:
>has received and exhibits many gifts from God;
>has gifts that are manifestations of the Holy Spirit indwelling;
>rests in God's gifts rather than in God Himself;
>is buried with Christ in baptism (Romans 6:4);
>is full of light (deep experiential understandings of God's word and ways), and is ardent in God's love;
>is active and effective in ministry;
>vigorously repels temptations;
>bears trials with great strength;
>gladly sacrifices for God & for others;

> buts trust in those gifts rather than more deeply pursues God;
>
> is greatly admired by others & is often diverted to think too much of importance of own ministry; and
>
> has yet to learn that life in God goes much deeper than possessing and exercising gifts of the Holy Spirit.

Since the indwelling Holy Spirit of Christ Jesus dwells in our human *spirit*, His influence on us is only to the extent that we (our soul) thus responds by yielding. But since our soul is not *directly* involved yet, our grasp of "so great salvation" is still primarily *intellectual* (doctrinal), and our views of Christ are largely *historical* (Calvary) and *futuristic* (His Parousia return), not primarily in the *present tense*.

10. Unto Spiritual Reality

God's purposes for us in this second general stage of sanctification are: (1) that we fully apprehend, deeply and experientially, full *spiritual reality*, interacting (as empowered by the indwelling Holy Spirit) with all other spiritual entities; and (2) that we become unclogged, unimpeded and freely-flowing *channels* of the spiritual light, life and love of Christ, first unto us, and thence through us unto others, when/as/how He chooses and directs.

The cycles of vision-loss-struggle-surrender-revisitation-consummation of the first stage were all to the purpose of our apprehending our freedom by *yielding*. Without these cleansing cycles, our natural tendencies of response are to work/strive as if to "earn" so rich a salvation. However, it is "*not* by works, lest anyone should boast; for we are *His* workmanship ..." (Ephesians 2:9-10). Oh, our workings/strivings are all *good* (the "good" part of the fruit of the "Tree of Knowledge ..."): devotional activities centered on prayer and study of God's Word, ministering to others especially for "winning souls for Christ" and faithful support of our local church, etc. But the end result of His workings in that first stage was that we must stop our striving on human strength and wisdom, and learn to *yield to His initiatives* in us.

The second general stage of the workings of the indwelling Holy Spirit to sanctify us, though an extension of this yielding to His initiatives, is of a significantly different emphasis: now it is to apprehend *our dynamic involvement* in full *spiritual reality.*

First of all, just what *is* "spiritual reality"? The major characteristics of the spiritual "domain" are incredible *intelligence* and tremendous *power* - God is *spirit* (John 4:24) and He *created* (power) by His *spoken word* (intelligence). Second, what do we mean by "our dynamic involvement"? Eternal life is not just mental understanding; it is *life* - the ability to dynamically interact, both ways, with one's environment. Whereas before (in the first general stage of the workings of the indwelling Holy Spirit to sanctify us) our yielding was primarily by mental understanding as applied to both the past and the future; now our yielding is to be by our entire person including our inherent *spiritual* facilities, and in the *present tense* as well.

11. Initial Filling And Spirit Release

Whereas in the first stage the entrance vision or revelation to us by our Lord Christ Jesus is *regeneration*, now it is our being *baptized into the Holy Spirit*. Whereas regeneration involves our human *spirit* becoming filled with the newly-indwelling Holy Spirit of Christ Jesus, now it is our *soul* that is thus filled. This is why in our discussion on the baptism into the Holy Spirit in Chapters Six and Seven earlier in this volume, we emphasized our *soul* - our seat of *self-awareness* - being *saturated* or *impregnated* by that already present Holy Spirit of Christ Jesus. This distinction is so important that we deemed it necessary to spend so much exegetical effort on the human *spirit vs soul vs* human *"heart"* in Chapters One and Seven and Appendix One of this volume.

Our dynamic involvement now with full spiritual reality means dynamic involvement with *all three* aspects or portions of spiritual reality: (1) the *very Godhead via* Christ through His Holy Spirit in us; (2) the *evil spiritual forces of satan*, over whom/which we now have Christ's power and authority; and (3) *human spirits*, both of ourself and of others, of which we are to grow in discernment (1 Corinthians 12:10). Initially we are usually surprised to discover that we, sinners saved but by grace, actually have such spiritual power and authority. We "naturally" tend to respond by exercising that power and authority according to own (human) wisdom. Hence, the usual emphasis on believers in this stage is on *Holy Spirit empowered ministry*. We readily acknowledge that the "ministry gifts" are of the Holy Spirit in us; but we need yet to learn the subtle distinction between our exercising those "ministry gifts" upon *our* initiative and our allowing He in us flowing His light, life and love through us upon *His* initiative.

It is necessary for our soul to be "released" unto the Holy Spirit of Christ Jesus in a Baptism into the Holy Spirit. This releasing must involve spiritual *phenomena* that the soul cannot dominate (that the mind cannot understand, and is outside our emotions) but that is recognized as real and Christ-centered.

Thomas a Kempis[32] comments why we so utterly fail to make the distinction between initial Holy Spirit filling and Holy Spirit release, and hence why we so rarely obtain victory in our spiritual battles:

> "We are too much held by our own passions, and too much troubled about transitory things. We seldom overcome even one vice perfectly, and are not set on fire to grow better every day; and therefore we remain cold and lukewarm. If we were dead unto ourselves, and not entangled within our own selves, then we should be able to relish things divine, and to know something of heavenly contemplation.
>
> "The greatest impediment is that we are not disentangled from our passions and lusts, neither do we endeavor to enter into the perfect path of the saints. ... If we would determine like brave men to stand in the battle, surely we should behold above us the help of God from Heaven. For He Himself who gives us occasions to fight, to the end we may get the victory, is ready to succor those who strive and trust in His grace."

So, in this stage our Lord subjects us to two of the major vision-loss-striving-surrender-revisitation-consummation cycles that I call: (1) a Mount Moriah trial; and (2) what we call "inner heart healing". Both our exegetical studies and our personal experiences attest to these two general "cycles" during the second general stage: (a) shifting from our *serving* our Lord by *our* ministries to being vessels/channels of *Him* ministering *through* us, that we call our "Mount Moriah" trial; and (b) inner heart healing to *release* the indwelling Holy Spirit to flow through us unto others with less impedance, a significant step in reckoning our *self* crucified with Christ. Our "Mount Moriah" trial is when we finally obey our Lord's command to surrender our "ministry gift(s)" back to Him in total sacrifice, so that subsequently all that we do is not us but He in us doing the doing when/as/how He chooses. And our "inner heart healing(s)" is our being purged of all that would otherwise hinder and impede that flowing of His light, life and love though us unto others in all of our interpersonal relationships.

Note that both of these cycles may be - in fact for most of us indeed are - quite iterative and involve many sub-cycles. Also, the time sequence of our being subjected to these cycles varies from believer to believer, and are not necessarily of the order in which we discuss them in the following subsections. Although the order of these two may be reversed in the lives of some believers, both are clearly of the "Way of Light" or second general stage/plane.

12. Unto Mount Moriah

God (Christ Jesus) gives us our ministries. His will is not that *we* minister according to our ministry, but rather that *He* do the ministering *through* us. As long as it is *our* ministry that He has given us, then we do the doing - and thus restrain Him from flowing freely through us as He wills. So, we must become broken to the point where we, ***willingly***, lay down our very ***ministry*** to Him. And do so without any expectation of Him *ever* giving it back to us. This is part of dying to self, but so deep a working of the Lord in our souls that few ***willingly*** allow Him to accomplish it.

Our ***surrender*** is a vital qualification for ***spirit-empowered ministry***. By this we do not mean *just* surrendering our self-will to the will of the indwelling Holy Spirit of Christ Jesus: that He desires of *every* mature ministry in the Body of Christ, whether of the public recognition or eldership type, or of the other hidden callings. Rather, we also mean surrender of one's ***ministry*** itself!

A clear typical illustration of this is Abraham sacrificing Isaac on Mt. Moriah (Genesis 22:1-18). Isaac was the physical embodiment of God's full ***purpose*** for Abraham's life, just as our ministry is the physical embodiment of God's purpose for our present life. But did Isaac ***truly*** belong to the Lord YHWH, or did Isaac actually belong to Abraham? That is the issue. Is my ministry mine in reality, or is it truly the Lord's in me? If it is mine, then what gets accomplished is atrociously limited by my human understandings and willingness, and is polluted by my self-seeking; but if it is truly His, then what He does through me can be virtually unlimited, hindered only by my hesitations in blindly yielding to Him! "Moriah" in the Hebrew (MWRYH) means "provided and guided by YHWH".

13. Inner Heart Healing

The sanctification process is the indwelling Holy Spirit of Christ Jesus dealing with what drives the sins that so easily beset us: our self-seeking, our self-protecting, our self-control, the accompanying embedded emotional empowerments, and all else in us that is not of the God-ordained servanthood walk according to the "Tree of Life". The purpose is indeed to restore us unto that original servanthood.

One major step of that is *inner heart healing*. We studied this in much detail in Chapters 5 through 10 of Volume I[33] of this series. For each specific area of self that we submit to our Lord for inner heart healing, it is a vital surrendering cycle. Note the three main components of *repentance*: (1) repentance *from* our intrinsic aversion against God due to our shame/guilt over our sin nature, and *unto* full appreciation of God's continual forgiveness and apprehension of God's grace; (2) repentance *from* our sin of unbelief that thinks Christ is not really sufficient or willing to provide all our needs and protection against all that is not in His will for us, *unto* a deep-seated trust in Him in all things at all times; and (3) repentance *from* self, specifically from our self-protecting strategies that distance us from God and from one another, *unto* full enjoyment of Christ both in us and in one another. Note also the difficulties usually involved in dealing with the emotional aspects of the third: the power of those emotions usually remain with us for years without our conscious awareness, and make it difficult to dump them onto Christ without the help of another Christian acting as a prayer partner.

Nori[34] also sees clearly the current urgency of this inner heart healing for us to fully exude the *Presence* of Christ and His Light, Life and Love:

"The whole crux of the [current] restoration movement ... is the *restoration of hearts*. If our hearts are not genuinely and radically restored to the Lord Jesus, then all other restoration becomes meaningless. ... He wants our hearts. ... God wants to heal us from within. ... There is healing for the human heart. There is healing that flows from the throne of God so that God's people can be whole.

"When we are scarred in our emotions, unless Jesus is allowed to heal us, our entire lives will remain affected by that scar. ... It is frequently dismaying to see people I counsel with choosing to stay hurt. They don't seem to know that there's [emotional] healing at the cross. ... [But] The very heart of what God is doing is the restoration of our hearts toward Him.

"If we want to be energized and motivated and controlled by His Life so that we overflow with His Love, His Power and His Character, we need to go before His Presence. In His Presence the river of the water of life flows, and this is what we need.

"God is restoring the hearts of His people. The healing of our hearts takes place in God's presence. It is there that we find the power to change and all the blessings of God has for us, including the wholeness He has for us. How we need to *live* in His Presence. How desperately we need His manifest Presence!"

This inner healing is, of course, impossible without first both regeneration and Holy Spirit infilling as prerequisites; hence it is a part of the second general stage, not the first. But it is also not a part of the third, since it only goes so far as to remove **barriers** in our inter-personal relationships so that we become unclogged and impedance-free channels of our Lord Christ Jesus' flow of His spiritual light, life and love through us unto others. The sanctifying dealings of the third stage, that we discuss shortly, go much deeper and pertain to our intrinsic holiness and Christ-likeness.

14. Personal Characteristics Of Second Stage

In terms of Table Two, Guyon's model does not *precisely* match our general three-stage concept. Both our exegetical studies and our personal experiences attest to two "degrees" or "cycles" of the workings of the Holy Spirit indwelling during the second general stage: (a) this "Mount Moriah" trial; and (b) inner heart healing. Both are clearly of Guyon's "Way of Light" or second general stage/plane. Guyon, writing primarily from personal experiences and without the benefits of our exegetical research, makes no mention of either of these two specific trials; but her "Souls of the 1st Degree" in the "Third Class" or "Way of Faith" matches that of our "Mount Moriah" trial. We have "corrected" this discrepancy by the diagonal lines in Rows [d] and [e] of Table Two and included both of these specific trials/cycles in the second part of our second general stage.

With this in mind, now note how Guyon describes the inner struggles of the believer during the vision-loss-struggle-surrender-revisitation-consummation cycles of this stage. A "Soul of the First Degree":
>is ardent in love for God;
>seeks and enjoys inner silence and peace with God;
>prefers prayer to duty;
>is so loaded with spiritual gifts and talents, but has
>>more difficulty entering into life of pure faith

than less mature souls;
esteems own spiritual possessions, and that esteem is a major obstacle to overcome;
has not yet fully learned the distinction between true Holy Spirit initiations and their own soulishness in serving Christ;
would forsake all worldly pleasures and possessions to walk more fully with God;
wants to suffer for Christ to satisfy Him;
yet has a secret, deeply subtle but hard contempt toward others who are not at his/her own level of experience;
cannot help weak souls at their level;
exacts too much of others;
expects others to see and accept spiritual things beyond their capacity at the time;
has true grief for one's sins however minor; and
is restless for more of God.

One more point needs to be emphasized before we leave the second general stage: what is the proof that we have consummated the second general stage? We have received Him by faith (Galatians 3:2-3), yes; but what are the essential *manifestations* of His indwelling presence? Are they the "gifts" of ministry? Tongues? Etc.?

Here is how Penn-Lewis[35] interprets Guyon's answer to this:

"... [We must] real[ly] surrender to obey Him, and putting ... all obstacles out of the way of His fullest working; removing the hindrances, wrong things in life put away, [as are] progressively revealed by Him."

The second stage, once consummated, is hence but the entry to the third, where that surrender and emptying is effected in yet deeper ways unto more complete Christ-likeness.

We are somewhat arbitrary in our model of the three general stages of sanctification, in how we define precisely where this second ("natural" or "soulical") stage ends and the third ("spiritual") stage begins. This is because both the latter part of the second stage, and the early part of the third stage, involve one or more cycles of vision-loss-struggle-surrender-revisitation-consummation. For illustrative purposes, we herein define the second stage to "end" when the vision first experienced upon Baptism into the Holy Spirit reaches some form of "consummation". This often takes the form of a distinct "event" that clearly marks the beginning of the third stage, even though this event is typically "buried" in those emptying cycles. That "event" is when our Lord Christ Jesus burns into our hearts, for the first time with significant vividness and clarity, a vision of what it really means for us *in this here-and-now* to be *"positioned with Christ in the heavenlies"* (Ephesians 1:3). This is a slight modification of the Guyon-Penn-Lewis concepts.

But also, while still here on earth we are to function as His sent and anointed *agents* ("Greater things than these shall ye do" - John 14:12). The emptying cycles of this third stage are for the purpose of working Christ's crucifixion *into us* (as we discussed in Chapter Two earlier in this volume), for only to that extent can we actually walk in His *agency!*

15. The Third Stage: Emptying And Outpouring

The third plane Guyon defines in terms of two sub-stages, that she calls the "Path of the Cross" and "Ascension", respectively. She also calls both stages the "Way of Faith". It is the stage where the indwelling Holy Spirit of Christ Jesus works to bring us unto God's original and ultimate intention for us in the first place.

Here is Penn-Lewis' interpretation of Guyon's definition of these two sub-stages[36]:

> "... [the] plane of the *'path of the cross'* [is] where the believer experimentally apprehends his position in Romans 6 in fellowship with Christ's death; [and] is brought into 'conformity' to His death [Philippians 3:10]; he learns the fellowship of His sufferings, and is led to walk in the path of the cross in every detail of practical life. Here the believer is able to lead others to know Romans 6 and 2 Corinthians 4:10-12 in *experience*.

> "... the plane of spiritual warfare ... is really the *'ascension'* plane, where the believer knows his union with Christ, seated with Him 'far above all principality and power'; and where, in service, he is in aggressive warfare against the powers of darkness; learns to have spiritual discernment to detect the workings of the devil; and learns the authority of Christ over all the power of the enemy (Luke 10:19)."

16. Emptying Of Our Self-Nature: Our Atonement Offerings

As stated in Row [c] of Table Two, God's purposes for us in this third general stage of sanctification are: (1) that we understand, and walk accordingly in the here and now, our position with Christ in the heavenlies (Ephesians 1:3); (2) that we concurrently act as His *agents* or mature *sons* here on earth; and (3) that we become prepared to be a part of His multi-membered *Bride*. In other words, God's ultimate intention for our salvation is to bring us unto Sonship (Agency) and Bridehood. We discussed this in depth in Chapter Four earlier in this volume.

Note in the above reference to Guyon, however, that the path to that glorious ultimate intention is that we fully embrace the Cross, that all residual aspects of our *sin-nature* be truly reckoned as crucified with Christ, that we experientially share the sufferings of Christ. It is one thing to have the vision. But to walk in true and full union with Christ appears *hopeless*, as it indeed is without these deep purgings by the indwelling Holy Spirit of Christ Jesus!

We follow Guyon, therefore, in discussing this third general stage of sanctification in terms of two sub-stages. We call her "Path of the Cross" our *emptying of self-nature*, and her "Ascension and Spiritual Warfare" our *standing in the divine presence.*

The general cycles of vision-loss-struggle-surrender-revisitation-consummation of this stage, with many local iterations usually the case, are a more complete emptying of our *self*, of our *self-nature*, of our soulishness, so that the outpouring of the indwelling Holy Spirit becomes pure in the holiness and righteousness of Christ Himself.

These "emptying" cycles are the antitypical meanings of the KPhR (or *atonement offerings)* of ChTAhTh (or *sin offerings)* and AhShM (or *guilt/trespass offerings)*, that we study in detail elsewhere in this series (i.e., in Chapter Five of Volume IV[37] of this series. Leviticus Chapters 4 through 6 describe the ChTAhTh or "sin-nature" offering and the AhShM or "transgression against our neighbor" offering, that typify God's subsequent dealings in our lives. Those dealings are to bridge this holiness gap between Christ Jesus and us, and through that we acquire and fully assimilate His holiness and righteousness. "Not us, but He living fully through us" (Galatians 2:20).

We need to take note of four specific and closely related theological terms: *atonement* ("being in harmony with"), *expiation* ("making amends by paying the penalty for"), *propitiation* ("appeasement to make favorable"), and *reconciliation* ("restoration to communication and friendship").

The Old Testament Hebrew word used in various places in the original text for these concepts is KPhR. KPhR does *not* mean *positional* atonement or legal justification; nor does it mean simply being at-one-ment with God, as a current cliche says. It's root meaning in the Hebrew is to *cover: not* to cover to *hide* from view, but to cover in order "to render *ineffectual;* to reduce to having no effect, to make inconsequential". It has nothing to do with our *positional* relationship with God; rather it has to do with our *experiential* or *actual* state before Him. It is not a term of theology, but one of the practical nitty-gritty details of our very *essence* and existence!

In order for us to grow into *experiential* atonement, the ChTAhTh or "sin-nature" and AhShM or "trespass" offerings are required, as specified in Leviticus Chapters 4 through 6. The ChTAhTh or "sin nature" offering is an offering of a slain life (this time it is *our* self life), and it is offered by fire. It is to remove all in us that would hinder us from *full* fellowship with God. And the AhShM, involving monetary or tangible payments of restitution to those *people* whom we have offended, is to remove all in us that would hinder us from *full* fellowship with our fellow brothers and sisters in God: removal of *all* hindrances and offenses, not just those of which we are conscious, but those that are inadvertent, of which we are not necessarily cognizant of in ourselves. The "inner heart healing" emptying cycles are merely foretastes of this. A complete removal of *all* such hindrances is the very essence of Christ maturing and perfecting His Bride (us, His church); and He will not come upon His Parousia return until He accomplishes that!

Neither of these KPhR offerings are voluntary nor of a sweet savor unto God: they do not *benefit us* nor *honor God*. God does not expect us to seek or to voluntarily choose to embrace these offerings, nor to rejoice over them. Our rejoicing, of course, is in our Lord Himself. But our entering into these offerings is not something we do because we *want* to, rather because we *must* in order to be able to abide in the full presence of our Holy God. For they involve *deep sufferings* that *He* subjects us to; our act of offering them is tantamount to our *yielding* to Him and His purposes for them during those sufferings. Of course, if we choose voluntarily to reject God's full purposes in our lives, we can refuse these offerings also; in that sense they are "voluntary". But for all who truly seek His fullness in their lives, these offerings are inevitable *necessities*, and are invoked *by God* as part of His dealings in our lives to make us aware of yet-not-dealt-with-in-His-Blood offenses to Him and to our brethren. That is why they are called "compulsory", as distinct from the former offerings that are called "voluntary".

17. Baptism With Fire

Another Biblical type of these "emptying" cycles, is that of *"Baptism by fire"*, that we mention in Chapter Seven earlier in this volume. Maturing in our relationship with Him is a process of *adjustment* in our lives.

The symbol of God's dealings in our lives to work purity into us, is *fire*. When John the Baptist prophesied of Christ Baptizing into the Holy Spirit, he also said "'... He Himself will baptize you in the Holy Spirit *and fire*' (Luke 3:16). '... I have come to cast fire upon earth ....' (Luke 12:49). '... by which we may offer to God an acceptable service with reverence and awe. For our

God is a consuming fire' (Hebrews 12:28-29)." Fire denotes God's purifying us, removing the dross and self-will in the subsequent adjusting process He puts us through. In the Old Testament type of Pentecost, Moses encountered God's *fire* on Mt. Sinai. The three Hebrew children (Daniel 3:23-28) went through a Baptism in fire in order to experience the *physical*, experiential *Presence* of Christ. God's fire does not speak of *destruction*, but of *cleansing*; of a complete removal from us of all that is not of Him, not of dependence upon Him alone, of not yielding to His Will *alone* (i.e., wood, hay, stubble and chaff: 1 Corinthians 3:12-15 and Matthew 3:12 & Luke 3:17).

The final phases of our process of being adjusted unto maturity entail an emptying of our self, so that we become *completely* yielded to the Holy Spirit of Christ Jesus in us - that we become completely fused into Him. It is a matter of our *internal* holiness, holiness *into* Him, our losing ourselves *in Him*. Holiness *from* the world (even pious religiousness) is *not* the issue here.

Brown[38] expresses in very practical terms this purging of our natural ways through a "baptism into fire":

"Any servant of God must spend much more time on his face before God than he ever does in the work God gives him to do. Lack of holiness in our lives blocks the flow of the Holy Spirit and transforms our work into worthless ashes in the sight of God....

"Why is it that we so easily tolerate sin in our lives? Yes, we will always be liable to sin as long as we are here in our earthly bodies, but, in light of Christ's specific commandment to be perfect, why are we so comfortable with a certain level of sin in our lives? Why are we so willing to accept anything less...? ... because we want Christ to baptize us with the Holy Spirit, but we don't want Him to baptize us with *fire*."

"... Just how do we get this baptism with fire? We have to ask for it, and sincerely mean it. I find that I have had to ask for this baptism at various [several] times in my life. ... That's very humbling. ... This is an interaction between you and God, and no one else. If you are truly willing, the Holy Spirit will painfully convict you of the sins [falling short, if not actual disobedience] in your life. Our hearts are so deceitful [Jeremiah 17:9-10] that only the Lord can do this work, we cannot. [But] we cannot truly serve this God of ours if we have any sin remaining in our hearts. If we allow sin to remain in our lives, ... sooner or later satan will have a great victory over us.

"Power from the Lord comes through a cleansed heart. Let us seek this special work of the Lord, ..., let us ask Jesus to baptize us with *fire*."

How does the Holy Spirit actually baptize and cleanse us through fire? What actually happens in our lives? It requires a ***process*** of adjusting our thought patterns, and that adjusting is very involved. It's not that we are deliberately, willfully, calculatingly rebelling against the Lord Christ Jesus; it's just that He knows that our thought patterns have to be changed, that our nature has to be cleansed, that our own self and our own ideas must be crucified and that the "poise of our soul" must be re-oriented unto full ***spiritual realities!*** Yet, for our sake and because of His love for us, He must do it in a way that does not destroy us but rather edifies us. So, He confronts us with situations where there's no way out except for us to cry unto Him for help. He ***does*** help us, and as He does, we learn not to depend upon our own ideas and thinking and abilities, but upon Him and upon Him alone. We learn this step-by-step, first in little things, and eventually in matters of our very being.

Sin is not the primary issue. Rather, the primary issue is our thinking, our mentality, our understandings of ***Spiritual reality*** that up to now are heavily dragged down by our worldly experiences. Our concepts of Christ Jesus and His ways and His will for our lives are at best greatly distorted and limited, if not actually erroneous in many aspects. So, our patterns of thinking, our attitudes, our motives, our perspectives, all must be adjusted. That comes not primarily through mind-knowledge or didactic education. Rather it comes through a process of interaction between His dealings in the circumstances in our lives, the guidance and direction we daily receive from the Holy Spirit of Christ Jesus in our hearts, and our responses thereto in the midst of those dealings.

Look at Hebrews 12:5-11 and note how the writer speaks of the adjusting process as ***chastening*** by a loving Heavenly Father. Yes, the maturing process is painful at times. But the love of our Lord Christ Jesus toward us is ever more real during the chastening tribulations, and it is that love that ever deepens our union with Him. And we become settled and stable through it all.

18. Personal Characteristics Of Third Stage: Complete Emptying Of Self

Returning to Mme. Guyon's model that indeed illustrates these atonement offerings and fire purgings, we note in Table Two her association of "souls of the 2nd and 3rd degree" to these "emptying" cycles, and characterizes them chiefly by *powerlessness* and *loss/burial*. The actual experiences of believers in this stage vary considerably, and the "emptying" cycles are often many and highly iterative. Hence these concepts of hers are but one believer's experience-borne understanding. Nevertheless, they are excellent examples, and hence we give them here for illustrative purposes:

Guyon's "Souls of the 2nd Degrees" of *Powerlessness* have similar characteristics to those of the 1st Degree in the second general stage, but go deeper into various aspects of the self-nature yet to be reckoned crucified with Christ. They are:
    has vision of full union with Christ, but it appears to be helpless to acquire it;
    experiencing emotional turmoil;
    feel that God has left them;
    experience dryness, contradictions and rejections;
    powerless of will to regain spiritual gifts and abilities;
    finally brought to the point of ceasing to strive on own efforts;
    experiencing the presence of the Lord again.

The cycles repeat themselves with respect to some other aspect of the self-nature yet to be reckoned as crucified with Christ.

Guyon's "Souls of the 3rd Degree" of *Loss and Burial* experience yet deeper emptying. The are:
- hateful of self;
- feel totally lacking, not possessing anything of spiritual worth at all;
- lacking in power for service and/or personal virtue;
- not even able to pray properly and fully;
- takes no pleasure in anything;
- thinks loss is own fault (even though it isn't); but
- has not actually lost God (only *seems* forsaken).

All of these "emptying" or chastening cycles finally bring the believer to the point of utterly abandoning all self-seeking, all self-striving, and to ***utterly trust and depend upon Christ for everything***.

19. Personal Characteristics Of Third Stage: Standing In The Divine Presence

When our Lord determines that the believer has reached that state of heart, He then raises the believer up to a life of abundance in abiding union with Him. At last the believer ***experientially*** apprehends what is his/her position with Christ in the heavenlies, in the here and now (Ephesians 1:3). It is a walk in such union with Him in the spirit, of personal holiness of Christ-likeness, of victory over the forces of evil, and of the love of Christ for other souls.

Again we summarize Guyon's model in Table Two. She characterizes such believers as "Souls of the 4th Degree" of "apostle" ministry, and talks of them: (1) having life abundant; (2) abiding in Christ; and (3) in union with Him:
- possessed by God;

has all things in God;
lives without effort;
is in perfect rest;
has boundless joy in the lord;
is in harmony with divine Will;
is one with Christ/God;
lives in utter simplicity;
has a very "ordinary" exterior;
endures more and heavier trials;
faithfully cooperates with God;
accepts will of God in all details at all times;
avoids self-reflection and self-effort;
functions "naturally" as a "part" of Christ;
rests from: reasoning; desires out of harmony with God's Will; reproofs of conscience; all disquieting forces; conflicts with "providence" and circumstances; labor, unrest and turmoil;
has deep peace, because activity is "natural" without striving; and
has passed from meditation to contemplation, i.e., from "outer" forms of prayer, to deep inner communion with Lord.

Endnotes: Chapter Ten

[1.] A modern English reprint of Madame Guyon's *Spiritual Torrents* is found in Edwards, Gene, Ed., *Madame Guyon Spiritual Writings,* (Goleta, CA: Christian Books, 1982), pages 501-639. Copyright © 1982 by Gene Edwards.

2. Penn-Lewis, Jesse, *Life Out Of Death*, (Originally published 1896, and revised 1900, Poole, England: The Overcomer Literature Trust). A short (55-page) treatise, modern reprint distributed in USA by Christian Literature Crusade, Fort Washington, PA, 19034.

3. Jeanne Marie Bouvier Guyon, *MADAME GUYON - an Autobiology*, (Chicago: Moody Press, no date), ISBN: 0-8024-5135-7.

4. Gene Edwards, *THE SPIRITUAL GUIDE by Michael Molinos*, Volume 5 of LIBRARY OF SPIRITUAL CLASSICS, pages 32 and 36 (Goleta, CA: Christian Books, 1982). Copyright © 1982 by Christian Books.

5. Edwards, Gene, Ed., *Madame Guyon Spiritual Writings*, pp. 505-637.

6. Penn-Lewis, Jesse *Life Out Of Death*, p. 5.

7. Edwards, Gene, Ed., *Madame Guyon Spiritual Writings*, pp. 505-506.

8. Penn-Lewis, Jesse, *Life Out Of Death*, pp. 42-43.

9. Gordon P. Gardiner, *RADIANT GLORY - The Life Of Martha Wing Robinson*, (Brooklyn, NY: Bread of Life, © 1962 and 1987, 6*th* Edition 1982).

10. David Wilkerson, *Thge Death of A Promise*, a 3-message audio tape series, 1996. Write to *World Challenge, P.O. Box*

260, Lindale, Texas 75771.

[11.] Dr. Millicent Thompson, *Don't Die In The Winter - Your Season Is Coming,* (Shippensburg, PA: *Treasure House,* Destiny Image Publishers, 1996).

[12.] Sherrerd, Chris S., *The Christian Marriage - A Six-Fold Covenant Of Love-Motivated Servanthood,* Volume I of the series "Where Do You Fit In? Practical Commitments In The Body Of Christ" (Shippensburg, PA: Treasure House, Destiny Image Publishing Group, 1994). Copyright © 1994 by Shulemite Christian Crusade.

[13.] Kubler-Ross, Elisabeth, M.D., *On Death and Dying,* (New York: Collier Books, Macmillan Publishing Company, 1969, 1*st* paperback ed. 1970). Copyright © 1969 by Elisabeth Kubler-Ross.

[14.] Edwards, Gene, *THE SPIRITUAL GUIDE by Michael Molinos,* p. x.

[15.] Ibid. pp. 71, 73 and 109.

[16.] Ibid. pp. 66-67.

[17.] Ibid. pp. 113 and 133-134.

[18.] Sherrerd, Chris S., *The Christian Marriage.*

[19.] Edwards, Gene, *THE SPIRITUAL GUIDE* by Michael Molinis, p.16.

[20.] Ibid. pp. 47-48, 55 and 63-64.

21. Ibid. pp. 91 and 104-105.

22. Ibid. p. 136.

23. Penn-Lewis, Jesse, *Life Out Of Death*, pp. 43-44 and 45-46.

24. Ibid. pp. 42-43.

25. Ibid. p. 45.

26. Edwards, Gene, *THE SPIRITUAL GUIDE by Michael Molinos*, pp. 149-151.

27. See next Section 7 of this chapter for discussion on our "Mount Moriah" surrendering trials.

28. Such "percentages" are only "guestimates" based upon personal observations of Bible-believing Christians in the USA over the past three decades; they are given only for illustration and are not claimed to be accurate. Perhaps as we get deeper into the current "purging" move of God, these "percentages" might get higher, although this author personally doubts that. The only Biblical suggestion is in Ezra chapters 1 and 2 where the number of Israelites who returned from exile to rebuild the temple are given. Just 4 out of 24 orders of priesthood returned, suggesting "percentages" as high as 16%.

29. Penn-Lewis, Jesse, *Life Out Of Death*, p. 41.

30. Ibid. p. 41.

31. Ibid. pp. 10 & 11.

[32] Thomas a Kempis, *The Imitation of Christ*, as published in "Forethoughts In Actions", *The MorningStar Journal* Vol. 1 No. 6 (1991), page 14.

[33] Sherrerd, Chris S., *The Christian Marriage*.

[34] Don Nori, *His Manifest Presence*, (Shippensburg, PA: Destiny Image Publishers), 1988 & 1992, pp. 140, 141, 145 & 146.

[35] Penn-Lewis, Jesse, *Life Out Of Death*, p. 46.

[36] Ibid. pp. 41-42.

[37] Sherrerd, Chris S., *Spiritual Dynamics In The Body Of Christ*, Volume IV of the series "Where Do You Fit In? Practical Commitments In The Body Of Christ", to be published.

[38] Brown, Rebecca, M.D., *Prepare For War*, (Springsdale, PA:Whitaker House, 1987, originally published by Chick Publications, Chino, CA), pp. 73-74 and 76. Used by permission of the publisher, Whitaker House, 580 Pittsburgh Street, Springsdale, PA 15144.

Chapter Ten

Divine "Three"

This chapter is basically an extension of Chapter Eight earlier in this volume, wherein we give twenty-three depictions of the three general stages of the sanctification process. We now discuss an additional set of twenty-seven. We do this in seven categories: (1) our *love-relationship* with Christ Jesus; (2) offerings of New Covenant believers; (3) the meanings embedded in Holy Communion; (4) we becoming kings, priests, and a holy people; (5) temptations we overcome; (6) "Pilgrim's Progress"; and (7) the three Marys at the Cross.

These twenty-seven are tabulated in Sanctification Stages Charts Four through Six, which are basically extensions of Sanctification Stages Charts One through Three of Chapter Eight. In addition, we list here in Sanctification Stages Charts Seven through Nine a total of thirty-one examples from other authors.

Sanctification Stages Chart Four

Row #	Three "Types" Of Believer →	CARNAL/FLESHLY [SARKIKOS]	SOULICAL/NATURAL [PSUCHIKOS]	SPIRITUAL [PNEUMATIKOS]
[24]	Love Relationship Between Believer And Christ: Types In Song of Songs	Songs 1:1 - 2:7 "He Is Mine And I Am His"	Songs 2:8 - 5:1 "I Am His And He Is Mine"	Song 5:2 - 8:14 "I Am His, And His Desire Is Toward Me"
[25]	Reasons For Praising Our Lord Christ Jesus	Because Of What He Has **Done For Me**	Because I **Love Him**	Because He Is **Worthy** Of All
[26]	Basis Of Our Relationship With Christ	**Forgiveness** EROS Love	**Service & Sacrifice** PHILEA Love	**AGAPE Love** Love-Union With Christ
[27]	Love-Fruit Characteristics: Songs 4:13-14/Gal 5:22-23	Beauty	Flavor	Effects: Nourishment
[28]	Our **Fame/Reputation** As A Christian	**PHEME** (Luke 4:14) Rumor, Suspicion	**ECHOES** (Luke 4:37) Roar, Loud Strong Signal	**LOGOS** (Luke 5:15) Container Of Christ Himself
[29]	What We **Are** To Christ	Servant	Instrument	Vessel
[30]	Three **Mountains** We Approach (Confrontations With God)	From **Calvary** To Mt. **Sinai/Horeb**	From **Sinai/Horeb** To Mt. **Moriah**	From **Moriah** To Mt. **Zion**
[31]	Stages Of Our Being Molded By The Master Potter	**Blessed**/Accepted	**Contradicted**/Recreated	**Anointed**/Established
[32]	Our **Witness** Of Christ	Light Of His **Word**	Power Of His **Life**	His **Love**
[33]	Levels Of **Prayer**	Thanksgiving	Supplication	Intercession
[34]	Progression In **Beholding** Him	**Praised** (Thanksgiving)	**Shared** (In Body Of Christ)	**Worshipped** (Drawn Into God)
[35]	Levels Of Our **Worship**	Barrenness	Desire	Joy

1. In Love With Jesus

One remarkable book in the Old Testament is "Song of Songs." It is a *love story!* It is a story of the enfolding *love-relationship* between a "Shulemite maiden" and "my Beloved". It typifies how we, as individual believers, grow in personal relationship with our Lord Christ Jesus, *after* our initial conversion. No discussion of our three general stages of our sanctification would be complete without use of this resource.

However, a *precise* exegetical interpretation of the Song of Songs is not possible, because in many places it is impossible for us to unambiguously determine who is speaking to whom. There are currently at least two prevailing exegetical interpretations.

The first prevailing interpretation is that the main characters are: the Shulemite maiden typifying the individual believer (as a member of the bride of Christ while now still being prepared/perfected); the "daughters of Jerusalem" representing fellow Christians who are more focused on Christianity as an institutional *religious system* than on personal relationship with Christ; and Solomon, the King of Peace, *synonymous* with "my Beloved", typifying Christ who is wooing us and preparing us to be His Bride.

Some excellent and still currently available books representing this interpretation are: (1) "Song of Solomon" by Madame Jeanne Guyon[1]; (2) "Thy Hidden Ones" by Jesse Penn-Lewis[2]; (3) "Song Of Songs" by Watchman Nee[3]; and (4) "The Mountain Of Spices" by Hannah Hurnard[4].

The second prevailing interpretation makes a distinction between Solomon and "my Beloved". It points out that Solomon as King of Israel, and his harem, more accurately typify *institutional Christianity;* and "my Beloved", as a sheepherder and vineyard keeper, typifies Christ our divine *lover.* An excellent currently available resource of this viewpoint is "Our Tremendous Lover" by Charles Schmitt[5], who also refers to "The Song of Solomon" by John A. Balchin[6].

Of these two viewpoints, this author is tentatively convinced that the second is the technically correct one, as it much more closely reflects the actual Hebrew text. For this reason, we strongly recommend the above reference by Schmitt[7] for exegetical study. In this, Schmitt makes the very timely emphasis that our Lord Christ Jesus today is calling His Body out of dead institutionalism into total love-relationship with Him as His Body and future Bride.

2. Our Unfolding Love Relationship With Christ Jesus

Our emphasis here, with *either* of these two viewpoints, is on the *unfolding love-relationship* between us as individual believers and our Lord Christ Jesus, eschatological considerations notwithstanding. Of all publications currently available that emphasize that, none compares in excellence and anointing, in this author's opinion, than a further reference: "The Secret Of The Stairs" by Wade Taylor[8]. The efficacy of Taylor's work for this discussion is not dependent upon which of these two viewpoints is assumed.

The typologies in the *Song of Songs* follow our three-stage general sanctification pattern, but add considerable amplification to the third stage. Also, they do not consider *initial conversion* of the believer but start with the believer already in the first stage. They describe the beginning of *deeper* seeking after our Lord, and speak of the believer's inmost heart's spiritual longings for Him and communion with Him up to the final climax of fullest fellowship with Him in the Heavenlies. The issue here, then, is not victory over sin and satan, but rather increasing *fellowship* with our Lord Christ Jesus.

The unfolding love-relationship between us as individual believers and our Lord Christ Jesus is perhaps the most essential aspect of our sanctification process for us to understand and be totally committed to. It is also a most involved process, with many painful workings and many joyful experiences closely interleaved in detail. We set the stage here for a detailed discussion of it, with a very brief outline and a corresponding illustration in Row [24] of Sanctification Stages Chart Four.

The three general stages of a believer's spiritual growth as typified in *Song of Songs* are illustrated in Songs 1:1-2:7, Songs 2:8-5:1, and Songs 5:2-8:14, respectively. In *Song of Songs* we have unveiled to us the heart-history of a redeemed one who is led on to know the Lord intimately. It is veiled in a language to be understood only by the teachings of the Holy Spirit. In it we see how the Heavenly Bridegroom woos the soul for whom He died, leading it/her/us on from one degree of union to another, drawing it/her/us with Love to utterly forsake self and our own life and to experience one Life with Him. It follows the progress of a soul through the experiences of death and Resurrection unto total Oneness with Christ. It is a "motion picture" wherein the Holy Spirit flashes before us a series of portraits of the Glorified Christ, first from one standpoint and then from another, so that the soul may be transformed from one image to a yet more mature image, "from glory to glory."

A most beautiful illustration of the growth of the Shulemite maiden (us) in her (our individual) personal love-relationship with our Lord Christ Jesus, is the three successively deepening key testimonies she gives of her "my Beloved" in Songs 2:16, Songs 6:3 and Songs 7:10, respectively. We list these in Row [24] of Sanctification Stages Charts Four through Six: (2:16) "He is mine and I am His;" (6:3) I am His and He is mine;" and (7:10) "I am His and His desire is toward me." Taylor[9] summarizes the significance of this progression:

> "Three key testimonies reveal the progressive levels of spiritual growth to which the Bride has developed; each of these confessions sets the stage for the intervention of the Lord to bring her up into the next level. Her first testimony expresses her *self-importance:* 'My Beloved is mine, and I am His,' S.S. 2:16. In her second testimony, some progress is evident, as a partial change in her priorities has taken place. Now she is able to *put Him first*, and say: 'I am my Beloved's, and my Beloved is mine,' S.S. 6:3. However, there is still an element of self-centeredness ruling over her priorities. Her third testimony expresses a total change, with the *Lord becoming all in all to her*: 'I am my Beloved's and His desire is toward me,' S.S. 7:10. Her self-life has been completely dealt with and no longer controls either her desires or actions.

"Notice that there is a complete reversal of positions in the progression of these testimonies. In her first confession, she serves the Lord for her own benefit. Therefore, she said, 'My Beloved is mine.' In effect, she ... loves the Lord because He gave her the things that she wanted. This reveals a selfish or a self-serving attitude towards the Lord. ... she views the Lord on a far lower plane of experience than He desires for her. He seeks her fellowship, while she seeks that which He can supply to please her.

"In her final testimony, she is able to say, 'I am my Beloved's, and His desire is toward me.' Now He has become the center of her life. Instead of possessing the Lord, she is possessed by Him. She has changed from a place of self-centeredness, where she tried to use the Lord for her own purposes, and has grown into a love-relationship in which she is sold out to Him. She has submitted her life to the Lord that she might be available to Him for times of fellowship and communion with Him, and also to become a partaker with Him in the outworking of His plan and purpose for mankind, and for the ages to come."

Taylor[10] further expands on this in terms of the three kinds of "love" reflected in three distinct Greek words. We list these in Row [26] of Sanctification Stages Chart Four:

"We all seek for the highest, but we must start at the beginning, where the lord first found us. Thus, the Bride in her first confession revealed her spiritual condition at that time, and said 'He is mine,' S.S. 2:16. Her level of growth had brought her to the place where she was only able to express a one-way love, which can be understood by the concept of 'Eros.' This was a love that moved toward her, in which she was receiving. She loved all of the blessings and the gifts that the Lord provided, and was satisfied with these, apart from Him.

"Then the Lord began to bring about changes within her, so she could become His Bride and love (Phileo) Him as a person rather than loving (Eros) Him because of all the things that He was able to provide for her. After He tenderly corrected her, she was able to say in her second confession, 'I am His, and He is mine,' S.S. 6:3.

"Now, she had progressed to the 'phileo' level of experience. She was responding to His love, and was beginning to notice Him as a Person, but was still very interested in all of the blessings and gifts that were available to her.

"Finally, He brought her into the level of spiritual maturity and experience where she was able to say, 'I am His, and His desire is toward me' S.S. 7:10. Now, her love (Agape) had become outgoing, with no expectancy of return. He had become her all in all, and she had entered into intimate communion with Him and shared His love (Agape) that reaches out to the world. She has become ready to cooperate with Him in His purposes."

We also are encouraged by our Lord Christ Jesus to walk this path of growth in Him.

In this "division" of *Song of Songs* into three parts corresponding to our three general stages of the sanctification process, the beginning of the second stage is typified in Song of Songs 2:8-17 by the sudden appearing of the Shepherd "my Beloved" (*vs.* 8-15) and the Shulemite maiden's response to Him (*vs.* 16-17). This is not a typological reference to the Second Coming of Christ, for *that* occurs to everyone worldwide, whereas this appearing is private to the Shulemite maiden alone. It is a time of great excitement to her. It is also a time of "new beginnings".

In other discussions of the three general stages of the sanctification process (i.e., in Chapter Eight above), we link this step in the believer's life to receiving the **Baptism Into the Holy Spirit**. See Row [15] of Sanctification Stages Chart Two. This typology is indeed of that! For the essence of the Baptism into the Holy Spirit is our *soul*, the seat of our awareness, emotions, thinking and will; we being immersed into or saturated with the Holy Spirit Whose primary task is to reveal Christ to His Bride. Hence, a significant increase in awareness of the *reality* and *presence* of Christ as a Person is what we should expect in the Biblical type. And the *suddenness* of His appearing denotes this to be a singular event in the Believer's life, a special time and event where we initially become aware of Him to this extent. Hence we have the Shulemite maiden's marvelous second testimony of Him in S.S. 2:16. These are some of the very characteristics of this Baptism into the Holy Spirit that we studied in Chapter Seven earlier in this volume.

This is in stark contrast to the type of the beginning of the *third* general stage of the sanctification process, as found in Song 5:2, namely a *silent* coming of Him into our hearts:

"I sleep, but my heart is awake. It is the voice of my Beloved. He knocks! 'Open for me, my sister, my love. My dove, my perfect one! For my head is covered with dew, My locks with the drops of the night.'"

He now gently calls us to open our hearts to Him in a deeper way (*vs.* 2b), that stirs in us an awareness of our inner fears of being unready for Him (*vs.* 3). He departs (actually it is our *awareness* of Him that leaves us), whereupon we are aroused to a most intense search for Him at all costs.

We studied this in depth in Chapter Nine. Whereas we enter the second stage with a dramatic event upon His initiative, our initiation into the third stage of inner purification is by deep inner stirrings in our hearts, to which *we* must respond! More specifically as we described in Chapter Nine, the "event" that clearly marks the beginning of the third stage, though typically "buried" in the midst of the emptying cycles of the second and third stages, is when our Lord Christ Jesus burns into our hearts, for the first time with significant vividness and clarity, a vision of what it really means for us *in this here-and-now* to be *"positioned with Christ in the heavenlies"* (Ephesians 1:3) and to function as His sent and anointed *agents* ("Greater things than these shall ye do" - John 14:12).

Rows [25] and [26] of Sanctification Stages Chart Four summarize these *associated* aspects of our growth in love-relationship *walk* with our Lord Christ Jesus, again in terms of the three general stages of the sanctification process. Row [25] reflects the Shulemite maiden's growth in her(our) reason for loving Him: (1) because of what Christ has *done for me;* (2) because I love Him as a *person;* and (3) because He is *worthy* of all. And row [26] lists the underlying bases we have for loving Him as we grow in these ways: (1) His *forgiveness* of us; (2) His call to *serve Him;* and (3) the *love-union* with Him into which He has drawn us.

3. Spices, Fragrances And Fruit Of Love

An associated rich typology in Song of Songs is the reference to the Shulemite maiden's heart being "my Beloved's" *garden of spices* (Song 4:13-14). An excellent and detailed study of these holy spices, that we highly recommend for the reader's edification, is "The Mountain of Spices" by Hannah Hurnard[11]. We briefly mentioned and summarized them in Table One of Chapter Three earlier in this volume.

The Bible uses the concept of odor to typify our thoughts. Our "spiritual fragrance" is that "spiritual aura" about us, *discernible* in *subtle* ways by God, by the Holy Spirit, by other human spirits if sensitive and discerning enough, and by evil spirits. It refers in the Bible to our *thought* life: our goals and aspirations, our framework of thinking, our true inner thought life, what we actually are. It does not refer primarily to what we *say* verbally or *do* in actions; those things only follow our thoughts.

As we pray or worship (or, negatively, murmur or complain or despair), God hears our *thoughts*, not our actual audible spoken sounds. Throughout the Law of Offerings in Leviticus Chapters 1 through 9, for example, the concept is frequently repeated of our offerings being of a "sweet savor" or "fragrant odor" unto the Lord. Ephesians 5:2 and 2 Corinthians 2:14-17 tell us that Christ, and knowledge of Him, is a "sweet aroma". 1 Corinthians 12:17 lists "smelling" (i.e., discerning of spirits) as one of the manifestations of the Holy Spirit in the Body of

Christ ministries. Romans 12:1-2 links our offering ourselves, as a living and "sweet-savor" *offering*, to: (1) our ***worship;*** (2) our ***separation from worldliness*** in our ***thinking;*** and (3) our being transformed by the ***renewing of our mind*** or patterns of thinking.

Many fragrances are mentioned in the Scriptures that are described as "sweet fragrances" unto God. In Song 4:13-14 are listed nine "holy spices" or aromas. Many are related to specific fruit and spices. Although most fruit and spices are also to be tasted, 90% of our physical sense of taste is really our sense of smell. So also with our spiritual inter-personal relationships, in which our spiritual flavors play an important role.

Hence there is a direct, and very enlightening, parallelism between these nine spiritual fragrances that our Lord Christ Jesus seeks to cultivate in His garden (our hearts), and the nine fruit of the Holy Spirit listed in Galatians 5:22-23. Fruit speak of a source of ***nourishment*** received by the partaker; and these fruit, to be also cultivated in our hearts by the indwelling Holy Spirit of Christ Jesus, are all aspects of ***Love.***

Love, here, is Agape love, not Philea nor Eros nor Storge love. Agape love is totally impossible for any of us to humanly produce. Agape is manifested through us ***only*** by Christ in us (*via* His Holy Spirit abiding) loving His love through us (Romans 5:5); hence it requires us fully yielding to the Holy Spirit, not us struggling to do it ourselves. That love is always ***specifically*** directed: to God the Father Himself, or to one another as specific individuals with specific needs and contributions. So often we confuse a "general compassion" we have for people, such as to "save souls" or to "preach the Gospel", for this. Those are rather forms of Philea love (i.e., for our ministries); though perhaps linked to our special callings (Romans 12:3-8), they are *not per se* the Agape love-fruit of the Holy Spirit of Christ Jesus.

The significance of the flavor characteristics of the love-fruit of the Holy Spirit in our hearts (Galatians 5:22-23) and of the holy spices in the Lord's gardens of our hearts (Song of Songs 4:13-14) is a separate and enlightening study. We illustrated the parallels between these two lists of nine fruits and spices in Table One of Chapter Three. The nine fruit-spice pairs have a logical grouping into three categories: (1) the ***beauty*** that attracts others to Christ living within us and radiating through our outward behavior; (2) the ***flavor*** of Christ in us as reflected in our inner emotions and thought patterns; and (3) the ***effects*** of He in us working through us in our interpersonal relationships. We summarize this in Row [27] of Sanctification Stages Chart Four.

4. Visibility Of Our Message Of Christ

A parallel concept to our "spiritual fragrance unto God" is our "fragrance" to men and women about us in this world, i.e., our ***fame or reputation*** as disciples and witnesses of Christ. Hall[12] gives us an excellent exegetical study of three increasing levels of our witnessing of Christ (as would be seen by others in the world), based on Jesus' increasing fame during His ministering in Galilee in Luke Chapters 4 and 5; we summarize these in Row [28] of Sanctification Stages Chart Four.

In Luke 4:14 we read "And Jesus returned to Galilee in the power of the Spirit; and ***news*** about Him spread through all the surrounding district." The word "news" in the Greek is

Pheme; it has the weak and uncertain connotation of "rumor or suspicion." When we *first* witness of Christ in the power of the indwelling Holy Spirit of Christ Jesus, those about us begin to see and hear our *message* about Christ, but *uncertainly* at first.

Later in Luke 4:37 after Jesus' preached for some time throughout Galilee, we read "And the *report* about Him was getting out into every locality in the surrounding district." The word for "report" in the Greek is Echos. This is a much stronger word than Pheme; it literally means a "loud roar, a clearly heard signal." Indeed, as we *persist* in witnessing in the power of the indwelling Holy Spirit of Christ Jesus, the *message* of Christ's reality becomes increasingly and clearly heard and believed by those about us.

Finally, in Luke 5:15 we read "But the news about Him was spreading even further, and great multitudes were gathering to hear and to be healed of their sicknesses." The word here for "news" in the Greek is Logos, that elsewhere means the *very word/presence of Christ*. John 1:1 uses Logos to refer to Christ Himself. As we mature in our personal relationships with/in Christ and continue to walk in the power of His indwelling Holy Spirit, those about us not only increase in the clarity by which they hear the gospel message: now they see *Christ Himself* in us, and seek Him through us to minister healing and deliverance to them in His power.

5. Growing In Christ-Likeness

Rows [29] through [32] of Sanctification Stages Chart Four give some further aspects of our growth in our personal relationships with our Lord Christ Jesus as a result of our

Divine "Three"

growth in His love. Row [29] summarizes what we are to Him in these separate stages. At first we simply *serve* Him by the fruits of our labors; however, we are to gradually allow Him to lead us in that service, and we become *instruments* in His hands; yet the ultimate goal is that He do everything through us, as we become impedance-free yielded *vessels* or channels of His Life, Light and Love, first unto us, and then through us unto others when/as/how He chooses.

In Row [30] we use the **typology** of *mountains* we approach, i.e., the *experiential goals* toward which He is drawing us as we grow through these stages in our love relationships with Him. At first, after Calvary we grow in living according to His *Law,* as typologized by Mt. *Sinai* (SYNY meaning "hidden from sight") which is also called *Horeb* (ChRB meaning "desolate") - i.e., Exodus Chapters 19 and 34, Numbers Chapter 10, etc.. But as our wills become linked with His Law, He now draws us unto total surrender unto Him of even our service/ministries, as typologized by Abraham's sacrifice of Isaac on Mt. *Moriah* (MWRYH meaning "YHWH provides") - Genesis Chapter 22. Yet even that is not His ultimate goal. His ultimate goal is that we be a strong fortress through which/whom He will establish His Kingdom on earth over the residual forces of satan; that strong fortress is typologized by Mt. *Zion* (TsYWN meaning "strong, conspicuous tower") (2 Samuel Chapters 6-17, etc.).

Varner in his book *Prevail*[13] uses this typology, but with Mt. *Ophel* (HIPhL - meaning a "high place") symbolizing the first stage, patterned by King Jotham's building there (2 Chronicles 27:3). But Mt. Ophel was where Mt. Zion was later located and denotes the third, not the first, stage of sanctification.

These successive goals each require a totally new framework of our thinking, a metamorphosis of our paradigms, a complete remolding of our very essence. We depict this in Row [31] as our being *remolded* as clay in the hands of He our Master Potter (Jeremiah Chapter 18). At first we feel richly *blessed* as we simply accept all He has done for us; but then He starts to recreate our thinking and we experience much *contradiction* between His ways and ours (Isaiah 55:8-9, etc.); finally, His ultimate goal for us is that we be established as fellow *anointed* ones, as He in us does all things when/as/how He chooses.

According to our growing in His thoughts and ways, we shift the nature of our being His witnesses (Row [32]). We first are witnesses of His *Light*, or mental understanding of His ways; as we grow in our actual apprehension of His ways in our lives, we increase as vessels of His *Life* or very presence in us; and finally as our self is totally set aside, we more freely be channels of His Agape *Love*.

6. Growing In Communication With Him

Rows [33] through [35] of Sanctification Stages Chart Four reflect our growth in our *communications* with our Lord Christ Jesus, i.e., our prayer, our gazing unto Him, and our worship of Him as we grow in our love relationship with Him. As we emphasized in Chapter Nine earlier in this volume, the essence of our growing in faith is our learning to *see* our Lord, to *gaze* upon Him in the Spirit, our *beholding* His reality. Hallelujah!

Row [33] indicates the levels of prayer that characterize us in these stages: (1) *thanksgiving* for what He has done for us;

Divine "Three"

(2) ***supplication*** to Him as a current provider; and (3) ***intercession*** with Him on behalf of others.

Row [34] suggests differences in how we behold Him: (1) we ***praise*** and thank Him; (2) we ***share*** Him, in ministry, to one another as members of the Body of Christ; and (3) we are drawn into true ***worship*** of Him.

Row [35] describes the depth of our worship of Him in each stage: (1) ***barren***, for we do not yet behold Him as a real ***presence***; (2) we now ***desire*** Him as a person; and (3) finally we worship Him in radiant ***joy***, so deep now is our love-relationship with Him in us.

7. New Testament Believers Are To Offer Offerings

We now address ***offerings*** pertaining to the three general stages of sanctification. (In Chapter Five of Volume IV[14] of this series, we study the Biblical references to offerings in detail.) We denote those offerings, as pertains to Christians, in Row [36] of Sanctification Stages Chart Five.

As we grow in our love relationship with our Lord Christ Jesus, we concomitantly grow in our ***offerings*** unto Him, since the essence of offerings are various ***expressions of our love*** unto Him.

The Old Testament is full of offerings; but so is the New Testament. Romans 12:1-2 is a keynote passage. In it we see that ***we*** are to offer our Soma - total physical body - as a living and holy sacrifice acceptable to God, our spiritual service of worship. But for our complete selves to be acceptable to God and to constitute our spiritual service, God requires of us: (1)

Sanctification Stages Chart Five

Row #	Three "Types" Of Believer	CARNAL/FLESHLY [SARKIKOS]	SOULICAL/NATURAL [PSUCHIKOS]	SPIRITUAL [PNEUMATIKOS]
[36]	**Offerings** (QRBN) We Give To Deepen Our Personal Relationship With God (Leviticus Chapters 1 - 9)	ILH/MNChH Christ On Calvary Our ALAH/**Ascent** Offering Ourselves Our MINCHAH **(Service)** Offering	Souls As Our ShLM/ThWDH (Wholeness & Thanksgiving) Offerings Of **Consecration** Of Our Entire Beings To Him	Our Entire Being As Our ChTAhTh (Sin-Nature) And AhShM (Guilt-With-Our-Neighbor) Offerings Of **Propitiation**
[37]	Christ Our **ASCENT** Offering	Turtle-Dove	Paschal Lamb	Bullock
[38]	Our Apprehension Of Christ's Atoning Work On Calvary	Acceptance	Involvement	Commitment
[39]	The **Blood** Of Jesus Is:	Sacrificed For Us	Shed Into Us	Shared Through Us
[40]	The **Body** Of Jesus Is:	Bruised On The Cross For Our **Wholeness** (Isaiah 53:4-6)	Multiplied As His Many-Membered Body On Earth	Functionally & Cohesively Unified In Harmony And Rapport
[41]	Levels Of Understanding Of The **Lord's Supper** Or Holy Communion	Recall That He Died For Remission Of My Sins (Forgiveness)	Be A Living Memorial Of Him On Earth During His Absence Due To His Death	Function As Him On Earth During His Absence

entire consecration; (2) active service; (3) worship as a "sweet aroma sacrifice"; and (4) our thought-life transformed (i.e., full repentance).

> "You also, as living stones, are being built up as a spiritual house for a holy priesthood, to offer up spiritual sacrifices acceptable to God through Jesus Christ" - 1 Peter 2:5.

Some other New Testament references are: (1) Ephesians 5:1-2 (following Christ's example of giving Himself as an offering and sacrifice to God as a fragrant aroma); (2) Romans 15:16 (...that Paul's ministry ... be an acceptable offering sanctified by the Holy Spirit); and (3) 1 Peter 2:5 as quoted above (as living stones in the temple of God, we are to offer up spiritual sacrifices acceptable to God through Christ Jesus).

As God matures the Body of Christ and adjusts us together, He is expecting *spiritual* offerings and sacrifices from *us*. This passage does not refer to our tithes and material offerings, for those things are physical, not "spiritual". It means more than even our prayers and intercessions. It also goes beyond our offering our "bodies" (Romans 12:1). What does it mean? What are the *spiritual* offerings required by New Covenant believers in Christ Jesus?

The *physical* sacrifices of the Old Testament are specifically linked to *spiritual* sacrifices of the New Testament. For example: (1) Hosea 14:2 - "present the bulls of our lips" links the Old Testament sacrifices to our praise, worship, and word ministries; (2) Hebrews 13:15-16 - "continually offering up sacrifices of praise, the fruit of our lips, giving thanks to His Name, doing good and sharing, for such sacrifices please

God"; and (3) Revelation 5:8 & 8:3-4 - "the prayers of the saints" (you and I) are compared to the smoke of the incense of the Old Testament offerings, going up before God as "a sweet aroma". Throughout the Bible, our ***thoughts*** are typified by our "spiritual aroma" or "savor". Hence, the "spiritual sacrifices" we are to offer always involve righteousness in our ***thoughts, attitudes, and intents***, as reflected in what we actually say and do.

Even the Old Testament offerings pointed not to ritual but to compassion, mercy, humility and righteousness, as the following passages of Scripture point out: Matthew 9:13 - "...I desire compassion, and not sacrifice; for I did not come to call the righteous, but sinners"; and Matthew 12:7 - "... if you had known what is meant by 'I desire compassion and not a sacrifice', you would not have condemned the innocent". In these two verses, Jesus is quoting Hosea 6:6. Also related to this are Micah 6:6-8 and Amos 5:21-24, that emphasize that such righteous attitudes as justice, kindness, humbleness, knowledge of the Lord, and mercy, are ***much*** more preferred from us by God than ILH (and other) sacrifices.

But *why* are offerings, even of justice and righteousness, desired from us by God? What ***purposes*** do offerings serve? What are the general ***principles*** behind offerings?

8. The Primary Essence Of Offerings

The primary essence of offerings is to establish and/or improve our personal ***relationship*** with God. We read in Leviticus 1:2, "When any man of you brings an ***offering*** to the Lord...." The Hebrew word for "offering" here is QRBN which has the basic meaning not of what we give up or relinquish possession of, but rather of something we do to improve our personal relationship with another person (in this case with God though Christ Jesus). QRBNs (offerings), therefore, are what we do to improve our relationship with God. If we don't care about that, then QRBNs are of no value. If we *do* care about that, then we must explore how the Old Testament QRBNs are shadows or types of New Testament QRBNs.

Leviticus Chapters 1-9 speak to those who desire to improve their personal relationship with God. We are not commanded to do this out of *duty;* rather, God wants and waits for us to *desire* and *seek* Him, before He will work in our lives (Jeremiah 29:13).

The *essence* of all of our QRBN offerings are our thoughts and *attitudes* toward God and toward one another. Our offerings and our repentance are closely related. Our thoughts and attitudes are typified by our "spiritual aroma" or "savor" or "odor" as perceived by God. Throughout the Law of Offerings in Leviticus Chapters 1 through 9, all of the offerings (except the sin-nature and trespass offerings) are described as being of a "sweet savor" or "fragrant odor" to the Lord. Ephesians 5:2 and 2 Corinthians 2:14-17 tell us that Christ, and knowledge of Him, is a "sweet aroma". For us ourselves as offerings to be a "sweet savor" to God means that our thought life must be in *harmony* with, and pleasing to, God. That in turn means that the very core of our thought life must be fused into oneness with Christ in *holiness*. "Come let us reason (think) together, says the Lord" - Isaiah 1:18.

9. Levels Of Offerings

The Old Testament identifies many kinds or types of offerings, each of which has a New Testament antitype. However, Leviticus Chapters 1-7 describe in some detail six specific major offerings, that we now discuss under three "levels". All other offerings in the Old Testament are either *elements* of these six (for example, drink or libation, wave and heave offerings), or simply *attributes* of these six (for example, votive or free-will, compulsory, slain and fire offerings).

Leviticus Chapter 1 describes the ILH or "ascent" offering (mistranslated "burnt offering"). This typifies our offering Christ crucified as our substitute to pay the death penalty for our sins, thus improving our personal relationship with God from absolute *zero* (Romans 3:23 & 6:23 and Ephesians 2:1-3), to a *covenant* relationship of regeneration. Leviticus Chapter 2 then describes our MNChH or "grain" or "fruit of our labors" offering (mistranslated "meat" offering), and typifies our service *for* God and of His preparation of us for that service. Leviticus Chapters 3 and 7 then describe the ShLM or "wholeness" offering (mistranslated "peace offering"), and its ThWDH or "thanksgiving" variation. This is an offering wherein *we*, our self or soul-life, is the offering (Leviticus 3:2), it typifies our yielding to the Holy Spirit of Christ Jesus Who indwells us since regeneration, and it begins upon our Baptism into the Holy Spirit. Leviticus Chapters 4 and 5 then describe the ChTAhTh or *"sin-nature"* offering and the AhShM or "transgression against our neighbor" offering, that typify God's subsequent dealings in our lives (that are *impossible* for any of us to endure until after we offer our ShLM), those dealings being to bridge the holiness gap between He and us, and through which we acquire His holiness and righteousness fully assimilated in us - "Not us, but He living fully through us" (Galatians 2:20).

Ascent And Service

In Row [36] of Sanctification Stages Chart Five we associate the ILH/MNChH offerings with the first general stage of sanctification.

In order for us to ascend to God, we must first undo or satisfy the Adamic Curse of death, since otherwise all of us, through sin, are hopelessly cut off from God. A slain offering, without blemish (sin), is needed as our ILH. Only Christ on Calvary can be that for/as us.

God *most* wants us to have Christ's righteousness *imputed to* us and then *appropriated by* us. The ILH or "ascent" offering of Leviticus Chapter 1 (our appropriating Christ on Calvary) imputes His righteousness to us, as His Holy Spirit comes to indwell in our hearts (in our human spirit). But further offerings are then required of us: that His righteousness become more than merely our legal justification; namely that it becomes our actual *nature*, that it permeates our very thoughts and behaviour.

After the ILH, the next specific form of QRBN offerings described in the Law of Moses is found in Leviticus Chapter 2. Many English language Bibles call it a "meat" offering, that, like the "burnt" offering of Leviticus Chapter 1, is an almost totally erroneous translation. The Hebrew word here is MNChH, that simply means a material gift or present or tribute that does not involve the shedding of blood. The MNChH is a QRBN of *labor* from the Earth under the

Adamic Curse. This is the meaning of the type of the grain or meal offering (MNChH) of Leviticus Chapter 2: our offering of *service*, of ourselves unto Christ Jesus as our appropriate service (Romans 12:1). In this QRBN, it is *fruit*, not life, that is given up. We are here to give to God *man's* allotted portion (Genesis 1:29), not returning to God *His* allotted portion (Genesis 9:4).

As an offering it is a QRBN: something God accepts us as doing in order to improve our personal relationship with Him. Our first permissible QRBN is to offer Christ crucified as our ILH or ascent offering, whereupon we improve our personal relationship with God, from absolute zero to one of communication and covenant Jesus. But now our personal relationship with Him is deepened from a legalistic standing in His presence to one of a *love* relationship, and the beginnings of being given responsibilities and the authority to act on His behalf, in His Name, for His purposes in this world.

A further implication in the Hebrew word MNChH is that it is a gift or tribute or presentation given by an inferior to his *superior*. Hence, we here acknowledge the *Lordship* of Christ over us, and our surrender to His Lordship as His slaves. This is amplified in Psalm 141:2 and Malachi 1:10-13, 2:12-15 & 3:2-4, where incense and lifting up of our hands in praise and worship is linked with the MNChH offering. Lifting of our hands denotes *surrender*; and our praise and worship, done in surrender and adoration, is our tribute indeed to our beloved Lord.

Consecration

In Row [36] of Sanctification Stages Chart Five we associate the ShLM/ThWDH offerings with the second general stage of sanctification.

Leviticus Chapters 3 and 7 describe the ShLM or "wholeness" offering (mistranslated "peace offering"), with its ThWDH ("thanksgiving") and NDR ("service") variations. Some specific Scripture references to this are Exodus 29:10-46, Leviticus Chapter 3 (the entire chapter), 6:12 & 7:11-34, and Ezekiel 43:18-27 & 45:15 through 46:24.

Upon a first glance, this ShLM offering appears to be quite similar to the ILH or ascent offering, that is Christ. But here is a *significant* difference: this is an offering wherein *we*, our self or soul-life, is the offering (Leviticus 3:2). It typifies *our* yielding to the Holy Spirit of Christ Jesus Who indwells us since regeneration, and it *begins* or is enabled upon our Baptism into the Holy Spirit.

In Leviticus 3:1-3, 6-8, & 12-13, we see that it is the *offerer* who *brings* the ShLM and who *slays* it. And we do it *publicly*, "at the doorway in front of the tabernacle or tent of meeting." In this, *we* must take the initiative. There are no prescribed times specified in the Scriptures as to *when* we should bring ourselves as a ShLM unto the Lord. We do it when and as we choose to, when and as we recognize our love debt to Christ Jesus and our total futility without Him indeed being our all. And *we*, publicly as well as in the innermost center of our thoughts and attitudes, slay our self-interests unto Him.

Let us be more specific. It involves a drastic change in our patterns of thinking, such that we willingly *yield* to the influence and *control* by the Holy Spirit of Christ Jesus in us. For us to yield to that control requires a cutting or removing of certain barriers in our hearts. Those barriers of our hearts, that must be cut in order for us to walk in wholeness in Christ, are those of the control our self-nature has over us. Our self, ever vying with the indwelling Holy Spirit of Christ Jesus to control us, must be removed. We must die to all self-rights, all self-exaltations, all self-aspirations. But we must also rise up to His rights, His exaltations, His aspirations.

The ShLM is a voluntary offering; one done upon the free-will and *initiative* of the offerer. It is not something our Lord and High Priest Christ Jesus does for us, nor commands us to do for Him; it is something we *want* to do on our own, out of our love debt to Him and out of our recognition that He is worthy of our all and a far better Lord over our lives than we can ever be.

Two variations of the ShLM offering are described: the Hebrew words used are ThWDH (Leviticus 7:12-15) and NDR (Leviticus 7:16-17). ThWDH means "praise, confession, and thanksgiving, openly and freely given"; and NDR means "vow, service, or harvest". These variations refer to our response or reaction or subsequent attitudes following our giving ourselves as our ShLM offering. Our first reaction (ThWDH) is gratitude to our Lord Christ Jesus for His drawing us unto this companionship relationship with Him, unto this vivid awareness of Him as a marvelous, loving and strong Person. We recognize and acknowledge our love-debt to Him. But our subsequent response must also be a determination (NDR) to persist in all of its ramifications, regardless of how unpleasant or costly. NDR typifies our ministries to one another within the Body of Christ. For to walk with Christ is to be yoked with Him and to be cleansed by Him.

KPhR (Propitiation): Experiential Atonement

Full victory in spiritual warfare, and overcoming the evil one, has yet a further prerequisite over and above our offering ourselves as a ShLM offering unto Christ Jesus. This additional requirement is the very holiness and righteousness of Christ Himself: that the holiness gap between He and us be bridged *experientially*.

A Biblical example of this requirement is the first battle of Ai in Joshua Chapter 7. Was this a cruel judgment by God for a seemingly minor incident? The issue is this: to whatever extent there be yet unconfessed and unyielded sin in our lives, to that extent and in those very areas we are *vulnerable* to satanic influence; for he thrives on darkness in our attitudes and motives and thoughts. God does not yet dare, for His Holy Name's (reputation and glory)'s sake, entrust us with His power and victory, lest satan through those areas of darkness in our lives exploit God's power manifested in us.

This is of immediate import to Spirit-led Christian fellowships today. Few of us at most have indeed reached a level of maturity in Christ commensurate with the responsibilities of our being in leadership of such fellowships (even though we each tend to think that we have). As certain individuals among us are from time to time projected into key roles of effective leadership, they are particularly vulnerable to satanic attack in whatever areas of weakness they happen to have in their walk with Christ Jesus. I personally have observed this very thing (both in myself and in others) on *many* occasions over the past several years. Yes, unless or until the holiness gap between Christ Jesus and us is bridged *experientially* to a *significant* extent in our lives, even if we indeed have offered ourselves as a ShLM offering, we will still by and large not personally experience the power of God and victory over satan for which we yearn.

In Row [36] of Sanctification Stages Chart Five we associate offerings known as ChTAhTh and AhShM with the third general stage of sanctification.

Leviticus Chapters 4 through 6 describe the ChTAhTh or "sin-nature" offering and the AhShM or "transgression-against-our-neighbor" offering, that typify God's subsequent dealings in our lives (that are impossible for any of us to endure until after we first offer ourselves as a ShLM offering). Those dealings are to bridge this holiness gap between Christ Jesus and us, through which we acquire and fully assimilate His holiness and righteousness. "Not us, but He living fully through us" (Galatians 2:20).

These ChTAhTh and AhShM offerings are related to KPhR or experiential atonement. Hence they apply to the personal *relationship* between us and God. In one sense, "atomenent" applies to *all* of the offerings described in Leviticus Chapters 1 through 7: the Hebrew general word for offering, QRBN, means something we do in order to establish and/or improve our personal relationship with God. *Positionally* we *achieve* atonement by offering Christ Jesus on the Cross as our ascent offering or ILH QRBN. But *experientially* we *begin to grow* in atonement through our subsequent offerings: of our *labors*

Divine "Three" 351

as MNChH, and of our *selves* as ShLM QRBN's.

In order for us to grow into *experiential* atonement, the ChTAhTh or "sin" and AhShM or "trespass" forms of KPhR offerings are required. Like the other offerings, these of course typify Christ Jesus on Calvary, Who is these offerings *for* and *as* us. But here we emphasize also that *we* are typified by these offerings: *we* are the *offering* as well as the *offerer*, and Christ Jesus on Calvary is our *example* Whom we follow.

Compared to our ShLM offerings that are offerings of our *self* - our self-rights, self-interests, self-orientation of our thoughts and attitudes - these KPhR offerings are offerings of our very sin *nature* and behaviour. They deal with not our willful rebellion against God, but our indifference and/or our *inadvertent* violations of His perfect will and holiness!

The ChTAhTh or "sin nature" offering is in some ways a deeper and more stringent extension of the ShLM: it is an offering of a slain life, and it is offered by fire. It is to remove all that would hinder us from *full* fellowship with God. And the AhShM, involving monetary or tangible payments of restitution to those *people* whom we have offended, is to remove all that would hinder us from *full* fellowship with our fellow brothers and sisters in God. That means removal of *all* hindrances and offenses, not just those of which we are conscious, but those that are inadvertent, of which we are not necessarily cognizant of in ourselves. Throughout Chapter Nine earlier in this volume, we refered to emptying cycles of vision-loss-striving-surrender-revisitation-consummation as our Lord's primary way of removing these hindrances and offenses.

Our giving unto God of these ILH/MNChH, ShLM, and KPhR offerings is an *iterative* process in time. We *grow* into the deeper levels of apprehension of *each* of these service-self-atonement offerings as we mature in *all* aspects of our walk with Christ Jesus and our consequently increasing understandings of what He requires of us individually.

The Baptism into the Holy Spirit is a necessary *prerequisite* for all levels of apprehension of our KPhR offerings. It being a prerequisite is not a "moral" law nor a mere desideratum on God's part, but a "physical" law: it is physically and spiritually *impossible* for us to proceed into death to self, experiential atonement, and mature service as love-slaves of Christ Jesus, without our first yielding our souls (soul-spirit barriers) unto the influence and control of the Holy Spirit of Christ Jesus Who indwells us. These latter offerings are not required of us at *set* or prescribed times, but only after these necessary conditions are first fulfilled.

10. This Cup Is My Covenant

Of course, the most foundational and ever-pervasive offering for New Testament believers is Christ, offering Himself on Calvary for our atonement. This we commemorate in many ways, but most visibly by Holy Communion, i.e. the Lord's Supper (Matthew 26:26-29, Mark 14:22-25, Luke 22:14-20, John 13:1 and 1 Corinthians 11:23-26) as we are commanded to commemorate (1 Corinthians 11:24-25). The Old Testament offerings, as we have just briefly discussed, are types of our Lord's sacrifice - particularly the ILH or *ascent* offering of Leviticus Chapter 1.

Divine "Three"

Little recognized, however, is that there are different "levels of apprehension" at which we commemorate the Lord's Supper, and these different "levels" correspond directly to the several stages of sanctification that we depict throughout this volume. To understand this, we briefly go back to review yet another aspect of those Old Testament offerings.

Principle of Different Levels of Apprehension

In each of the six main Old Testament offerings, different extents or magnitudes of the offering were permitted according to how much the offerer could *afford*. These different levels of ability to afford typify our different levels of *apprehension* of the meanings of the offerings. (By "apprehension" we mean understanding in *experience*, not just with our *minds*.) We have this principle: whatever be our level of apprehension of Christ and our offering, it is *fully* acceptable to God as a QRBN *if* we indeed offer at our level, but *not* acceptable to Him if we offer at a lesser level. Of him to whom much is given, much is required (Luke 12:48).

The clearest example of this is the three kinds of animals (dove, sheep or goat, and bull) that typify Christ on the cross as our ascent offering. The dove (Leviticus 1:14-17) is a bird of flight, and typifies Christ as *divine* (the "Son of God"). Here Christ's *divinity* is emphasized, and He is acting as the Spirit of peace. For the sheep or goat level of apprehension (Leviticus 1:10-13), the emphasis is on the *sacrifice* He made for us, and on us *partaking* of Christ. His Lamb Nature consists of total submission (i.e., to the will of the Father) and His meekness and gentleness; and His goat nature consists of persistence and determination to follow a set course (i.e., the Father's will). For the bullock or ox (Leviticus 1:3-9), the emphasis is on Christ as the strong but gentle and suffering servant of mankind, exhibiting patience and untiring labor as the love-slave of the Father.

These three levels of apprehension of Christ as the ascent offering on our behalf are summarized in Row [37] of Sanctification Stages Chart Five:

> (1) turtledove - divine Son of God and the Spirit of peace;
> (2) lamb - the Paschal (sacrificial Passover) Lamb of God;   Christ stepping *into* our hearts; and
> (3) bullock - Christ the strong, gentle, but suffering burden-bearer of mankind, with whose sufferings and ministry *we* identify.

These three levels of apprehension of Christ as our ascent offering determine the emphases in which we are to celebrate the Lord's Supper, as we now discuss in the following three subsections.

Our Initial Apprehension Of Christ's Atoning Work On Calvary

The first level of emphasis in Holy Communion, that is most common among many traditional Protestant denominations, is our merely *accepting* Christ's atoning work on the Cross individually (see Row [38] of Sanctification Stages Chart Five). Here the priests (or presiding minister and elders) serve us the elements where and as we are. We commemorate Christ on Calvary, and we rejoice in our justification before God through Christ's dying for our sins, thus satisfying the Adamic Curse for each of us. Little detail is given of who

Christ was except as the sinless One and God's divine agent for our salvation. Hence, the emphasis corresponds to the turtle-dove level of apprehension of Christ as our ascent offering.

Our sights are on Calvary: we note the Blood of Christ sacrificed or shed (i.e., spilled) *for (i.e., on behalf of) us*, and His Body was broken (i.e., crucified) for (i.e., on behalf of) us, as we remember Christ's death (i.e., the *act* of His dying). We illustrate this in Rows [39] and [40] of Sanctification Stages Chart Five. (But as we subsequently note, these concepts are *not* those of the Greek words used to record Jesus' and Paul's actual exhortations to us on Holy Communion.) Our apprehension of Christ's atoning work on Calvary here is simply that of our *recalling* that He died for remission (forgiveness) of our sins, as we denote in Row [41] of Sanctification Stages Chart Five.

Our Personal Involvement In Christ's Atoning Work On Calvary

The second level of emphasis in Holy Communion, as indicated in Row [38] of Sanctification Stages Chart Five, is one that emphasizes our *involvement* with one another in the Body of Christ, i.e., as we, functioning together, be the physical manifestation of Christ on Earth (i.e., His "Body") now, while He Himself "remains in the Heavenlies ..." (Acts 3:20-21).

We celebrate Holy Communion at the sheep or goat level of apprehension of Christ as our ShLM offering (see Row [37] of Sanctification Stages Chart Five). Here our sights are not on Calvary, but on Pentecost.

Total Union With Christ

The third level of emphasis in Holy Communion goes yet a step further and exemplifies our ***total commitment*** to Christ and to one another: that as fellow members of the Body of Christ, each containing Christ, we *serve* one another with meekness and humility. We emphasize this commitment in Row [38] of Sanctification Stages Chart Five.

In this case, we celebrate Holy Communion much as in the second level above, but with more love toward and sensitivity to the needs of one another, and in addition, following Holy Communion immediately with foot-washing (John 13:3-17). Our feet typify our points of contact with the world in our daily walk, and foot-washing typifies how we each help one another from becoming, and remaining, polluted in attitudes by those contacts. We do this through mutual encouragement, intercessory prayer and exhortation.

This particular emphasis is on the Philippians 2:3-8 attitude that we are to hold toward one another. It is the attitude that Christ Jesus desires to bring us unto, and will be essential in the coming persecution days. In it we see, and emulate, Christ as the bullock - strong yet gentle and meek suffering servant of mankind - in our apprehension of Him as our ascent offering. This we emphasize in Row [37] of Sanctification Stages Chart Five. Meekness in Biblical Greek (Praus) does not mean being of low estate, but rather being of great strength and authority but being very gentle, sensitive, merciful and loving in its exercise, purely to edify others even at our personal expense!

Divine "Three"

Our emphasis here is also on our identification with the *sufferings* of Christ, that through death of self we choose to permit Him to flow unhindered through us unto others. The bread is much that of above, but with more oil (Holy Spirit anointing) and salt (demonstration of righteousness). As we mature, our attention is less on our selves, even our sanctified selves, and more on Him in His totality.

11. Kings And Priests - A Holy People

We have studied how our *offerings* are expressions of our love for our Lord Christ Jesus, and that our commemorating the Lord's Supper includes our expressions of that love not only unto Him but also to one another in His Body. We now study further aspects of our expressing that love to one another.

The Biblical types we use here are we being: (1) kings; (2) priests; and (3) anointed servants. These concepts are closely interlinked. In Exodus 19:6 we read "... you shall be to Me a kingdom of priests and a holy nation." And we are called both "a royal priesthood" in 1 Peter 2:9 and "an holy priesthood" in 1 Peter 2:5: "Ye also, as lively stones, are built up a spiritual house, an holy priesthood, to offer up spiritual sacrifices, acceptable to God by Jesus Christ." Hence the apostle Peter is emphasizing that as He draws us apart unto Him in holiness, He gives us His authority as King to act as *priests*. And even more, as a priesthood, we form the very temple of God, i.e., the domain in which priests function.

Kings

"Repent, for the Kingdom of God/Heaven is at hand (i.e., can at last be grasped by you)!" - the salient message of the New Testament, first by John the Baptist, and then by Jesus.

Just what does the "Kingdom of God" mean? Actually, "the Kingdom of God now able to be grasped by men and women on earth" *is* the New Testament message; "being born again" is one of many details of insight on *how* that kingdom can now be grasped by us.

The real meaning is in terms of the ***personal relationships*** in a righteous (i.e., a "perfect") kingdom. Those personal relationships can be quite simply stated. A (righteous) king uses his authority to maximize the ***well-being*** of all of his people: peace from military conquest from the outside, economic stability, enforcement of justice and fairness, education of the people, mercy when called for, etc. The people, in exchange for that well-being, provide that authority to the king by virtue of their willingness to *obey* him and to help and support one another.

For us, therefore, the "Kingdom of God" is a matter of us individually ***choosing*** to be totally submissive to the Lordship of Christ Jesus in all areas of our lives, to surrender to Him our "rights", our tendencies to run our own lives, in exchange for total well-being, the "peace that surpasses all understandings" (Philippians 4:7). This "trust and obey" issue is the essence of our "Kingdom of God" relationship with Christ Jesus. It is for "here and now" (i.e., can *now* be grasped by us), although it will be ***completed*** "then and there". Though far from being a vague mystical notion, this is an area that we must be taught to walk in - and that learning continues during our entire lives here on earth. Christ's process of sanctifying us is a key reality.

When we think of *royalty*, i.e., of members of a king's family, we immediately associate it with *authority*. We as adopted members of God's family, are indeed part of the Kingdom of God now on earth. As such, we are given the authority of His name.

The *essence* of our being "royal" members of His Kingdom is not just exercising the *authority* of the Name of our Lord Christ Jesus. Rather, it is our being *servants*! We are to walk in this servanthood "here and now" as a "royal priesthood", we indeed walk in His authority - for His authority is essential for that servanthood to be of practical effect. Nevertheless, just as there are different levels of our love-relationship with Him, as reflected in different levels of our offerings and of our apprehension of the Lord's Supper, there are different levels of our appropriating His authority. And those different levels of our appropriating His authority correspond directly to the three general stages of sanctification as depicted throughout this volume.

These three levels of our appropriating His authority are: (1) His *Word* that we follow *legalisticly* by human will and strength; (2) His *life* that flows through us to give our actions divine *power;* and (3) His *love* that flows through us from His indwelling *Presence* when and as and how He alone chooses. We illustrate these three levels of our appropriating and walking in His authority by three Old Testament Kings of Israel (see Row [42] of Sanctification Stages Chart Six): Saul, David and Solomon.

Sanctification Stages Chart Six

Row #	Three "Types" Of Believer →	CARNAL/FLESHLY [SARKIKOS]	SOULICAL/NATURAL [PSUCHIKOS]	SPIRITUAL [PNEUMATIKOS]
[42]	Three Kings	Saul	David	Solomon
[43]	What We Rule By	His Word	His Life	His Love
[44]	Three Priesthoods	Aaron	Zadok	Melchizedek
[45]	Priestly Ministries	To Those Of The World	To The Believer	To God
[46]	Three Anointings	Leper's (Leviticus 14:14-18)	Priest's (Exod. 28:41, 29:7,30;40:13&15)	King's (1 Samuel 9:16, 10:1, 16:1 & 12-13)
[47]	Three Levels Of Overcoming	From Temptation Of The Flesh	From Deceptions Of The Soul	Unto Spiritual Power And Discernment
[48]	Pilgrim's Progress	Regeneration & Struggles w Carnality (Sections 1-4)	The Spirit-Dependent Walk (Sections 5 - 10)	Vision Of The Heavenlies (Sections 11-16)
[49]	Pilgrim's Trust Is In:	God's Word (Knowledge)	Indwelling Holy Spirit	Position Christ In Heavenlies
[50]	What The 3 Marys At The Cross Presented To Us	Magdalene News Of His Resurrection	Mother Of James The Lesser Apostle/Messenger Of Gospel	Mother of Jesus Presence Of Jesus

Saul, popularly sought out by God's people outside of divine guidance (and in direct contradiction to the prophetic word given at the time through Samuel), operated totally *by human wisdom and with human strength*. Yet God allowed it, and accomplished much in the eyes of the world through him. King Saul is a type of denominational Christianity today: lacking divine unction and power, but still reflecting to some extent God's Word.

David, rejected by his half-brothers, loved God and His ways above all else and was divinely protected and raised up by God Himself. It was through David, a humble and obedient servant warrior, that God conquered all of the area originally promised to Abraham (compare 2 Samuel 8:1-15 and 1 Kings 4:20-21 to Genesis 13:14-17 and 15:18-21) and hence fully established the *nation* of Israel on earth. David is a type of Christ as Captain of His army. And though David at times succumbed to his sin-nature (as indeed we also do), He was one of the most Godly of all Old Testament kings of Israel.

Solomon, *born* into the Davidic kingdom, was characterized primarily by the unusual and tremendous *anointing* upon him to rule with divine wisdom and love. As such he is a type of Christ as head of His Body and His Kingdom. Until late in his kingdom when his lusts for women brought his downfall, his kingdom was a reign of great peace and economic well-being (which is what his name ShLMN means in the Hebrew).

But each of these kings are also types of the extent to which we individually walk with Christ, either by His word, by His life, or by His love and anointing. This we note in Row [43] of Sanctification Stages Chart Six.

Priests

But also, we are called to be royal *priests*. To be a royal priest, a Christian must himself be born anew in Christ. He/she must also have Christ's ***authority***. That authority is ***not*** a political nor institutional authority over other people, not even over other Christians. Rather, it is the spiritual authority which comes from the indwelling ***Presence*** of Christ. He does not separate His authority from His Presence.

What does it mean to be a priest? Word etymology does not help us much here; the Greek word Iereus means simply that: "a priest". And religious tradition does not help us here either, because of gross distortions rooted in Baal. A Biblical priest is not one who has political or institutional authority over another person or persons, as is the common pattern today.

The Old Testament priest is a type of the New Testament priest. The Hebrew word KHN, based on a root verb meaning "to stand in a gap", means one who stands between two parties to mediate between them. The priest is one who stands between people and God. The Old Testament High Priest stood between the entire nation of Israel and God; Christ, as our High Priest now stands between you/I and God the Father (Hebrews 4:14-5:10 and 5:20-6:28). The lesser priests stood between individual Israelites and God as teachers, guides and assistants in their offerings of their sacrifices. You and I today, as New Testament priests, stand between one another (and/or those still of satan's Kosmos) and God (through our Lord Christ Jesus living in us) in the whole gamut of Body of Christ ministries.

Divine "Three" 363

As one who stands between men/women and God, a priest has two main functions: (1) sacrifices; and (2) intercession. We studied the first of these above. In this section we now address intercession.

Hebrews 4:14-16 assures us that since Christ is our High Priest, we can enter boldly in Him before God. Hebrews 5:3-10 establishes that God the Father raised up Christ to the position of High Priest through His (Christ's) offering Himself as a sacrifice on our behalf. Hebrews 5:10, 7:11-25 and 9:11 indicate that Christ's Priesthood is of a glorious new order, of which (see Hebrews 7:26-8:6) the Old Testament priesthood was but a type or shadow or image. Romans 8:27 and 34 then give us a glimpse of how Christ as our High Priest, and His Holy Spirit, constantly intercede before God for us.

But *we* are to function as priests for others in addition to Christ functioning as a priest for us. What does that mean? Simply that until Christ's return (Acts 3:21), *we* are to allow Christ to **manifest** His new-order priesthood on Earth through us His Body.

Since the Old Testament priesthood was but a type or shadow or image of Christ's new-order priesthood, we need to see how that functioned in order to start understanding what is required of us, Spirit-filled believers, today. Of course we do not now offer the blood of bulls and goats; nevertheless, the Old Testament priesthood intrinsically has many valuable lessons for New Testament believers.

The Old Testament priesthood actually had three distinct "orders" or periods of development, which we denote in Row [44] of Sanctification Stages Chart Six: Aaron (AhHRWN),

Zadok (TsDWQ) and Melchizdek (MLK-TsDQ). Each is a type of an aspect of *Christ* being our High Priest today. But here we also note that these three have direct and important antitypical meaning to *us* today, as *we* are matured by Christ into functioning as priests of intercession.

The first order of priesthood was that of *Aaron* (see, for example, Exodus Chapters 4 though 7 and Leviticus Chapters 8 through 10). Aaron in Hebrew (AhHRWN) means "enlightened (one)". In type, then, the priesthood "of the order of Aaron" symbolizes Christians who have significantly matured in apprehension of the word of God and are enlightened in the ways of God. Such a believer is able to knowledgeably direct his prayers and acts of intercession and properly focus his attention and priorities on the needs and burdens of others.

The second order of priesthood was that of *Zadok* (see, for example, 2 Samuel Chapter 15 and verses 19:11 & 20:25; 1 Kings Chapter 1 and verses 2:35 & 4:2 & 4; 1 Chronicles 16:39 & 29:22; and Ezra 40:46 and Chapter 43). Zadok in Hebrew (TsDWQ) means "righteous (one)". This type, the priesthood "of the order of Zadok", symbolizes Christians who have been significantly matured in righteousness of character and attitudes. Such believers are more effective priests of intercession than those of the preceding order, since our Lord Christ Jesus is now able to more significantly trust them with His authority and power in actual practice to *effect* many of the answers to the prayers of intercession. This is a more supernatural ministry and involves flowing in the prophetic word, in discerning and exorcising spirits, and in healing and other miracles.

The Zadokite priesthood speaks of two distinct ways in which He would have us minister: unto *Him* in the "inner court"[15]; and unto *people*, in the "outer court". We indicate this in Row [45] of Sanctification Stages Chart Six. Ministry unto *Him* is to precede, *as a prerequisite*, our ministering unto people!

The third order of priesthood was that of *Melchizedek* (see Genesis 14:18, Psalm 110:4, and Hebrews 5:6 & 10, 6:20, 7:1, 10, 11, 15, 17 & 21). Note that we regard the Melchizedek order as most superior, even though it preceded the other two in time and in Scripture; Hebrews 6:20 is our basis for that. Melchizedek in Hebrew (MLK-TsDQ) means "my king is righteous". He is also identified as the King of (Jeru)Salem, or King of (habitation in) peace, wholeness." The Scriptures do not explicitly identify Melchizedek for reason of the comparison with Christ that is given in Hebrews 7:3. But the ancient non-canonical Hebrew scriptures identify him as Shem, son of Noah, in his latter years. This is highly plausible considering the stated lifespan of Shem and the territory allotted to him. And Shem in Hebrew (ShM) means "name" or "reputation" or "authority".

In type, the priesthood "of the order of Melchizedek" symbolizes the Christian who *lives* as a citizen of His Kingdom, *walks* (experientially) in His righteousness, *knows* His peace, and *reigns* in the Name of Christ (i.e., in His presence).

Hebrews 5:5-10 and 7:1-22, quoting Psalm 110:4, does not conflict with this concept that the Melchizedek order was the most *superior* of the Old Testament orders of priesthood. Three separate issues are being emphasized in Hebrews 5 and

7, neither of which pertains to the orderings *within* the Old Testament. First, Christ Jesus of the New Covenant, is a High Priest of an order "higher" than *any* Old Testament priesthood, since He instituted a new and *better* covenant (Hebrews 7:22, 8:6, 11 & 15). This supports our suggestion that Christ Jesus is the typical *fulfillment* of all three Old Testament orders of priesthood, Melchizedek included. Second, the author of Hebrews is emphasizing that Christ's priesthood is not a priesthood under *law*, but transcends the law by a sovereign act of God. Christ came to *personify* the law (literally "be its fulfillment" in the Greek of Matthew 5:17-18). Both the Aaronic and Zadokite orders of priesthood were under the law, whereas the Melchizedek preceded (and hence *transcended)* the law; he was made a priest directly by God (long before God established the law in written form). Ephesians 1:19-23 tells us this same thing about Christ Jesus. And third, Hebrews 5:5-10 and 7:1-22 emphasizes the all-encompassing or all-inclusive reach of Christ Jesus's priesthood. Christ beckons all whosoever ... to come unto Him (John 6:37, Acts 2:21, etc.). Melchizedek is depicted in Genesis 14:18-20 as worthy of respect and homage by *all* peoples, not just Abraham and his kin. The Aaronic and Zadokite orders, on the other hand, are more restrictive orders, as they reflect deeper personal relationships between the priests and God.

We are to function as priests! *We* are to manifest Christ's new-order priesthood on Earth! We are: to do all that will satisfy God in our personal relationship with Him; to become washed by the water of the Word of God unto personal holiness of behaviour; flow in Body ministries; share the word of God freely; lift thoughts of thanksgiving and praise and worship continually unto God; go through personal crucifixion of our own fleshly attitudes and drives; and then enter freely into the very presence of God to represent and to intercede on behalf of others.

To function as priests of the order of Zadok and/or Melchizedek requires a deep level of maturity in our yieldedness to Christ in us, a level that most of us have not yet reached. That is why our being priests of intercession is a new concept to most of us. What is such a priest of intercession like? What are his chief characteristics? How does he acquire that functioning maturity?

To be an intercessor is the height of our calling. An intercessor takes the place of those he intercedes for, and is responsible for bridging the gap between them and God. But an intercessor is also an *ordinary* man. He is specially *commissioned* to stand in the gap in specially appointed situations; but it is Christ in ordinary men, you and I, doing it. He is "taken among men" (Hebrews 5:1), that is, out of this world, to contain Christ *via* the indwelling Holy Spirit. Then he is ordained *for* men, that is, he is conscious of some special commission relating to some special people or situation. He is ordained for men in things pertaining to God, that is, to be responsible to join other men to God. We, both men and women in Christ, are all priests, because we all have commissions for others. We are royal priests because we have our authority from the Ascended Christ, are directed and enabled by the Indwelling Christ, and so function in His Name.

12. Anointings

As a "royal priesthood" ministering as kings and priests, we must be anointed by our Lord Christ Jesus for our specific ministries.

The Biblical concept of *anointing*, typified by the *pouring of oil*, is that of the Holy Spirit of Christ Jesus in us ministering though us in wisdom and power. It is not a static concept but rather a highly *dynamic flow*. It is not something usually associated with us as persons nor something that we "obtain"; rather it is an aspect of our *doing*, an important part of our *ministering* in servanthood.

Just as there are different "levels" of our acting as kings and priests, there are different "levels" of our anointing and our ministering. These we illustrate in Row [46] of Sanctification Stages Chart Six.

The first anointing is typified by the *Leper's* anointing of Leviticus 14:14-18. Here we see our anointing is by the *blood* of the ILH or *ascent* offering (of Christ on Calvary), that we ourselves first have our sins forgiven by His shed blood. This is our necessary preparation for the preaching of the Gospel aspect of the Great Commission. In this leper's anointing, we see the application of that blood is on our head, hand and foot, symbolizing our presentation of the Word of God as we walk.

The second anointing, appropriate when we are ministering to one another within the Body of Christ, is typified by the *priest's* anointing alluded to in Exodus 28:41, 29:7, 30:30, 40:13 and 40:15. Here the emphasis is heavily on the outpouring not of blood but of *oil*, i.e., the Holy Spirit. This is our necessary preparation for the ministering the *life* of Christ in His power.

The third anointing is typified by the *king's* anointing described for King David in 1 Samuel 9:16, 10:1, 16:1 and 16:12-13. Here we see a more intense outpouring of *oil* on the *person* receiving the anointing. The person himself was divinely selected by God and is being raised up by God to share in the administering of the "inheritance of the saints" (Ephesians 1:18). Afterward, the anointer (Samuel) went to Ramah (HRMH, that means "the divine heights"), leaving the anointed one to carry on the work. Hence, here the *person* himself is anointed, not just his ministering acts.

13. Overcoming Temptations

In His messages to *each* of the "Seven Churches" (or church characteristics or periods of church history in typology), our ascended Lord Christ Jesus promised great rewards to "he who overcomes and keeps My deeds until the end" (Revelation 2:7, 11, 17 & 26 and 3:5, 12 & 21). In the prophecy of the New Heaven and New Earth (Revelation 21:7) this promise is repeated. Those great rewards include sharing in the power and authority of His government/kingdom over Heaven and Earth.

A closer look at the New Testament shows that it is specifically *satan* whom we believers are to overcome. 2 Corinthians 11:3 and Ephesians 6:11 tell us to guard against being led astray by the wiles of *satan*. Romans 12:21, 1 John 2:13-14 and Revelation 12:11 specifically tell us to overcome the evil *one*. And 1 John 5:4-5 tells us to overcome the "world" (which in the Greek is Kosmos meaning satan's *organization)*. Hence, God's children are to overcome the person of satan.

How? We assert that believers must overcome three ways in which satan works to destroy us: *temptation* that makes us vulnerable to satan; *deception* from satan, and the *power* of satan. The first two of these "levels" of overcoming are required of each believer *individually;* and the third level involves believers acting *corporately*. Here, as summarized in Row [47] of Sanctification Stages Chart Six, we discuss the first of these.

All temptations fall under one or more of three basic categories: temptations of the human *flesh;* of the human *soul;* and of the human *spirit*. These three temptations, in three representations of each, are summarized in Table Three. Note that there is a progressive *sequence* involved here.

These are the three temptations that the serpent used (alas, successfully) to tempt Eve and Adam (Genesis 3:6). "Serpent" in the Hebrew (NChSh) that means "enchanter" or "beguiler". He also confronted Jesus with these same three temptations; but Jesus overcame them all. We also, in Him, are to likewise overcome! Most of us never get past temptations of the *flesh* by *fully* appropriating Romans 6, *via* baptism, reckoning our flesh crucified with Christ and our life lived in the resurrected life of Christ. Temptations of the *soul* involve placing "good" things higher in priority to our relationship with Christ, such as art, beauty, superficial social fellowships, "good works", respectable aspects of our culture. Temptations to the human *spirit* come primarily through love in its various forms. They are also especially great dangers to mature, *anointed* ministers of God who refuse to lay down their ministries, their Isaacs, on the altars on Mt. Moriah before God, as He for our sake may at times require of us.

Table Three

Our Three Great Temptations

Nature Tempted	Temptation of Eve/Adam (Gen. 3:6)	Temptation of Jesus (Luke 4:1-13 & Matt 4:3-10)	Our Provision From God For Overcoming: "Hidden" In Ark (Heb 9:4)
Lust of **Flesh** (Physical)	Good For Food	Command Stones to Become Bread	Manna (God's Provision Of Daily Bread)
Lust of **Soul** (Esthetics & Power)	Delight To Eyes	Glory Of Kingdoms of World	Tables of The Covenant (God's Wisdom & Righteousness)
Lust of **Spirit** (Life, Wisdom, Rightness)	Desirable to Make One Wise As Gods	Throw Self Down; Angels Will Protect You	Aaron's Rod That Budded (Holy Spirit's Fruit In Us)

Our provisions from the indwelling Christ to enable us to overcome these three temptations is represented by the artifacts in the Ark of the Covenant (Hebrews 9:4). Manna (God's provision of daily bread - Exodus 16:31-34) pertains to the *flesh*. The tables of the Covenant (Exodus 31:18, 32:15-16, & Deuteronomy 9:9, 11 & 15) pertain to God's wisdom and righteousness (for us to choose to live by). Aaron's rod that budded (Numbers 17:2-10) pertains to the fruit of the Holy Spirit in us.

14. "Pilgrim's Progress"

One popular Christian source that portrays many of the stages of the sanctification process, is the allegory or "visionary biography" in John Bunyan's 19th century book "Pilgrim's Progress"[16]. Here we briefly summarize, from Part I of that allegory, how Bunyan relates a Christian's experiences from initial conviction of the need for a saviour to final translation to be with Christ in the heavenlies. Row [48] of Sanctification Stages Chart Six sketches this. We quote the summary headings of each numbered section in the original.

Also, in Row [49] of Sanctification Stages Chart Six we list the different objects of *trust* the believer has during his progress, first just in his intellectual **knowledge of the Word of God**, then in the wisdom and power of the **indwelling Holy Spirit of Christ Jesus**, and finally upon his **position with Christ in the heavenlies**, he now being but a pilgrim or traveler in this world that is no longer his home.

Divine "Three"

Conviction To Enlightenment Of Calvary:

In Sections 1 through 3 we see the seeker's initial conviction of his need for a savior, but also his hopelessness. He sees the harshness of religious legalism that ever deepens his hopelessness. Finally he is enlightened about so great salvation by Christ on the Cross:

> "1. (pp. 46) Christian, feeling his burden, and alarmed at this danger, flees from the City of Destruction - Is met by Evangelist, who directs him to the Wicket-gate - Obstinate and Pliable go after Christian, to fetch him back - Christian persuades Pliable to go with him - They fall into the slough of Despond - Pliable, discouraged, returns home - Christian, assisted by Help, gets out of the Slough on the side next the gate.
>
> "2. (pp. 59) Christian is met by Mr. Worldly Wiseman, who condemns Evangelist's counsel, and prefers morality to the strait gate - Christian is snared by his words, and turned out of the way - He comes to Mt. Sinai, and fears it will fall on his head - Evangelist again meets him, and puts him in the right way - Christian arrives at the Wicket-gate - Conversation between Christian and Goodwill.
>
> "3. (pp. 75) Christian arrives at the Interpreter's house - The Interpreter shows and explains to him various representations and emblems of spiritual things, as the picture of the pilgrim's guide, the dusty parlour, Passion and Patience, the fire, the man in the iron cage, etc."

Regeneration And Struggle With Carnality:

In Section 4 we see the seeker, by trusting in this knowledge of God's *Word*, accepts Christ's atoning work for the forgiveness of his sins. But he almost immediately encounters the Romans 6 *vs.* 7 struggle of flesh *vs* spirit:

> "4. (pp. 89) Christian loses his burden at the cross - Is saluted by three shining Ones, who give him a change of raiment, etc. - Going on his way he finds Simple, Sloth, and Presumption, asleep - Meets Formalist and Hypocrisy - Climbs the hill Difficulty - Falls asleep in the Arbour, and loses his roll - Meets Timorous and Mistrust fleeing back - He misses his roll and returns to find it."

The Spirit-Dependent Walk

In Sections 5 through 10 we see the Christian, who now realizes his understanding of God's Word is insufficient, learns by trials and errors (i.e., the vision-loss-striving-surrender-revisitation-consummation cycles that we discussed in Chapter Nine above) to trust and depend upon God alone. At first he fails to realize how *close* God is to him (i.e., dwelling within his very heart). The entry into the Palace Beautiful in Section 5 is a type of Baptism into the Holy Spirit. In Sections 7 and 9 we see the practical help he receives from other believers in Body of Christ ministry. In Sections 6, 8 and 10 we also see his still struggling with intellectual faith, with self (his need for inner heart healing and for Mt. Moriah surrenderings) and with the demonic powers of satan.

"5. (pp. 103) Christian arrives at the palace called Beautiful - His converse with the Porter - Admission into the palace - Discourse with Piety, Prudence, and Charity - The supper - The records of the house - Visit to the armoury - View of the Delectable Mountains - Christian is furnished with armour, and prepares to proceed on his journey.

"6. (pp. 117) Christian, accompanied by Piety, Prudence, and Discretion, leaves the Beautiful Palace - Goes down the hill, into the Valley of Humiliation - His terrible conflict with Apollyon - His perilous passage through the Valley of the Shadow of Death - He passes without danger the cave of giants Pope and Pagan.

"7. (pp. 133) Christian overtakes Faithful - Their talk about the country whence they came - How Pliable was accounted of when he got home - How Faithful was assaulted by Wanton, and by Adam the first - Also, in the Valley of Humiliation, by Discontent and Shame.

"8. (pp. 145) The pilgrims fall in with one Talkative of Prating-Row - Faithful enters into conversation with him, and is at first deceived by his fine discourse - Christian discovers to Faithful the real character of his new companion - Faithful begins to discourse with him about heart-religion, with which he is not pleased, and they soon part.

"9. (pp. 159) Evangelist overtakes the Pilgrims - He predicts the troubles they will meet with in Vanity-Fair, and encourages them to steadfastness - Account of Vanity-Fair - The Pilgrims enter the Fair - The Fair is in a hubbub about them - They are taken prisoners and put in the cage - The trial - Faithful is put to death.

"10. (pp. 177) Christian finds another companion in Hopeful, who accompanies him from Vanity-Fair - They overtake By-ends, with whom Christian enters into discourse - By-ends leaves the Pilgrims and falls in with company more to his mind - Demas invites the Pilgrims to turn aside to see a silver mine - By-ends and his companions go to the mine and are seen no more - A strange monument."

Vision Of The Heavenlies:

In the remaining sections 11 through 16 we see a slow transfer of his trust from even the indwelling Holy Spirit unto Christ Himself in the Heavenlies. He first envisions the practical aspects (in the here and now) of his position with Christ in the heavenlies (Ephesians 1:3), but that envisionment is yet distant, i.e., "across a river". Slowly that vision becomes a part of him, and he learns to rest in it. In sections 13 and 15 he also sees the urgency to reach out to others with the new-found power of his faith. Finally in section 16 he prepares for his final transition.

"11. (pp. 193) The pilgrims [Christian and Hopeful] come to a pleasant river, and travel awhile by its side - Finding the way difficult after they leave the river, they turn aside into By-path Meadow - They are caught by Giant Despair trespassing on his grounds, and are thrust into Doubting Castle - Their sad condition there - Deliverance comes at last.

Divine "Three"

"12. (pp. 207) The Pilgrims come to the Delectable Mountains - Their talk with the Shepherds - The Shepherds welcome them - The names of the Shepherds - The Mountain of Error - Mount Caution - A by-way to Hell - The Shepherds' perspective glass - A two-fold caution.

"13. (pp. 213) The Pilgrims meet with Ignorance - Christian has some talk with him - The destruction of one Turnaway - Christian tells his companion a story of Little Faith - The Flatterer seduces the Pilgrims - They are taken in a net - A Shining One lets them out - They are whipped and sent on their way - Atheist meets the Pilgrims.

"14. (pp. 231) The pilgrims come to the Enchanted Ground - To prevent drowsiness they fall into good discourse - Hopeful relates his experience - His life before conversion - He falls under conviction - Endeavours to mend his life - Finding no relief, he breaks his mind to Faithful, who tells him the way to be saved - He doubts of acceptance - Is better instructed, and bid to pray - Christ is revealed to him.

"15. (pp. 243) The Pilgrims have another conference with Ignorance, who will not be convinced of his error - The good use of right fear - Why ignorant persons stifle conviction - Talk about one Temporary - The reasons why such as he turn back - How the apostate goes back.

"16. (pp. 257) The Pilgrims, having got over the Enchanted Ground, enter the country of Beulah - They come to a river without a bridge, which they must pass - Christian's conflict at the hour of death - He is delivered from his fears - The angels wait for them as soon as they are passed out of this world - Their admission into the City - Ignorance comes up to the river - Vain-Hope ferries him over - What becomes of him."

15. Mary, Mary, Mary!

A further although indirect and somewhat surprising[17] source of insights into the three general stages of our sanctification by the indwelling Holy Spirit of Christ Jesus, is John 19:25:

> "... there were standing by the Cross of Jesus His mother, and His mother's sister, Mary the wife of Clopas, and Mary Magdalene."

Comparing this passage with its parallel accounts in Matthew 27:55-56 and Mark 15:40-41, we see that four women were among the very few followers of Jesus we know of who remained close to Him during His crucifixion. Three of them were named *Mary*.[18] Is there any significance to this, and if so, what?

First of all, who were these Marys? The first was the mother of Jesus and the wife of Joseph; she was used by God to present Jesus Himself (His Presence) to the world. Another, "Mary the wife of Clopas", was most probably she who is elsewhere identified as the mother of the apostle James the Lesser, and wife of Alphaeus[19]; she was used to present one of the apostles to the Lord. And the third, "Mary of Magdala" was the first to bear witness to the resurrection of Jesus (John 20:1-2). So we have here women who played a major role in witnessing or presenting to the world the presence, ministry and resurrection of our lord.

There is no clear Biblical indication of a progression between these three Marys paralleling our three general stages of sanctification. In fact, the three Biblical accounts are mutually inconsistent in their order: the Matthew and Mark accounts list Mary Magdalene first, and the John account lists her last. However, we suggest the Matthew and Mark accounts could imply an upward (from human toward divine) progression and the John account a downward (from the divine toward the human) progression. This suggests this progression in terms of our three stages, which we show in Row [50] of Sanctification Stages Chart Six:

> Stage 1: Mary Magdalene, a devoted disciple of Jesus who first presented to the world the *good news* of the resurrected Christ;
> Stage 2: Mary the mother of James the Less, who presented to the world one of the *apostles* **or** *messengers* of the gospel;
> and Stage 3: Mary the mother of Jesus, who presented to the world the *presence* of Jesus on Earth.

The etymology of the name Mary is significant. "Mary" is the English form of the Latin and Greek names "Maria" and "Miriam", that in turn are forms of the Hebrew name "MRYM". MRYM is the Old Testament name we have in English as Miriam, the sister of Moses. Modern Hebrew concordances tell us that MRYM means "bitterness", it being a noun from the Hebrew root verb MRH, "to be bitter", used in Exodus 15:23. But there is yet another possible source and meaning of the Hebrew word MRYM: the prefix M-combined with the root RWCh would mean "to be high, exalted." This suggests the additional meaning that those who willingly submit to the "emptying" cycles, and having done so become powerful in presenting the good news, ministry and Presence of Christ to the world, also become greatly exalted and lifted up - indeed into our position with Christ in the heavenlies!

16. Some Other Authors' Divine "Threes"

All of the seventy portraits of the three general stages of our sanctification that we delineate elsewhere in this volume, were formulated in the mid-1970s but not published until now. In the meantime, other anointed authors have also pursued this theme and published some excellent resources. It is not our intent to "steal their thunder" herein. But it *is* our intent to be as *comprehensive* as practicable in this volume; therefore we now briefly summarize thirty-one additional examples of the "divine threes" from such authors, and tabulate them in Sanctification Stages Charts Seven through Nine[20].

(a) Walking In Faith

One such example is found in Bishop T. D. Jakes' 1993 publication *Woman Thou Art Loosed!*. Based on Hebrews 11:4-7, he notes on page 83 therein a progression in walking in faith (see Row [a1] of Sanctification Stages Chart Seven):"Abel *worshipped* God by faith. Enoch *walked* with God by faith. You can't walk with God until you worship God. The first calling is to learn how to worship God. When you learn how to worship God, then you can develop a walk with God. ... Enoch walked and by faith Noah *worked* with God. You can't work with God until you walk with God.

Sanctification Stages Chart Seven

Row #	Three "Types" Of Believer	CARNAL/FLESHLY [SARKIKOS]	SOULICAL/NATURAL [PSUCHIKOS]	SPIRITUAL [PNEUMATIKOS]
[a1]	Walking in Faith (Heb. 11)	Abel Worshipped God	Enoch Walked With God	Noah Worked With God
[b1]	On Mt. Of Transfiguration (Luke 9:30-31)	Moses: Law Didn't See Prom. Land	Elijah: Prophet Caught Up To Heaven Alive	Jesus: Messiah Both Law And Prophet
[b2]	Jesus w. Bread (Luke 24:30)	Accepted It (Us)	Broke It (Us)	Gave It (Us)
[b3]	How We Worship Jesus	Thanksgiving What He's Done For Us	Praise Who He Is To Us	Rejoicing Radiating His Presence In Us
[b4]	Paul's Prayer That We Know:	Hope Of Our Calling	Riches Of Our Inheritance	Greatness Of His Power To Us
[b5]	What We Rejoice During:	Temptations	Tribulations	Fiery Trials
[c1]	Jesus Himself In Each Stage	Babe	Youth	Man During 3½ Years Ministry
[c2]	What Jesus Is To Us	Saviour	Anointer And Sanctifier	Lord And Captain
[c3]	What Jesus Imparts To Us	Justification	Sanctification	Glorification
[c4]		New Birth	Holy Spirit Baptism	Maturity
[c5]		Divine Healing	Divine Health (Cleansing)	Divine Life (His Presence)

You can't walk with God until you worship God. If you can worship like Abel, then you can walk like Enoch. And if you walk like Enoch, then you can work like Noah."

(b) On The Potter's Wheel

Another writer on this theme is Mark Hanby. His recent book *The House That God Built*[21] is a study of the rich typology of Moses' Tabernacle in the Wilderness, a theme which we study also in the following Chapter 12. Hanby also includes several "divine threes" in another recent book *Perceiving the Wheel of God*[22]. We summarize in Rows [b1] through [b5] of Sanctification Stages Chart Seven five examples that Hanby mentions therein:

First Hanby comments on what the three personages on the Mount of Transfiguration represent[23] (see Row [b1] of Sanctification Stages Chart Seven):

> Moses represented the *Law*, Elijah represented the *prophets*, and Jesus fulfilled them **both** on a tree. ... Moses died without ever going into the Promised Land. ... Elijah knew what it was like to be carried up to Heaven alive. Jesus would be resurrected and caught up to Heaven."

Hanby[24] notes the stages of Jesus' dealing with the bread at the Lord's Supper (Luke 24:30-31), comparing how He likewise deals with us as "little breads" or propagators of Him (see Row [b2] of Sanctification Stages Chart Seven):

> "He *took* [accepted] it, He *broke* it, and *gave* it."

Divine "Three"

Likewise, He accepts us when we make Him our Lord, breaks us, and then gives us unto servanthood (i.e., Ephesians 4:11-12, etc.).

Next are noted three phases of worship[25] (see Row [b3] of Sanctification Stages Chart Seven). These parallel but somewhat differ from our concepts indicated in Rows [33] through [35] of Sanctification Stages Chart Four earlier in this chapter:

> "1. *Thanksgiving*, or personal supplication. The first is what we feel He is to us, and what we are to Him.
> 2. *Praise*, giving laud and praise about what He is. The second is what He is to us.
> 3. *Rejoicing*. The third phase encompasses everything from dancing to laughing in the Holy Ghost. ..."

Hanby[26] comments on three stages of Paul's prayer for the saints (us) in Ephesians 1:18-19 (see Row [b4] of Sanctification Stages Chart Seven). We have here a progression in our apprehending what we have in Christ:

> "1. He [Paul] wanted them to know what was the *hope of the calling* of the Lord.
> 2. He wanted them to know the *riches of the glory of His inheritance* in the saints ...
> 3. He wanted them to know what is the *exceeding greatness of His power* to us who believe."

Hanby also comments on what we encounter, and are to rejoice in the midst of, during *suffering*[27]. In Row [b5] of Sanctification Stages Chart Seven we reverse the order of his first and second:

"The Scripture teaches us to rejoice in *tribulation* [Romans 5:3], *temptation* [James 1:2], and *fiery trials* [1 Peter 4:12-13]."

(c) Prevailing In Christ

Yet another prolific current writer on these three general stages of sanctification is Kelley Varner, who throughout his several books notes a strong parallelism between the three division of Moses' Tabernacle, the three major Feasts of the Lord, and the three stages of the wanderings of the Israelites from Egypt to the "Promised Land". Those three typologies, with several ramifications, we study in detail in the following Chapter Eleven.

In his book *Prevail*[28] Varner lists forty examples of "divine threes", including several that we have discussed so far in this volume and/or discuss in Chapter 12 following. In his book *Unshakeable Peace*[29] he lists several further examples, including nine that are paralleled in Aaron's high priestly vesture. For completeness, we list as follows (and in Rows [c1] through [e6] of Sanctification Stages Charts Seven through Nine) twenty-four of the examples given in these two sources that we do not otherwise specifically address elsewhere in this volume. For detailed studies of these, we recommend those sources to the interested reader.

In Row [c1] of Sanctification Stages Chart Seven are suggested Jesus Himself in each stage: Jesus the *babe* and child; Jesus the *young man* (age 11 up to age 30); and Jesus the *man* (during His 3½ years of active ministry), respectively.

Divine "Three" 385

What is Jesus to us in each general stage of sanctification? In Row [c2] are suggested: (1) our ***Saviour***; (2) our ***Anointer*** and ***Sanctifier***; and (3) our ***Lord*** and Captain, respectively.

Varner gives us several concepts of what Jesus imparts to us during each stage. These parallel but differ somewhat from our corresponding entries in Rows [11] and [12] of Sanctification Stages Chart Two. Here in Sanctification Stages Chart Seven, we have Row [c3]: (1) *justification*; (2) *sanctification*; and (3) *glorification*, respectively. In Row [c4]: (1) our new *birth*; (2) the *baptism into the Holy Spirit*; and (3) He bringing us unto *maturity*, respectively. In Row [c5]: (1) divine healing of our sins and *carnality*; (2) divine health through cleansing of our *self*-seeking and self-protecting; and (3) His indwelling Divine Life and ***Presence***, respectively.

What does the Holy Spirit impart to us during each general stage of our sanctification? In Row [c6] of Sanctification Stages Chart Eight are listed: (1) our new birth (as in Row [c4] - it is actually the ***Holy Spirit*** being sent by Jesus into us which constitutes that new birth); (2) *fruits* of the Holy Spirit (that are all attributes of Agape love); and (3) ***fullness*** of Christ-likeness, respectively. Actually, as shown in Row [c7], we increase in manifesting the fruit of the Holy Spirit during all stages, differing between the three stages in the extent or degree to which that fruit is manifested in our lives.

Varner also lists several aspects of our appropriating our inheritance as Paul mentions in Ephesians 1:11. As listed in Row [c8], in the first stage we are simply heirs to a future inheritance *via* our new ***birth***; in the second stage we receive an earnest or ***"down payment"*** or partial amount toward our

Sanctification Stages Chart Eight

Row #	Three "Types" Of Believer	CARNAL/FLESHLY [SARKIKOS]	SOULICAL/NATURAL [PSUCHIKOS]	SPIRITUAL [PNEUMATIKOS]
[c6]	What Holy Spirit Gives To Us"	New Birth	Fruits	Fullness
[c7]		Some Fruit	More Fruit	Much Fruit
[c8]	Appropriating Our Inheritance	Born An Heir	Earnest Of Inheritance	Full Possession
[c9]		Birthright	Blessing	Inheritance
[d1]		Born Of The Spirit	Being Developed	Matured
[d2]		Gleanings	Harvest	Firstfruits
[d3]	Our Walk In The Spirit	Faith	Hope	Love
[d4]		Little Faith	Great Faith	All Faith
[d5]		Walk	Run	Mount Up
[d6]		Way	Truth	Love
[d7]		Thanksgiving	Praise	Worship

inheritance; in t*he third stage we begin to actually experience our* inheritance without external or theoretical limits. In Row [c9] of Sanctification Stages Charts Seven through Nine: (1) first we are **assured** of our *birthright*; (2) then we begin to *experience its blessings* in our lives here and now; and (3) finally we begin to understand what our inheritance entails in its *fullness*. In Row [d1] we list what our inheritance entails in the here and now, namely our personal relationship with Christ *in the spirit:* (1) first we are born in the spirit, and hence have the *capability* to dynamically interact two-way with the Godhead; (2) we develop in that two-way *spiritual* relationship; (3) toward *maturity* in Him. And as a consequence of that growth in our personal relationship with Him, we also see increasing results in what He accomplishes through us, as seen in Row [d2]: (1) gleanings of other souls brought to basic salvation through our *witnessing*; (2) a more significant harvest of souls through our Spirit-empowered *ministries*; and (3) finally first-fruits of other souls being brought unto spiritual *maturity* in Christ, respectively.

How our walk in the Spirit increases during the three general stages of our sanctification is the next topic listed in Sanctification Stages Charts Seven through Nine. In Row [d3], we grow from *blind faith*, through increasingly realized *hope* (assurance of His promises to us), finally exuding His *Love* through us unto others. Row [d4] emphasizes that we ever grow in faith, i.e., *seeing* Him in His spiritual reality, *depending* upon Him for all things, and sensitively *obeying* Him. Row [d5] puts that in different words: (1) *walk* in faith (belief); (2) *run* in faith (dependence and obedience); and (3) *mount* up with Him (in His Presence), respectively. How others see us is indicated in Row [d6]: (1) we *lead* the way unto salvation in Christ; (2) we *demonstrate* the truth (and righteousness) of Christ and how it is superior to whatever the world has to offer; and (3) again as in Row [d3], we are *channels* of His Agape love, respectively. Our inner feelings (see Row [d7]) grow from *thanksgiving* (of what He has done for us), through *praise* (of Who He is), unto *worship* (unity in the Spirit with Him), as we indicate in a slightly different way in Row [33] of Sanctification Stages Chart Four.

Rows [d8] through [e2] of Sanctification Stages Chart Nine address what we are collectively in these three general stages of sanctification. Row [d8] lists the disciples of Jesus who we pattern: (1) the *multitude* of followers of Jesus, who followed Him for His miracles, feeding them, etc.; (2) the *disciples* who were more serious in their commitment to Him; and finally (3) the *three* disciples who remained closest to Him. Row [d9], based on Jesus' parable in Matthew 25:1-13, suggests that: (1) in the first general stage of sanctification, we are patterned by the five *"foolish"* virgins in that we lack the oil (anointing of the Holy Spirit) even though we be born of Him; (2) in the second stage we are patterned by the five *"wise"* virgins in that we now have that oil (anointing) of the Spirit; and (3) in the third stage we grow into being able to *discern* the times and spirits as watchmen. Row [e1] uses some typology from both the Old and New Testaments to indicate how close we are to "ruling and reigning with Christ" as His "Israel": (1) in the first stage we, as *gentiles*, are far from ruling and reigning with Him; (2) but as His people, we are *"called apart"* (the meaning of Ekklesia or "church") to become His Israel; and (3) finally we draw so close to Him we begin (though now only in part) to *rule with Him* in His Power and Love. In more practical terms, we grow from being simply *workers* for Him, to *warriors* against the enemy,

Sanctification Stages Chart Nine

Row #	Three "Types" Of Believer →	CARNAL/FLESHLY [SARKIKOS]	SOULICAL/NATURAL [PSUCHIKOS]	SPIRITUAL [PNEUMATIKOS]
[d8]		Multitude Of Disciples	The Nine Disciples	Peter, James & John
[d9]	What We Are Like	Foolish Virgins	Wise Virgins	Watchmen
[e1]	Collectively	"Gentiles"	The Ekklesia	"Israel"
[e2]		Workers	Warriors	Worshippers
[e3]	Naomi, Orpah & Ruth Typology	Orpah Stayed In Comfort Zone	Naomi Went Back Where Came From	Ruth Remained Faithful In Love
[e4]	Peace	Loves	Lifts	Laughs
[e5]	That:	Gives	Guards	Governs
[e6]	What We Are Sealed With	Circumcision of Water Baptism	Holy Spirit Of Promise	Name & Mind Of Christ On Forehead
[f1]	Being Quickened By Indwelling Holy Spirit	Repentant Sinner	Longing & Desire	Unencumbered Joy

and finally unto *worshipers* (in Spiritual unity with Him), as indicated in Row [e2].

The three women in Ruth Chapter 1 are types of our commitment to Christ, as indicated in Row [e3] of Sanctification Stages Chart Nine. Orpah chose to *remain* behind in the land of Moab, even though she was part of the family of Naomi. This reflects how many of us choose the "comfortable religion" of institutional Christianity, rather than the wilderness walk with Christ. Naomi chose to *return* to her land of origin, and this reflects how some of us will choose to travel through the wilderness to return to what our Lord created us for - oneness with Him. Ruth also chose to return, but with the additional characteristic of love-motivated *servanthood* unto Naomi. This reflects how the more we mature unto Christ, the more we become servants of Him and of those to whom He sends us, no matter what the cost.

In *Unshakeable Peace*[30] Varner emphasizes how the closer we come to Christ, the more we tangibly experience His peace, the peace that passes all understanding. That is because we have been created for fellowship with God in Christ, and hence when we actually walk in that fellowship, we live most "naturally" without internal conflict. Rows [e4] and [e5] reflect how we grow in that tangible experience. In Row [e4] we grow in how we experience His peace ourselves: (1) His *love* for us becomes apparent; (2) His *lifting* us from our sins and selfishness then follows; and finally (3) we can rejoice (*laugh*) in the face of worldly trials. In Row [e5] we grow in how we reflect that peace unto others: (1) we start in *giving* ourselves in service; (2) we *guard* and protect others from being destroyed by sin; and (3) we start to *govern* in His Kingdom with Him, respectively.

Varner[31] also addresses what we are sealed with, or secured in our relationship with Christ, during the three general stages of our sanctification (see Row [e6] of Sanctification Stages Chart Nine). First, we are sealed through *water baptism*, which is our "first heart circumcision" as we discussed in Chapter Six earlier in this volume (see Romans 4:11 and 6:1-11). But with the baptism into the Holy Spirit comes our being sealed with *His promise* (see Ephesians 1:13 and 4:30). Finally, the His very *Name* and Mind is implanted on our forehead (in our minds) - see Revelation 7:3, 14:1 and 22:4.

Hallelujah!

(d) Other Summaries

Yet another author we briefly quote is Piper[32], who describes three "levels" of worship, related to degrees with which we are quickened in our soul by the Holy Spirit through our human spirit. We list them in Row [f1] of Sanctification Stages Chart Nine, in reverse order from Piper:

> Third (lowest) level: "... the *barrenness of soul* that scarcely feels any longing, and yet is still granted the grace of repentant sorrow for having so little love."
>
> Second (middle) level: "... we do not feel fullness, but rather *longing and desire*. ... we recall the goodness of the Lord - but it seems far off. ... for now our hearts are not very fervent."
>
> First (highest) level: "... we feel an *unencumbered joy* in the manifold perfections of God - the joy of gratitude, wonder, hope, admiration."

End Notes: Chapter Eleven

1. Contained in *The Spiritual Writings of Jeanne Guyon*, Edwards, Gene, ed., pages 385-499 (Goleta, California: Christian Books, 1982), ISBN 0-940232-07-3.

2. Penn-Lewis, Jesse, *Thy Hidden Ones*, originally published 1899, modern reprint avaialable through Christian Literature Crusade, Fort Washington, Pa.

3. Watchman Nee, *Song of Songs*, Translated from Chinese by Elizabeth K. Mei and Daniel Smith, (Fort Washington, Pa.: Christian Literature Crusade, 1965).

4. Hurnard, Hannah R., *The Mountain of Spices*, (London, England: The Olive Press, 1964).

5. Schmitt, Charles P., *Our Tremendous Lover*, (Grand Rapids, Michigan: Fellowship Publications, 1981).

6. Balchin, John A., "The Song of Solomon", in D. Guthrie and J. A. Motyers (eds.), *The New Bible Commentary: Revised*, 3rd ed., completely revised (Grand Rapids: William B. Eerdmans Publishiang Company, 1970, p. 579.

7. Schmitt, Charles P., *Our Tremendous Lover*.

8. Taylor, Wade E., *The Secret of The Stairs*, (Salisbury Center, New York: Pinecrest Publications, 1988).

9. Ibid. pp. 25-27, emphasis added.

10. Ibid. pp. 29-30.

11. Hurnard, Hanna R., *The Mountain of Spices*.

12. Hall, Dudley, *Out Of The Comfort Zone - The Church In Transition* (Pineville, NC: MorningStar Publications, 1991).

13. Varner, Kelley, *Prevail - A Handbook for the Overcomer*, (Shippensburg, PA: Destiny Image Publishers, 1982), p. 85. Copyright © 1982 by Kelley Varner.

14. Ibid.

15. This is a use of the typology of Moses' Tabernacle in the Wilderness, that we study in Chapter 12 following in this volume.

16. Bunyan, John, *THE PILGRIM'S PROGRESS From This World To That Which Is To Come, Delivered Under The Similitude Of A Dream*, Part I first published 1638, our quotations from a 1856 publication (New York: Carlton & Porter).

17. Surprising, at least, to this author.

18. The fourth, mother of the apostles James and John, was Salome (the Hebrew form being ShLMI or "my peace"), sister of Mary the mother of Jesus.

19. See the discussion on *Mary* found in *The International Standard Bible Encyclopaedia,* Volume III, p. 2001 (Grand Rapids, Mich.: Wm. B. Eerdmans Publishing Co., 1939). The Hebrew/Aramaic forms of the Greek names *Alphaeus* and *Clopas* are nearly identical.

20. We use a different designation of Row numbers in Sanctification Stages Charts Seven through Nine than we do in Tables Two, Four, Seven and Ten, to distinguish these examples of other authors from those originally gathered together and formulated by this author.

21. Hanby, Dr. Mark, *The House That God Built,* (Shippensburg, PA: Destiny Image Publishers, 1993). Copyright © 1993 by Dr. Mark Hanby.

22. Hanby, Dr. Mark, *Perceiving the Wheel of God - The Suffering Series,* (Shippensburg, PA: Destiny Image Publishers, 1994). Copyright © 1994 by Dr. Mark Hanby.

23. Ibid., p. 55, emphases added.

24. Ibid., p. 64, emphases added.

25. Ibid., p. 75, emphases added.

26. Ibid., p. 77, emphases added.

27. Ibid., p. 79, emphases added.

28. Varner, Kelley, *Prevail - A Handbook for the Overcomer.*

29. Varner, Kelley, *Unshakeable Peace - The Life and Times of Haggai the Prophet,* (Shippensburg, PA: Destiny Image Publishers, 1994). Copyright © 1994 by Kelley Varner.

30. Varner, Kelley, *Unshakeable Peace,* p. 223.

31. Ibid., p. 223.

32. Piper, John *Desiring God - Meditations Of A Christian Hedonist* (Portland, OR: Multnomah Press, 1986), pp. 75-76. Copyright © 1986 by Multnomah Press.

Part IV

Typological Perspectives And Personal Examples

In each of Chapters Eight and Ten we have briefly explored fifty-one Biblical depictions of the three general stages of our being sanctified in our personal relationship with our Lord Christ Jesus. The twenty-three of Chapter Eight were direct Biblical teachings, and the twenty-eight of Chapter Ten were various Biblical types to enrich our basic understandings. Also in Chapter Ten were listed thirty-one further examples from other authors. Chapter Nine in-between discussed several experiential aspects, especially of the second and third general stages.

We have yet some additional typological depictions of the three general stages which we now explore in Chapters Eleven and Twelve following. In Chapter Eleven we present fourteen further Biblical types; in Chapter Twelve we then give seven personal examples from the Old Testament with the help of Biblical typology.

Chapter Eleven

Divine Perspectives

This chapter is basically an extension of Chapter Ten. The fourteen Biblical types we now discuss depict the three general stages of the sanctification process according to further perspectives. Those perspectives are:

> three stages of *personal holiness* as typified in the Tabernacle in the Wilderness (six aspects)
> our *psychological perspective* of the three stages as typified in the story of the Book of Esther;
> aspects of our *walk in this world* as typified in Psalms 120 through 134;
> perspective of stages of our being *separate* from this world as typified by the Holy Convocations observed by Old Testament Israel;
> a *theological* perspective of the three stages as typified by key incidents in Exodus and Joshua;
> our *view of Christ* as we progress in our personal relationship with Him;
> the parallel stages of spiritual growth typified by an Old Covenant *Israelite's* life;
> parallel aspects typified in *Church age* periods; and
> similar parallels typified in God's *periods of dispensation* for His people.

These fourteen are tabulated in Sanctification Stages Charts Ten and Eleven, which are basically extensions of Sanctification Stages Charts One through Nine in earlier chapters. Additional Figures and Tables are used to further delineate these aspects.

1. The Tabernacle: Holiness In Perspective

"who [He, Jesus our High Priest] was faithful to Him [God the Father] Who appointed Him, as Moses also was faithful in all his house. For this One has been counted worthy of more glory than Moses, inasmuch as He who built the house has more honor than the house. For every house is built by someone, but He who built all things is God. And Moses indeed was faithful in all his house as a servant, for a *testimony* of those things which would be spoken afterward; but Christ as a Son over His own house, *Whose house we are,* if we hold fast the confidence and the rejoicing of the hope firm to the end" (Hebrews 3:2-6).

This key passage introduces a powerful Biblical type. We, the believers, the Body of Christ, are a house or a temple to contain Christ. That temple (us) is parallel in details with the "Tabernacle in the Wilderness" which was built by Moses according to strict instructions he received from God. Most of those details are found in Exodus Chapters 25 through 31 and 35 through 40. Hebrews Chapter 9 is devoted to how Christ our High Priest is typified by the High Priest and we by the priesthood associated with Moses' tabernacle.

Comparisons of the many details of construction of Moses' tabernacle and the priesthood functioning therein, with the

Body of Christ and the interpersonal relationships between us and Christ our High Priest, are among the most rewarding Bible studies I have done. *Every* detail of that Tabernacle in the Wilderness has some significant typological meaning for the Body of Christ today.

Several books are available for those who wish to pursue such studies. The three "classics" most useful to this author were: Soltau (*The Holy Vessels and Furniture of the Tabernacle*[1] - 1851) on the Tabernacle's instruments; Soltau (*The TABERNACLE - The Priesthood and the Offerings*[2] - 1855) on the Tabernacle priesthood; and Cornwall (*Let Us Draw Near*[3] - 1977) on our personal relationship with Christ. Some more recent publications are: Varner (*The More Excellent Ministry*[4] - 1988), an anointed study of the ministries performed by the priesthood which are types of our functioning today within the Body of Christ; Varner (*The Priesthood Is Changing*[5] - 1991), an anointed study of the priesthood which served in the Tabernacle that are types of our ministries today; and Hanby (*The House That God Built*[6] - 1993), an excellent general introduction to the types of the Tabernacle.

The Tabernacle in the Wilderness describes in great detail three areas of truth pertaining to the Body of Christ under the New Covenant: (1) the Person, Nature and Ministry of Christ Jesus our High Priest; (2) the nature, functions, and various ministries of His church; and (3) the three stages of growth of a believer in Christ and the processes He puts a submissive believer through to "perfect" or mature or sanctify him. For the first two of these areas of truth, we refer the interested reader to the above references by Varner. In this brief study we concentrate on this third area of truth. Rows [51] through

Sanctification Stages Chart Ten

Row #	Three "Types" Of Believer	CARNAL/FLESHLY [SARKIKOS]	SOULICAL/NATURAL [PSUCHIKOS]	SPIRITUAL [PNEUMATIKOS]
[51]	Three Stages Of Holiness: Types In Tabernacle (Exodus 25-31 & 35-40)	Courtyard: Holiness of Hope Assurance & Reconcil.	Holy Place: Holiness Of Domicility (Of Righteous **Life-Style**)	Holy Of Holies: Holiness Of Christ's **Divine Presence** In Us
[52]	Christ The **Entrance Way** Area = 100 Cubic Cubits	**Gate** 5 High, 20 Wide	**Curtain** 10 High, 10 Wide	**Veil** 10 High, 10 Wide
[53]	**Light** Shed On Ministries	**Natural** Light	**Artificial** (Lampstand)	**Divine**
[54]	Who Does The **Ministry**	Men **Alone** (Priests)	Men **Plus** Holy Spirit	**God** Alone
[55]	Who Is **Served** By Ministry	Priests To All **Israel**	High Priest To **Priests**	God To **High Priest**
[56]	**Seals** Or Signets On **High Priest** Designating:	Breast Plate (Over His **Heart**) All Tribes Visualized	Onyx Stones (On His **Shoulders**) All Tribes Engraved In Gold	Gold Plate (On His **Forehead**) "Holy Unto The Lord" Engraved
[57]	**Psychological** Perspective: Types In Esther (Unregenerate: 1:1-2:16)	Esther 2:17 - 7:16 (Regeneration: 2:17) (Dying to Self:7:7-10)	Esther 8.1-8:17 (H.S. Baptism: 8:2)	Esther 9:1 - 10:3 (Victory: 9:1-10:3)

Figure Three
Tabernacle General Layout

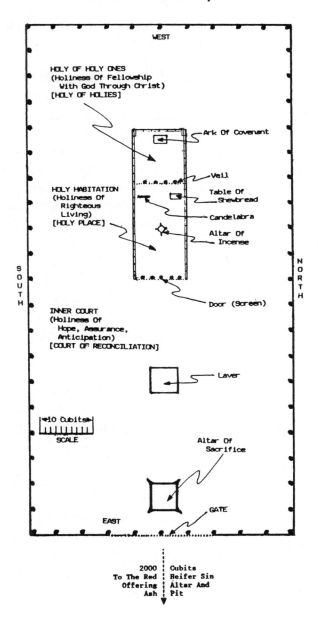

[56] of Sanctification Stages Chart Ten list a few such aspects. However, we barely scratch the surface.

General Layout And Court Of Reconciliation

A sketch of the general layout of the Tabernacle is given in Figure Three. The outer boundary of the tabernacle area was a linen "fence" or wall, five cubits in height and 50 cubits by 100 cubits. The center 20 cubits of the Eastern end was open to form a "gate" of entry. Hence its total surface area (including this "gate") was 1500 square cubits, the number of years of the Old Covenant Law. It was supported by a total of 60 posts, all spaced 5 cubits center-to-center. The posts were of "shittim wood", a native "acacia" wood that grows all twisted and knotted, set in sockets of brass. Shittim in Hebrew (ShTH) means "to turn aside; depart"; it typifies sinners who have turned aside from their sins and followed Christ. The bronze that typifies Christ's judgment on satan, i.e. the brazen serpent of Numbers 21:9.

The "fence" was of fine-twined linen which typifies the righteousness of Christ, and was supported by the posts with rods and hooks of silver which typify our atonement by Christ and our lifting Jesus up before the world. The "gate", 20 cubits wide, was on the Eastern end, immediately outside of which was camped the Tribe of Levi, the priestly tribe. Furthermore, 2000 cubits further east (i.e., "outside the camp"), the altar of the Red Heifer Sin Offering (Numbers 19:1-10) and the ash pit (where the ashes of all burnt offerings were deposited) were located. This speaks of Christ's crucifixion on Calvary and burial in a cave, all on the *Mount of Olives*[7].

In the general layout (see Figure Three) we see the three areas within this enclosure, a courtyard and two compartments of a "building" called the "tent of the meeting".These are called the Court, Holy Place, and Holy of Holies. The Hebrew word for Court, ChTsR, means an enclosed place of *congregation and protection*, and reminds us of the "green pastures" of Psalm 23. The Hebrew for Holy Place, MQWM QDSh (Exodus 29:31 for example) means *holiness of standing*, holy stature, holy *way of living*. And the Hebrew for Holy of Holies, QDSh HQDShYM (Exodus 26:33 for example), means holiness of the Holy Ones or *holiness of Holy Presence*. This reflects the three levels of holiness characterized by our three stages of Christian growth: carnal, soulical and spiritual. We illustrate these three stages of holiness in Row [51] of Sanctification Stages Chart Ten.

The carnal Christian is typified by any of the rank-and-file Israelites who entered the *court* to offer sacrifices at the altar. The sacrifice we offer is Christ, as our sin-forgiver, ransomer, reconciliator by virtue of His dying for our sins. Indeed, the altar of the "burnt" or "ascent" (ILH) offering is located *immediately* upon entry of the court through the "gate". Here we have a holiness of reconciliation, i.e., of hope, assurance, anticipation of a yet-to-be-completed salvation. Hence we call this the *Court Of Reconciliation*.

If we as carnal Christians seek to grow in Christ unto royal priesthood, however, we must reckon our flesh crucified with Christ (Romans 6) - the only way the flesh can be "cleansed" or sanctified. This is typified by the priests washing their own hands and feet at the laver, a large basin or reservoir of water located further in the court before the "tent of the meeting". The obvious type is that of water baptism. The shape and size of the laver was not specified in Exodus: there is no set "pattern" for Christian water baptism; only the requirement is that we submit to it as a watery grave of burial of our self-nature and from which we rise in resurrection to life in Christ. (Since the temple of Solomon's counterpart was known to be rectangular, we use that shape in Figure Three.)

Tent Of The Meeting

The "building" or "tent of the meeting" located further in the court, was of substantial construction. Its North, West and South walls were formed out of upright boards or planks of dimension ¼ cubit thick, 1-½ cubit wide, and 10 cubits high (that's approximately ½ foot thick, a yard wide, and 20 feet tall)[8]! The outer dimensions of the construction were 10 cubits in width by 30 cubits in length by 10 cubits in height. The total number of boards was 48, all alike, each set in a socket of silver which again typifies our atonement paid by Christ on Calvary). The boards also were made out of "shittim wood", but here with two additional details: (1) sawed and worked smooth (in type, we having been purified by the indwelling Holy Spirit of Christ Jesus as our sanctifier); and (2) overlaid with Gold (typifying the preciousness of Christ). These boards typify key members of the church, Christ's Body, living stones rightly fitted together (1 Peter 2:5) in the temple of God.

The two corner boards in the NW and SW corners were twinned, i.e. each were actually two boards tightly fitted together. Exodus 26:23-24 and 36:29 in the Hebrew means "And they shall be twinned beneath, and together they shall be aligned upon its head to the same ring." For the key "corner" ministries with most responsibility, Christ pairs or twins *two* believers into such unity they act as one! For example, Paul and either Barnabas or Mark or Luke, Peter and John, etc.

The boards were held in place by horizontal bars, also of highly worked "shittim wood". No specifications were given on the size of these bars, but they are also matured members of the Body of Christ, set in linking and strengthening and edifying and coordinating ministries such as teacher, prophet, intercessor, encourager, exhorter, etc.

This awesome wall of boards was covered by a total of four curtains or coverings which formed the ceiling/roof of the tabernacle. The innermost part was seen only by the priests. It was of linen, with patterns of blue, purple and scarlet; linen typifies the ***righteousness*** of Christ, and the colors typify both the divinity (blue) and humanity (scarlet) of Christ blended (purple) into one. Taches of gold (typifying the ***preciousness*** of Christ) joined the sections of this curtain together. It was draped 1 cubit down from the top in the Eastern or "door" end; on all other sides it hung down to within 1 cubit of the ground (i.e., within reach of but never actually touching those of earth).

The next layer, completely covering and overhanging this inner "tabernacle" layer, was of "goat hair" (actually fine-textured leather of goat skin). It was called the "tent". It typifies Christ as our "scapegoat". Christ's righteousness and our refuge in Him is completely hidden from view except to those who first accept His sin-forgiveness and atonement.

The third and outermost layers (simply called "coverings") were for protection only. The third was of ram's skins dyed red, typifying the outward aspect of the affliction and sorrow of Christ on the cross as seen by men. The fourth or outermost layer was of "badger's skin" (the Hebrew word ThChSh actually means "hasten; come quickly", which typifies how all should come to the Temple of Christ, and also how our Lord will return when the last trump sounds.

Two-thirds of the way back in this "tent of the meeting" was a vertical curtain, called the "veil", that separated the area into two "rooms". This veil was of the same material (linen with patterns in blue, purple and scarlet) as the innermost curtain or "tabernacle".

The floor of the "tent of the meeting" was bare desert dirt. Compared with the beauty of God's dwelling place (i.e., the Body of Christ), the world (earth) is utterly barren.

The entry into the "tent of the meeting", called the "door" or "curtain", consisted of 5 pillars set in sockets of brass (judgment) with tops of Gold (purity and preciousness of Christ). Hung on these pillars was another curtain, of the same material and colors as the tabernacle curtain and veil, but without intricate embroidery in its patterns.

Of note is comparison of the cross-sectional areas of the gate into the court, this door or curtain, and the veil: all three were 100 square cubits, typifying the *perfection* of the work of Christ. The same Christ is our entry into each stage of holiness. But whereas the gate into the court was low (5 cubits high) and wide (20 cubits), both the door or curtain and the veil were high (10 cubits) and narrow (10 cubits). We show this in Row [52] of Sanctification Stages Chart Ten. Jesus said: "Enter by the narrow gate; for the ... way is broad that leads to destruction, and many are those who enter by it. For the gate is small (pressured) and the way is narrow that leads to life, and few are those who find it" (Matthew 7:13-14).

Holy Place

Inside the first "room" of the "tent of the meeting" were three items or articles of "furniture: a candelabra or lampstand, a table of "shewbread" (the actual Hebrew means "bread of faces"), and an altar of incense. The lampstand provided light night and day by burning of oil, and it typifies the indwelling Holy Spirit of Christ Jesus being manifested through us. The table of shewbread was a display of twelve loaves, typifying our "cereal" (fruit of our labors) or MNChH offerings and our "consecration" or ShLM and ThWDH offerings of ministries of servanthood. The altar of incense was used to provide a pleasant aroma (our thoughts and praises and prayers and intercessions unto God). The orientation and position of the altar of incense was not given; in Figure Three we show it central to the Holy Place because most attention was given to it by the priests.

The door was entered daily by all of the tabernacle priests. Entry typifies the Baptism into the Holy Spirit, for the only light inside was that provided by the lampstand which typifies the indwelling Holy Spirit of Christ Jesus manifested through us. Hence, those priests who entered typify the *soulical* Christian of our second general stage of sanctification. The soulical Christian, having accepted Christ now as *sanctifier*, now experiences partaking of Christ, both directly and through other believers. The three items or articles of furniture denote that. And the emphasis is in holiness and righteousness in our interpersonal relationships, in our behavior, in our life-styles.

Holy Of Holies

The *veil* with four pillars separated the Holy Place from a smaller room called the Holy of Holy Ones. These four pillars typify the four views of Christ presented to us in the four Gospels: saviour and judge, servant-bearer, man (our high priest), and divine (Son of God). These pillars, like the boards, were also of highly finished "shittim wood", set in sockets of silver, with hooks of gold to hold the veil.

Behind this veil was an item called the "Ark of the Covenant". This was a box (made of "shittim wood" overlaid inside and out with gold), containing three items, and having a "lid" with two cherubim wrought in gold facing each other. The items within the box were: (1) a sample of the *manna* during the 40 years of wilderness wanderings of the Israelites; (2) the two tablets of *Law* that Moses received (the second time) from God on Mount Sinai; and (3) Aaron's *almond rod that budded* (Numbers 17:1-11).

All of this denotes the *Presence of God* among His people in a very specific way: God as giver of His Covenant of atonement. Manna typifies Christ as our bread of life, and of His provision of our needs; Aaron's rod that budded typifies our fruitfulness in ministry when it is Christ in us doing it; and the tablets of law typify God writing His law on our hearts.

The lid of gold cherubim, often called "mercy seat", typifies our total encompassment in Christ. The Hebrew for "mercy seat" (KPhR) really means "propitiatory cover". It means to cover, not to *hide* from view necessarily, but to *render ineffective.* All of this typifies Christ in us rendering ineffective the *written* law for us, He in us *being* our law. It also typifies our self-struggles to obtain our provisions and to minister unto others, He in us doing all of these things.

Only the High Priest could enter behind the veil, and then only on one certain day of the year, the Day of Atonement (tenth of Tishri). He typifies our entering into the very presence of God, but only after we have been purged through sanctification enough to withstand His awesome holiness. If we as soulical Christians seek with our entire hearts to fellowship with God through Christ, then our soul powers (mind, emotions, will) must totally yield to the indwelling Holy Spirit of Christ Jesus.

But until the veil was rent in twain from top to bottom on the completion of Christ's sacrifice and death on the Cross (Matthew 27:50-51), men could not on their own fulfill their part of the Old Covenant Law. Hence, the Law had to be kept covered in the Ark and the Ark virtually inaccessible to the rank-and-file, lest they perished under those Old Testament Law terms. But now, under the New Covenant of Grace, that Old Testament Law has been rendered ineffective by the Presence of Christ Himself, and we have free access to God! Hebrews 10:19-22 says it this way:

> "Since therefore, brethren, we have confidence to enter the holy place by the blood of Jesus, by a new and living way which He inaugurated for us through the veil, that is, His flesh, and since we have a great priest over the house of God, let us draw near with a sincere heart in full assurance of faith, having our hearts sprinkled clean from an evil conscience...."

Although the veil typifies Christ on Calvary, it does not refer to *basic* salvation, i.e., to the forgiveness of our sins; entering the gate of the courtyard and offering Christ as an ILH or "ascent offering" at the altar typifies that. On Calvary afternoon, the veil was rent in two from top to bottom *after* Christ had died. The veil being torn goes far beyond our forgiveness of sin; it signifies our free access to intimate *fellowship* with God in Christ Jesus by virtue of the inner workings in our hearts by the indwelling Holy Spirit of Christ Jesus.

Who ministers to whom in the three areas is also highly illustrative, as we show in Rows [54] and [55] of Sanctification Stages Chart Ten. In the Court of Reconciliation, men (the priests of the Tribe of Levi) minister to all others of Israel, and minister according to Law. In the Holy Place, the High Priest (typifying Christ) ministers to the other priests (servants of His), and the priests minister to one another, as anointed by the indwelling Holy Spirit. This involves ministry of a *mixture* of God and man, as Varner[9] suggests. In the Holy of Holy Ones, God does *all* ministering, and only to the High Priest (i.e., once each year on the Day of Atonement). Now in the New Covenant, however, we (all believers) have the invitation to go through the (torn) veil directly into the Holy of Holy Ones, to be ministered to directly by Christ Himself.

Some Other Types

There are several other interesting types which parallel our three general stages of sanctification. Hebrews Chapters 9 and 10 are rich sources.

For example, the light, which typifies our source of understanding of what we're doing in our personal relationships with Christ (Ephesians 1:18-19), differs in each of the three areas of the Tabernacle. As we show in Row [53] of Sanctification Stages Chart Ten, in the court of Reconciliation only natural light existed. Here we seek Christ and experience water baptism by the mental understandings we have acquired by hearing and reading the Word. In the Holy Place, the light came from the burning of oil in the lampstand. This typifies understanding coming from our being anointed by the indwelling Holy Spirit Who is "burned" through us as we minister to others. Varner[10] calls this light "artificial" - it involves a *mixture* of both human knowledge and divine revelation. In the Holy of Holy Ones, the only light was from the divine presence of God (in Christ). No human activity at all was involved in producing it.

The Old Testament priests wore special *garments* while serving. Our garments typify how we appear to others: our attitudes that we convey, exude, make manifest; our *countenance*. That is, our garments identify what we *are* to others, including to God. They are closely linked to the Hebrew concept KPhR which has the meaning of "covering in order to render powerless and ineffectual". Our true self-attitudes must be rendered of none effect and be replaced by Christ-attitudes, in order for us to flow in both forms of ministry.

It is the *inner-court* (Holy Place and Holy of Holines) *ministry garments* (our countenance) that is the issue of our ShLM offering: sanctification by Christ, righteousness as Christ, humility of Christ, waiting upon Christ[11], and worship unto Christ. They are garments of peace and rest (no sweat);

i.e., totally without struggle in the flesh. They are garments of total trust in and dependence upon Christ; they are garments in which we offer our "best parts" (fat) and "life" (blood); and they are garments of simply enjoying Him in His fullness.

It is the *outer-court* (Court of Reconciliation) *ministry garments* (our countenance) that is the issue of our ILH, MNChH, ChTAhTh and AhShM offerings. These are garments of walking in faith, aggressiveness in prayer and warfare, anointed proclamation of God's word, and Agape-love to people. But we must first flow in inner-court ministries as a prerequisite for outer court ministries!

Following Varner[12], we denote in Row [56] of Sanctification Stages Chart Ten some aspects of the High Priest's inner court ministry garments. On his chest close to his *heart*, he wore a breast-plate which included stones representing each tribe of Israel. This typifies Christ's *love* for "all whosoever ..." On his shoulders (that typify load-carrying or burden-bearing) he wore two Onyx stones (Hebrew ShHM, meaning "their name/reputation") with all tribes' names engraved. This typifies Christ *representing* all of us believers. But on his forehead (typifying his mind), only "Holiness unto the Lord" was present. This teaches us how Christ alone should be ever central to our thinking, motivations, prayers, praise and worship!

There is tremendous power to our prayers, *providing we first* minister unto Christ in the inner court, in peace and adoration. Prayer is *first* ascertaining what the perfect will of our Lord Christ Jesus is in and for specific situations, and then in our thoughts and actions indicating our identification with that Will and our willingness to flow in oneness with Him. It is in

Divine Perspectives

the inner court with Him that we first ascertain His will.

The necessity of inner-court ministries unto ***Christ***, as a ***prerequisite*** to effective outer-court ministries unto people, cannot be overstated. Praise is essential to the release of our faith unto victories through prayer. The power for victory requires our appropriating the ***glory*** (manifestation of the Presence) of God. Ever-increasing approximation to God in character, glory, and love, require our spending time with Him in praise and worship. Praise and worship decentralize self, shift the center of our thoughts from self to Him, and dispel self-pity, defenses, hostility, and all negative spiritual power that our thoughts radiate to hinder God's purposes.

2. The Esther Story: Psychological Perspective

Our next typology of the three general stages of a Christian's sanctification by the indwelling Holy Spirit of Christ Jesus is found in the story of Esther in the Old Testament. This was first brought to this author's attention through a 1969 book "If I Perish, I Perish" by Thomas[13]. A more recent and excellent resource is Penny Smith's 1992 book "Gateways To Growth"[14].

In type we gain rich insights on our ***psychological*** experiences as we grow from stage to stage. We summarize this in Row [57] of Sanctification Stages Chart Ten.

First, the basic typology. King Ahasuerus (see Ezra 4:6) typifies a believer's ***soul*** with its functions of mind, emotions and will. The "127 provinces" of his kingdom typify the believer's physiological ***body***. Hamman typifies the believer's ***carnality;*** Amalek (Esau's grandson and Hamman's ancestor) typifies satan, the arch-enemy of those with God-given birthrights and blessings because he resents they having supplanted him. On the other hand, Mordecai typifies the indwelling *Holy Spirit* of Christ Jesus, ever working to sanctify the soul, in type to bring King Ahasuerus's thinking and decisions to righteousness in all things. Queen Vashti, and later Esther, typify the believer's human *spirit*,[15] Vashti the unregenerated human spirit, and Esther the believer's spirit after regeneration and hence totally in one with God's Will (made known to her by Mordecai).

We suggest: Esther 1:1 through 2:16 typify the *unregenerated* state of the believer; 2:17 through 7:16 the *carnal* stage; 8:1 through 8:17 the *soulical* stage; and 9:1 through 10:3 the *spiritual* stage.

Unregenerate

In Esther Chapter 1, the unregenerate soul (King A.) discovers that the natural intuition, conscience and common sense of his unregenerated human spirit (Vashti) are unreliable and unsatisfying. The soul is restless for more meaning and fulfillment in life, and refuses to pay any further attention to his spirit (rejects Vashti). But in Chapter 2 he discovers that to be totally without intuition and conscience (a queen at his side) is not good either, and he seeks another. Esther, adopted by Mordecai, is encouraged by him to prepare herself for the King.

Regenerate But Carnal

Finally, in 2:17-18, the soul accepts as totally worthy of his attention a human spirit that has been adopted and prepared by

Divine Perspectives

the Holy Spirit of Christ Jesus (i.e., Esther related to and "prepared" by Mordecai). His regeneration is publicly proclaimed (King A. holds a banquet celebrating his new queen Esther). At first, however, the soul is not *aware* of the indwelling Holy Spirit of Christ Jesus (Mordecai) having adopted his spirit (Queen Esther - 2:20). Nevertheless, the Holy Spirit (Mordecai) through the regenerated human spirit (Esther) saves the soul's life (King A. - 2:22-23) from death, i.e., the consequences or penalty of sin (Romans 6:23).

Nevertheless, the flesh (Hamman) warreth against the spirit (Mordecai) as we are told in Galatians 5:17; satan through the flesh seeks to destroy all vestiges of Christ in the new believer. Chapter 3 unfolds this warfare. In Chapter 4, the indwelling Holy Spirit of Christ Jesus (Mordecai) grieves in order to bring to the soul's (King A.'s) attention the danger. The regenerated human spirit (Esther) is sensitive and obedient to the Holy Spirit (Mordecai), but the soul (King A.) is not, except when he chooses to listen to her. So, the spirit (Esther) prepares for a day of reckoning to "force" the soul (King A.) to listen to Christ's Holy Spirit (Mordecai) and know consciously of the flesh's (Hamman's) destructive intent. If the soul (King A.) *willfully* rejects this revelation, he will lose his regeneration (Esther).

The next step unfolds in Chapter 5: the soul (King A.) recognizes that Christ's Holy Spirit (Mordecai) should be honored out of gratitude for His having saved his life. The second step is described in Chapter 6: the will/volition function of the soul (King A.) forces the flesh (Hamman) to honor/praise/worship the indwelling Holy Spirit of Christ Jesus (Mordecai). Our human will has control over our flesh, if only we will exercise that control.

Finally, in Chapter 7 we see a step of *consecration* by the soul to that control over the flesh by rejecting the flesh's demands. The believer's soul (King A.) recognizes consciously the full evil nature of flesh (Hamman) and *wills* (reckons as in Romans 6) that it be destroyed (rendered ineffective). The indwelling Holy Spirit of Christ Jesus (Mordecai) does not bring this awareness about by *force* - God never forces us against our will - but rather, in conjunction with the regenerated human spirit (Esther) and through circumstances in the believer's life, issues arise in which the soul (King A.) cannot fail to see the contrast and conflict between flesh and spirit.

Soulical Stage

In 8:2 we see the culmination of this flesh-spirit warfare, when the soul chooses to give the spirit full authority in his life. This typifies the Baptism into the Holy Spirit. That means the soul is *saturated* with the indwelling Holy Spirit of Christ Jesus and chooses to yield to Him in all things. By this willful act of the soul (King A.), the Holy Spirit (Mordecai) is given full reign over the entire body (the 127 provinces of the kingdom). The remainder of Esther Chapter 8 typifies the actual working out of this yielding of the soul. But the 127 provinces are still not fully purified.

Emptying Unto Spiritual Victory

Chapter 9 of Esther continues the story of purification of the kingdom. The Holy Spirit (Mordecai), now in control, gives power throughout the entire body (127 provinces) to resist the last vestiges of temptation (friends of Hamman's household). Finally, commemoration of the final victory starts in 9:25. The full spiritual walk in this victory continues to the end of the

Divine Perspectives 419

Book of Esther, verse 10:3.

We are somewhat arbitrary in how we define precisely where the second ("natural" or "soulical") stage ends and the third ("spiritual") stage begins. We define the second stage to "end" when the vision first experienced upon Baptism into the Holy Spirit reaches some form of "consummation". This often takes the form of a distinct "event" that clearly marks the beginning of the third stage. That "event" is when our Lord Christ Jesus burns into our hearts, for the first time with significant vividness and clarity, a vision of what it really means for us *in this here-and-now* to be *"positioned with Christ in the heavenlies"* (Ephesians 1:3), and while still here on earth we are to function as His sent and anointed *agents* ("Greater things than these shall ye do" - John 14:12). This third stage is for the purpose of working Christ's crucifixion *into us*, for only to that extent can we actually walk in His *agency!*

3. Psalms Of Degrees Of Ascent: Our Walk In This World

Another typology of the three general stages of a Christian's sanctification by the indwelling Holy Spirit of Christ Jesus is found in a series of fifteen Psalms known as the "Psalms of Steps Or Degrees", namely Psalms 120-134. In type we gain rich insights in the practical aspects of our *walk* as Christians in this world as we grow from stage to stage. We summarize this in Row [58] of Sanctification Stages Chart Eleven. We also detail this typology in Table Four following.

Two scholars who have published meditations on these fifteen Psalms are Kaung[16] and Mumford[17]. We include the essence

Sanctification Stages Chart Eleven

Row #	Three "Types" Of Believer →	CARNAL/FLESHLY [SARKIKOS]	SOULICAL/NATURAL [PSUCHIKOS]	SPIRITUAL [PNEUMATIKOS]
[58]	Perspective Of Our Walk In This World: Types In Psalms Of Degrees (Psalms 120 - 134)	**Regeneration:** 120 New Desire For God 121 He Has The Answers 122 See His Objectives 123 Grace-Disciplined 124 Living By Doctrine	**Empowerment:** 125 Becoming Establ. In God 126 Christ In/Through Me 127 Spiritual Usefulness 128 Full Of Holy Spirit 129 Afflicted And Suffering	**Union:** 130 Waiting In Brokenness 131 Weaned By Humility 132 I In Christ In Union 133 Union With Our Brethren 134 Ministering Unto Lord
[59]	Perspective Of Our Calling To Be Separate From World: Types In Holy Convocations Of Israel (Leviticus Chapter 23)	Passover: Deliv. From **Penalty** Of Sin 1st Fruits: Deliv. From Sin's **Presence**	Pentecost/Weeks/1st Fruits: God Writing His Law In Our **Hearts**, As His Holy Spirit Himself; Deliv. From **Power** of Sin	Trumpets: Call To **Deeper Life** Atonement: Refiner's Fires Of **Death Of Self** Tabernacles/Booths: **Dwelling In Christ**
[60]	**Theological** Perspective: Types In Exodus-Joshua	Passover Night To Mt. Sinai (Law)	Mt. Sinai To Jordan (New Generation)	Jordan Crossing & Gilgal To Full Conquest Of Promised Land
[61]	Our **Progress** In Christ	Christ Is My Shepherd	Christ Is My Indwelling **Power**	Christ Is My Heavenly Companion
[62]	**Old Covenant** Maturing Stages	First 8 Days	Being Tutored (In Law)	**Agent** Of Inheritance
[63]	**Church Age** Periods	Christ Incarnate	Church Age To Now	"End Times"
[64]	Perspective Of Patience In God's Dealings With Men: Periods Of Dispensation	Abrahamic & Mosaic Covenants To Pentecost	Pentecost To Christ's Parousia Appearing	Millenial Reign Of Christ

Table Four

Christian Maturing Concepts
As Seen In The Ascent Psalms

STEP-DEGREE	STAGE	Psalm #	American Stand. Vers. (Bible) Title Of Psalm	Stephen Kaung "The Songs Of Degrees" Key Word	Stephen Kaung Message	Bob Mumford "15 Steps Out" Summary	Other Comments On Emphasis Of The Psalm
1	REGENERATION	120	Prayer For Deliv. From The Treacherous	Deliverance	Awakening of Desire	Seeing God In Things Present	New Desire For God
2		121	The Lord Is The Keeper Of Israel	Keeping	Going And Keeping	Learning Where To Get Your Answers	He Has The Answers
3		122	Prayer For The Peace Of Jerusalem	Peace	Companionship	Recognizing God's Objectives	Seeing His Objectives
4		123	Prayer For The Lord's Help	Gracious	Being Under Discipline	Learning To Wait	Disciplined By Grace
5		124	Praise For Rescue From Enemies	Escaped	Reminiscence	Translating Doctrine Into Experience	Experiencing One's Doctrine
6	EMPOWERMENT	125	The Lord Surrounds His People	Trust	Inner Conflict & Victory	Becoming Established In God	Becoming Established In God
7		126	Thanksgiving For Return From Captivity	Turn	Two Sides Of The Cross	Turning Of The Tide	Christ Into And Through Me
8		127	Prosperity Comes From The Lord	Build	Building And Growing	Experiencing Spiritual Usefulness	Spiritual Usefulness In Ministering
9		128	Blessedness Of The Fear Of The Lord	Fruitful	Full Of The Holy Spirit And Very Fruitful	Experiencing Spiritual Maturity	Full Of The Holy Spirit
10		129	Prayer For The Overthrow Of Zion's Ennemies	Afflicted	Life Of Spirit vs Life Of Flesh	Embracing Suffering As A Balancing Factor	Afflicted And Suffering
11	UNION WITH CHRIST	130	Hope In The Lord's Forgiving Love	Wait	Brokenness	Allowing God To Reveal Ourselves To Ourselves	Waiting In Brokenness
12		131	Childlike Trust In The Lord	Weaned	Humility	Finding Our True Selves & Our Place In Body Of Christ	Weaned By Humility
13		132	Prayer For The Lord's Blessing Upon The Sanctuary	Habitation	Mutual Desire And Fulfillment	Union With Christ	I In Union With Christ Indwelling
14		133	The Excellency Of Brotherly Unity	Unity	Body Of Christ Life Is A Blessing	Union With Our Brethren	Union With Our Brethren
15		134	Greetings Of The Night Watchers	Bless	Ministering Unto The Lord Through The Night	Bless The Lord!	Ministering Unto The Lord

of both Kaung's and Mumford's summaries of these Psalms in Table Four, along with the Psalm Titles given in the American Standard Version of the Bible, plus our additional comments. We here also categorize these 15 Psalms according to our three general stages of our sanctification by the indwelling Holy Spirit of Christ Jesus: (1) Psalms 120-124 to the Carnal Stage, with the emphasis upon *regeneration;* (2) Psalms 125-129 to the Soulical Stage with the emphasis upon *empowerment* by the indwelling Holy Spirit of Christ Jesus as our soul allows; and (3) Psalms 130-134 to the Spiritual Stage with the emphasis upon *union with Christ.*

This is a parallel but slightly different categorization than that made by Kaung[18]: (1) Psalms 120-124 of a *Stage Of Purification;* (2) Psalms 125-129 of A *Stage Of Enlightenment;* and (3) Psalms 130-134 of A *Stage Of Union*. We do not disagree with Kaung's categorizations, and we highly recommend his book to the interested reader. Indeed we use many of his interpretations. We only point out here that both our first and second general stages of sanctification involve *both* purification and enlightenment.

Regeneration

Psalms 120 through 124 take the Psalmist (1) from crying out for deliverance from the treacherous (sin), (2) through deliverance and regeneration by the Shed Blood of Christ, (3) discovering Christ's sustaining and providing power, (4) seeking His help, and (5) experiencing true peace in one's saving relationship with Him.

Psalm 120 is a weary cry for one's soul's deliverance by the Lord unto peace. It reflects a *desire* for the Lord and knowing that only the Lord can provide that deliverance. Such understandings come only when revealed inwardly to the soul by the Holy Spirit of Christ Jesus (Matthew 16:17). Psalm 121 is still *a cry of distress*, but reflects absolute assurance that one's salvation shall be kept or preserved by the Lord, and He alone has the answers to all of life's problems. By Psalm 122 the Psalmist sees the *peace* of belonging to "Jerusalem", the "city of peace", the Body of Christ. Hence, the Psalmist seeks the Lord's help and *waits* upon Him (Psalm 123). Finally, in Psalm 124 he rests *assured* of his deliverance. Thus, these first five Psalms of Degrees brings us, in type, into regeneration and our first general stage of sanctification.

Empowerment

Nevertheless, the believer soon experiences the conflict between the flesh and the spirit, even though he is now assured of his salvation in Christ. In Psalm 125, the Psalmist starts out with the assurance that by trusting utterly in the saving power of Christ our Lord, he will *overcome* temptations of the flesh and live in the righteousness of the Lord. That comes, however, only as and to the extent that one *chooses* to yield to the indwelling Holy Spirit of Christ Jesus in all things, that yielding being the essence of our receiving the Baptism into the Holy Spirit. Through this the believer truly becomes established in the Lord. And indeed, in Psalm 126, he rejoices in the Lord *turning* the tide of his carnality. In Psalms 127 and 128 he further rejoices, this time for the *prosperity* and *usefulness* the indwelling Lord is giving to him. Rejoicing means radiating the empowerment and anointing and love of the indwelling Holy Spirit of Christ Jesus, and the Psalmist indeed has learned this.

But, oh oh, his spiritual walk is soon challenged, and in Psalm 129 we see the beginnings of a deeper level of spiritual *conflict*. This is the beginning of the emptying cycles of loss-struggle-surrender-revisitation-consummation that we studied in Chapter Nine earlier in this volume.

Union With Christ

When the believer reaches the "surrender" stage of this emptying cycle, he cries out to the Lord in a depth of soul never before experienced. This we see beginning in Psalm 130, wherein the Psalmist, broken, simply waits in *surrender* for the Lord to make the next step. That brokenness leads to humility, and the Psalmist in Psalm 131 begins to understand why the Lord has allowed these new trials: he sees himself as being *weaned* like a child so that he can stand as a son/agent of the Lord.

Psalm 132 brings him to even sharper understandings, and he chooses to dwell in the Lord. Before, he simply allowed the Lord *in him* to take the initiatives; now he sees *himself in the Lord* as a co-inheritor, a son/agent who is being adopted (Romans 8:23) and who is now expected to bear the responsibilities of such. In Psalm 133 he sees that those responsibilities are primarily toward fellow believers, and can be met only through the spiritual *anointing* that is now upon him.

Finally, as we see in Psalm 134, the Psalmist is in such union with the Lord and with fellow believers, that all he can do is simply rejoice in praise and *worship*!

4. Several Types Of The Sanctification Process Time Sequence

The next six typologies of the three general stages of our being sanctified by the indwelling Holy Spirit of Christ Jesus, which we now briefly study, specifically include the *chronological* aspects: how we progress from stage to stage *over time*. The first is the set of Holy Convocations of Old Testament Israel, as specified in Exodus 23 and Leviticus 23. The second is the story of the Israelites in Exodus and Joshua. Thirdly, a personal aspect of the Holy Convocations typifies our progress as a Christian. Closely related is how an Israelite matured under the Old Covenant. Our fourth is a prophetic aspect of the Holy Convocations for the church. Parallel to that is the sequence of different dispensations of "Israel" over all of time.

We summarize these six in Rows [59] through [64] of Sanctification Stages Chart Eleven. We also use Figure Four, following, to capture more details, particularly how they unfold over time.

5. Israel's Holy Convocations: Our Separation From The World

The first set of such typologies we study is that of the Holy Convocations of Old Testament Israel, as specified in Exodus 23 and Leviticus 23. We briefly illustrate them in Row [59] of Sanctification Stages Chart Eleven, in Row [i] of Figure Four, and in Table Five, also following.

Figure Four

Types Of The Sanctification Process Time Sequence

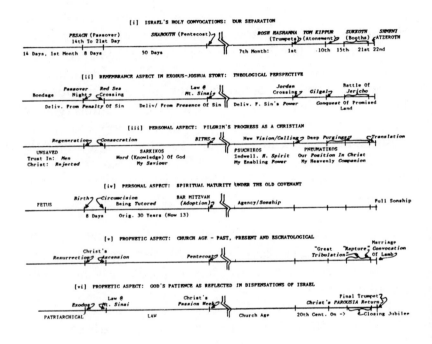

Table Five

Israel's Holy Convocations And Their Typological Aspects

SEASON (Ex. 23)	HOLY CONVOCATION (Lev. 23)	REMEMBRANCE ASPECT	PERSONAL ASPECT	PROPHETIC ASPECT
UNLEAVENED BREAD	PASSOVER	LORD STEPS INTO HOMES DELIV. FROM ANGEL OF DEATH	ACCEPTING CHRIST AS SAVIOUR DELIV. FROM *PENALTY* OF SIN	CHRIST'S CRUCIFIXION: FROM "PALM SABBATH" TO CRUCIFIXION & BURIAL & RESURRECTION
	UNLEAVENED BREAD	MARCH OUT OF EGYPT	WITHDRAW FROM SINFUL INVOLVEMENTS BY RECKONING FLESH CRUCIFIED	APPEARANCES OF CHRIST TO DISCIPLES
	(1ST OF) FIRST FRUITS	RED SEA CROSSING	RECKONING FLESH CRUCIFIED WITH HIM DELIV. FROM *PRESENCE* OF SIN	ASCENSION OF CHRIST
HARVEST	PENTECOST/WEEKS/ FIRST-FRUITS	RECEIVING OF LAW ON MT. SINAI	BAPTISM INTO HOLY SPIRIT; GOD WRITING HIMSELF ON OUR HEARTS DELIV. FROM *POWER* OF SIN	HOLY SPIRIT OUTPOURING ON SAINTS IN ACTS 2,3
INGATHERING	TRUMPETS (1ST TISHRI)	GOD INSTRUCTING JOSHUA TO MOVE BEHIND ARK	PRAISE & WORSHIP NEW VISION OF *DEEPER LIFE*	HEALING & CHARISMATIC RENEWALS IN 1950'S THROUGH 1970'S
	YOM KIPPUR (ATONEMENT) (10TH TISHRI)	CROSSING OF THE JORDAN	UTTER DEATH OF SELF: TOTAL *COMMITMENT* TO CHRIST JESUS	ECONOMIC, SOCIAL, POLITICAL & MILITARY CHAOS PERSECUTIONS OF CHRISTIANS IN THIS LAND
	SUKKOTH (TABERNACLES/BOOTHS) (15TH THRU 21ST TISHRI)	BATTLE OF JERICHO	COMPANIONSHIP AND MILITARY *WALK IN CHRIST*	ARMY OF GOD IN SPIRITUAL OFFENSE
	SHMENI ATZEROTH (22ND TISHRI)	FALL OF JERICHO	*TRANSLATION* TO HEAVEN	"RAPTURE" AND MARRIAGE CONVOCATION OF THE LAMB

Three special seasons of "Holy Convocations" were specified during each year for ministering unto the Lord. The Hebrew word used for such occasions is ChG, which means "to move in a circle; to dance, to celebrate". They were *"solemn* (of thanksgiving) *assemblies"* of God's people. They took place on days called in Hebrew "Moad" (MWID) that literally means "appointed time or place to meet; to betroth".

In particular, a total of seven festivals are specified in the Ceremonial Law, those seven occurring in three seasons of appointed times. The first season, known as the season of "Unleavened Bread", included the festival called "Passover", "Unleavened Bread", and "First of First Fruits". The second season, called the season of "Harvest of First Fruits", was called "Pentecost". And the third season, known as the season of "Ingathering", included the festival called "Trumpets" (Resh Hashannah: RAhSh HShNH, "head of the year"), "Day of Atonement" (Yom Kippur: YWM KPhR), and "Tabernacles or Booths" (Succoth: SKH, "booths"). Examples of portions of Scripture that delineate the Law of these Holy Convocations are Exodus 23:14-17, all of Leviticus chapter 23, Numbers 28:16 through 29:40, and Deuteronomy 16:1-17.

The Holy Convocation season of "Unleavened Bread" was in the first month of the year, Abib (AhBYB, or "sprouting; green") that is roughly our month of April. Passover was on *14th* Abib at evening; "Unleavened Bread" was the *15th* through *21st* Abib, and the "First of First Fruits" was on the Sunday (i.e., the first day after the Sabbath) of or following *21st* Abib. Pentecost was on the *49th* day after First of First Fruits, also on the first day of a week (i.e., a Sunday). Trumpets was on the *1st* of the *7th* month of the year, Tishri[19]

(ThShRY, "dominion"); Atonement was on the *10th* Tishri; and Succoth was from 15th through 21st Tishri. The 22nd Tishri, known later by Israelite scribes as Shmeni Atzeroth (ShMNY ITsRTh which means "eighth restraint"), was also a special day. See Row [i] of Figure Four.

But so what? Of what significance to *us today* are these details of when the Israelites celebrated Holy Convocations unto YHWH in Old Testament days, since Christ Jesus has *replaced* the entire Old Testament Ceremonial law with the law of the *Spirit* under a new and better covenant of grace (Hebrews 7:22-25)?

As with many passages of Scripture, these details of ancient Israelite Holy Convocations have more than one application or way in which they may be interpreted. Their *direct* application, of course, is *ceremonial:* that which the Ceremonial Law of Moses required of the Israelites during the Old Testament days. In addition, they have direct *historical* meanings, plus at least two typological or symbolic *spiritual* interpretations. Both these ceremonial and historical details also serve as a rich source of lessons, through typology, that they teach us regarding our Lord Christ Jesus' dealings with His children throughout history. For they have distinct parallels in the process through which Christ draws in Him those of His *individual* believers who would go on to full maturity in their walk in Him. We call those lessons the *personal* or "soteriological" (i.e., "pertaining to salvation") fulfillment of the ancient Holy Convocations. And they also have distinct parallels in His dealings *corporately* with His church throughout the New Testament era or "church age" to mature His Bride. We call those parallels the *prophetic* fulfillment of the ancient Holy Convocations.

We briefly study these historical, personal and prophetic aspects of the fulfillment of the ancient Israelite Holy Convocations in the following discussions, with references to Figure Four and Table Five as appropriate.

6. Remembrance Aspect In The Exodus-Joshua Story: Theological Perspective

We first briefly suggest a further typology in the festivals themselves: how they indicate different "levels" or degrees of our *separation* from the world (John 15:19, John 17:14-16 and 1 John 2:15-16; see also Romans 12:2 and James 1:27).

These "stages" of our separation are seen theologically by the corresponding events in Exodus and Joshua that they were ordained by God to be remembrances of. For this, see Row [60] of Sanctification Stages Chart Eleven and Row [ii] of Figure Four.

The historical interpretation of the season of "Unleavened Bread" is the story of the Israelites described in Exodus chapters 12 through 15, from the first Passover, through their crossing the Red Sea, until they came to Mt. Sinai. The historical meaning of Pentecost is Moses receiving the Law on Mt. Sinai, the account of which begins in Exodus 19:1. And the historical significance of the "Ingathering" season of Holy Convocations in the month Tishri is found in the first 9 chapters of Joshua. It is this set of historical events underlying these Holy Convocations that enables us to more fully understand the details of the Ceremonial Law, as it was understood by the Old Testament Israelites.

Divine Perspectives 431

The theological implications are those various levels of our *deliverance from sin*. As stated in Row [59] of Sanctification Stages Chart Eleven: (1) the season of *Unleavened Bread* typifies our deliverance from both the *Penalty of Sin*, namely death of our "First-Born", of our souls (Passover Night) and our deliverance from the immediate *Presence of sin* (Unleavened Bread); (2) deliverance from the *Power of Sin* by having God's Law written on our hearts (Pentecost) and the Indwelling Holy Spirit *empowering* us; and (3) deliverance unto a *Deeper Life* in Christ by being called (Trumpets), purged (Yom Kippur), and separated from the world to be covered by Christ (Succoth).

In Chapter Twelve following in this volume, we will revisit the story of the Israelites' wanderings in the wilderness, there from the point of view of them being sanctified unto singleness of purpose - the Perfect Will of God.

7. Personal Aspects: Our Progress In Spiritual Maturity

The various stages of our deliverance from sin, unto deeper life in and fellowship with our Lord Christ Jesus, are shown in parallel in Row [iii] of Figure Four and in the fourth column of Table Five. The original Passover night typifies our deliverance from the *penalty* of our sins, i.e. death of our "first-born" (soul-spirit combination) according to Romans 3:23, as a consequence of our "pleading" the shed blood of our PhSCh or Passover Lamb our Lord Christ Jesus. That is suggested by our displaying on the entrance-way of our hearts, for the Lord to see, a "welcome sign" unto Him to enter - see Revelation 3:20. But it took the march out of Egypt, including the Red Sea crossing (i.e., water baptism - see

Romans 6:3-11), to deliver us from the *presence* of sin, i.e., the immediate influence of our sin-nature on our actions and outward behavior by virtue of the mental discipline of reckoning our flesh and sin-nature crucified with Christ. But then, it still takes God writing His Word, His Holy Spirit, on the "tablets of our hearts" in the Baptism into the Holy Spirit (Mt. Sinai), and the subsequent "soaking" of our hearts by that indwelling Holy Spirit during our wilderness walk, in order for us to be fully "filled" (saturated) with Him, and consequently delivered from the *power* of sin. Yet even that is not the final goal: a deeper emptying experience, typified by our stepping into the Jordan River on faith (*before* the waters were held back) before we can reach our Gilgal of worship celebration of our *union* with Christ. Then at last, by virtue of our position in Christ in the heavenlies, we are about to inherit our promised land.

Row [61] of Sanctification Stages Chart Eleven further emphasizes this according to how our experiential view of our Lord Christ Jesus expands during this progress after we apprehend so great salvation: from He as my *shepherd* (protector and provider), through He as my indwelling *power*, to He as my heavenly *companion*. Actually, in this third stage we do not see Him as *our* companion so much as we see ourselves as *His* companion.

The Old Testament scriptures have yet another typology of this progression, albeit somewhat incomplete. This is illustrated in Row [62] of Sanctification Stages Chart Eleven and Row [iv] of Figure Four. We refer here to the several "rites of passage" of the Israelite male child (that by virtue of the masculine gender typifies the "rites of passage" of our human spirits). First comes our birth (typifying our human spirit being regenerated) and circumcision (i.e., marked by Christ as belonging to Him, and having the soul-barrier to the dispersal of the seed of eternal life - foreskin- removed). Then one entered a period of being tutored and matured (unto faith by the indwelling Holy Spirit - Galatians 3:23-24) until the time came when he could be trusted with the responsibilities of the Father's affairs. At that time (*originally* at age 30 years) an "adoption" rite of passage occurred whereupon those responsibilities, plus the concomitant authority of the Father's Name, were bestowed. Likewise we, upon the Baptism into the Holy Spirit, acquire the responsibility of Body ministries and the power and authority of the Name of Christ to enable us to meet those responsibilities. But we actually mature in these responsibilities during the third general stage of sanctification. Note, however, this typology does not extend to cover our third general stage of sanctification. *Full sonship* did not occur until late - the father's death in the natural Old Testament tradition.

8. Prophetic Aspects: God's Patience As Reflected In Dispensations

The Holy Convocations of Old Testament Israel, in addition to having significance in terms of remembrance of the events of the story of the Israelites in Exodus and Joshua and significance in terms of our personal sanctification, also has a *prophetic* interpretation. The primary prophetic significance of these Holy Convocations we illustrate in Row [63] of Sanctification Stages Chart Eleven and in Row [v] of Figure Four. We also list them in the final column of Table Five.

Regarding the prophetic fulfillment of the ancient Israelite Holy Convocations, two of the three seasons *have already*

been fulfilled in human history. The season of "Unleavened Bread", historically dated to about 1485BC, prophetically pointed then to Jesus Christ's first coming, crucifixion, resurrection, ascension, and the days immediately thereafter. The season of Pentecost, also dating historically to about 1485BC, had its prophetic fulfillment in the first and second chapters of Acts: the first Baptizing of the disciples into the Holy Spirit.

But the season of Ingathering, that dates historically to about 1445BC, has ***not*** yet been completely fulfilled! The yet-future (actually now in progress) prophetic fulfillment of the season of Ingathering, is a major study of its own, to which we devote an entire separate volume[20] in this series. There we show the parallelisms of the pattern of sequential events between ***three*** sources: the Holy Convocations, the Exodus-Joshua story, and the Book of Revelation. The reader is referred to that separate volume for details of these "End Times" prophetic aspects. Table Five gives only a very cursory suggestion of the more salient attributes.

Yet one further set of parallelisms is available to us, however, that we suggest in Row [64] of Sanctification Stages Chart Eleven and Row [vi] of Figure Four. We refer here to an overview of the several dispensations or distinct periods of time during human history from the patriarchal dispensation, unto the "end times", from the perspective of the unfolding of revelations of God's ways to us, and that reflects God's tremendous patience with mankind. Here we see the events of Exodus including Mt. Sinai as typifying our initial entering unto a dispensation of ***Law***, Christ's Passion Week as typifying our entering the dispensation of ***Grace*** (Church age), and the "End Times" culminating with the closing Jubilee.

Our primary reason for including this portrait is simply to emphasize how vital it is for believers to embrace the emptying experiences of our third general stage of sanctification in order to "overcome" and be effective witnesses of our Lord Christ Jesus during these end times, that we are now already in!

End Notes: Chapter Twelve

[1.] Henry W. Soltau, *The Holy Vessels and Furniture of the Tabernacle*, (London, England: Yapp and Hawkins, 1851, modern reprint available from Kregel Publications, Grand Rapids, Michigan 49503).

[2.] Henry W. Soltau, *THE TABERNACLE - The Priesthood and the Offerings*, (London, England; 185?, modern reprint available through Kregel Publications, Grand Rapids, Michigan 49503).

[3.] Judson Cornwall, *Let Us Draw Near*, (South Plainfield, NJ: Bridge Publishing, Inc., 1977). Copyright © 1977 by Bridge Publishing, Inc.

[4.] Varner, Kelley, *The More Excellent Ministry*, (Shippensburg, PA: Destiny Image Publishers, 1988). Copyright © 1988 by Kelley Varner.

5. Varner, Kelley, *The Priesthood Is Changing*, (Shippensburg, PA: Destiny Image Publications, 1991). Copyright © 1988 by Kelley Varner.

6. Hanby, Dr. Mark, *The House That God Built*, (Shippensburg, PA: Destiny Image Publishers, 1993). Copyright © 1993 by Dr. Mark Hanby.

7. That was the only geographic location in Jerusalem area which satisfied all these requirements, plus being the only place where the centurion, at the foot of the cross, could visibly see the veil being torn, over half a mile to the west (Luke 23:44-47).

8. There were several different definitions of the cubit in use in ancient times, both in Egypt and in Israel. The cubit used here was approximately 25 inches in length. More precisely it was remarkably close to 1.0×10^{-7} times the earth's polar radius. The "English" foot was originally ½ cubit.

9. Varner, Kelley, *Unshakeable Peace - The Life and Times of Haggai the Prophet*, (Shippensburg, PA: Destiny Image Publishers, 1994), p. 195. Copyright © 1994 by Kelley Varner.

10. Varner, Kelley, *Prevail - A Handbook for the Overcomer*, (Shippensburg, PA: Destiny Image Publishers, 1982), p. 84. Copyright © 1982 by Kelley Varner.

11. In Isaiah 40:31, "wait on the Lord" in the Hebrew means "to *entwine* one's life with the Lord".

12. Varner, Kelley, *Unshakeable Peace*, p. 223.

13. Major W. Ian Thomas, *If I Perish, I Perish*, (Grand Rapids, Michigan: Zondervan Publishing House, 1967, Fifth Printing 1969). Copyright © 1969 by Zondervan Publishing House.

14. Smith, Penny, *Gateways To Growth - Keys to Christian Growth and Maturity from the Book of Esther*, (Salisbury Center, NY: Pinecrest Publications, 1992). Copyright © 1992 by Penny E. Smith.

15. This typology fits well, even though it is a contradiction to the fact that Biblical Hebrew and Greek words pertaining to the human soul are in the feminine gender and words pertaining to the human spirit are in the masculine gender.

16. Kaung, Stephen, *The SONGS of DEGREES - Meditations on Fifteen Psalms*, (Hollis, New York: Christian Fellowship Publishers, Inc., 1970). Copyright © 1970 by Christian Fellowship Publishers, Inc.

17. Mumford, Bob, *15 Steps Out - A Study of Subjective Christianity; A Testimony of a Spiritual Itinerary*, (Plainfield, NJ: Logos International, 1969). Copyright © 1969 by Logos

International.

[18.] Kaung, Stephen, *The SONGS of DEGREES*.

[19.] "Tishri" (ThShRY, meaning "dominion") was the Chaldean/Babylonian name for the 7th month. Here we use it, rather than the Hebrew name "Aythenim" (AhYThNYM, meaning "permanent; firm; constant"), because "Tishri" is in common use today by Jewish Scholars.

[20.] Sherrerd, Chris S., *Unto The Mountain Pass - A Theology Of The End-Time Purposes Of God*, Volume VI of the series "Where Do You Fit In? Practical Commitments In The Body Of Christ", to be published..

Chapter Twelve

Our Cloud Of Witnesses

Of the many different concepts of the three general stages of the sanctification process that we have discussed so far (i.e. a total of sixty-four in Chapters Eight through Eleven - plus thirty-one from other authors), each gives a unique viewpoint or framework of understanding each stage. This total set is presented for general understanding of the sanctification process; but no one of these concepts precisely applies to any one person. Each individual believer experiences these stages differently from each other; our Lord Christ Jesus tailors the dealings of His indwelling Holy Spirit to each of our unique situations as He chooses. It is therefore appropriate for us to also comment briefly on how the general process of sanctification *differs* from person to person.

Perhaps the best way to do this is to look at individual cases. For this reason we include, in Rows [65] through [71] of Sanctification Stages Chart Twelve of this concluding chapter, summaries of seven Old Testament Biblical "personages" from this three-stage point of view. Sanctification Stages Chart Twelve is basically an extension of Sanctification Stages Charts One through Eleven.

Sanctification Stages Chart Twelve

Row #	Three "Types" Of Believer →	CARNAL/FLESHLY [SARKIKOS]	SOULICAL/NATURAL [PSUCHIKOS]	SPIRITUAL [PNEUMATIKOS]
[65]	Life Of Abraham Unto *Faith*	Shechem, Covenant, Battles In Siddim (Genesis 12:6-14:16)	Melchizedek, Ishmael Born, El Shaddai, Isaac B., Mt Moriah (Genesis 14:17-22:19)	Sarah Dies, Bride For Isaac, Keturah, Blesses Isaac (Genesis 23:1-25:8)
[66]	Life Of Jacob Unto *Righteousness*	Birthright, Departure, Tarry At Luz (Genesis 25:27-28:10)	Vision @ Bethel, Serving Laban, Birth of Sons, Departure (Genesis 28:11-32:2)	Jabbok Crossing, Peniel, Shechem, Benjamin, Egypt (Genesis 32:3-50:14)
[67]	Life Of Joseph Unto *Forgiveness*	Age 17, Coat, Dreams, Sold Into Slavery (Genesis 37:3-37:6)	Potipar's Steward, False Accusations, Prison Dreams (Genesis 39:1-40:25)	2 More Years Prison, Pharoah's Appointment, Brothers, Etc. (Genesis 41:1-50:26)
[68]	Life Of Moses Unto *Overcoming* Ungodly Demands By People	Rescued From River, In Palace, Midian Desert (Exodus 2:5-3:11)	Burning Bush, Plagues etc., Passover, Red Sea Crossing (Exodus 3:2-15:18)	Marah, Elim, Mt. Sinai, Wilderness Walk, Mt. Nebo (Exodus 15:19-Deut. 34:5)
[69]	Israelites In Wilderness Unto *Singleness Of Purpose*	Passover, Elim, Mt. Sinai (Exodus 12:1-15:18)	Pillar Of Cloud & Fire, Manna, To Paran, Spies Sent Out (Numbers 10:33-13:24)	Spies Report, 38 Years, All Die, Jordan Cr., Gilgal, Jericho, etc. (Numbers 13:25 - Joshua 26:27)
[70]	Life Of David Unto *Victory*	Life As Shepherd Lad (Events Not Recorded) (1 Samuel 16:1-16:12)	Anointing, Serving Saul, Victory Over Goliath (1 Samuel 16:13-17:58)	Fugitive, Enthroned, Tabernacle, Family Problems, Final Conquests (1 Samuel 18:1 - 1 Kings 2:12)
[71]	Life Of Elijah A *Prophet's* Testings	(Events Not Recorded)	Prophecy To Ahab, 3 Years In Hiding, Mt. Carmel Events (1 Kings 17:1-18:46)	Flight From Jezreel, Wilderness Walk, Discipling Elisha, Bethel (1 Kings 19:1 - 2 Kings 2:14)

1. Meanings Of Old Testament Names

In this chapter we will be making much use of Old Testament Biblical typology in our examples. Therefore we need first to comment on what we know and don't know about the meanings of the many Hebrew place and person names involved. Many years ago when I was doing the Biblical exegetical research for Volume III[1] of this series, I noticed what to me then was an incredible and remarkable fact: even the proper nouns (names of people and places) of the Bible, treated as words in the original language, have significant meanings related to the contexts in which they appear. Just how significantly meaningful they are will be apparent in the following as we study the lives of some of the great men of God in the Old Testament. We need, however, to be very careful in unraveling the original meanings of those Old Testament names.

It is far from the simple matter of looking up those names in a Hebrew Lexicon. It also requires in most cases seeking insight from the indwelling Holy Spirit of Christ Jesus, *via* "praying through". That is because for clear historical reasons the "standard" current Lexicon meanings of many Hebrew words and names reflect a significant departure from their original meanings. Two historical reasons are: (1) the underlying ***paradigm*** intrinsic to the ***original*** Old Testament Hebrew language is so vastly different from the underlying paradigms intrinsic to most modern languages, including both modern English and New Testament Greek, and different in a way that has been ***doctrinally denied*** over the centuries by Hebrew scholars both Jewish and Christian; and (2) Old Testament Hebrew ceased being a ***spoken*** language for several centuries, and modern pronunciation symbols (points) were added many centuries later and reflected much "guess work".

We first address the intrinsic paradigms. The language spoken by a people bears with it a pattern or perspective or framework of thinking that is distinct and unique to those people and to that language. The framework of thinking that is intrinsic to the Hebrew language and to the Old Testament Hebrew-speaking peoples was that of the *God-man relationship* from *God's* perspective. That framework is deeply embedded in the language both by the subtle form of meanings of the verbal action roots, and also by the structure of the language itself as based on those verb roots. In sharp contrast, the framework of thinking that is intrinsic to our English language (and also the New Testament Greek language) is the *human experience* from *man's* perspective. That framework is embedded for example in the precision with which physical concepts and human experiences can be articulated.

This means that if we would fully grasp Christian truths pertaining to the *God-man* relationship from *God's* perspective, we must study those truths in the Old Testament Hebrew words and types that pertain to them. But to capture the *original* meanings we must go back to the original unpointed texts, and work from there with the help of the indwelling Holy Spirit of Christ Jesus. Throughout this volume, we give the unpointed Hebrew words themselves in all cases. A table at the beginning of this volume gives the English representations we use for the Hebrew letters.

An important characteristic of Old Testament Hebrew is the affixing of certain prepositions to the beginning of nouns (i.e., as part of the word itself). Examples of this are: *AhLY-* for "God (EL) of [or is/has/does]"; *AhBY-* for "father of"; *YAhChY-* for "brother/kindred of"; *B-* for "in" or "into"; *D-* for "this"; *H-* for "the"; *DAh-* or *ZH-* for "this [one]"; *W-* for "of"; *L-* or *LW-* for negation, i.e., "not" or "no"; *YW-* for "God (YHWH) of [or is/has/does]"; and *M-* or *MH-* to denote interrogation, i.e., "who?" or "what" or "why?" or "how?", or to denote reflexive action which is done to the object of the noun. Interpretation of words with these beginnings requires determining whether that beginning is an affixed preposition, or is a part of the verb root.

The language ceased as a widely spoken medium of communication at certain times, resulting in pronunciation changes over the centuries, with changes in structure and word spellings accordingly. Examples of such times were just prior to the reign of King Josiah, during the Babylonian Exile, and the few centuries prior to the time of Christ. It was much later than that, namely between the 7th and 10th centuries A.D., that the "modern" pronouncement symbols (called "points") were added, namely by Masorete scholars.

For these reasons, our current knowledge of Hebrew, both its pronunciation and its meaning, reflects later reconstructions of the language. That reconstruction is based on century-long shifts in local pronunciations (i.e., a so-called "Syriac dialect"). That reconstruct is also based on the Masorete doctrinal beliefs that included a ***denial of any God-man relationship*** except through Mosaic Law. But as we said above, the very paradigm intrinsic to the verb roots of the language is a personal dynamic relationship between God and His people.

Hence, the *meanings* of many *verb roots* as well as many proper nouns are today inaccurately represented.

One of many examples that illustrates this is the Hebrew word PhSCh, translated "Passover". The closely associated verb root means "to step" (i.e., as in walking). The sense of its use in Exodus Chapter 12 is that the Lord "steps through" the believer's doorway in order to enter, and it is His Presence in the home that keeps the destroying angel (God's agent to enforce the Adamic curse) out. But Masoretic doctrine forbade, as utter blasphemy, any consideration of God speaking of His Presence that close to any mortal believer. Hence, over the years the meaning of PhSCh has shifted to some *remote* concept of "passing *over*" such as "giving approval" or "remotely protecting". Those are true associated concepts, yes; but the real meaning of the Passover account is almost totally lost.

Our efforts to reconstruct the *original* meanings of Old Testament Hebrew proper nouns and other words, as used in the following sections of this chapter, were very tedious and far from straight forward. Wherever it "made sense" in the context, we used as a starter, Strong's Concordance[2] definitions of the *verbal roots*. Where that was inadequate (including for words of non-Hebrew origin), we used Davidson's Lexicon[3] and a modern version of Robinson's translation of Gesenius.[4] And for the actual Old Testament Hebrew text, we referred to Kittel.[5]

However, we virtually ignored the Masoritic "points" out of distrust, and we investigated various other ways in which the specific proper nouns could have been constructed from verb roots and prefixes. Since these sources still reflect the

Masorite reconstructions, in all cases our constant prayer was for guidance by the indwelling Holy Spirit of Christ Jesus. But we cannot guarantee absolute accuracy, so in the following we use the phrase "has as one meaning" or "one meaning of which being".

An additional typology is that of a king or patriarch being a type of our human *soul* and his queen or wife being a type of our human *spirit*. We also use that on occasions in this chapter. This seems at first glance to contradict the gender of the words used for "soul" and "spirit" in the Bible: in both the Old Testament Hebrew and New Testament Greek, the words used for "soul" are in the *feminine* gender and the words used for "spirit" are in the *masculine* gender. Our typology does not intend to ignore that, but simply reflects the patriarchal *culture* of Old Testament days together with the *will/volition/choice* function of the *soul*. The type is that our sanctification is reflected by the extent to which we (our *soul*) chooses to yield to the indwelling Holy Spirit of Christ Jesus *via* our human *spirit*. The corresponding anti-type of this is the extent to which one's wife *appealed* to him as worthy to be heeded, and in which ways she anti-typically reflected the indwelling Holy Spirit of our Lord Christ Jesus.

2. Abraham: Unto Faith

Our first example is that of the patriarch Abram/Abraham, whose story is given in Genesis 11:26 through 25:8. Here we study his life as an example of the indwelling Holy Spirit of Christ Jesus *unto faith*. See Row [65] of Sanctification Stages Chart Twelve which summarizes how we relate his life to the three general stages of sanctification.

Faith, as used in the Bible, does not mean *mind assent to the truth of some proposition;* it means, rather, a *choice* we make, a choice *to be totally dependent upon and obedient to our Lord Christ Jesus!* It is not a verbal action of our mind, nor of our emotion; rather it is a decisive action of our *will/volition.* And that choice is necessary in order for our Lord Christ Jesus to be *released* to work when/how/as *He* chooses.

Our Lord has chosen to not override our human wills. Hence, for His purposes to be accomplished in us, the indwelling Holy Spirit of Christ Jesus must first work to change our will to conform ours to His. That working, a major aspect of His sanctifying us, is so beautifully seen in the life of Abram/Abraham, as we study his life both historically and typically.

Regeneration And Carnal Stage:

We begin our story of the life of Abram/Abraham in Genesis 11:26-32, where we find him in Haran. Haran (Hebrew: ChRN, one meaning of which being "mountaineer, from hilly country or high regions") typifies one who has been powerfully enlightened about his/her sinful state and need for a savior. He responds to that enlightenment by stepping out in faith, at age 75, to seek for and start a new life (Genesis 12:1-5).

His first stop was at the high trees of Moreh in Shechem (Genesis 12:6-7). Moreh (Hebrew: MWRH) has as one meaning "rebel", and Shechem (Hebrew: ShKM) has as one meaning "place of burden". The Cross is where we place our sin-burden due to our rebellion against the Lord's word. That we initially approach with repentance to find He provides so great a forgiveness and the lifting of our burdens of fear and guilt.

But notice in Genesis 12:8, that immediately thereafter he settles in the Negev between Bethel and Ai. Negev (Hebrew: NGW) has as one meaning "famine due to being parched, i.e., without rain"; Bethel (Hebrew: BYThAhL) has as one meaning "dwelling place of God"; and Ai (Hebrew: HIY) has as one meaning "the heap of ruins". How often after we initially reach Calvary we withdraw in unbelief, thus finding ourselves in a dry land, and oscillate between yielding to the indwelling Holy Spirit of Christ Jesus, our heart being His dwelling place, and being ruined through temptations. The result? Egypt - a sojourn in sin. But the Lord sovereignly and mercifully preserves us from losing our human spirit, as is typified by his wife Sarai (Hebrew: ShRY/SRY, one meaning of which being "dominating, one in control" - Genesis 12:9-26). So, sin no longer being where we belong, we return to the parched land of Negev, and settle once again between being the dwelling house of God (Bethel) and being ruined by temptations (Ai - Genesis 13:1-3).

This time, however, that struggle is resolved by the leaving of Lot (Genesis 13:7-1). Lot (Hebrew: LWT) has as one meaning "veil or covering". The veil of our blindness must be lifted so that we can see Christ for He really is and our desperate need for Him. So Abram moves on, and settles in the area of Hebron, next to the high trees of Mamre (Genesis 13:18). Hebron (Hebrew: ChBRWN) has as one meaning "congregation or place of congregation", and Mamre (Hebrew: MMRAh) has as one meaning "firm, vigorous". So at last we see our soul joined with others in a local congregation of the Body of Christ, wherein we grow firmly and vigorously in faith.

Soon, however, our newly-vigorous faith is challenged. In Genesis 14:1-16 we see a battle between two groups of kings in the general area, in which Abram joins forces if for no other reason than to rescue Lot. Note the kingdoms involved. Side #1, that Abram eventually joins, are of the kingdoms of: (1) Ellasar (Hebrew: AhLSR, one meaning of which being "God is sad and grievous"); (2) Elam (Hebrew: IYLM, one meaning of which being "God is distant and hidden"); and (3) the gentiles (Hebrew: GWYM, one meaning of which being "the masses of people"). Side #2 are of the kingdoms of: (4) Sodom (Hebrew: SDM, one meaning of which being "scorched by fire"); (5) Admah (Hebrew: AhDMH, one meaning of which being "earthy, worldly"); (6) Zeboiim (Hebrew: TsBWYM, one meaning of which being "enticements - literally gazelles or beautiful creatures"); and (7) Bela (Hebrew: BLI, one meaning of which being "destruction") or Zoar (Hebrew: TsIR, one meaning of which being "small, belittled"). The battles all took place in the valley of Siddim (Hebrew: ShDYM, one meaning of which being "wide spaces or plains"). In type, then, Side #2 represents the results of temptations into sin, i.e., our being destroyed or scorched (ultimately in hell) through worldly enticements such as sexual lusts, covetousness, etc. Side #1 appears at first to be the "good" side, but not really: it is our attempts to overcome those temptations *through human effort* because God seems too far away to help us. Wide is this way: so many of us - the masses of carnal Christians - try to overcome flesh by Law, only to fail. We only partially obtain victory of sorts this way; at least we do not become destroyed by temptations. Galatians 3:23-25 summarizes this

Our Cloud Of Witnesses 449

by our being protected by Law until we grow in faith.

He went as far as Dan (Hebrew: DN, one meaning of which being "judge") in Hobah (Hebrew: ChWBH, one meaning of which being "hiding place") north of Damascus (Hebrew: DMShQ, one meaning of which being "sorrowful; intricate scheming"). By pursuing the forces of evil in our subtle and secret ways we finally see God's *judgment* prevail. But God has so much more for us.

Natural (Soulical) And Spiritual Stages

Genesis 14:17-20 tells us how, after this victory, Abram is met by Melchizedek, to whom Abram tithes, and who in return blesses Him. Melchizedek has as one meaning "King of Righteousness", and He is also identified as the "King of Salem", one meaning of which being "King of Wholeness ('peace')". This typifies Christ Himself, the *Person* of Christ, whom Abram now meets face-to-face. We suggest that this typifies our Baptism into the Holy Spirit. In Chapters Six and Seven of this volume above we showed how the essence of that baptism is our increased awareness of the reality of Christ in the here and now.

That this event fortifies Abram's faith is indicated by the next event: in Genesis 14:21-24 we read how he resisted the offer (of temptation to much material gain) from the "King of Sodom"; satan is our "king of the scorched place (Hell)."

This refusal in turn brings upon Abram rich blessings from God (Genesis 15:1). He meets Eliezer (Hebrew: AhLYIZR, one meaning of which being "God of help" - Genesis 15:2). He receives God's promises of a rich inheritance in the future

(Genesis 15:4-6), and enters into a covenant of total commitment with God (Genesis 15:7-21).

His wife was still Sarai (Hebrew: ShRY/SRY, one meaning of which being "dominating"). And he listens to her, and as a consequence by *human* efforts they try to fulfill God's promises. This is so typical of Christians of the second or "natural" or "soulical" stage of sanctification: though we are rich in anointings of guidance and power from the indwelling Holy Spirit of Christ Jesus, nevertheless we strive to do the doing of our ministries ourselves, we being too intense on that to seek the Lord in deeper ways. The result (Genesis 16): Ishmael (Hebrew: YShMIAhL, one meaning of which being "God will give attention to" - as in answer to prayers) is born of Hagar (Hebrew: HGR, one meaning of which being "foreign guest").

God allows us to minister on *our* terms, but *only for a season*. Our *human efforts* to minister, even under the anointing of the indwelling Holy Spirit of Christ Jesus, are foreign to our Lord's perfect will for us. So sooner or later God humbles us. Our ministries, even though under the anointing of the indwelling Holy Spirit of Christ Jesus, fail to produce the expected results, and we approach "burnout"

Finally we take the time to deeply seek the Lord, at all costs. We get into our prayer closets and stay there until He answers. And answers us clearly. What is His answer? We simply read "I am El Shaddai; walk before Me ..." (Genesis 17:1), followed by a renewal of His promises to us (Genesis 17:2-21). El Shaddai? El simply has as one meaning "Almighty". But Shaddai (Hebrew: ShDY) has as one meaning "your nursing breast". God is not here associating

Himself with the feminine gender; but what He *is doing* is inviting Abram into the most beautiful, close interpersonal relationship with Him, one in which by our willingly yielding to Him in all ways we receive total provision, nurture, protection and love. Wow!

Not only that, but God also then confirms His covenant promises to us in even more powerful ways. A covenant between two parties involves an exchange from each to the other of something very precious to each. What is more precious to any of us than our *name?* God and Abram exchanged portions of their names. From that time thereafter, God referred to Himself as the "God of Abraham" (later as the "God of Abraham, Isaac and Jacob"). But also, God inserted into both Sarai's and Abram's name the "AH" syllable of His Name (YHWH, the "I AM"), whereupon their names became Sarah (Hebrew: ShRH, one meaning of which being "noble princess"), and Abraham (Hebrew: AhBRHM, one meaning of which being "father of many"). Before she was "Sarai", strong-willed; now she is "Sarah", a noble one. Before, he was just "Abram" (its meaning in the Hebrew acknowledged that God was his father); now he is "Abraham", a spiritual father himself.

Abram accepted that invitation, and his immediate act is to commit his entire household to God, including his human efforts of ministry (as typified by Ishmael); this we see by the first act of circumcision that typifies our being *marked* or *sealed* as *belonging* to and *used by* God (Genesis 17:22-27).

The third general stage of sanctification involves one or more cycles of vision-loss-striving-surrender-restoration-culmination. This story is no exception. In Genesis 18:1-19, when challenged by the Lord (a messenger or angel), Sarah laughs in derision out of unbelief over the promise that at her age she will still bear a child (son). In Genesis 18:20-33 Abraham argues with God over His pending judgment over sinners. In Genesis 19 we see the story of Lot and his loss and sorry state for having stayed in the world too long.

But perhaps Abraham's greatest test at this time is alluded to in Genesis 20:1-2. His dwelling place in Hebron by the high trees of Mamre no longer satisfied him, he having seen clearly the coming judgment of all worldliness - Sodom and Gomorrah (Hebrew: GMRH, one meaning of which being "fissure, trap"). So he moved on. But to where? Back into the land of the Negev ("dry wilderness without rain"), and settles between Kadesh (Hebrew: QDSh, one meaning of which being "holy sanctuary") and Shur (Hebrew: ShWR, one meaning of which being "wandering about aimlessly"), in the valley of Gerar (Hebrew: GRR, one meaning of which being "ruminating, meditating, mulling things over"). Here he finds himself not yet quite apprehending his state as a *holy* sanctuary of God, wandering about seeking it, and constantly meditating on the Word of God. This dry wilderness walk is not without its rewards, for they meet Abimelech (Hebrew: AhBYMLK, one meaning of which being "father of the King"), who typifies God the father Himself who blesses them (Genesis 20:3-18).

Isaac was finally born - the embodiment of God's purpose for Abraham's life on earth (Genesis 21:1-5). This occurred when Abraham was 100 years of age - "100" has as one meaning "completion". Sarah laughed a second time over Isaac, but this time out of joy and rejoicing (Genesis 21:6-7).

Isaac still had to be weaned (Genesis 21:8). But more importantly, Ishmael had to be dealt with - the consequences of our trying in the past to minister to the Lord by our own human efforts (Genesis 21:9-21). This is a very painful step for us to take. But afterward, we again meet Abimelech (Father of the King - God the Father of our Lord Christ Jesus) and his commander-servant Phicol, who demand a full commitment with total honesty from then on out (Genesis 21:22-30). Phicol (Hebrew: PhYKL) has as one meaning "speaking mouth of all" and refers to the indwelling Holy Spirit of Christ Jesus guiding us unto all wisdom. We make that oath, and publicly announce it (Genesis 21:31-33).

However, yet again a testing - this one the most severe of Abraham's entire life - to give Isaac back to God. How *totally* do we mean our oath of total oneness with our Lord Christ Jesus? Genesis 22:1-19 gives the story of Abraham and Isaac on Mt. Moriah. Only when we go that far in our surrender to Him, the surrender of our very purpose for having lived, will that purpose be worked out *supernaturally* by Him. That is truly the emptying processes at the end of the second general stage of our sanctification.

Sarah ("our noble princess") died in Kirjarth-Arba (Hebrew: QRYTh-AhRBI, one meaning of which being "city of four", the number four symbolizing the "fulfillment of our human lives on earth" - Genesis 23:1-2). This is yet a further experience of breaking us, for we must bury her in a grave from Heth (Hebrew: ChTh, one meaning of which being "broken prostrate"). And we must insist on buying it ourselves, not just allowing our Lord to give it to us. We must persist in our KPhR or atonement sacrifices.

The resulting union with our Lord, though, is very fruitful. We live to see our now-Christ-initiated ministries (Isaac) fulfilled in *beauty* (one meaning of the Hebrew RBQH for Rebekah) - Gen. 24.

In his later years Abraham took as a new wife Keturah (Hebrew: QTWRH, one meaning of which being "being perfumed with the odor of incense" - Genesis 25:1-8). This typifies our spirit now being obsessed with the pleasant aroma of intercessory prayer and worship. But note the fruit of that union, as listed in Genesis 25:2:

(1) Zimran (Hebrew: ZMRM, one meaning of which being "musical");

(2) Jokshan (Hebrew: YQShN, one meaning of which being "ensnaring", i.e., of souls to the Kingdom of God);

(3) Medan (Hebrew: MDN, one meaning of which being "discord and strife", i.e., as we experience misunderstanding and rejection by fellow Christians and are engaged in the spiritual warfare against satan);

(4) Midian (Hebrew: MDYN, one meaning of which being "contention and quarreling", i.e., again of the warfare we are now fully in);

(5) Ishbak (Hebrew: YShBQ, one meaning of which being "he (i.e., satan) will quit, leave us alone", finally as we persist in our warfare against him);

(6) Sheba (Hebrew: ShBAh, one meaning of which being "carrying away as captive" as we win souls from the enemy);

(7) Dedan (Hebrew: DDN, one meaning of which being "walking gently as judge", the true meaning of "meekness");

(8) Asshurim (Hebrew: AhShWRM, one meaning of which being "those who are successful in righteousness");

(9) Letushim (Hebrew: LTWShM, one meaning of which being "those who are hammered and oppressed" - yes we will know persecution in the world, as He our Master knew);

(10) Leummim (Hebrew: LAhMYM, one meaning of which being "community gatherings", i.e., of local groups of the Body of Christ);

(11) Ephah (Hebrew: AhYPhH, one meaning of which being "obscurity", as in the world we have no renown, being covered only by Christ);

(12) Epher (Hebrew: IPhR, one meaning of which being "of dusty color", denoting our walk in the world as one on a "dusty" pilgrim's path, from that we need foot-washing - John 13:5 & 12-15);

(13) Hanoch (Hebrew: ChNWK, one meaning of which being "disciplined", as we indeed must become);

(14) Abida (Hebrew: AhBYDI, one meaning of which being "Father of Knowledge, wisdom", referring to our being true prophet-elders in the Body of Christ); and

(15) Eldaah (Hebrew: AhLDIH, one meaning of which being "God of knowledge and wisdom", Who will manifest Himself through us as those prophet-elders in the Body of Christ).

3. Jacob: Unto Righteousness

We next turn our attention to the patriarch Jacob/Israel, whose story is given in Genesis 25:24 through 50:14. Though he was set aside from birth by God for a special purpose, he was quite scheming and selfish in the flesh. His name was initially Jacob (Hebrew: YIQB, one meaning of which being "one who supplants; follows with evil intent; deceives"). But after harsh dealings in his life, God renamed him Israel

(Hebrew: YShRAhL, one meaning of which being "he will rule as God" - literally: "man in regal relationship with God", or simply "prince of God"). So the primary lessons of his life are how our Lord molded him into a righteous servant suitable to be Israel, "prince of God." See Row [66] of Sanctification Stages Chart Twelve which summarizes how we relate his life to the three general stages of sanctification.

Regeneration And Carnal Stage:

At the time of Jacob's birth, Isaac and Rebekah lived by Beer-lahai-roi (Hebrew: BAhR-LChY-RAhY, one meaning of which being "well or spring of my vision") which typifies that they were holding fast to the vision God had given them, even though Rebekah had been barren for 20 years (Genesis 25:11-23). Jacob was the second-born of twins, his brother being Esau (Hebrew: IShW, one meaning of which being "rough to touch or handle" - Genesis 25:24-26). *By law* Esau was to inherit the family "birthright", even though God had promised it to Jacob.

At an age of accountability, Jacob deceived Esau out of his birthright inheritance (Genesis 25:27-34). Although done through deception, that act was *legally binding* and was to play a major role in driving Jacob's life. His error, of course, was trying to fulfill God's promises by human means (including guile and dishonesty), rather than by trusting and waiting on God in faith. Oh how many times we also act that way! Nevertheless, Jacob acquiring the "birthright" typifies our being regenerated, our acquiring our "eternal birthright" in our Lord Christ Jesus, instead of the geneological Israelites who "should have" by Law.

Shortly after this, the family moves to Gerar (Hebrew: GRR, one meaning of which being "ruminating or meditating or mulling things over"), and settled by Beersheba or the "well of Shibah" (Hebrew: ShBIH, one meaning of which being "fullness in that which God has sworn or promised" - Genesis 26:17-33). There more intrigue took place, this time by Rebekah, who with Jacob's help "tricks" the aged Isaac to actually bestow the family birthright on Jacob rather than Esau (Genesis 27:1-35). Esau's anger is cause for Jacob to depart (Genesis 27:36-28:5). In the meantime, Esau settles down, marries Mahalath (Hebrew: MChLTh, one meaning of which being "sickness"), a daughter of Ishmael (Hebrew: YShMIAhL, one meaning of which being "God will pay attention to"). So Esau, though remaining in close companionship with "sickness", is indeed not abandoned by God. Oh how marvelous is our Lord's patience with us, even when we choose wrong paths in life!

Natural (Soulical) And Spiritual Stages:

So, Jacob departed. His mother Rebekah did not want him to settle in an area where he would likely marry a "daughter of Heth" (Hebrew: ChTh, one meaning of which being "broken; prostrate"), so she sent him back to her home land. Oh how much unnecessary suffering we might avoid if we would allow our Lord Christ Jesus to humble and prostrate us in the first place. Nevertheless, he goes back to Haran (Hebrew: ChRN, one meaning of which being "mountaineer; from a high region" - Genesis 27:10), that route being through Paddan-aram (Hebrew: PhDN-AhRM, one meaning of which being "high plateau"), a type of the "mountain-top" experiences our Lord sometimes blesses us with in order to sustain us when He knows we will be in the desert in the future. He is returning to Laban (Hebrew: LBN, one meaning of which being "maker of fired white bricks; worldly employer"), son of Bethuel (Hebrew: BThWAhL, one meaning of which being "dwelling in God - Genesis 28:5). Indeed he was to serve there for over 20 years.

But what a "mountain-top" experience first. The story of Jacob's Ladder" is found in Genesis 28:11-22. At a place called Luz (Hebrew: LWZ, one meaning of which being "turned aside; perverse" - that Jacob certainly was at that point in his life), God gave him a vision of his access to heaven. He saw that he was in the *presence* of God. He renamed the place Bethel (Hebrew: BYThAhL, one meaning of which being "dwelling place of God"). To be plunged into a vivid awareness of God is the essence of our being Baptised into the Holy Spirit by our Lord Christ Jesus!

Jacob fell in love with Laban's second daughter Rachel (Hebrew: RChL, one meaning of which being "female traveler or wanderer, as a sheep or goat"). But after 7 years of labor he first married Laban's first daughter Leah (Hebrew: LAhH, one meaning of which being "weary; tired; disquieted", as all of us become when trying to serve by human strength). One week later he marries Rachel, but ends up serving Laban 13 more years (Genesis 29:1-30). Jacob prospers during this time, *via* "legal guile" (Genesis 30:25-43), but finally has to leave due to contention between he and Laban (Genesis 31:1-9). Those of us in the "spirit-filled" walk find ourselves in increasing contention with our worldly employment.

Before we trace his departure and subsequent dealings by God in this life, let is quickly review the fruits of his years of labor under Laban. The sons and daughter born of his wives

Our Cloud Of Witnesses

(Genesis 29:32-30:24) were:

(1) Of Leah (weariness): Reuben (Hebrew: RAhWBN, one meaning of which being "to directly behold a son who will build the family name"). Optimistic encouragement is indeed a good start!

(2) Also of Leah: Simeon (Hebrew: ShMIWN, one meaning of which being "hearing intelligently; receiving discernment"). Yes, spiritual discernment indeed is one of the consequences of our being Baptised into the Holy Spirit.

(3) Again of Leah: Levi (Hebrew: LWY, one meaning of which being "united; twined with; attached to; joined with"). Another fruit of the Holy Spirit in our lives is to be an increased union with our Lord Christ Jesus.

(4) Fourth of Leah: Judah (Hebrew: YhWDH, one meaning of which being "use of hands to celebrate and/or praise"). Yes, even though we labor in weariness, we bear some fruit and we praise Him!

Rachel (our wanderings), in the meantime, remained barren. But of her servant Bilhah (Hebrew: BLHH, one meaning of which being "timid; terrified; fearful" - a state we often reach during our wanderings), were born:

(5) Dan (Hebrew: DN, one meaning of which being "vindicated; judged and approved").

(6) A second son by Bilhal is Naphtali (Hebrew: NPhThLY, one meaning of which being "struggling as in wrestling; twisting; entwining").

Yes, even in our fearfulness during wanderings, God blesses us with awareness of our vindication and of our lives increasingly being entwined with our Lord Christ Jesus, as "wait on the Lord" in Isaiah 40:31 means.

In our weariness we continue to bear fruit. Leah's maid was Zilpah (Hebrew: ZLPhH, one meaning of which being "oozing, dripping, as myrrh", and that speaks of the beginnings of our death of self). Out of that came:

(7) Gad (Hebrew: GD, one meaning of which being "distribution of provisions"); and

(8) Asher (Hebrew: AhShR, one meaning of which being "blessed, bubbling; demonstrating charisma").

As we embrace our Lord's emptying us of self, we increasingly discover the richness of his provisions toward us and we bubble over in exuding the Life of the indwelling Holy Spirit of Christ Jesus unto others.

Three further fruit of Leah (weariness) yet continued:

(9) Issachar (Hebrew: YShShKR, one meaning of which being "reward; compensation; salary");

(10) Zebulun (Hebrew: TsBLWN, one meaning of which being "residence; habitation"); and

(11) a daughter Dinah (Hebrew: DYNH, one meaning of which being "tribunal, justice, plea").

Though we labor and serve in weariness, if we faithfully persist, we see ever clearly our rewards (position with Christ in the heavenlies), and that the very Holy Spirit of Christ Jesus dwells in us, bringing justice.

Finally our wanderings bear fruit directly:

(12) of Rachel (our wanderings), Joseph (Hebrew: YWSPh, one meaning of which being "adding; augmenting; increasing"). "God has taken away my reproach", said Jacob; and indeed with us as we see the Kingdom increased by our *Lord's* use of us. (We will discuss (13), Benjamin, in a

moment.)

It was not easy for Jacob to leave his serving Laban, and it is never easy for us to leave our serving those in the world about us and totally abandon ourselves unto God. It first requires specific directions from God (Genesis 31:10-13). Those directions, however, involved going *via* Paddan-aram again (another walking in the "high places" with God) unto Gilead (Hebrew: GLID, one meaning of which being "visible witnessing or testifying" - Genesis 31:14-21). We finally have to make our peace with the world, as Jacob did with Laban at Jegar-Sahadutha (Hebrew: YGR-ShHDWThAh, that also has as one meaning "dwelling as a testimony of worthlessness"). We finally see that our self-efforts are worthless. But our witnessing is no longer by our efforts; it is a result of our Lord, dwelling in us, doing the doing. Furthermore, our witness is of *Christ Himself in us* (not just words of knowledge *about* Him)!

Jacob reached Gilead and sees angels; as a result he calls that camp Mahanaim (Hebrew: MChNYM, one meaning of which being "double encampment" - Genesis 32:1-2). The culmination of the vision we receive upon being Baptised into the Holy Spirit, and the vision for our third stage of sanctification, is that we see ourselves no longer servants of the world (Laban), but as vessels through whom He, our Lord Christ Jesus dwelling in us, does the serving. "It is no longer I who lives, but Christ lives in me; and the life that I now live in the flesh I live by faith in the Son of God, who loved me, and delivered Himself for me" shouts Paul in Galatians 2:20. We are a double encampment, yes; but finally *He* in us now waxes stronger than does the "I" in each of us.

Yet we are still in the world, and much of the world is still in us. Hence the next steps are emptying cycles. Esau, typifying the world still in us, is in Seir (Hebrew: ShIYR, one meaning of which being "rough") in Edom (Hebrew: AhDM, one meaning of which being "mankind" - Genesis 32:3-21). We are facing the brook Jabbok! Jabbok in the Hebrew is YBQ, one meaning of which being "emptying; pouring *out of*". What does Jabbok empty? A valley (Hebrew: BQIH, that might be translated "a cleft place, a place without a clear vision"); hence a place of confusion and indecision. That valley is between Gilead (Hebrew: GLID, one meaning of which being "visible witnessing or testifying" as we said above) and Ammon (Hebrew: IMWN, one meaning of which being "fellows; multitude", i.e., of the world). We even have to be emptied of *our* indecision between *witnessing* of Christ, on one hand, and *fellowshipping* with the world's ways, on the other hand.

We first send all we ourselves can across that emptying. Then we must face it alone (Genesis 32:24-32). But as a result of our struggling with the Lord in the darkest night of our soul, He not only becomes our ruler and Lord indeed, but he calls us to rule with Him. That is the true meaning of Israel (Hebrew: YShRAhL, one meaning of which being "he will rule as God; man in regal relationship with God almighty"). As we now see us in our heavenly position with Christ, we see Him face-to-face at Peniel (Hebrew: PhNYAhL, one meaning of which being "direct appearance of God; seeing God face to face").

Our relationship with the world now changes. Esau greeted Jacob (Genesis 33:1-16), but basically in peace. For the world no longer has us in bondage, nor has our fear of men. Oh, we still know sufferings in this world, even more intensely (Genesis 33:17-35:8): warfare against Hamor (Hebrew: ChMWR, one meaning of which being "rearing up, as a he-ass or mule"); sins and warfare among our family members, and everything that is orderly in our lives. Our Deborahs (Hebrew: DBWRH, one meaning of which being "to set or arrange in order") die and are buried in sorrow (Allon-Bachuth, Hebrew AhLWN-BKWTh, one meaning of which being "oak of mourning"). But once again God blesses us, now as "Israel", and confirms His promises (Genesis 35:9-15).

In route to Ephrath (Hebrew: AhPhRTh, one meaning of which being "fruitfulness"), Rachel gave birth during *severe* labor, and then died. Though our wanderings in this world are over, we soon see that *our* Ben-oni (Hebrew: BN-AhWNY, one meaning of which being "son of my sorrows") is to be *God's* Benjamin (Hebrew: BN-YMYN, one meaning of which being "son of the right hand; son of strength"). So, our wanderings over, we settle in Bethlehem, "house of bread of God" (Genesis 35:19-20). We live to see our sons, the fruit of our life, settled and blessed by God through us (Genesis 49:1-28). In due time, we are removed to Atad (Hebrew: AhTD, one meaning of which being "pierced, as a love-slave" - Genesis 50:10-14). Our life has not been in vain; we even end up in God's "hall of fame" (Hebrews 11:21). Hallelujah!

4. Joseph: Unto Forgiveness

The story of the patriarch Joseph is found in Genesis 30:22-24 and 37:3 through 50:26. Perhaps the most outstanding characteristic of Joseph was *forgiveness:* of Potiphar's wife who falsely accused him; of the Pharoah's cupbearer who failed to help him get out of prison at first; and most of all, his brothers who sold him into slavery out of jealousy in the first place. So certain was he of God being in control of his life, that we have no record in the Word of resentment toward his enemies nor of his exploitation of others over whom he had authority. Surely his life is worth scrutiny as to the dealings of God in his life that wrought such marvelous characteristics. See Row [67] of Sanctification Stages Chart Twelve which summarizes how we relate his life to the three general stages of sanctification.

As mentioned above, Joseph in the Hebrew is YWSPh, one meaning of which being "adding, augmenting; increasing". Upon his birth, his father Jacob shouted "God has taken away my reproach", for at last he had the (first) fruit of Rachel's womb (Genesis 30:22-24). Rachel represents Jacob's wandering as a pilgrim in this world, our position actually being with Christ in the heavenlies (Ephesians 1:3 and Phillippians 3:20).

Regeneration And Carnal Stage:

The first event of significance in Joseph's life that we encounter in the Word is recorded in Genesis 37:3, where we read that his father placed upon his shoulders a "coat of many colors". The Hebrew of "coat" here is KThNTh, one meaning of which being "covering of the burdens/roles we must bear" - literally "covering of the shoulders". That translation was indeed prophetic, for he was to bear many burdens, though he knew God's covering through them all. But also implicit in the phrase "coat of many colors" is a ceremonial token of rank, given to him in some public (family) ritual. It implies a recognition that Joseph, not the firstborn son Reuben, was

Our Cloud Of Witnesses 465

ultimately to inherit the family "birthright". At any rate we see it as a type of *regeneration*. Joseph was 17 years of age at the time, and his mother Rachel had previously died after giving birth to his youngest brother Benoni/Benjamin. His father Jacob/Israel loved him more than his brothers. So, of course, his brothers hated him with intense jealousy. And to make matters more intense, Joseph had a dream that in time he would rule over all of his brothers in authority (Genesis 37:4-11).

In Genesis 37:12-17, we see some very interesting types of many evangelical Christian churches today. Jacob/Israel, typifying God our father, sent Joseph to his brothers to see about their welfare. Where are they? In the valley of Hebron (Hebrew: ChBRWN, one meaning of which being "place of the congregation") in Shechem (Hebrew: ShKM one meaning of which being "place of burdens") at Dothan (Hebrew: DThYN, one meaning of which being "legalism"). Oh how many of us, deeply steeped in Christian legalism, are trying to bear the burdens of one another by human efforts!

But do the brothers *want* to be helped, be set free? No! They want nothing to do with their brother. Reuben, who would normally inherit the Birthright, argued to save Joseph's life (Genesis 37:21-22); nevertheless, they sell him into slavery of traders of Midian (Hebrew: MDYN, one meaning of which being "contention"), who in turn sell him to Potiphar (Hebrew: PhWThYPhR, one meaning of which being "violate or break into pieces in contempt"). Often when we try to minister to fellow Christians, they turn against us, we get the "left foot of fellowship", and we end up serving the world just to survive.

Natural (Soulical) And Spiritual Stages:

But Potiphar blessed Joseph, and Joseph prospered as Potiphar's steward (Genesis 39:1-6). This being Joseph's first experience of having power and authority (under Potiphar's authority), can be a type of our receiving the Baptism into the Holy Spirit, the first time we under the authority of our Lord Christ Jesus demonstrate in our lives the power and authority of the indwelling Holy Spirit.

But our power and authority, our opportunities to "minister", soon are sacrificed on Mt. Moriah. Genesis 39:7-23 tells the story of how Joseph, tricked by false accusations, ends up in jail. How many Judas's have you known in your ministry?

Our days of infamy are many; the tunnel is dark and long. Joseph's lasted two full years. But God blessed Joseph where he was, albeit in prison. God blessed Joseph in prison by enabling him to minister to other prisoners, and peace and order reigned with all even while in bondage. How beautiful a picture that is of how we serve one another in the Body of Christ no matter what be our station in life, if we would be but faithful to whatever and whenever God has called us. He even blessed Joseph with the prophetic word, that in this case was in a dream and its interpretation regarding two fellow prisoners (Genesis 40:1-25).

Light came at last at the end of Joseph's tunnel. Genesis 41:1-13 tells the story of how his prophetic ministry came to the attention of Pharoah who heeded it. Joseph faithfully obeys his God, and is elevated by Pharoah to great stewardship over all of Egypt (Genesis 41:14-52). Joseph became the National Treasurer: certainly the culmination of the vision of the

Our Cloud Of Witnesses

Baptism into the Holy Spirit in type. He marries Asenath (Hebrew: AhSNTh, one meaning of which being "hurt one"), daughter of Potiphara (Hebrew: PhWTYPRI, one meaning of which being "delivered from contempt"), priest of On (Hebrew: AhWN, one meaning of which being "successful through self-exertion"). And two sons are born of this union: Manasseh (Hebrew: MNShH, one meaning of which being "causing to forget") and Ephraim (Hebrew: AhPhRYM, one meaning of which being "doubly fruitful"). "God has made me forget all my troubles and all my father's household". And "God has made me fruitful in the land of my affliction." Though his sufferings were real and very painful, Joseph saw vividly the mighty hand of God all throughout his life, and his faith remained strong as a result.

The next 14 years were fruitful indeed for all around, due to Joseph's faithfulness as Egypt's steward (Genesis 41:53-57 and 47:12-22). Joseph dispensed food first to his own family, then to all who would buy. He put the entire world into slavery under Pharoah (except the Egyptian priests). He also dispensed seed for all to plant, the harvest of which Pharoah is to receive a fifth.

Genesis Chapters 42 through 46 tell of Joseph being reconciled to his brothers and father, and their eventual settlement in Goshen (Hebrew: GShN, one meaning of which being "pinnacle"). Our forgiveness of others will bring them to a pinnacle of faith, if we be genuine servants of God and faithful stewards of His kingdom.

The story concludes in Genesis Chapters 48 through 50. When Joseph finally died (was translated), he was buried in Egypt. But not until he witnesses the rich blessings to come to his people. Jacob/Israel prophecied over his sons, and especially over the two sons of Joseph. He then assured his burial back in the land of his forefathers, and died. But the Hebrews remained in Goshen for several centuries, until God's time came once again for a remarkable deliverance.

5. Moses: Unto Overcoming People's Ungodly Demands

Moses, of course, stands out among the Old Testament men of God as one who received the greatest revelations from God and who knew God's ways so thoroughly as to give to God's people in writing the Old Testament Law. Indeed the first five books of the Bible are attributed to him as the one whom God used to write.

However, another characteristic of Moses also stands out: his withstanding the ungodly demands that people, both people of the world and the people of God, constantly placed on him. It wearied him, utterly at times; and in his weariness he even erred some. But in general he held fast to the ways of God as divinely revealed to him, and he steadfastly led and judged the people accordingly. It is this characteristic we now emphasize: how God dealt in his life to bring him to that. See Row [68] of Sanctification Stages Chart Twelve which summarizes how we relate his life to the three general stages of sanctification. In the succeeding section we in turn study how those dealings changed the Israelite people themselves.

Regeneration And Carnal Stage:

The story of Moses starts in Egypt in Exodus Chapter 1. The Israelites, brought to Egypt centuries earlier under Joseph, had settled in Goshen where they were respected for a while. However, a new Pharoah arose who no longer respected them; he actually feared them because they had out-populated the Egyptians in that area of the land. As a strategy to constrain them, he placed then into slavery, primarily in the making of bricks by firing a mixture of mud and straw. Two cities are mentioned for their slavery: Pithom (Hebrew: PhThM, one meaning of which being "breaking into pieces") and Raamses (Hebrew: RIMSS one meaning of which being "violently shaking"). How that often speaks of our sorry state as slaves to worldliness, before we come to Christ.

Moses was born of the tribe of Levi. That in itself is prophetic, for Levi in the Hebrew (LWY) has as one meaning "to join"; God used Moses mightily to unite His people with Him through the Mosaic covenant law. Exodus 6:20 gives us his father and mother; his father was Amram (Hebrew: IMRM, one meaning of which being "exalted tribe or group of people"), and his mother was Jochebed (Hebrew: YWKBD, one meaning of which being "glorified by God"). So Moses was indeed special to God even in the womb. And even his birth was special, seeing the midwives (Exodus 1:15): Shiphrah (Hebrew: ShPhRH, one meaning of which being "brightness") and Puah (Hebrew: PhWAhH, one meaning of which being "brilliance"). Nevertheless, due to persecution by the Pharoah who knew not the Israelites (a type of satan who rules the world but knows not the people of Christ), shortly after birth he was hidden in the river Nile (Hebrew: YAhWR, one meaning of which being "confinement"), also called Sihor (Hebrew: ShYChWR, one meaning of which being "dark; turbid").

Moses as a baby was rescued by a daughter of Pharoah's house, who saw him and in full knowledge of what she was doing took the baby to raise him (Exodus 2:5-11). She named him Moses (Hebrew: MShH, one meaning of which being "drawn out, as from confinement; rescued"). We see this as typifying our being born again, our being rescued from our confinement to our sins and from our guilt thereof. And he grew up as a prince in Pharoah's house, being highly educated according to Egyptian knowledge. How like us today in "affluent" America. He even had his own mother as his nursemaid, who taught him also of the ways of God.

In early manhood, he saw the sorry plight of his people in slavery to the system in which he had become a prince. But not yet knowing the power of God, he tried to deliver them by his own strength, the result being a fiasco (Exodus 2:11-15). Not only were the Egyptians after him now for having murdered one of them, but the Israelites themselves resented his interference. Oh how often even people chosen by God resent our attempts to lead them to a deeper walk with our Lord Christ Jesus!

So Moses escaped to the plain east of Midian (Hebrew: MDYN, one meaning of which being "contention"), in the south-west corner of the lands now occupied by the nation of Arabia. There he met the priest of Midian whose name is Reuel (Hebrew: RIWAhL, one meaning of which being "friend of God"), also called Jethro (Hebrew: YThRW, one meaning of which being "abundant"). How fortunate that even in our flight, even in the midst of contention, God provides his companionship and abundant provisions for us.

Moses married Reuel's daughter Zipporah (Hebrew: TsPhRH, one meaning of which being "hopping; skipping; as in happiness"). Two sons are born: Gershom (Hebrew: GRShWM, one meaning of which being "refugee; driven out of our possession"); and Eliezer (Hebrew: AhLYIZR, that might be translated "God is protection and covering" - Exodus 18:1-4). We must never forget that we are still refugees in this world under the supernatural covering and protection of God, even though we must spend many years "to the east of the Midian desert", contending with the affairs of this world.

Natural (Soulical) And Spiritual Stages:

On the *backside* (Hebrew: AhChWR, one meaning of which being "away from") of the Midian desert (Hebrew for "desert": MDBR, one meaning of which being "place driven to") is Mount Horeb (Hebrew: ChRB, one meaning of which being "desolate" - Exodus 3:1). Our wanderings finally take us there. When we are least expecting it, God calls us by confronting us with a burning ("fiery") but not consumed ("being devoured") bush (Hebrew for "bush": SNH, one meaning of which being "thorn or prick" - Exodus 3:2). This is yet another type of our receiving the Baptism into the Holy Spirit: we radiating the energy of the Holy Spirit in us (yet not being devoured by Him) and being a thorn or goad to non-Christians and nominal Christians about us.

God promised Moses several things (Exodus 3:7-9). He would use Moses as part of His workings to bring deliverance (Hebrew: NTsL, one meaning of which being "snatch away; rescue") from affliction (Hebrew: INY, one meaning of which being "depression; misery"), unto milk (Hebrew: ChLB, one meaning of which being "fat; choicest part") and honey (Hebrew: DBSh, one meaning of which being "stickiness; persistence"). His deliverance of His people will be *from:*

Canaanites (Hebrew: KNINY, one meaning of which being "humiliation"); Hittites (Hebrew: ChThY, one meaning of which being "confined"); Amorites (Hebrew: AhMRY, one meaning of which being "publicly exposed"); Perizites (Hebrew: PhRZY, one meaning of which being "aimlessness"); Hivites (Hebrew: ChWY, one meaning of which being "encampment, as in the world"); and Jebusites (Hebrew: YBWSY, one meaning of which being "trodden down"). God will use us, *via* His Holy Spirit in us, to bring such a wonderful deliverance to His people, if we will be faithful in our love-motivated and Spirit-empowered servanthood in ministry in the Body of Christ.

Next God sent Moses off to contend with Pharoah (Exodus 3:10-22). This is our commission unto spiritual warfare, wherein we will use our staff (Hebrew for "staff": MTH, one meaning of which being "extension" - we are an "extension" of our Lord Christ Jesus Himself - Exodus 4:2). We will not do it alone: our brother Aaron (Hebrew: AhHRWN, one meaning of which being "enlightenment" - the enlightenment that comes only from the indwelling Holy Spirit of Christ Jesus) will accompany us all the way. And even though we still are refugees (Gershom) in this world, we must be especially marked and certified (circumcised) as belonging to God, lest we perish (Exodus 4:14-26).

As we get into the spiritual warfare and we demand of Pharoah (satan) to "let God's people go", our relationship with God is very special: He is our El Shaddai (Hebrew: AhL ShDY), one meaning of which being "almighty nursing breast" - a relationship of total provision, total protection, total nurturing, providing we totally yield unto Him (Exodus 6:3).

The plagues that God sends against satan in this warfare are typified in Exodus Chapters 8 through 11; they consist of harassments and annoyances of increasing severity, finally resulting in devastation, darkness, and death of all that is dearest to those of the world. But God's provision for His people, those who obey Him, is marvelous in the midst of this, as the Passover story of Exodus Chapter 12 describes. Also the remarkable deliverance as typified by the Red Sea crossing, where Pharoah's army (satan's forces) cannot follow us (Exodus Chapters 13-15). The song of Moses (Exodus 15:1-18) upon seeing the results of God's deliverance of His people through our ministry, is indeed a culmination of the vision of the Baptism into the Holy Spirit.

Our emptyings and God's miraculous providings are just beginning. In Shur (Hebrew: ShWR one meaning of which being "wanderings about") we encounter bitter water, that He turns to sweet (Exodus 15:22-26). At Elim (Hebrew: AhYLM, one meaning of which being "strength") we rest and gain strength in God. We must go through the wilderness of Sin (Hebrew: SYN, one meaning of which being "uncomfortable, as thorny"), but when we reach Mount Horeb (formerly "desolate") it is now Mount Sinai (Hebrew: SYNY, one meaning of which being "cloudy; hidden as behind a veil"). There *we* see God face to face, though those we leave behind cannot.

The many details of the following wanderings of the Israelites we study in the next section. Here we note that as far as Moses was concerned, those forty years were very vexing. First of all, those years were *unnecessary*, having been caused by the Israelites **lack of faith**. Second, they were *grievous*, seeing how God had often had to deal harshly with their *rebelliousness*. And third, they were *aimless*, for God had to deal with their hearts before He could lead them according to His purposes for them. Yet, through it all, God indeed guided them, and provided their food and water.

How did Moses overcome these unnecessary and grievous vexations placed on him by the ungodly among God's people? *We* do by learning to trust in our Lord Christ Jesus for *all* things and to work all things to good for those who love and trust Him and are called according to His purpose (Romans 8:28).

The story of Moses closes in Deuteronomy 34:5, where he died on Mt. Nebo (Hebrew: NBW, one meaning of which being "prophecy of God"). That is our ultimate rest: what saith the Lord!

6. Wandering Israelites: Unto Singleness Of Purpose

In the preceding chapter in this volume, we briefly discussed how the story of the Israelites wanderings, as documented in the Biblical books Exodus through Joshua, give in type a *theological* perspective of our three general stages of personal sanctification by the workings of the indwelling Holy Spirit of Christ Jesus. We pointed out how the events from Passover night through the Red Sea crossing give us rich insights on many theological aspects of our *regeneration* by our Lord Christ Jesus. We further pointed out how the receiving of the Law through Moses on Mt. Sinai typified our being *Baptized into the Holy Spirit* by our Lord Christ Jesus. And we also showed how the events from the Jordan crossing up to and including the victory of Jericho, pointed to our final victory in *appropriating our position in Christ* in the heavenlies now.

Here we revisit the story of the Israelites' wilderness wanderings from Mt. Sinai through Gilgal to Jericho, but now from a different point of view. Here we focus on the details of the wilderness walk itself, as those details typify our experiential emptying and mountain-top experiences during the second and third general stages. See Row [69] of Sanctification Stages Chart Twelve which summarizes how we relate their escapades to the three general stages of sanctification. Though the Israelites had richly and repeatedly experienced the Hand of God to protect and provide for them, nevertheless they had many aspects of their lives (specifically of their thought patterns) that needed to be changed. In essence, like so many of us after we have received the Baptism into the Holy Spirit, we desire the *blessings* of God but still resist appropriating His *purpose* for our lives. Hence, we need to be purged of self-seeking purposes, and become single-minded in yieldedness to His Will in ways that are often beyond our understandings and are always contrary to our desires of the flesh.

Let us first recall how God guided them during their forty years. Exodus 13:18-22 talks about a pillar of cloud by day and of fire by night. Pillar in Hebrew is IMWD, one meaning of which being "standing (hence highly visible) column"; cloud in Hebrew is INN, one meaning of which being "covering"; and fire in Hebrew here is AhSh, that not only means "fiery; hot" but also one other meaning of which is "covertly covering". Hence God, in a highly visible way, covered them in all they did, and kept them hidden from the enemy except for those times when His will directed otherwise.

Let us also recall how God provided their needs during their forty years. Exodus 16: 13 & 31 mention quails and manna for food. Quails in Hebrew is ShLYN, one meaning of which being "sluggish; slow in flight (hence easy to capture)"; manna in Hebrew is MN, one meaning of which being "what?; how?" and denotes bafflement as to what it was. Deuteronomy 29:5 is also astonishing and baffling: "... forty years in the wilderness; your clothes have not worn out on you, and your sandal has not worn out on your foot." So, even though *how* God provided their needs lies beyond our intellectual understanding and involved sustained supernatural miracles, it was real and totally met their needs.

But were they satisfied? No! Are we? We don't like the uncertainty of walking in blind faith! And although we know God provided and protected in the past, do we really know that He will do so *now in this present trial?* I smell the age-old lie of satan here: "Hath God *really* said?" (Genesis 3:1). Oh our intrinsic sin of unbelief: does Christ really intend to meet my needs and keep me from being hurt beyond my ability to withstand? And if He is *able*, will He *actually do so?* This sin of unbelief is rooted in my sin of intrinsic aversion to God in the first place: I don't fully apprehend His tremendous forgiveness, love and acceptance of me, a sinner, as I now am.

These sin-rooted dissatisfactions quickly became apparent in three ways: (1) thirst when a source of drinking water was not *immediately* apparent; (2) fear when *danger* appeared; and (3) nostalgic longings in the face of everything being *unfamiliar*, those nostalgic longings being primarily in the form of *religious practices* and *food tastes*.

The first arose almost immediately after they left the Red Sea crossing. Exodus 15:22-26 tells us of how the people grumbled at Marah when they discovered the waters too bitter with mineral content to be fit to drink. God used Moses to sweeten the waters. But not until after the people bitterly grumbled against Moses for having brought them out there. Yet God not only sweetened those waters, He then led them to Elim, a marvelous oasis in the desert, for rest and refreshment.

Okay, God provided for us last week and yesterday. But now we're in the wilderness of Sin (Hebrew: SYN, one meaning of which being "thorny, prickly; uncomfortable"), camped at Rephidim (Hebrew: RPhYDYM, one meaning of which being "those that are spread all over the place") before Mount Horeb (Hebrew: ChRB, one meaning of which being "desolate; parched") with absolutely no water anywhere in sight (Exodus 17:1-7). God can't possibly get us through this testing! So, grumbling again! But God *did*, once again. "And they named the place Massah (Hebrew: MSH, one meaning of which being 'testing; temptation') and Meribah (Hebrew: MRYBH, one meaning of which being 'provocation; strife'" - Exodus 17:7). Maybe someday we might actually learn to really trust in God.

And then again, maybe not. For now Amalek (Hebrew: IMLQ, one meaning of which being "misery; sorrow") fights against us, and we are having a grand old "pity party" (Exodus 17:8-13). But God, once again! This time He used Joshua (Hebrew: YHWShWI, one meaning of which being "saved by YHWH-God") and Hur (Hebrew: ChWR, one meaning of which being "made white," i.e., by the shed blood of our Lord Christ Jesus), together with Moses' undergirding (i.e., a type of intercessory prayer ministries). Victory was obtained, and we now see God as our Jehovah-Nissi (Hebrew: YHWH-NSY, one meaning of which being "God is my military banner/flag/standard").

Okay, that was three months ago. Now again I'm at Rephidim before Mount Horeb (Exodus 19:1ff). Yeah, it's now called Mount Sinai, "the mountain of anointing". And yeah Moses has given us some marvelous words that he heard from God up there. But now we're in the midst of horrible earthquakes and volcanic eruptions, and Moses is up there out of sight, probably perishing in the violence. Help! Maybe if we can quickly reconstruct the kind of religious services we used to know twenty years ago in denominationalism, and serve God as we used to, there's hope. But we'll have to act quickly. At least that's what Aaron, our "enlightened one", is telling us to do (Exodus 32).

Did that work? "Then the Lord smote the people, because of what they did with the calf that Aaron had made" (Exodus 32:35). What? Even though it's Aaron's fault for leading us that way, God smotes *me?* Well, if I had laid hold of God's purpose for my being out here in the first place, I wouldn't have been led astray!

But God, once again! He forgives and re-promises. He gave to Moses His Law once again, and this time even added to it (Exodus 33-40). Out of this comes a marvelous tabernacle in which to worship God, one in which each of us, no matter how mature we are in our relationship with Him, can worship Him appropriately. And God leaves us alone there for a whole year (Numbers 10:11-13)!

But don't rejoice too soon. Although that year in God's Presence should have left us fully settled in Him and His new ways for us, now come the real trials!

The first comes simply because God uproots us. We're now in the wilderness of Paran (Hebrew: PhAhRN, one meaning of which being "make an example of" - Numbers 10:12). But the people again started to complain, bringing some severe chastisements from God on them (Numbers 11:1-3). Those complaints became most widespread, this time over boredom *re* nothing but manna to eat (Numbers 11:4-35). Moses calls a fast and special consecration, but the people's greed grieved Moses. So God sent them quail which the greedy ones snatched up to eat to their death. So the place became Kibroth-Hattavah (Hebrew: QPRWTh-HThAhWH, one meaning of which being "place of burial of our desires" - Numbers 11:34-35). So, before we can go on to Hazeroth (Hebrew: ChTsRWTh, one meaning of which being "protected pastures"), we have to learn again to reckon our flesh crucified with Christ and buried with Him (Romans 6:5-11).

Oh no; now what's up with Miriam and Aaron? Moses's very sister and brother take it upon themselves to judge Moses in legalism (Numbers 12:1)! But God quickly teaches them the lesson, that *relationship with God* is the issue, not legalism, and that our role to one another is to *forebear one another in love* (John 15:17, Ephesians 4:2, Colossians 3:13, etc.) and leave the judging up to His Holy Spirit (John 16:8). It often seems that the closer we become to a Christian brother or sister, the more we tend to do that "judging" and the less we tend to do that "loving" (out of possessiveness).

Now at last we're ready for the final spiritual warfare against satan, and conquer the promised land? We're now at the north edge of the wilderness of Paran, at the very southern edge of the promised land (Numbers Chapters 13 and 14), at a place that Numbers 32:8 calls Kadesh-Barnea (Hebrew: QDSh-BRNI, one meaning of which being "holiness of life-style"). So, let's go!

But first, let's spy out the land, to see what we're up against. Twelve spies went out full of enthusiasm; ten returned defeated in attitude, only two still with enthusiasm. Murmuring like we've never heard before. Majority rules in favor of the sin of unbelief. May God deliver us from *democratic* procedures in the Body of Christ: He, not "the majority", is the Head! After two years of supernatural provision and protection by God; shame on us! So, instead of taking the land after two years of wandering, we must yet wait another 38 years! Furthermore, it won't be *us* who does it then; it will be the generation after us (Numbers 32:13). In the meantime, the enemy comes in and drives us off to Hormath (Hebrew: ChRMH, one meaning of which being "sanctification" - Numbers 14:45) for yet more dealings by the indwelling Holy Spirit of Christ Jesus.

Next came Korah's rebellion in Numbers 16:1-35. Korah (Hebrew: QRCH, one meaning of which being "stripped, bald, smooth") said to Moses and Aaron in vs. 3: "... all the congregation are holy, every one of them, and the Lord is in their midst; so why do you exalt yourselves above the assembly of the Lord?" Moses challenged them to a test as to who the Lord had chosen to lead, and the result was the Lord confirming Moses and causing an earthquake to destroy Korah and his followers.

Our Cloud Of Witnesses 481

That was during Old Testament times. Then only a specific few individuals (including Moses and Aaron, but not including Korah) are explicitly identified as having the Holy Spirit of the Lord in them. So Korah's claim that "all the congregation are holy, every one of them, and the Lord is in their midst" was *false,* was a lie. It was because of that *false claim* that the Lord destroyed them. But today under the New Covenant in Christ Jesus, *every* born-again believer, by virtue of the New Birth, *does* have the Spirit of Christ dwelling in him/her.

The remaining testings during the 38 years were many. In Numbers 16:36-17:13 we have a follow-up rebellion by the Israelites against Moses, that God answered by a purging plague, and a test wherein only Aaron's rod budded In Numbers 20:1-13 we see how the people again complained about no water, this time at Meribah (Hebrew: MRYBH, one meaning of which being "provocation; strife"), whereupon Moses, in exasperation, *struck* the rock instead of speaking to it. God answered by providing water, but the act cost Moses seeing the promised land (Numbers 20:8-13). That rock (Hebrew: SLI, one meaning of which being "elevated one") is Christ (1 Corinthians 10:4).

Miriam and Aaron, Moses' sister and brother, both died (Numbers 20:1 & 28); hence the Israelites lost two servant leaders on whom they had relied heavily for worship and enlightenment.

The king of Edom (Hebrew: AhDM, one meaning of which being "humanity") blocked the Israelites from passing through his territory (Numbers 20:14-21); we cannot expect help from people of the world when we are this far with our Lord. The Israelites had victory over the king of Arad (Hebrew: IRD, one meaning of which being "individual fugitive"); we should expect success in ministries on a one-to-one basis (Numbers 21:1-3). The people again complained about no food and water (though they still had manna), and God chastened them with fiery serpents. Our only deliverance from them is the lifting up of Christ dying on the Cross (Numbers 21:9 and John 3:14).

Numbers Chapters 21 through 32 list many other trials, and Chapter 33 summarizes the wanderings. Finally, 40 years after their deliverance from Egypt, they reached the western edge of the land of Moab, just across the Jordan river from Gilgal where they were to enter the land. Moses gave final instructions (Numbers 34:1 through Deuteronomy 34:5), and died on Mt. Nebo. Joshua ("salvation in YHWH-God") took over the leadership.

They passed through the Jordan (Hebrew: YRDN one meaning of which being "descending"), but only by *following* the *Presence of God in their midst.* That is our greatest emptying cycle, for after that final death of self and total obedience to God, we reach Gilgal (Hebrew: GLGL, one meaning of which being "trusting; commitment"). Thereafter, by totally trusting in God and obeying Him, we see tremendous victories, including Jericho (Hebrew: YRYChW, one meaning of which being "fragrant, fruitful"), and ultimately over the entire promised land.

But there was yet another, more fundamental issue, beyond their faithfulness. It was that they understood God's *purpose*. God's purpose is *not* for *us* "in faith" to possess the promised land; rather it is that *He through us* obtain that victory. That may be a small step in wording, but it is a mighty leap in meaning. Full sanctification is not for the faint-hearted. Who *truly* is Lord? Me, or Christ in me?

Another important detail: of the over two million Israelites who were delivered from Egypt by the sovereign hand of God, how many saw Gilgal and the promised land victories? Exactly two: Joshua and Caleb (Hebrew: KLB, one meaning of which being "hearty; forcible; aggressive"). They were the only two of the twelve spies who did not lose heart, who did not rebel against God, who did not complain nor murmur. All others died in the wilderness; it was the next generation, their sons and daughters, who possessed the land.

7. David: Unto Victory

David stands out among the Old Testament patriarchs as the great conqueror after Joshua. Indeed, as we see in 1 Kings 4:20-21 and 2 Chronicles 9:26, the area ruled over by his son Solomon after David died was exactly the territory promised by God to Abraham's seed. How did God prepare David for such a task?

See Row [70] of Sanctification Stages Chart Twelve which summarizes how we relate his life to the three general stages of sanctification.

We know that David himself came from very humble beginnings, even though his father Jesse was a wealthy and well-established man of Judah. David's exact genealogy is a bit confusing in the scriptures. For one thing, 1 Chronicles 2:13-15 lists David as the *seventh* son of Jesse, whereas 1 Samuel 16:10-11 specifies David to be the youngest son of Jesse out of *eight*. Also, 1 Chronicles 27:18 lists Elihu as one of David's brothers, but Elihu is not listed in 1 Chronicles 2:13-15 as one of the there-listed six bothers of David. It appears in the final analysis, therefore, that David was the youngest of eight sons of Jesse.

Another uncertainty is the identity and nationality or tribe of David's mother. 1 Chronicles 2:16 and 17 list two sisters of David: Zeruiah and Abigail (whose sons Abshai, Joab, Asahel and Amasa were to play major roles in David's army); but 2 Samuel 17:25 lists David's sister Abigail, and probably Zeruiah, as "daughters" (female decedents) of *Nahash*. Both of these passages list Ithra/Jether (variations of the same name in the Hebrew) as the father of Amasa by Abigail. Hence we know it is the same "Abiail" in both passages. Nahash is identified as king of the Ammonites, the sons of Ammon, in 1 Samuel 11:1-2, 1 Samuel 12:12, 2 Samuel 10:1-4 and 1 Chronicles 19:1-6. And although Nahash often warred against the Israelites, and at times harassed David, nevertheless David seems to have had some special relationship with him, because in these last two scriptures David determined to show kindness to Hanun, Nahash's son after Nahash died. Also, in 1 Samuel 22:3-4, when severely threatened, David left his aged mother and father in Mizpah for security, an area of Moab in which the Ammonites had settled. Yet a further strange detail: in Psalm 51:5 David referred to himself as having been "conceived in sin", that reference seeming to be more than just a reference to all of us having the intrinsic Adamic sin nature.

David's mother is not explicitly identified, but the most likely way to unravel these incongruities is to suggest that she was the daughter of a wife or concubine of Nahash, king of the Ammonites in Moab, and who married Jesse as his second wife, then a widower, probably *after* she conceived David. Hence she may have been a Moabitess as was Ruth, David's great grandmother.

These details and this speculation is of interest for several reasons. (1) It emphasizes the *humble* origins of David, that he was not born with a highly recognized and regarded "birthright" to begin with. Hence all of us can identify with David in that sense. (2) It underlies David not having originally been regarded as an equal to his seven older brothers in 1 Samuel 16: 5-11, and the lack of familial respect those older brothers had for David, as for example in 1 Samuel 17:28. (3) It tends to explain some of David's foreign ties, i.e. with Moab. (4) It would make sense that his mother would not have been explicitly identified in the Hebrew geneological records. And (5) it tends to explain why David had such a lowly and lonely task (shepherd of Jesse's sheep) as a boy.

Nevertheless, God works all things to good for those who love God and are called according to His purposes (Romans 8:28).

Here are some key names. David in the Hebrew is DWD, one meaning of which being "beloved; loving". Samuel, the prophet of God who was to play a major role in David's life, is in the Hebrew ShMWAhL, one meaning of which being "hearing intelligently from God". Saul in the Hebrew is ShAhWL, one meaning of which being "demanding". Jonathan in the Hebrew is YWNThN, one meaning of which being "given by YHWH". Michal in the Hebrew is MYKL, one meaning of which being "promising, as an empty container". Bathsheba in the Hebrew is BThShBI, one meaning of which being "daughter of promise/commitment".

And Solomon in the Hebrew is ShLMH, one meaning of which being "well-being; peace; wholeness".

Natural (Soulical) Stage:

The first mention of David is 1 Samuel 16:1-13, in which Samuel, upon the sovereign initiative and direction of God, anointed David to be a future king over Israel. We would liken this in type to our being Baptized into the Holy Spirit, since it involves an anointing of authority, even though its fulfillment would be yet many years. Sometime earlier, as a shepherd boy, David learned to deeply love, praise, and depend upon God, as we know from his musical abilities including singing songs of praise to God, and also from his victory over a lion and a bear.

Saul was not aware of this anointing having occurred. Nevertheless, David was chosen to serve as Saul's musician and armor-bearer. A member of his palace staff had recalled that a son of Jesse was a skillful musician and the Lord was with him (1 Samuel 16:14-23). This was how Saul first learned about and met David. Saul loved David, and David soothed Saul on many occasions. According to 1 Samuel 17:15, David was not continuously with Saul, having traveled back and forth between Gibeah where Saul's home was, about five miles north of Jerusalem, and Jesse's flock near Bethlehem, about the same distance but south of Jerusalem. Even when we have an anointing of God, we still must be faithful in serving those whom God appoints for us, both at home and abroad, until He leads otherwise.

God did soon lead otherwise: Goliath in the Hebrew is GLYTh, one meaning of which being "disgracefully exposed".

His challenge to disgracefully expose Israel had Saul's entire army in fear. David's remarkable defeat of Goliath is recorded in 1 Samuel 17:1-58.

Several results followed quickly. Saul at first latched onto David "full-time" (1 Samuel 18:2 & 5). Jonathan, Saul's son and rightful successor of Saul as King, bonded himself to David in covenant. And David married Michal (Saul's daughter and Jonathan's sister), who loved David (1 Samuel 18:20-29).

But David's popularity, both as an excellent musician/singer and as a national hero, quickly stirred up Saul's jealousy, that jealousy being based on a fear that David would become more popular than he and usurp his throne. Saul still knew nothing about Samuel's having anointed David, and David did nothing to seize the throne (he never did).

The chase was on. In 1 Samuel 19:1-17, Jonathan and Michal saved David's life by helping him escape Saul's house. David briefly visited Samuel, and David and Samuel went to Naioth (Hebrew: NYWTh, one meaning of which being "beautiful place to rest"). But Saul also went to Naioth, so David left, this time going back to discretely visit Jonathan (1 Samuel 20:1-17). Saul returned home. Jonathan warned David to leave again, that he did (rest of 1 Samuel 20).

Next stop: in Nob (Hebrew: NB, one meaning of which being "sprout; germinate as seed"), to the priest Ahimelech (Hebrew: AhYMLK, one meaning of which being "kindred of the king"), who fed him from the shewbread of the tabernacle and armed David with Goliath's sword (1 Samuel 21:1-9). Of course, for anyone other than a priest to eat the shewbread violated the Law; but we are not under the Law of Moses: we are anointed under the Law of the indwelling Holy Spirit of Christ Jesus, to show (glorify) Him.

David's next stop was to foreign land, to Achish (Hebrew: AhKYSh, one meaning of which being "to smite down"), king of Gath (Hebrew: GTh, one meaning of which being "trodden down"). No respite here; David pretended madness in order to save himself (1 Samuel 21:10-15). Even though we are under the anointing of the indwelling Holy Spirit, when at times we feel so trodden down and suppressed, we weaken in faith and try to protect ourselves by human means. That of course makes victory even more impossible. The purpose of these dealings of God in our lives is not to teach us to walk in our own strength in faith, but to let God establish His ways *through* us.

He next went to Mizpah ("stronghold") of Moab, where he left his aged father and mother for protection (see our comment above). David then went on to the forest of Hareth (Hebrew: ChRTh, one meaning of which being "forest; source of building materials"), having been warned by a prophet that Saul plans to attack him (1 Samuel 22:1-5) Saul indeed started his attack, slaughtering all the priests of Nob, including Ahimelech but excepting Abiathar (Hebrew: AhBYThR, one meaning of which being "father who provides liberally") who escaped and informed David (1 Samuel 22:6-23).

By this time David was acquiring a few followers and supporters, including his maternal nephews, who were forming a small army. We need to remember that in Christ we are never alone; not only do we have His indwelling Presence, He also provides a few supporters who will walk with us through our trials if we swallow our pride and ask and allow them to. David used his army, however, not to defend himself but to liberate other Israelites, namely those at Keilah (Hebrew: QIYLH, one meaning of which being "enclosed; confined" - *vs.* 23:1-5).

Saul continued to chase him (1 Samuel 23:6-24:22). First to Ziph (Hebrew: ZYPh, one meaning of which being "flowing; melting"), where David melted with fear (*vs.* 23:17). Then south of Jeshimon (Hebrew: YShYMWN, one meaning of which being "desolation") to the hill of Hachilah (Hebrew: ChKYLH, one meaning of which being "intensely agitated"). Next David went to the strongholds of Engedi (Hebrew: IYN-GDY, one meaning of which being "fountain of pasture", and that typifies Christ as our source of living water and as our great shepherd/protector), and rested in a cave. But even though David's faith was wavering to the point of fleeing for his life rather than trusting the Lord to save Him, nevertheless when he had the opportunity to kill Saul, he did not, out of respect for "God's anointed" (*vs.* 24:10).

David had a heart of both mercy and justice, as was demonstrated in 1 Samuel Chapter 25 *re* Nabal and his wife Abigail, and also *re* Michal his wife who Saul had reneged on and given to another man. Even though our faith may be weak almost unto death at times, let us at least continue to live in respect of God and His law and mercies.

1 Samuel Chapter 26 describes almost a repeat of the events in *vs.* 23:19-26. David with one of his maternal nephews stole into Saul's camp at night, and once again had the opportunity to slay Saul but did not. The next day, though, he taunted Abner, Saul's captain. David and Saul parted in peace for a

season.

David was regaining his faith to a slight extent. Nevertheless, he returned to Gath, where before he pretended madness to escape. He was now received kindly, we suspect due to maternal family influences. So, he and his small army of followers and their wives settled in Ziklag (Hebrew: TsQLG, one meaning of which being "tied up; bound"). But for a season David and his army covenanted with the Philistines. That cost him the capture of Ziklag, which he had to recapture (1 Samuel Chapters 27 and 30). We must be careful to never be yoked with the world (2 Corinthians 6:14 and Galatians 5:1); when we do, our problems only become confounded! Nevertheless, even in victory, David dispensed the spoils of his victories according to God's laws and not for his own personal gain.

In due course of time, despite our vain struggles, God gives us the victory! Not only these victories over the Philistines (i.e., over the forces of satan in our lives), but also over our enemies among the people of God, those who persecute us out of selfish ambitions, jealousy and spiritual deception. 1 Samuel Chapters 28, 29 and 31 tell us of Saul's death, totally apart from anything David did. And yet, even though Saul was David's enemy, he was of God's people, and hence David genuinely grieved over his death (2 Samuel 1:1-27). We must never gloat over the sufferings of fellow Christians, even those who persecute us; rather we are to love them, i.e., ever seek their spiritual wholeness and well-being (Matthew 5:44, Luke 6:27 & 35, etc.).

Spiritual Stage:

God having removed Saul the persecutor, the elders of Judah then publicly anointed David as their king (2 Samuel 2:1-7). This second anointing (out of three total) is a type of the culmination of the vision of our Baptism into the Holy Spirit. But it is also the beginning of another stage of emptying cycles.

Abner (Hebrew: AhBNR, that might be translated "father of lamplight; glistening, enlightening"), Saul's captain, tried to hold onto Saul's family rule by enthroning one of his sons for two years. But Joab, a maternal nephew and faithful follower of David, challenged them and ultimately removed them (2 Samuel 2:8-32 and 3:6-39). A long war between the houses of Saul and David followed, with David slowly winning. In the meantime, David settled at Hebron (Hebrew: ChBRWN, one meaning of which being "place of assembly"). And his family grew (2 Samuel 3:1-5).

The rest of David's life demonstrated a continued determination to live according to God's ways, despite his intrinsic human weaknesses. He honored his covenant with Jonathan *re* Mephibosheth (Hebrew: MPhYBShTh, one meaning of which being "dispeller of shame" - 2 Samuel 4:4). He executed the murderers (*vs.* 4:1-12). He also tried to glorify God, by capturing and building Zion (Hebrew: TsYWN, one meaning of which being "conspicuous stronghold") from Jebus (Hebrew: YBWSI, one meaning of which being "trodden down"), and renamed it "Jerusalem" (Hebrew: YRWShLM, one meaning of which being "dwelling in peace"). To glorify our Lord Christ Jesus, to lift Him up before the world, is always our goal.

He also brought back the Ark of Covenant (which meant the Presence of God in the midst of His people), although he quickly learned that that could be done only in God's ordained ways (2 Samuel Chapter 6). It had been in the house of Abinadab (Hebrew: AhBYNDB, one meaning of which being "father of liberal provision") in Baale-Judah (Hebrew: BILY-YHWDH, one meaning of which being "possessor/master of praise"). But David now brought the SHEKINAH (Hebrew: ShKNYH) Dwelling Glory-Presence of God before the entire people, to be *worshiped*, not just praised. Of course, even this is costly to us: those close to us, our Michals, will misunderstand, think us to be fools, and despise us. But let *God* bring the retribution (in Michal's case, she remained barren for the rest of her life - 2 Samuel 6:16, 20-23).

God even restores the prophet ministry to us (2 Samuel 7:1-29). Samuel having died, He now sent Nathan (Hebrew: NThN, one meaning of which being "given; provided; sent").

Final victories over our external enemies followed (2 Samuel 7 and 1 Chronicles 18).

However, it is often in the midst of our most glorious moments that God subjects us to yet another emptying cycle or cycles, to yet purify us. This time, however, the enemy is *within* us. It is within our geneological family. 2 Samuel 10 and 1 Chronicles 19 tell of humiliation caused to David's servants by the son of his maternal grandfather.

2 Samuel 11 tells of his sins with Bathsheba and Uriah, that exposed intrinsic sins of lust and dishonesty still lurking beneath the surface of David's heart. The immediate fruit of such sins become sick and die (2 Samuel 12:1-23), even

though the ultimate fruit, after our deep repentance, may well be our Solomon (Hebrew: ShLMH, one meaning of which being "prosperity; well-being") that in God's sight is a Jedidiah (Hebrew: YDYDYH, one meaning of which being "beloved of YHWH-God" - 2 Samuel 12:24-25).

2 Samuel Chapters 13 through 20 tell us of deep troubles that David's immediate family, his own sons and his maternal nephews, caused him, and the deep grief it cost him. We today tend to judge David when we read this, thinking it was his own fault for not having been faithful to his Christian responsibilities as a father to discipline his sons while they grew up. There indeed is truth to that. However, he dealt with his sons exactly the way God deals with us: never directly overriding our human wills but constantly trying to draw us by His love; telling us His ways so that we know how; but using circumstances in our lives to discipline us, not to punish us *per se*.

Yet even more of an issue here is that God is using whatever is closest and dearest to us to purge us of whatever is still in our hearts that is not fully yielded to our Lord Christ Jesus. We must not try to defend ourselves from those purging and emptying cycles, but embrace them and the lessons they teach us, so that the days of our final victory will be hastened.

Those days of final victory finally came to David (2 Samuel Chapter 21 through 1 Kings Chapter 1). God's purpose for his life was fully accomplished in his conquests of all lands promised to Abraham's seed. And his son Solomon followed Him, to rule to the glory of God for forty years, until the next stage of God's dealings with His people was to unfold.

8. Elijah: Prophet's Testings

One of the major workings of our Lord Christ Jesus today is the restoration of the *prophet* ministries to His Body. So it behooves us to take a few moments to study how He specifically prepares His servants for that ministry. One of the best examples to use for that study is Elijah. We find his story in 1 Kings Chapters 17 through 2 Kings Chapter 2. See Row [71] of Sanctification Stages Chart Twelve which summarizes how we relate his life to the three general stages of sanctification.

In 1 Kings 17:1, Elijah (Hebrew: AhLYHW, one meaning of which being "God almighty YHWH"), is identified as a "Tishbite" (Hebrew: ThShBY, one meaning of which being "returned; restored; converted") of Gilead (Hebrew: GLID, one meaning of which being "memorial of promises, testimonies, witnessings"). In type we see him as if already both regenerated and Baptized into the Holy Spirit.

We now study his life in terms of the victories and trials that a prophet of our Lord Christ Jesus is often subjected to, both to prepare him, and as part of his ministry.

The first event we read of his ministry was his confrontation with Ahab (Hebrew: AhChAhB, one meaning of which being "kindred of the father", and hence typifies those who are of our Adamic human heritage). All he told Ahab was that there would be a severe drought in the land until such a time as the Lord spoke through him (Elijah). What a picture of most of institutional Christianity today: though we are rich in the written Word of God and the fruits of His workings of the past, there is today a drought of the Logos and Rhema Word of God, and that condition will persist until the time comes when God will choose to speak forth through His prophetic ministries (that He is *now* raising up).

When will that be? Elijah then disappeared from Ahab for three and one-half years. During that time Ahab, like Christianity steeped in humanity, continued on his own efforts. That is trying to live without the living waters offered to us richly by our Lord Christ Jesus. Worshiping the Gods of Baal instead that are strongly forced upon us by the whore riches and power and religion of Babylon (Revelation 18:2-3) which has become so dear to us through our Jezebel (Hebrew: AhYZBL, one meaning of which being "dwelling with in cohabitation"). See our cautions against the darknesses of Baal and Jezebel in Chapter Eleven of Volume I[6] of this series.

During those three and a half years, God *also* had to prepare Elijah, the prophet ministries. 1 Kings 17:2-24 gives the story. He was first sent by the Lord eastward (Hebrew: QDYM, one meaning of which being "returning to basics, to one's origins"), where he hid by the brook Cherith (Hebrew: KRYTh, one meaning of which being "to covenant"), and had his needs provided by ravens (Hebrew: IRB, one meaning of which being "interwoven; braided with") (1 Kings 17:2-7). If we would go from Spirit-empowered ministries unto being prophets of God, we must return to the basics of the Word of God, abandon ourselves to our New Covenant relationship with our Lord Christ Jesus, and entwine our lives with Him. Then, in His timing, He will lead us to Zarephath (Hebrew: TsRPhTh, one meaning of which being "refined, as metal ore") in Zidon (Hebrew: TsYDWN, one meaning of which being "to ambush; to catch, as fish"). 1 Peter 1:7 talks about how, through trials, our faith becomes purified as ore by a refiner's fire. If we would be "fishers of men", we must witness not by our words but by our Christ-radiating lives, out of a purified faith.

Even then we cannot minister to others until those others *seek* it of us, and seek with a seeking that is sincere and intense. But when the widow did feed him, miracles followed, including resurrection of her firstborn son (1 Kings 17:8-24). If we would have our spirits resurrected, like the widow of Zidon we must seek out God's prophetic ministries and yield thereto, more and more so in the closing decade of this twentieth century and in the decade following.

At last God uses us to reach humanism-encrusted Christianity and others in bondage to Babylon (1 Kings Chapter 18). Elijah returned to Ahab. Ahab, having tried these years to watch over Samaria (Hebrew: ShMRWN, one meaning of which being "watch-station") as best he could under Baal domination, was really feeling the drought and famine. In the meantime, Obadiah (Hebrew: IBDYH, one meaning of which being "bondservant"), who greatly feared God, tried to protect and feed many prophets who would otherwise be destroyed by the priests of Baal. There are many faithful servants of our Lord Christ Jesus in His Body today who have been faithfully trying to protect those who He is raising up, from having been destroyed in faith by humanism during this drought of the prophetic word. Elijah first went to him (Obadiah), to: (1) encourage him; and (2) use him as a messenger to Ahab *re* his arrival. Indeed many faithful servants in the Body of Christ today are beginning to see the coming forth of the prophetic ministries, are encouraged by them, and are shouting forth the clarion call to all who will listen within humanism-encrusted Christianity.

The inevitable then happened: a direct, full-fledged, knock-down-drag-out confrontation between Elijah, the prophetic ministries of our Lord Christ Jesus, and the priests of Baal, the servants of satan. And where did it take place? Mt. Carmel (Hebrew: KRML, one meaning of which being "garden or harvest field of increase"), the harvest fields of souls of the world yet to be reached for our Lord Christ Jesus. But God came forth. Not Elijah; God! It is not the efforts of the prophetic ministries that accomplishes the Will of God; rather, it is God working through them. How important it is for us to see that difference!

God even set a trap for the priests of Baal, i.e., at the brook Kishon (Hebrew: QYShWN, one meaning of which being "to set a trap"). The fire to purge humanism-encrusted Christianity comes from God, not satan, even though most evangelical Christians today will not be able to understand how and why *God* would take away their familiar Churchianity ways!

After that purging fire, and only *after* it, the rain comes forth, profusely. All throughout the land will then hear the prophetic word of God. The prophetic ministries will, by God's doing, even outrun Ahab, the former church leaders, back to Jezreel (Hebrew: YZRIAhL, one meaning of which being "to disseminate, as seed"), i.e., in now spreading the seed of the Gospel (Matthew 13:3-9 & 18-23; Luke 8:4-8 & 11-15).

In 1 Kings Chapter 19, however, we see that Elijah, the new prophetic ministries, were still very human. After the new outpouring of God's rain subsides a bit (as it will, so that *fruit* of the Spirit will grow and ripen in the land), the very human weaknesses tend to become apparent. So God has to do some more purging of our lives. Before, our purgings had to do with refining our *faith*, our seeing, obeying, and depending upon our Lord Christ Jesus and only upon Him. Now they have to do with other aspects of our intrinsic sin-nature, so that we become Christ-like in *character*. Why does God bother with that, now that His most important thing to be accomplished by Him through us seems to have been accomplished? Because there are many believers, younger in the faith than us, who *have their eyes on us*, and who God is raising up to follow in our footsteps to minister in His *next* movings. So, we need to spend some more intimate time with our Lord Christ Jesus, being discipled a bit more by Him, before He will transfer our mantles of anointing onto the Elishas (Hebrew: AhLYShI, one meaning of which being "to cry to be set free") after us, to those who are crying for our help in discipling them to also become free of *their* sin-nature.

Elijah fled Jezreel (the harvest or mission field) and went to Beersheba (Hebrew: BAhR-ShBI, one meaning of which being "well of promise or fulfillment"). We leave the ministry, and submit ourselves to the final stages of sanctification by the indwelling Holy Spirit of Christ Jesus. For a while this means a walk in a wilderness, yoked with Christ by a "Juniper" (Hebrew: RThM, one meaning of which being "to be yoked to"). During that time we are supernaturally fed in otherwise desolate circumstances, i.e., near Mount Horeb (Hebrew: ChRB, one meaning of which being "desolate"). We lodge in a cave. The number 40 (i.e., days and nights) speaks of the time of *completion* of God's purposes in human affairs.

The Lord shows Himself to us in *wind* and *earthquake* and *fire*, namely in His ways of *shaking* all that can be shaken (Hebrews 12:26-29). "Shake all that can be shaken"? Wow!

That's far more than what happened on Mt. Carmel. The Elishas after us will indeed need a "double-portion" of the anointing that is on us! And *we* are to be used to pass it onto them! How? Look at 1 Kings 19:15-18 as a starter. Go to Damascus (Hebrew: DMShQ, one meaning of which being "quietly drinking of water"), go to those who are persistently partaking of the living water of Christ. Take the son of Nimshi (Hebrew: NMShY, one meaning of which being "drawn out, revealed"), who is Jehu (Hebrew: YHWAh, one meaning of which being "The Lord YHWH is He"), and anoint him king over all of Israel. Disciple all who are followers of our Lord Christ Jesus, to make sure that He becomes Lord of *everything* in their lives. And take Elisha, son of Shaphat (Hebrew: ShPhT, one meaning of which being "to judge; litigate") of Abel-Meholah (Hebrew: AhBL-MChWLH, one meaning of which being "meadow of dancing, as in worship") and anoint him as prophet in your place. Help to prepare, and even minister by the laying on of hands in anointed identification, those who have been judged and prepared by God and are now worshiping Him. Help them take your place by being their advocate. There are still 7000 in the land who have not yet submitted to Baal.

So, in 1 Kings 19:19-21, Elijah did just that for Elisha.

1 Kings Chapters 20-22 and 2 Kings Chapter 1 are an interesting turn of events. God used a foreign Pharoah to attack Ahab. God will use the nations of the world to attack the Christian nations. Why? For at least two reasons: (1) to destroy Baal; and (2) to train Elisha. But remember, it is God who does that, not us. We in the midst of such chaos about us are to remain faithful as vessels/channels of the Light, Life and Love of Christ through us unto others when, as, and how He

chooses. That will be mostly on a one-to-one basis. And it will be in ways that baffle our natural understandings. But eventually, total victory is obtained, we are transferred to heaven, and the Elishas after us take our place (2 Kings 2:1-14). Our translation, when it occurs, will be "no big deal" for us at that time, for we will have been walking in the here and now according to our position with Christ in the heavenlies right along.

9. New Testament And Other Examples

These few Old Testament examples are only a small sampling of Biblical personages whose lives reflect our Lord bringing them through all three levels of sanctification. Indeed Hebrews Chapter 11, in the context of lives illustrating a walk *in faith* with our Lord Christ Jesus, lists so many others by name. Nor do we need stop with the Old Testament. The New Testament also contains examples. And many more examples are contained in the last 19 centuries of church history.

Space does not permit us to delineate such other examples. But to do so would be a fruitful experience for the diligent reader. Here are a few suggestions for that.

Even Jesus Himself followed the general pattern. He, of course, was regenerated right from birth, even from conception. His Baptism into the Holy Spirit was immediately after His water baptism by John. And the Mount of Transfiguration event consummated His earthly ministry prior to Calvary, and certified the vision of His ultimate ministry at Calvary. Gethsemene was certainly his greatest emptying experience, but we also know that he suffered on many other

Our Cloud Of Witnesses

occasions (Hebrews 5:8),

Peter and John, with the other disciples except Thomas, were regenerated in John 20:22, and baptized into the Holy Spirit in Acts 2:4. We suggest Peter's original ministry to the Jews was consummated, and his vision for his fuller ministry was certified, as a result of his House of Cornelius experience in Acts chapter 10. John's original vision was fulfilled, and his vision for his further ministry certified, on Patmos (Book of Revelations). Both Peter and John had many emptying cycles during their lives.

Paul apparently was regenerated on the road to Damascus (Acts 9:3-6) when he first heard the Lord. His vision for ministry came shortly after when he was filled with the Holy Spirit upon the ordination by Ananias (Acts 9:17). His vision of his full ministry came when he was called on his missionary journeys to establish churches among the gentiles (Acts 13:2-3). Many emptying cycles followed during the rest of his life, including being stoned to death, and subsequently resurrected, at Lystra (Acts 14:19-20).

We could continue with many other examples during church history. St. Augustine, Thomas Aquinas, the saints we mentioned in Chapter Nine above, Martin Luther, Menno Simmons, Jacob Amman, John Wesley, Count Zinzendorf, George Whitfield, Dwight Moody, etc. - their lives all attest to these three general levels of sanctification, with many emptying cycles, at the hands of their Lord Christ Jesus. The list goes on and on. Again, we have not the space here to delineate them.

10. Those Who Saw Not The Vision Fulfilled

But Hebrews 11 ends with several verses on quite a different note. Verses 35-40 refer to many whose lives also attest to walking in faith, but though intensely persecuted *they did not see* their vision fulfilled in this life. Verses 39-40 tells us of them: "And all these, having gained approval through their faith, *did not receive what was promised*, because God had provided something better for us, so that apart from us they should not be made perfect."

Huh?

Well, first of all, this tells us that not all of us will go through *all three* stages in this life! In fact, *the vast majority of us will not!* All but a very few of us will be cut off by intense persecutions before we reach *in this life* the final stage of full victory with Christ in the heavenlies. Hebrews 10:32 warns us of that: "... after being enlightened, you endured a great conflict of sufferings...." This in spite of the fact that now we have a far better New Covenant than the Old Covenant (Hebrews 8:6).

The vast majority of believers never proceed to the second and/or third general stage of sanctification at all during this life. Two vital questions immediately arise, therefore: (1) Why then should we even bother to seek full maturity? and (2) How can others in the future both benefit by our sufferings and in turn assist in our perfection?

To this first question, a correct but far from satisfying answer is simply "because the Word of God admonishes us to". For example:

2 Corinthians 4:1-2 tells us "Therefore since we have this ministry, as we have received mercy, *we do not lose heart*, but we have renounced the hidden things of shame, not walking in craftiness nor handling the word of God deceitfully, but by manifestation of the truth commending ourselves to every man's conscience in the sight of God."

Galatians 6:9-10 adds: "And *let us not grow weary while doing good*, for in due season we shall reap if *we do not lose heart*. Therefore, as we have opportunity, let us do good to all, especially to those who are of the household of the faith."

Again, in 2 Thessalonians 3:13: "... brethren, *do not grow weary in doing good.*"

But how can I not "grow weary" if I know that most probably I will not see the final victory in my life here and now?

Re-examine the vision, if you will. It is our Lord Christ Jesus, and only He, Who knows the end results not only for each of us individually but also for His Body collectively. And the essence of being in the third or "spiritual" general stage of sanctification, is *not that we will see results* in our personal lives here and now, but rather that *He accomplish His will* through us, always when, as and how He alone chooses. The essence is therefore that we be so lost in Him, so yielded to Him as vessels of His light, life and love flowing through us as He chooses, that any results are no longer of concern to *us*. If we need any assurances that that will not be in vain, that assurance is what the Spirit is trying to tell us in the second part of Hebrews 10:32. No way can we figure out how we will be "perfected" by others after us and they perfected by us; but He knows.

This is a difficult enigma: even *our desire* to go all the way in this life is a *self*-desire, a *self-seeking goal* that must be yielded to Him as part of our sin-nature! The *purpose* for our seeking inner heart healing, and for our enduring all of the other loss-striving-surrendering-revisitation-consummation cycles of the sanctification process that he chooses to subject us to, is not *our being blessed;* rather it is that we become pure vessels/channels for He to pour Himself through unto others. Any other motives we might have than that, are motives that yet need those very cycles in order to remove from us!

What, then, shall we do?

(1) Ever seek to grow as far along this route as He permits. Hebrew 6:1-3, a powerful admonition for us to ever seek to grow more maturely in our relationships with Him, includes the phrase "if God permits." It is His business, not ours, to what extent "God permits." Even that we must leave up to Him.

(2) Embrace all cycles to which He does subject us to, but especially the cycles of inner heart healing. For only to the extent that we commit to the areas of surrender-repentance thereof, to that extent can we be useful to Him as pure vessels/channels. It is our sin-*nature*, not just sins *per se*, that impede and clog us and hinder our being those vessels/channels.

(3) Ever "see" Jesus and lift Him higher. Never forget, even in the darkest of our moments, that He, alone, is our everything!

(4) Note that this volume was not written to provide the reader with a "three or twelve step program" by which one can achieve spiritual maturity. Indeed, none of us would knowingly *seek* the emptying cycles of the second and third stages. Rather it has been written to provide the reader with understandings of the dealings of the indwelling Holy Spirit of Christ Jesus in our lives, so that he/she may more freely be able to cooperate therewith, and be encouraged to endure the emptying cycles of those dealings.

Amen!

End Notes: Chapter Thirteen

[1] Sherrerd, Chris S., *From Sheepfold To Bride: Christ Maturing His Church,* Volume III of the series "Where Do You Fit In? Practical Commitments In The Body of Christ", to be published.

[2] James Strong, *THE EXHAUSTIVE CONCORDANCE OF THE BIBLE: Showing Every Word of the Text of the Common English Version of the Canonical Books, and Every Occurrence of Each Word in a Regular Order; Together With A Comparative Concordance of the Authorized and Revised Versions, Including the American Variations; Also Brief Dictionaries of the Hebrew and Greek Words of the*

Original, With References to the English Words, (New York & Nashville: Abingdon Press, 1890, 27th Printing 1967).

3. Benjamin Davidson, *The Analytical Hebrew And Chaldee Lexicon,* (London: Samuel Bagster & Sons Ltd., Reprinted 1967).

4. Francis Brown, S. R. Driver and Charles A. Briggs, *A HEBREW AND ENGLISH LEXICON OF THE OLD TESTAMENT WITH AN APPENDIX CONTAINING THE BIBLICAL ARAMAIC, Based on the Lexicon of William Gesenius as Translated By Edward Robinson,* (Oxford: Clarendon Press, 1907, 1968 Printing).

5. Rudolf Kittel, *BIBLIA HEBRAICA,* (Stuttgart: Wurttembergische Bibelanstalt, 1937, 1962 Printing).

6. Sherrerd, Chris S., *The Christian Marriage - A Six-Fold Covenant Of Love-Motivated Servanthood,* Volume I of the series "Where Do You Fit In? Practical Commitments In The Body Of Christ" (Shippensburg, PA: Treasure House, Destiny Image Publishing Group, 1994). Copyright © 1994 by Shulemite Christian Crusade.

Epilogue

When the very first conception of this volume came to me back in the early 1970s, the Lord also burned into my heart a prophetic vision of a new thing He was about to do throughout the land, for which He would have to do a major work of sanctification in the lives of His saints. Those were the days of the crest of the "Charismatic Movement", when we all thought we "had arrived" at all He has for us. So blind we all were!

Nevertheless, I have waited for nearly 2-½ decades to see that "New Work" both: be shared in vision by other leaders in the Body of Christ; and begin to actually unfold. I was certainly not the only one who had that vision. But it was not until the mid 1990's when I personally first saw signs of it. We are now in the beginnings of a very powerful and significant fresh move of our Lord Christ Jesus among His people. It will be the most significant characteristic of this and the next decade.

It will not be at all like the previous major outpourings of the Holy Spirit during this century. All of the previous outpourings in this century had *high visibility* to the world, and have been primarily focused to *reach the lost for Christ.* Azuza street and the rise of Pentecostalism in the first two decades, the rise of formal Fundamentalism in the 1920s, the great healing-evangelism ministries of the late 1940s and the 1950s, the Charismatic movement of the 1960s and the 1970s, are still in the memory of many of us, and still excite us when we recall them.

But then the outpouring seemed for the most part to stop! The 1980s turned out to be the great "silent decade". Why? What was happening to the many saints which the Lord had raised up during these previous outpourings of His Spirit, and had called them and anointed them to vibrant ministries? The vast majority of them seemed to be merely biding time, they having been removed from their previous ministries for some reason or another, and not able to find other opportunities. Why did the Lord allow that?

Now we begin to see, though yet through a glass darkly. The Lord has had so many of us in this wilderness walk, most of us for over a full decade or two, *to prepare us for His new work!* And now at last it is beginning.

But don't be too quick to rejoice about it! For this new work will *not* have the high visibility of the others. Its *results* will, but not the move of God itself. And those caught up in it will not have the public recognition, the large congregations, the big churches, the radio and TV ministries, the publishing houses, of which we now see almost *ad nauseam*. It will not be doctrine dominated, nor even "goose-bump" oriented. It will be one thing only: the indwelling Lord Christ Jesus, and He only, working when/as/how He chooses, through whoever He chooses, for whatever He alone knows.

The emphasis of this New Work among His people has already started, and it is this: inner heart healing and sanctification unto *intimate union* with Him. It is the full transition from our being "natural" or "soulical" Christians to being "spiritual" Christians in the sense described in this volume. And He is doing that primarily one believer at a time.

Epilogue

There is a rise, at last, of the prophetic and apostolic ministries today, but their focus at least for now is to edify the saints, individually, in terms of this inner heart sanctification. Starting new churches will *not* be its main thrust, at least in terms of our current understandings of what a "church" is.

As I have begun to share this vision with others, and read the literature of others who are likewise thus sharing, however, I find the reaction of most "rank-and-file" believers to be not what I had expected. Most are already aware that our Lord is about to do *some* "new work". Most are aware that our Lord's purgings of His church, especially here in America, are long overdue. They do not need a "clarion call" *per se*. But what they *do need*, what they are crying out for, is guidance and help in knowing *what they need to do in order to properly respond to our Lord Christ Jesus these days!*

How to respond? What must I do in order to become the "third level" believer He want's me to be? How can I better cooperate with the indwelling Holy Spirit of Christ Jesus as He sanctifies me? Indeed, am *I* to do anything *myself,* since we say repeatedly throughout this volume that the essence is for us to *yield to Him doing the doing?* This is truly an enigma.

One issue is a misunderstanding of what "eternal life" is. Eternal life, first of all, is *life.* Life is not mind understanding ("light" is the Biblical type of that). Life is not thorough knowledge of God's Word. Life is not correct doctrine, carefully defended. Life is not feeling good about God. Life is not obeying His commands. Life is not even "serving Him" as most of us understand what serving Him means.

Life is *the ability to fully, dynamically, interact two-ways with one's environment!*

Eternal life, then, is the ability to fully, dynamically, interact two-ways with Christ in the *spiritual* environment of the Godhead!

We all also have a misunderstanding of what our "spiritual environment" is. The spiritual environment, first of all, is *real, very real, reality.* What kind of reality? Its two main attributes are: *(1) incredible intelligence; and (2) astonishing and awesome power.* We see this by God's simply having created all creation by His "spoken Word."

We have been created with the ability to interact with that incredible reality! God is Spirit, and we have been created in His image. But unless we do it in total dependence upon and obedience to God *via* our Lord Christ Jesus, satan is quick to captivate us, in ways in which we are unaware; and he always ultimately leads us to destruction, terrible and painful destruction.

It is therefore time, in God's economy, for the Body of Christ to rise up to the warfare. But we cannot offer the world a way to detect the counterfeit until we offer them the genuine. The genuine, the Way of the Cross, the total *intimate union* with Christ *in the here and now,* is that to which this volume is directed: to lead us through the entire sanctification process unto that final stage of union and victory.

So be it.

Appendix One

The Human "Heart"

We have been created in the image of God. The "image" of God is the Holy Trinity. So is our "image" a triparte one. God's disciplinings and chastenings of us can be fully explained only in the context of three major and distinct aspects of our salvation that correspond to the three aspects of our triparte psychological nature.

The Old and New Testaments also use the words LB and Cardia (translated "heart"), respectively, to refer to the human psychological make-up. The basic concept here is not that of the physical organ that pumps our blood (although those words *literally* mean that), but is that of the "innermost" or central "core" of our psychological nature.

1. Body, Soul And Spirit

Actually, three specific aspects of our human nature are identified in the Scriptures by the terms (human) "spirit", "soul" and "body" or "flesh". Spirit, soul, flesh: *human* spirit, human soul, human flesh? The Greek words here are Pneuma for "spirit", Psuche for "soul", and Soma for "body". Elsewhere Paul often uses the Greek word Sarx for "flesh" to refer to the psychological power of the appetites of the physical body.

Throughout the Old Testament, three corresponding distinct Hebrew words are also used: RWCh for "spirit", NPhSh for "soul", and BShR for "flesh". However, this clear distinction of the three separate aspects of the human psychological nature was not familiar to Old Testament writers. Only occasional such understanding appears before the time of Paul. Indeed it is to the Holy Spirit through Paul that we primarily owe this understanding.

The basic meanings of RWCh And Pneuma are of wind, physical air in motion; but the words are also used to denote "life" and "spirit" because the manner in which our Lord YHWH/Christ (Who *is* spirit - John 4:24) imparts life to us is by "breathing" life into us [Genesis 2:7 and John 20:22]. The basic meaning of NPhSh is that of a "living creature", that which results when RWCh is in-breathed into us; NPhSh is therefore often used to refer simply to a living human being. Psuche in the Greek mainly refers to the human "soul" as distinct from the rest of our nature. BShR in the Hebrew basically means "flesh" in the physiological sense, i.e., muscle, bone, "meat", etc. Soma in the Greek means the body in an overall sense: our entire being. Sarx specifically refers to our *carnality*, that is, the appetites of our physical body and how they influence our feelings, thoughts and decisions.

Note: I have prepared separate Appendices 2, 3 and 5 that list the Biblical texts wherein these Hebrew and Greek words are used to refer to the human spirit, soul and carnality, respectively. I have also prepared a separate Appendix 4 that lists the Biblical texts wherein the Hebrew and Greek words are used to refer to the human "heart" in this context. The following is a very brief summary of those separate appendices. Copies of them are available upon request. They total 76 pages. Please include $10.00 to cover actual costs of photo-copying plus shipping and handling.

2. The Human Spirit In The Bible

Throughout the Old and New Testaments, the Hebrew word RWCh and the Greek word Pneuma have many uses. Four primary meanings in particular are: physical *wind* or *breath*; satanic spirits *(demons);* the *Holy* Spirit of YHWH/Christ; and the *human* spirit.

In separate Appendix 2 we list 89 uses from the Old Testament and 95 from the New Testament that, we assert from their context, refer to the *human* spirit. Both the noun and adjective/adverb forms are included in that listing. The quotations are from the King James translation, with the English word that is translated from RWCh or Pneuma italicized. We do not include in that listing the uses of RWCh/Pneuma that refer to either wind/breath, satanic spirits, nor the Holy Spirit.

There is a definite development in the concept of the human spirit during the Old Testament. At first, RWCh referred simply to our breath or breathing, as a sign of our living; that results from God's method of imparting life into us (i.e., He breathed the breath of lives into us - Genesis 2:7). By Job's time and later, RWCh took on the meaning of a specific, recognizable "something" in our "hearts" or innermost consciousness. Yet all throughout the Old Testament times the functions of the human spirit were poorly distinguished from the functions of the human soul, if at all.

Only in the New Testament times were the specific functions of that "something", called our human *spirit*, identified. The context is almost always in reference to the human element of the God-man relationship, with "divine" or "eternal" *life* the key issue. But it is the writings of Paul that mainly distinguish the human spirit from the soul, and imply the distinct functions of each.

We illustrate these several functions of the human spirit implied in the Biblical use of these Hebrew and Greek words under *eight* specific categories:
> (1) 6 Old Testament and 5 New Testament references to the human spirit as denoting *life;*
>
> (2) 13 Old Testament and 47 New Testament general references to the human spirit simply as a distinct *entity;*
>
> (3) 17 Old Testament and 23 New Testament references to the human spirit as our seat of *God-orientation* (our spirit being enlivened or quickened by the Holy Spirit of Christ Jesus, or our seeking God or rejoicing in Him or worshiping Him, our being stirred up by Him, and our determination to serve Him or do His will);
>
> (4) 18 Old Testament and 5 New Testament references to the human spirit as the seat of our *conscience;* a broken or contrite or humble "heart" with a right attitude toward God, or in a right moral condition because of the operation of our Holy-Spirit-enlivened conscience;
>
> (5) 11 Old Testament references to the Adamic human state where the human spirit is not quickened

by the Holy Spirit, and the conscience is hence not functioning - a "heart" being ***hardened, corrupt, perverse, proud, haughty***, etc.;

(6) 4 Old Testament and 1 New Testament references to human ***courage***, more specifically it failing in fear due to overwhelming imminent destruction;

(7) 17 Old Testament and 4 New Testament references to our being ***grieved***, confounded, troubled, sorrowful or wounded in the human spirit; and

(8) 3 Old Testament and 10 New Testament references to the ***intuition*** function of the human spirit.

3. The Human Soul In The Bible

The Old Testament Hebrew word for the human soul is NPhSh. It has several uses throughout the Bible, and its use shows a development of understanding of the human nature during historical times. The most prevalent use of NPhSh is indeed to refer to the human "soul", with a few translations into "heart" and into some of the functions of the soul such as "mind", "desire" and "will".

In the New Testament the Greek word translated "soul" is Psuche, with its adjective form Psuchikos. It nearly always refers specifically to the soul as described in this book.

In separate Appendix 3 we list 440 references from the Old Testament and 93 from the New Testament, using the King James translation, with the English word that is translated from NPhSh or Psuche italicized. We do not include in that listing the uses of NPhSh/Psuche to refer simply to a living person or "man" or sometimes any living creature.

We illustrate the several functions of the human soul implied in the Biblical use of these Hebrew and Greek words under *seven* specific categories:

(1) 88 Old Testament and 36 New Testament references to the soul as denoting physical *life* or a living person;

(2) 133 Old Testament and 37 New Testament references to the soul as a separate psychological entity, the seat of *"self"*, and that which is the object of salvation;

(3) 16 Old Testament and 1 New Testament references to the soul's *mental* activities (knowledge, understanding, wisdom) or its oral expression (speaking);

(4) 72 Old Testament and 8 New Testament references to the soul's act of volition or will or **choice**, i.e., to do a certain thing, to seek the Lord, to turn unto Him, or to bless or covenant with or submit to another person;

(5) 89 Old Testament and 6 New Testament references to the soul's *emotions*, ranging from joy, rejoicing, and love, to grief, sorrow, bitterness - even fainting from fear;

(6) 26 Old Testament and 4 New Testament references to fleshly *lusts* and pleasures; and

(7) 16 Old Testament and 1 New Testament reference to the soul's *poise* - humble *vs* proud, satisfied *vs* "thirsty", content *vs* idle or alienated, etc.

4. The Human "Heart" In The Bible

The Old and New Testaments use the words LB And Cardia (translated "heart"), respectively, to refer to the human

The Human "Heart"

psychological make-up; more specifically to the "innermost" or central "core" of our psychological nature. The overwhelming Biblical use of these words can be seen to refer to the human *soul*; only a few of these references are to functions that are normally associated with the human *spirit*. In fact, "heart" is used more often than "soul" to refer to the human soul.

In separate Appendix 4 we list 779 references from the Old Testament and 157 from the New Testament, using the King James translation, with the English word that is translated from LB or Cardia italicized.

We illustrate these several functions of the human soul implied in these Biblical uses of the Hebrew and Greek words for "heart" under *ten* specific categories:

(1) 38 Old Testament and 17 New Testament references to the human "self" as *a distinct entity;*

(2) 108 Old Testament and 21 New Testament references to the *mind: knowledge, understanding, wisdom and discernment;*

(3) 30 Old Testament and 5 New Testament references to *carelessness of the mind,* such as foolishness and being deceived;

(4) 81 Old Testament and 12 New Testament references to human **concern and choice**: exercising our will or volition or determination in a general sense;

(5) 113 Old Testament and 16 New Testament references to human choice in the sense of *communion with and/or commitment to* God and/or to fellow believers;

(6) 71 Old Testament and 22 New Testament references to our human will being *humbled, broken, contrite* and "circumcised";

(7) 61 Old Testament and 10 New Testament references to our emotions in a positive sense, such as *merriment, gladness and rejoicing;*

(8) 177 Old Testament and 34 New Testament references to human choice in an evil sense, such as *being proud, haughty, and/or vindicative;*

(9) 14 Old Testament and 12 New Testament references to our emotions in a longing sense, such as our *seeking, desires and lusts;* and

(10) 86 Old Testament and 8 New Testament references to our emotions in a negative sense, such as *sorrow, discouragement and fear.*

Bible scholars have traditionally associated "heart" with the human *spirit* rather than soul. I indeed did so, until I made this detailed categorized listing. But all of these uses, except perhaps for some of the 113+16=129 uses of category (5), are clearly for references to the *soul*. This confusion has come about partly due to the often-repeated Biblical phrase "with all your heart and with all your soul", which on the surface implies that the writer considers the "heart" and the "soul" to be two distinct entities. However, particularly in Old Testament Hebrew, the same thought is very often repeated in the same verse with different but nearly-synonymous words; ancient scribes commonly used that technique for emphasis. Hence, such phrases as this do *not* necessarily indicate distinction between "heart" and "soul", but rather primarily emphasize the utter importance of soul-*righteousness*.

One point of particular interest is the numerous references to the soul in the Mosaic law: the human soul is the main issue in salvation!

5. The Human "Flesh" In The Bible

The basic Old Testament Hebrew word for "flesh" is BShR. It is is used mainly in a purely physiological sense, i.e., for "muscle", "bone", "meat", etc. Only in a very few passages does it refer to "flesh" in a psychological sense. "Flesh" in a psychological sense (i.e., "carnality") is primarily a New Testament concept. There the Greek word used is Sarx, with its adjective form Sarkikos.

Paul does at times use Sarx to refer to the human physical body, when he talks about "members" of our bodies (see Romans 6:13 & 19, Romans 7:5 & 23, and Colossians 3:5; see also James 3:5 & 6 and 4:1). In such passages, the Greek word for members is Melos, which literally means "limb" or "extension", and is the same word used to refer to us believers as "members" of the Body of Christ in Romans 12, 1 Corinthians 6 and 12 and Ephesians 4 and 5.

In separate Appendix 5 we list 15 uses of "flesh" from the Old Testament and 89 from the New Testament that, we assert from their context, refer to the psychological uses of BShR, plus all uses of Sarx and Sarkikos. We do not list the other uses of BShR; we exclude in particular most of the references simply to the human physiological body and to human genealogical relationships. All quotations are from the King James translation, with the English word which is translated from BShR or Sarx/Sarkikos italicized.

We illustrate those references under *four* specific categories:
> (1) 2 Old Testament and 36 New Testament references to flesh as our very beings;
>
> (2) 3 Old Testament and 37 New Testament references to the longings of our flesh;
>
> (3) 4 Old Testament and 15 New Testament references to the intrinsic evil in our flesh; and
>
> (4) 6 Old Testament and 1 New Testament references to our knowing God even in the flesh.

Our "flesh" can have both good and evil manifestations. Its good manifestations are those that cause us to care for the body, so that our Lord in us can use our entire beings for His glory. Appetites for food, rest, withdrawal from pain, etc., when disciplined and controlled, are examples of such.

Nevertheless, the scripture references to the "flesh" are overwhelmingly given as warnings of how evil it usually is. For example, Galatians 5:16-21 lists many of the more common *evil* "works" or manifestations of our flesh: the results when our passions, inflamed by the power of sin, dominate our soul's function of will. Note the list:

Adultery (Moicheia) - sexual relations in direct violation of marriage relationships.

Fornication (Porneia) - sexual relations not involving marriage.

Uncleanness (Akatharsia) - a general defilement of the whole personality involving impure thoughts; repulsiveness.

Lasciviousness (Aselgeia) - a love of sin so reckless and audacious that one no longer cares about whatever God or other people think.

Idolatry (Eidololatreia) - worship of created things rather than of the Creator. Worship is an act that normally is beautiful, but not when used in a Godless and sinful way.

Witchcraft (Pharmakeia) - use of drugs to stimulate otherwise normal body functions. The word strictly means *any* use of drugs, even for medicinal purposes; but the emphasis in Galatians 5 is on their misuse, to obtain "spiritual" experiences outside of the Holy Spirit of Christ Jesus.

Hatred (Echthra) - being an enemy to; enmity; hostility; prejudice; precisely the opposite of AGAPE love.

Variance (Eris) - strife; divisions in personal relationships; contentions; this is the "natural" result of the attitude of Echthra.

Emulations (Zelos) - zealousness; jealousness; possessiveness. This could be good if properly directed, but here it refers to passionate possessiveness. (Note: a Christian, being a slave of our Lord Christ Jesus, has no rights to possess anything or anyone.)

Wrath (Thumos) - outbursts of passion; bad temper; fits of rage; fury; being moved to anger.

Strife (Eritheia) - striving for the sole purpose of how much one can gain; selfishness; intrigues; selfish and cunning ambition.

Seditions (Dichostasia) - personal divisiveness; dissension; factions; standing apart; precisely the opposite of Koininea fellowship.

Heresies (Hairesis) - division by groups; party factions; the "natural" outcome of Dichostasia.

Envyings (Phthonos) - envy; jealousness; severe forms of

Zelos.

Murders (Phonoi) - Taking the life of any human being (even one's own in suicide) except where God's law specifically allows.

Drunkenness (Methe) - excessive drinking of intoxicating beverage to the point of losing control of one's behavior.

Revelings (Komos) - orgies; riotous feasting; disorderly dancing and/or carousing.

6. What Are They, Really?

It is quite natural for one to ask, at this point, "Just what *are* the human ***RWCh/Pnneuma, NPhSh/Psuche,*** and ***BShR/Sarx?*** In this study, we see that the Bible characterizes these three aspects of human nature by their *functions or purposes or activities*, and not by their actual substance or construct. Modern biomedical research in physiology and neurology has given us much data on the substance/construct of the human ***BShR/Sarx*** in terms of molecular (chemical) biology. But the ***NPhSh/Psuche*** substance/construct is still mostly unknown to modern science (psychological research on the brain notwithstanding), and the human ***RWCh/Pneuma*** is a *total* mystery to modern science.

There are a few hints, however, in the Scriptures. For one, we see clearly taught in the Scriptures that although the human ***BShR/Sarx*** is subject to death, the human ***NPhSh/Psuche*** and ***RWCh/Pneuma*** are not, but live on together as a distinct entity, spiritually perceivable and recognizable after death. And after resurrection they acquire a (new) physical embodiment. As astonishing to our natural mind this fact may be, it is a clear teaching of the Scriptures. Among its

The Human "Heart"

implications are that: (1) their existence and substance/construct are independent of any particular physical embodiment; but (2) their function purpose/activities are intrinsically related to and dependent upon their particular physical embodiment at a given point in time.

Hence, in terms of its substance/construct, the human *NPhSh/Psuche* can perhaps best be compared to the mathematical concept of "information": a uniquely definable "thing" quite independent of its form of encoding and the physical forms of that encoding; yet its value/function is highly *related* to that physical encoding form and the physical context of it as it exists at any given point in time. Perhaps such a concept as this is about as far as our natural mind can go in grasping understanding concerning the substance/construct of the human *NPhSh/Psuche*: until we learn (through divine revelation) more about the physical nature of the higher "spiritual reality" and just how the four-dimensional "physical reality" is a subset or "hyperplane" thereof, we can go no further in our understanding.

We are even more limited in the ability of our natural mind to understand the substance/construct of the human *RWCh/Pneuma*. But both the Scriptures and personal experience clearly bear out the basic fact that, whatever it may be "physically", it is chiefly manifested as a propensity or capability of the human *NPhSh/Psuche* to be *influenced* (as it deliberately allows itself to be) informationally if not controlled by it. Actually, that influence, if not also control, is by either of two types or forms of purely spiritual forms of intelligence: the *Agion HRWCh/Pneuma HQDWSh* (Holy Spirit) and *Diamonia* (demonic spirits); and *both* of those forms can bear heavy influence on an individual's

NPhSh/Psuche. We are also taught by both the Scriptures and personal experience that each of these types of spiritual forms of intelligence are as spiritually perceivable and recognizable as are the human *NPhSh/Psuche* apart from the *BShR/Sarx*.

The "hyperplane" concept of four-dimensional "physical reality" being an embedded subset of the higher-dimensioned "spiritual reality", is about as sophisticated a concept our natural mind can grasp in truth concerning this. Clearly certain "things" exist apart from their "physical" embodiment but whose functions/purposes depend on their embodiment. And their embodiment in the "full spiritual reality" may (but need not necessarily) intersect or involve the 4-dimensional "physical reality subset" thereof (and hence be observable in substance/construct to our natural mind). But one thing is clear from the Scriptures about this "full spiritual reality": its main characteristics are incredible ***intelligence*** and tremendous *power*. This is real, very real, reality!

It is sheer human intellectual *pride* for our natural mind to insist upon further intellectual understanding than this. But it is also sheer intellectual dishonesty to *deny* the reality of these aspects of human nature because one cannot further understand them, for to do so requires an unjustified denial of the real evidence we do have of their functional veracity.

Volume 1 of the series, *Where Do You Fit In?*
Practical Commitments in the Body of Christ

The Christian Marriage
A Sixfold Covenant of Love-Motivated Servanthood

Why do people marry? The vast majority of us enter into marriage not to build up our partners but to fulfill our own needs. Many of us have deep-seated emotions and behaviors that drive us to maintain distance in all our interpersonal relationships—but especially in marriage.

Our own hearts need healing before we can be free from seeking to gratify self and have a truly blessed marriage. We need an "inner heart healing" to be able to commit totally to Christ, and thus to our marriage partners as true, love-motivated servants.

The Christian Marriage explains how the principles that apply to the Christian walk are vital to your marriage. Learn how, by faith and as an act of your will, you can determine to obey Christ in all situations and in your reactions to them—including those that involve your spouse.

For more information or to purchase this book, contact:

Chris Sherrerd
1420 Armstrong Valley Road
Halifax, PA 17032

Ph: 717-896-8386   FAX: 717-896-8676
E-mail: sherrerd@epix.net
www.chrissherrerd.com

**Volume 4 of the series, *Where Do You Fit In?
Practical Commitments in the Body of Christ***

Spiritual Dynamics In The Body Of Christ
Dynamic Interactions With Christ Indwelling

Salvation is a *process* whereby the Adamic curse we are each under is being nullified, and we are restored, in all aspects of our nature and relationship with God, to that which Adam and Eve had in the Garden before the Fall. It is completed upon our bodily resurrection in Christ. In the meantime, our Lord ever works that we become *agents of His Life, Light and Love* while still here on earth.

The most vital aspect of being His agent is having Christ Himself, *via* His Holy Spirit, live *within us.* We are to allow Him, within us, full freedom to live His life in and through us when and as He chooses. That is the essence of "the Kingdom of God" and "walking in faith".

In this volume, we concentrate on the positive aspects of such spiritual dynamics. The bottom line is that we must learn to *live in union with Christ Indwelling.* So we give the basic spiritual truths and principles of Christ living within us. We study our spiritual foundations in Christ, how we are to walk in the Spirit, and the dynamics of our spiritual relationship with our Lord Jesus Christ. We also include some understandings of the tactics of the enemy.

Chris Sherrerd
1420 Armstrong Valley Road
Halifax, PA 17032

Ph: 717-896-8386   FAX: 717-896-8676
E-mail: sherrerd@epix.net
www.chrissherrerd.com

Volume 6 of the series, *Where Do You Fit In?*
Practical Commitments in the Body of Christ

Unto The Mountain Pass
A Theology of the End-Time Purposes of God

The breaking of the seals of the scroll (Rev. chaps. 4 to 11) trigger the events associated with our Lord redeeming all of creation from the Fall. That sequence of end-time events is discussed from three perspectives: (1) the vantage point of heaven (Book of Revelation); (2) as experienced by believers on earth (Book of Joshua); and (3) as related to our personal relationship with God (prophetic fulfillment of the Israel Holy Days in the month Tishri). We are now already almost a century into those events, and the breaking of the third seal (release of Black Horseman) will soon begin God's Yom Kippur purging of His people.

God's purpose behind all of this is to prepare a Bride for His Son. Only those of us who become an intimate extension of Christ will endure those events, let alone be used by Him in His purposes. We will find Him when, and only when, we seek Him with our ***whole heart.***

Chris Sherrerd
1420 Armstrong Valley Road
Halifax, PA 17032

Ph: 717-896-8386   FAX: 717-896-8676
E-mail: sherrerd@epix.net
www.chrissherrerd.com

BILL HAMON

THE DAY OF THE SAINTS

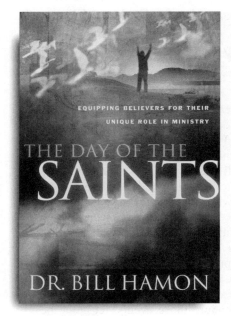

Many Christians are looking for "the Day of the Lord," but before that day comes the Lord is preparing His Bride for His Divine purposes in the earth. All creation longs for that day—*The Day of the Saints*. This day is on God's prophetic timetable and is the day when the Saints will fulfill all the Scriptures regarding Christ's glorious Church. *The Day of the Saints* is written with a sense of urgency and a surge of passion about God's great plans for His end-time people. With prophetic clarity, author Bill Hamon fits together the Biblical directives and the spiritual power that will prepare and propel the saints of God into the world. The saints of God are called to take the message of the Kingdom into the marketplaces of the world, and Dr. Hamon shows how all of history has been moving towards this magnificent end.

ISBN: 0-7684-2166-7

Available at your local Christian bookstore.

For more information and sample chapters, visit www.destinyimage.com

RICK JOYNER

BREAKING THE POWER OF EVIL

The gates of hell are the entrances through which evil gains access to the world. Rick Joyner, author of the best-selling book *The Final Quest*, dramatically exposes the insidious cruelty of evil as manifested in jealousy, fear, the spirit of poverty, spiritual authority, and religious spirits. *Breaking the Power of Evil* equips the Church with the tools necessary first to create a barrier to our world and then open a door into the heavenly realm. Joyner declares that the battle is one of territory—a struggle for the human heart. It is in the heart where evil must be broken. With prophetic precision, Joyner carefully casts a prophetic light that will dispel the darkness as it enlightens the soul.

ISBN: 0-7684-2163-2

Available at your local Christian bookstore.

For more information and sample chapters, visit www.destinyimage.com

TD JAKES

WOMAN, THOU ART LOOSED! GIFT SET

Writing to the hungry and hurting with a powerful anointing, T.D. Jakes has been firmly entrenched on the best-seller lists since his first best-seller, *Woman Thou Art Loosed!*, hit the charts in 1995. Now available from the original publisher of this best-selling author comes a new boxed gift set. This set includes T.D. Jakes's first three best-selling books, *Woman Thou Art Loosed!*, *Can You Stand to Be Blessed?*, and *Naked and Not Ashamed!* These three books have combined sales of over 1.5 million. Each book features a new cover design and is available separately.

ISBN: 0-7684-3036-4

Available at your local Christian bookstore.

For more information and sample chapters, visit www.destinyimage.com

BILL HAMON

PERSONAL PROPHECY SERIES

Dr. Bill Hamon
PERSONAL PROPHECY SERIES

THE CLASSIC GUIDE OF PERSONAL PROPHETIC MINISTRY

Dr. Bill Hamon, president of Christian International's schools and ministries, is one of the most widely recognized prophetic ministers in the Church today. He has functioned in the office of prophet for over 38 years and has personally prophesied to more than 25,000 believers, including hundreds of prominent believers. Now you can own *Prophets and Personal Prophecy*, *Prophets and the Prophetic Movement*, and *Prophets, Pitfalls, and Principles*, all in one complete boxed gift set.

ISBN: 0-7684-2054-7

Available at your local Christian bookstore.

For more information and sample chapters, visit www.destinyimage.com

BILL HAMON

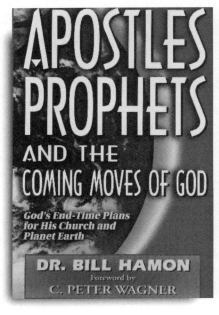

APOSTLES, PROPHETS, AND THE COMING MOVES OF GOD

Author of The Prophets Series, Dr. Bill Hamon brings the same anointed instruction in this new series on apostles! Learn about the apostolic age and how apostles and prophets work together. Find out God's end-time plans for the Church!
ISBN: 0-939868-09-1

Available at your local Christian bookstore.

For more information and sample chapters, visit www.destinyimage.com

MILLICENT THOMPSON

DON'T DIE IN THE WINTER

Don't Die in the Winter, by Dr. Millicent Thompson, explains the spiritual seasons and cycles that people experience. We need to endure our spiritual winters, for in the plan of God, spring always follows the winter!
ISBN: 1-56043-558-5

Available at your local Christian bookstore.

For more information and sample chapters, visit www.destinyimage.com

Additional copies of this book and other book titles from DESTINY IMAGE are available at your local bookstore.

For a complete list of our titles, visit us at www.destinyimage.com
Send a request for a catalog to:

Destiny Image® Publishers, Inc.
P.O. Box 310
Shippensburg, PA 17257-0310

"Speaking to the Purposes of God for This Generation and for the Generations to Come"